LANET PUBLICATIONS

MAT OAKLEY
JOSHUA SAMUEL BROWN

SINGAPORE
C I T Y   G U I D E

INTRODUCING SINGAPORE

Chefs at Raffles Hotel (p124) indulging, sating, fuelling Singapore's greatest obsession: food

Always the bridesmaid and never the bride, this perennial stopover city is reinventing itself as a destination in its own right.

Most people know about the shopping and the eating, but Singapore has taken a serious look at the subject of fun, decided that it is good, and set about converting itself into the ultimate 21st-century metropolis. And in a city for which constant change and improvement are almost a religion, decisions quickly turn into reality.

Almost every facet of this tiny island state is undergoing a renaissance: arts and entertainment, sports, tourist attractions, nature spots and, of course, food and shopping.

The once-staid entertainment scene has erupted into life, with new megaclubs and beach parties placing the city on Asia's nightlife map. Two vast new 'integrated resorts' promise to lure hordes of visitors to their casinos, theme parks and big-note attractions. Huge, modern new malls are jostling into every available space on the city's famous Orchard Road shopping strip. Arts and cultural festivals crowd the calendar. Suddenly Singapore is on the international sporting calendar, too, hosting Formula One's first night race and the 2010 Youth Olympics.

And always, everywhere, there is food, glorious food, the single overwhelming obsession that unites and defines all Singaporeans.

Yet, nestled among it all, and frequently overlooked, are the wonderful green spaces that make Singapore such a masterpiece of urban design, surprising anyone who thinks of this tiny island state as an urban jungle.

Whatever you thought you knew about Singapore, there's always a surprise around the corner.

CITY LIFE

Aside from the identity of their government, when Mr & Mrs Average Singapore step out the door of their Housing Development Board flat every morning, change – or the prospect of it – is the one constant in their lives.

The old, glowingly prosperous and comfortably insular days of the 1980s and early '90s are over. Prosperity remains, but the fickle winds of the global economy, as they are constantly reminded by politicians and the media, are blowing harder, and Singaporeans must learn to blow with them.

And those same global winds are blowing the rest of the world into Singapore, too. There are more foreigners these days, and they're no longer confined to the rich, expat havens of old, travelling by cab or company car. Now they're out in the heartland suburbs, catching buses and trains, eating in the food courts and hawker centres. And tourists too – lots of them, with even more to come, Mr & Mrs Average Singapore are told.

Everywhere there is construction and everywhere there is change. The casinos, the Universal Studios theme park, the world's biggest aquarium, the Singapore Flyer. A new MRT line nearly complete, work on another one about to start. A Formula One race. New roads, more traffic, higher road tolls. New condominiums everywhere. Drainage canals turned into water-themed leisure zones, new botanical gardens on the bay. High-tech industries moving in from Europe. Biomedical research hubs. Another terminal at the airport. New restaurant and entertainment developments. A new land-reclamation project announced. A sale at the brand new mall. A hawker centre closed for renovation. A museum upgraded and reopened.

Hang on, we were here six months ago, where did that building come from? And where did our favourite pub go? It was here last week.

Singapore is going places fast in its quest to become an even more modern, liveable city. For the visitor, this can only be a good thing. As for Mr & Mrs Average Singapore, well, it'll happen whether they like it or not, so they have no choice but to try and keep up.

Futuristic architecture at Peddler's Walk, Clarke Quay (see the boxed text, p57)

HIGHLIGHTS

① **The serious...**
Visit the Asian Civilisations Museum (p51) and the National Museum of Singapore (p56; pictured left) for some heavyweight culture reinvented

② **The sombre...**
Singapore's WWII experience is kept alive on the message board at Changi Chapel (p81)

③ **And the strange**
Try the Museum of Shanghai Toys (p70) or Haw Par Villa (p96; pictured below) for a peek at the city's quirkier side

MUSEUMS

Singapore can lay a convincing claim to be Southeast Asia's museum capital. From the grandest colonial-era showpiece to the tiniest, most moving memorial, the city's cultural exhibits could easily fill a week.

❶ Fish-head curry
The delicious local speciality is a lot better than it sounds

❷ All day, and all night
Plunge into the 24-hour retail madness of the Mustafa Centre (p111)

❸ Wanderlust
Take an aimless stroll – Little India (p67) never fails to fascinate

A SLICE OF THE SUBCONTINENT

Like India with the uncomfortable bits taken out, Little India, by far the best preserved of all Singapore's traditional ethnic districts, is a bustling, disordered network of lanes and alleyways filled with the scent of spices and garlands and thumping bhangra.

GREEN SINGAPORE

Many visitors are surprised by the city's lushness. The sheer number and brilliance of Singapore's green spaces make it one of the world's best-designed cities – an urban masterpiece that's continually being reinvented.

① Sungei Buloh Wetland Reserve
A bird-watcher's paradise in a pristine mangrove area – with the odd crocodile thrown in (p88)

② Singapore Botanic Gardens
A riot of flora near the end of Orchard Rd (p91)

③ MacRitchie Nature Reserve
A tropical rainforest habitat filling the centre of the island (p88)

④ Fort Canning Park
Once a forbidden hill, now a leafy city centre retreat (p55)

① **The fluoro-light fantastic**
No visit is complete without eating at a hawker centre or coffeeshop (p125)

② **Posh nosh**
Finest fare everywhere: 70 floors up at Equinox (p124), on a clifftop at The Cliff (p137), or in a cable car at Sky Dining (p137)

STUFF YOURSELF SILLY

If you don't check in at the airport puffing your cheeks and nursing a full belly, you've gone wrong somewhere. Singapore is food heaven, from the simplest, cheapest street snacks to the highest culinary arts – this city is obsessed with eating.

OLD FRIENDS REDISCOVERED

Travellers looking for a slice of old Singapore should head to Joo Chiat, the heart of the Peranakan Renaissance.

❶ Koon Seng Road Shophouses
Beautiful colonial-era homes restored to their former glory (p78)

❷ Katong Antique House
A fascinating insight into Peranakan history and culture (p78)

HOUSES OF THE HOLY

Spiritual diversity and mandatory cultural tolerance makes the Lion City a veritable one-stop shop of religious culture.

① Buddha Tooth Relic Temple
Sacred purity housed under 420kg of pure gold (p61)

② Sri Mariamman Temple
Riotous colour and detail at Singapore's oldest Hindu temple (p61)

③ Thian Hock Keng Temple
Heavenly bliss in the centre of town (p61)

④ Sultan Mosque
Awe-inspiring dome overlooking Kampong Glam (p70)

❶ Scale the heights
Get the best views of the city from the G-max Bungy (p156), the Singapore Flyer (p156; pictured left), and even a big 'yellow balloon' (p156)

❷ Cycling
Experience Singapore's extensive network of parks (p153), and dodge traffic, astride a bicycle

❸ Skate Singapore
Bring your skates (or rent a pair) and skate across the island on bicycle trails, park connectors and streets (p153)

DARE TO BE DIFFERENT

Not satisfied with the usual eat-shop-temple hop? Try something a bit different, from views on high to outdoor pursuits.

CONTENTS

Mat Oakley

Mat was born and raised in Watford by a Scouse dad and a Yorkshire mum, and has never forgiven either of them (though he is thankful his Dad persuaded his four-year-old self to support Liverpool, rather than his mum's home town of Leeds). Since escaping England in 1993, he has lived and worked as a journalist and author in Thailand, Laos, Australia and Fiji, and has spent the last four years in Singapore with his wife and three cats. Apart from the infinite possibilities of finding new places to eat in Singapore, he enjoys exploring the oases of greenery in the city, and hopping on his motorbike in search of a clear stretch of Singapore road (hard to find, but they do exist). Mat was the coordinating author and wrote the Introducing Singapore, Getting Started, Background, Shopping, Eating, Transport and Directory chapters.

MAT'S TOP SINGAPORE DAY

I'd start the day on the veranda of the Rider's Café (p135), part of the Bukit Timah Saddle Club, and probably the most peaceful, rural breakfast spot in Singapore. If it's a weekday, I'd ride to East Coast Park (p80) and have a few spins around the Ski360° (p157) lagoon on the waterskis for a couple of hours, then wander over to the East Coast Lagoon Food Village (p134) for a bowl of laksa for lunch.

In the afternoon I'd go into the city, spend a few hours browsing books and antiques at Tanglin Shopping Centre (p112), then wander through the National Museum (p56) and the Colonial District, hitting the Elgin Bridge just after dark, looking across the river at Boat Quay (p57) as it lights up, with the skyscrapers towering behind it. It's a magnificent sight.

Thirsty work, this walking, so where next? The Archipelago brewpub? Oosters for some Belgian beer? The upstairs lounge by the window at Harry's (p141)? Whatever the choice, it has to be Little India for dinner: Gayatri (p129), Anjappar (p129) or Andhra Curry (p129), washed down with a beer at the Prince of Wales (p144).

Joshua Samuel Brown

Joshua Samuel Brown is a writer and photojournalist who has tramped the globe since late adolescence, writing features articles for publications both illustrious and obscure. An on-again off-again expatriate, Joshua has been coming to Singapore since the late '90s. He currently divides his time between Asia and North America, with occasional forays into Central America. When not writing for Lonely Planet, Joshua lives with his wife, four dogs and six cats on an organic farm in rural Texas, where he writes political essays, short stories and endless emails, trying in vain to avoid manual labour. His blog, Snarky Tofu, is erudite, opinionated, bizarre and online at www.josambro.blogspot.com. Offering tales of betel-nut beauties and tips on avoiding jail time by impersonating a Mormon, his first solo book is *Vignettes of Taiwan*. Joshua wrote the Neighbourhoods, Drinking & Nightlife, Arts & Leisure, Sleeping and Excursions chapters and the Arts section of the Background chapter.

Singapore is a breeze – possibly one of the least challenging cities in the world to visit. Plonk some 10-year-olds at Changi Airport and chances are that within a couple of hours they'll be booked into a hotel, scooting around on the MRT, munching on chicken rice and deciding which movie to see first.

They'll need plenty of pocket money, though. Singapore is not the cheapest destination, though it's possible to cut costs dramatically by eating at hawker centres and using public transport. Accommodation can also fill up fast, so it's a good idea to book a room well in advance. If you're coming in September during the Formula One grand prix, reschedule or be prepared to pay well over the odds for a room.

WHEN TO GO

Any time's a good time to go to Singapore. There are cultural events and festivals all year round, from fashion to film to food, and because Singapore is home to so many ethnic communities, you can hardly step outside without bumping into a festival. The less spectacular, less extravagant aspects of traditional culture are visible, and even the casual visitor will notice the numerous little street shrines, with their incense sticks, offerings and pyramids of oranges, that are inserted sometimes into the most unexpected corners.

Practically on the equator, Singapore is constantly hot (the temperature never drops below 20°C) and humid and gets fairly steady year-round rainfall. The wettest months are supposedly November to January, when it's also a degree or two cooler, while the driest are supposedly May to July, but in reality there is little distinction between the seasons. Similarly, there is no high and low tourism season as such, though during local school holidays (see p196) and major cultural festivals things become noticeably more crowded.

FESTIVALS

Singapore is awash with festivals – religious, cultural, national and commercial. Religious festivals in particular are timed according to lunar calendars, but the Singapore Tourism Board's online what's-on guide usually lists precise days.

January
PONGGAL
A four-day harvest festival celebrated by southern Indians, especially at the Sri Mariamman Temple (p61) on South Bridge Rd or in Little India. It's traditional for people to greet each other by saying *'pal pongitha'* (Has the milk boiled over in your house?). Sweetened, spiced rice is cooked in milk and allowed to boil over to symbolise bounty, and the boiling over is accompanied by cries of *'pongollo ponggal!'*

THAIPUSAM
This is one of the most dramatic Hindu festivals, in which devotees honour Lord Subramaniam with acts of amazing masochism. In Singapore, Hindus march in a procession from the Sri Srinivasa Perumal Temple (p70) on Serangoon Rd to the Chettiar Hindu Temple (p57) on Tank Rd carrying *kavadis* (heavy metal frames decorated with peacock feathers, fruit and flowers). The *kavadis* are hung from followers' bodies with metal hooks and spikes that are driven into their flesh. Other devotees pierce their cheeks and tongues with metal skewers *(vel)*, or walk on sandals of nails.

February
CHINESE NEW YEAR
Dragon dances and pedestrian parades mark the start of the New Year. Families hold open house, unmarried relatives (especially children) receive *ang pow* (gifts of money in red packets), businesses clear their debts and everybody says *'Gung hei faat choi'* (I hope that you gain lots of money). Chinatown is lit up, especially Eu Tong Sen St and New Bridge Rd, and the 'Singapore River Hongbao Special' features *pasar malam* (night market) stalls, variety shows and fireworks.

CHINGAY
www.chingay.org.sg
Singapore's biggest street parade occurs on the 22nd day after the Chinese New

Year. It's a flamboyant multicultural event, with subliminal themes bolstering the social order, and held either along Orchard Rd or around the Colonial District, with flag bearers, lion dancers, floats and other cultural performers. Buy tickets in advance for a seat in the viewing galleries, or battle the crowds for a place at the roadside barriers.

March

MOSAIC MUSIC FESTIVAL
www.mosaicmusicfestival.com
Annual 10-day feast of world music, jazz and indie laid on by the Esplanade theatre, featuring acts local and international, renowned and obscure. The schedule is peppered with free concerts held in the Esplanade's smaller venues.

SINGAPORE FASHION FESTIVAL
www.singaporefashionfestival.com.sg
Not quite Paris, but probably as close as you'll get in Southeast Asia, this festival also features a fortnight of shows from local designers as well as prominent international names.

April

QING MING FESTIVAL
On All Souls' Day, Chinese traditionally visit the tombs of their ancestors to clean and repair them and make offerings. Singapore's largest temple complex, Kong Meng San Phor Kark See Monastery (p86), in the centre of the island, is the place to be on consecutive weekends throughout the month, when relatives descend on columbaria en masse, causing chaos on the surrounding roads.

WORLD GOURMET SUMMIT
www.worldgourmetsummit.com
Celebrating the national passion, the month-long Singapore Food Festival (www.singaporefoodfestival.com) from the end of March to end of April (though it has been known to switch months) has special offerings at everything from hawker centres to top-end restaurants. The two-week World Gourmet Summit is a gathering of top international chefs, with foodie events, classes and dinners.

INTERNATIONAL FILM FESTIVAL
www.filmfest.org.sg
Independent and art-house movies are pretty thin on the ground in Hollywood-obsessed Singapore, so this showcase of world cinema is a rare chance to see cinematic talent from some of the planet's other countries.

GOOD FRIDAY
A candle-lit procession bearing the figure of the crucified Christ takes place at St Joseph's Catholic Church (Map pp52–3) at Victoria St.

May

VESAK DAY
Buddha's birth, enlightenment and death are celebrated by various events, including the release of caged birds to symbolise the setting free of captive souls. Temples such as Sakaya Muni Buddha Gaya Temple (p70) in Little India throng with worshippers, but the centre of the activity is the Buddha Tooth Relic Temple (p61) on South Bridge Rd.

June

GREAT SINGAPORE SALE
www.greatsingaporesale.com
Runs from the end of May to the beginning of July (it seems to get longer and broader every year). Orchard Rd and the big malls are decked with banners, and retailers around the island cut prices (and wheel out the stuff they couldn't sell earlier in the year). Shoppers' paradise, or desperate tourist-board gimmick to bolster the city's weakening position among Asia's retail giants? Opinions are divided.

BIRTHDAY OF THE THIRD PRINCE
During this Chinese festival, the child-god is honoured with processions, and devotees go into a trance and spear themselves with spikes and swords. Celebrations are held at various temples and on Queen St (Map pp52–3).

DRAGON BOAT FESTIVAL
www.sdba.org.sg
Commemorating the death of a Chinese saint who drowned himself as a protest against government corruption, this

ADVANCE PLANNING

Checking the Singapore Tourism Board online calendar (www.visitsingapore.com), the Sistic website (www.sistic.com .sg) and the Esplanade theatre site (www.esplanade.com) will yield just about every upcoming concert, play or sports event in Singapore. Check a few weeks in advance and get your tickets booked.

If you're a jazz fan, take a look at the www.southbridgejazz.com.sg and www.blujaz.net for upcoming gigs.

If you're planning a fancy night out, some restaurants get booked out days, if not weeks, ahead, particularly at weekends. Au Jardin (p134) is a notable example. Singapore has enough restaurants for you to never be completely stuck, but phoning a week ahead is advisable to avoid disappointment.

festival is celebrated with boat races at Bedok Reservoir. Check the website for other races held throughout the year.

SINGAPORE ARTS FESTIVAL
www.singaporeartsfest.com
Organised by the National Arts Council, this is Singapore's premier arts festival with a world-class program of art, dance, drama and music.

July

SINGAPORE FOOD FESTIVAL
www.singaporefoodfestival.com
A month-long celebration of all things edible and Singaporean. Well-known restaurants lay on events and there are cooking classes, food-themed tours for visitors and plenty of opportunities to sample classic Malay, Chinese and Indian dishes – though if there are discounts or freebies on offer expect to be trampled in the stampede.

August

SINGAPORE NATIONAL DAY
www.ndp.org.sg
Held on 9 August (though dress rehearsals on the two prior weekends are almost as popular), this huge nationalist frenzy takes the whole year to prepare and sees military parades, extravagant civilian processions, air force fly-bys, frenzied flag-waving and a concluding fireworks display. Look out for the slightly unsettling rows of white-clad People's Action Party members surveying the proceedings. Tickets sell out well in advance.

WOMAD
Marking the end of National Day celebrations, this festival of world music usually takes place on Fort Canning Green (p55).

HUNGRY GHOST FESTIVAL
Marks the day when the souls of the dead are released to walk the earth for feasting and entertainment. The Chinese respond to this morbid notion by placing offerings of food on the street and lighting fires. Chinese operas and other events are laid on to keep these restless spirits happy.

September

FORMULA ONE GRAND PRIX
www.f1singapore.com
We're jumping the gun predicting this will be an annual event, but F1's first ever night race held in 2008 on the scenic street circuit around Marina Bay is vying to cement its place on the calendar.

BIRTHDAY OF THE MONKEY GOD
T'se Tien Tai Seng Yeh's birthday is celebrated twice a year at the Monkey God Temple (Map pp62–3) on Seng Poh Rd near the Tiong Bahru Market. Mediums pierce their cheeks and tongues with skewers and go into a trance, during which they write special charms in blood.

MOONCAKE FESTIVAL
Celebrated on the full moon of the eighth lunar month, and also known as the Lantern Festival. Mooncakes are made with bean paste, lotus seeds and sometimes a duck egg, though a endless variety of flavours are now available to suit modern tastes.

NAVARATHRI
In the Tamil month of Purattasi, the Hindu festival of 'Nine Nights' is dedicated to the wives of Siva, Vishnu and Brahma. Young girls are dressed as the goddess Kali; this is a good opportunity to see traditional Indian dancing and singing. The Chettiar Hindu Temple (p57),

Sri Mariamman Temple (p61) and Sri Srinivasa Perumal Temple (p70) are the main areas of activity.

October

DEEPAVALI
Rama's victory over the demon king Ravana is celebrated during the 'Festival of Lights', with tiny oil lamps outside Hindu homes and lights all over Hindu temples. Little India is ablaze with lights for a month, culminating in a huge street party on the eve of the holiday.

PILGRIMAGE TO KUSU ISLAND
Tua Pek Kong, the god of prosperity, is honoured by Taoists in Singapore, who make a pilgrimage to the shrine on Kusu in the ninth month of the Chinese lunar calendar, sometime between late September and November. At weekends the island almost sinks under the weight of pilgrims.

HARI RAYA PUASA
Also known as Hari Raya Aidilfitri, this festival celebrates the end of the Ramadan fasting month (it can also occur in September). Head to Kampong Glam (the Arab Quarter) for nightly feasts during Ramadan.

November

HARI RAYA HAJI
An event celebrating the conclusion of the pilgrimage to Mecca. Animals (mostly sheep shipped from Australia) are ritually slaughtered in the mosques, after which the Koran dictates a portion of the meat must be handed out to the poor. (The event will take place in November in the years 2009, 2010 and 2011.)

THIMITHI
At this fire-walking ceremony, Hindu devotees prove their faith by walking across glowing coals at the Sri Mariamman Temple (p61).

SINGAPORE BUSKERS FESTIVAL
Southeast Asia's largest showcase of street performing talent, from acrobats, artists, magicians and contortionists to the inevitable jugglers and mime artists, takes place principally along Orchard Rd and the Singapore River and in Marina Sq.

December

CHRISTMAS
Singapore has enthusiastically embraced everything we all love about Christmas: rampant commercialism, vacuous sentiment and gaudy municipal decoration. But no matter how cynical you are (and we are pretty cynical), the light display that stretches for a kilometre or more down Orchard Rd starting in late November is breathtaking.

COSTS & MONEY

Singapore can cater to all budgets, but compared with its Southeast Asian neighbours it's far from cheap, particularly since hotel rates skyrocketed in 2007.

On the tightest possible budget, it's possible to scrape by on $50 to $60 a day (assuming you actually want to do something other than sit in a hostel watching TV and eating instant noodles). A hostel bed costs from $16 at the grungy end to $30 for the best. Eating at hawker centres costs between $2.50 and $6 for standard fare, while meals at food courts in downtown shopping malls generally cost a little more – add an extra $2 as a rough estimate. Visiting museums during free times can cut your costs even further.

Midrange accommodation ranges from around $90 a night for a clean, functional room in one of the less swanky city neighbourhoods to $300 for a three-star hotel room. Add a few sights, some restrained shopping, a modest lunch and dinner in a good restaurant, plus a few taxi rides and you should budget for an extra $200 to $300 on top of your room.

Occupying a top-end hotel, splurging on shopping and going out to the city's fanciest restaurants and bars, you can drop more than $1000 in a day without much effort.

INTERNET RESOURCES

www.disgruntledsingaporean.blogspot.com Series of articles and musings from an opposition standpoint, plus links to dozens of other similarly dissenting blogs.

www.mrbrown.com Website of blogger and podcaster Lee Kin Mun, who achieved infamy when his column in the *Today* newspaper was canned after he wrote too frankly about rising living costs in Singapore. The podcast, accessible through the website, is still popular.

www.sistic.com.sg One-stop site selling tickets to pretty much every concert, play or other performance taking place in Singapore, with a useful events calendar.

www.stomp.com.sg Community site run by the official mouthpiece media company SPH, embodying the kind of carefully monitored 'open society' the government is trying to foster. For an insight into issues that preoccupy Singaporeans, check the 'Singapore Seen' section.

www.talkingcock.com The original satirical website that was actually debated in parliament. Ironic takes on the news of the day, plus the priceless Coxford Singlish Dictionary.

www.uberture.com Nightlife, entertainment, shopping, society and pics of people smiling in nightclubs.

www.visitsingapore.com Singapore Tourism Board information on the city's top attractions, plus a useful events calendar.

SUSTAINABLE SINGAPORE

Singapore is well equipped for visitors wanting to reduce their impact on the environment. If travelling from Malaysia, or even Thailand, consider coming by train. It's no more expensive and a lot more scenic.

Once in the city, use trains and buses as much as possible. The central city is also very compact for walking, but we wouldn't recommend hiring a bicycle to get around. Drivers can be highly aggressive and particularly unsympathetic to cyclists' space.

Air-conditioning is ubiquitous in Singapore – most hotels have it. However, it might be possible to switch it off and get a fan, or sleep with the windows open if there's a decent sea breeze blowing.

The island has slowly woken up to recycling – there are bins scattered around the city – but the average shop assistant and check-out worker retains a pathological obsession with handing out as many plastic bags as possible.

HOW MUCH?

Litre of petrol $2.01

Litre of bottled water $1.20

Bottle of Tiger beer (in a hawker centre) $5.50

Bottle of Tiger beer (in a city pub) $12-plus

Souvenir T-shirt $5

Bowl of Katong laksa $3.50

Latte at Coffee Bean $5.50

Kopi (coffee) at a kopitiam (coffeeshop) $1.25

Peak-hour taxi from Orchard to Chinatown $12

Most expensive MRT trip $1.90

HISTORY
PRE-COLONIAL SINGAPORE

Pretty much every museum you'll see in Singapore is devoted to post-colonial history, simply because there is not a great deal of undisputed precolonial history. It is known that the island waxed and waned in importance as empires to the north and south rose and fell – and archaeological digs have demonstrated there were substantial settlements there in the past – but there is little in the way of concrete historical material.

Malay legend has it that long ago a Sumatran prince visiting the island of Temasek saw a strange animal he believed to be a lion. The good omen prompted the prince to found a city on the spot of the sighting. He called it Singapura (Lion City).

Chinese traders en route to India had plied the waters around what is now Singapore from at least the 5th century AD, though the records of Chinese sailors as early as the 3rd century refer to an island called Pu Luo Chung, which may have been Singapore, while others claim there was a settlement in the 2nd century.

In 1292, Marco Polo visited a flourishing city that may have been where Singapore now stands, though it's by no means clear (and besides, Marco Polo's entire account of his travels has often been questioned). He called it Chiamassie, though the Venetian's only sure report is of the city of Malayu – now called Jambi – on Sumatra.

What is certain, however, is that Singapore was not the first of the great entrepôt cities in the region. By the 7th century, Srivijaya, a seafaring Buddhist kingdom centred at Palembang in Sumatra, held sway over the Strait of Malacca (now Melaka). By the 10th century it dominated the Malay peninsula as well. At the peak of Srivijaya's power, Singapore was at most a small trading outpost.

Raids by rival kingdoms and the arrival of Islam spelled the eclipse of Srivijaya by the 13th century. Based mainly on the thriving pirate trade, the sultanate of Melaka quickly acquired the commercial power that was once wielded by Srivijaya, becoming a cosmopolitan free port that valued money above any notions of cultural imperialism.

The Portuguese took Melaka in 1511, while the equally ambitious Dutch founded Batavia (now Jakarta) to undermine Melaka's position, finally wresting the city from their European competitors in 1641. In the late 18th century, the British began looking for a harbour in the Strait of Melaka to secure lines of trade between China, the Malay world and their interests in India. Renewed war in Europe led, in 1795, to the French annexation of Holland, which prompted the British to seize Dutch possessions in Southeast Asia, including Melaka.

After the end of the Napoleonic Wars, the British agreed to restore Dutch possessions in 1818, but there were those who were bitterly disappointed at the failure of the dream of British imperial expansion in Southeast Asia. One such figure was Stamford Raffles, lieutenant-governor of Java. Raffles soon procured permission to establish a station to secure British trade routes in the region and was instructed to negotiate with the sultan of nearby Johor for land.

TIMELINE

300	1200s	1390s
Chinese seafarers mark the island on maps, labelling it Pu Luo Chung, believed to have come from the Malay name Pulau Ujong, meaning 'island at the end'.	Prince of Sumatran Srivijayan dynasty founds a settlement on the island and calls it Singapura (Lion City), having reputedly seen a lion there. Later named Temasek (Sea Town).	Srivijayan prince Parameswara flees Sumatra to Temasek after being deposed. He later founds the Sultanate of Malacca, under which Temasek is an important trading post.

THE RAFFLES ERA

For someone who spent a very limited amount of time in Singapore, Sir Stamford Raffles had an extraordinary influence on its development. His name appears everywhere in the modern city – Raffles Place in the CBD, Stamford Rd, Raffles Hotel, the Raffles City shopping mall, the prestigious Raffles Institution (where Lee Kuan Yew went to school) – but his impact extends way beyond civic commemoration.

The streets you walk along in the city centre still largely follow the original plans he drew. The ethnic districts still evident today, particularly in the case of Little India, were demarcated by him. Even the classic shophouse design – built of brick, with a continuous covered verandah known as a 'five-foot way' and a central courtyard for light, ventilation and water collection – has been attributed to him. More importantly, Singapore's very existence as one of the world's great ports is a direct consequence of Raffles' vision of creating a British-controlled entrepôt to counter Dutch power in the region.

Even Raffles' delicate and adept diplomatic dealings with the Malay sultanate to the north, which dwarfed the tiny island, have echoes in the frequently fractious relations between the two countries today.

When Raffles landed at Singapore in early 1819, the empire of Johor was divided. When the old sultan had died in 1812, his younger son's accession to power had been engineered while an elder son, Hussein, was away. The Dutch had a treaty with the young sultan, but Raffles threw his support behind Hussein, proclaiming him sultan and installing him in residence in Singapore.

In Raffles' plans the sultan wielded no actual power but he did serve to legitimise British claims on the island. Raffles also signed a treaty with the more eminent *temenggong* (senior judge) of Johor and set him up with an estate on the Singapore River. Thus, Raffles acquired the use of Singapore in exchange for modest annual allowances to Sultan Hussein and the *temenggong*. This exchange ended with a cash buyout of the pair in 1824 and the transfer of Singapore's ownership to Britain's East India Company.

The sultan's family retained a home in Singapore until 1999, when they moved out. The building now houses the Malay Heritage Centre (see p67).

Along with Penang and Melaka, Singapore formed a triumvirate of powerful trading stations known as the Straits Settlements, which were controlled by the East India Company in Calcutta but administered from Singapore.

Raffles had hit upon the brilliant idea of turning a sparsely populated, tiger-infested malarial swamp with few natural resources into an economic powerhouse by luring in the ambitious and allowing them to unleash their entrepreneurial zeal. While it was to be many decades before Singapore's somewhat anarchic social conditions were brought under control, the essential Rafflesian spirit still underpins the city's tireless drive to succeed.

COLONISATION & OCCUPATION

Singapore Under the British

Raffles' first and second visits to Singapore in 1819 were brief, and he left instructions and operational authority with Colonel William Farquhar, former Resident (the chief British representative) in Melaka. When Raffles returned three years later, he found the colony thriving but displeasingly chaotic.

1613	1819	1823
Portuguese attack the town on the island and burn it to the ground. Singapura never regains its former importance while the Portuguese rule Malacca, and it slides into obscurity.	Sir Stamford Raffles, seeking a site for a new port to cement British interests in the Malacca Strait, lands on Singapura and decides it's the ideal spot.	Raffles signs treaty with the Sultan and Temenggong of Johor, who hand control over most of the island to the British. Raffles returns to Britain and never sees Singapore again.

RAFFLES THE MAN

Sir Stamford Raffles, cultural scholar, Singapore colonist, naturalist and founder of the London Zoo, died at his home in Hendon, North London, the day before his 45th birthday in 1826, probably from a brain tumour. Having fallen out with the East India Company, his death was ignored by London society, and it was eight years before a marble statue of him, commissioned by friends and family, was placed in Westminster Abbey.

The original bronze statue of Raffles in Singapore, unveiled on the Padang on 29 June 1887, now stands in front of Victoria Theatre and Concert Hall. A white stone replica on Empress Place supposedly marks the spot where he first set foot on the island.

Raffles himself was an extraordinary man, in many ways at odds with the British colonial mould. While he was a firm believer in the British Empire as a benevolent force, he also preached the virtues of making Singapore a free port and opposed slavery. Raffles was also a sympathetic student of the peoples of the region and spoke fluent Malay.

His character was probably shaped by his humble upbringing. He began his working life at 14 as a clerk for the giant East India Company, but was a tireless self-improver. In 1805, he was appointed as part of a group to cement emerging British interests in Penang. Within six years, through several promotions, he became the governor of Java, where his compassionate leadership won him enduring respect. From there he travelled to Sumatra, where he became governor of Bencoolen on the island's southern coast.

His life was marred by tragedy, however. While in Southeast Asia he lost four of his five children to disease, his massive natural history collection in a ship fire and his personal fortune in a bank collapse. The East India Company refused him a pension and after his death his parish priest, who objected to his antislavery stance, refused him a headstone.

His achievements as a statesman have often obscured his brilliance as a naturalist. He made an intricate study of the region's flora and fauna and though much of his work was lost, it is still honoured at the National University of Singapore, which maintains the Raffles Museum of Biodiversity Research (p95).

It was then that he drew out his town plan that remains today, levelling one hill to form a new commercial district (now Raffles Place) and erecting government buildings around another prominence called Forbidden Hill (now called Fort Canning Hill).

His plan also embraced the colonial practice, still in evidence, of administering the population according to neat racial categories. The city's trades, races and dialect groups were divided into zones: Europeans were granted land to the northeast of the government offices (today's Colonial District), though many soon moved out to sequestered garden estates in the western suburbs. The Chinese, including Hokkien, Hakka, Cantonese, Teochew and Straits-born, predominated around the mouth and the southwest of the Singapore River, though many Indians lived there too (hence the large Hindu temple on South Bridge Rd). Hindu Indians were, and still are, largely centred in Kampong Kapor and Serangoon Rd; Gujarati and other Muslim merchants were housed in the Arab St area; Tamil Muslim traders and small businesses operated in the Market St area; and the Malay population mainly lived on the swampy northern fringes of the city.

In time, of course, these zones became less well defined, as people decanted into other parts of the island.

While the British ran the colony, they needed the cooperation of their subjects, particularly the Chinese, for whom the British echoed the admiration other European powers had for the Chinese communities under their rule.

Just as the infamously harsh Dutch East Indies governor-general Jan Pieterszoon Coen described the Chinese residents of Batavia (Jakarta) as 'clever, courteous, industrious and obliging

1824	1826	1867
Anglo-Dutch Treaty carves up the region into different spheres of influence, effectively removing any lingering threat to the island and cementing British sovereignty over Singapore.	Penang, Melaka and Singapore combined to form the Straits Settlements, administered from India. Large waves of immigration wash over Singapore free port as merchants seek to avoid Dutch tariffs.	Social problems and discontent at ineffectual administration and policing of Singapore persuades the British to declare the Straits Settlements a separate Crown Colony, no longer administered from India.

people', the Chinese of Singapore particularly impressed Victorian traveller Isabella Bird in 1879, when she described the city's 'ceaseless hum of industry' and 'the resistless, overpowering, astonishing Chinese element'.

Despite its wealth, the colony was a dissolute place, beset by crime, clan violence, appalling sanitation, opium addiction, rats, huge poisonous centipedes, mosquitoes and tigers. Life for the majority was extremely harsh; the Chinatown Heritage Centre (p60) is probably the best place to appreciate just how harsh.

Raffles sought to cooperate with, and officially register, the various *kongsi* – clan organisations for mutual assistance, known variously as ritual brotherhoods, secret societies, triads and heaven-man-earth societies. (Many of them had their headquarters on Club St, and a couple still hold out against the area's rapid gentrification.) Labour and dialect-based *kongsi* would become increasingly important to Singapore's success in the 19th century, as overseas demand for Chinese-harvested products such as pepper, tin and rubber – all routed through Singapore from the Malay peninsula – grew enormously.

Singapore's access to *kongsi*-based economies in the region, however, depended largely on revenues from an East India Company product that came from India and was bound for China – opium.

Farquhar had established Singapore's first opium farm for domestic consumption, and by the 1830s excise and sales revenues of opium accounted for nearly half the administration's income, a situation that continued for a century after Raffles' arrival. But the British Empire (which has been called the world's first major drug cartel) produced more than Chinese opium addicts; it also fostered the Western-oriented outlook of Straits-born Chinese.

In the 19th century, women were rarely permitted to leave China; thus, Chinese men who headed for the Straits Settlements often married Malay women, eventually spawning a new, hybrid culture now known in Singapore as Peranakan (see p29).

Despite a massive fall in rubber prices in 1920, prosperity continued, immigration soared and millionaires were made almost overnight. In the 1930s and early '40s, politics dominated the intellectual scene. Indians looked to the subcontinent for signs of the end of colonial rule, while Kuomintang (Nationalist) and Communist Party struggles in the disintegrating Republic of China attracted passionate attention. Opposition to Japan's invasions of China in 1931 and 1937 was near universal in Singapore.

But just as political rumblings began to make the British nervous, war overtook events.

Singapore under the Japanese

When General Yamashita Tomoyuki pushed his thinly stretched army into Singapore on 15 February 1942, so began what Singapore regards as the blackest period of its history. For the British, who had set up a naval base near the city in the 1920s, surrender was sudden and humiliating – and some historians have pinpointed the fall of Singapore as the moment when the myth of British impregnability was blown apart and the empire began its final decline.

The impact of the Japanese occupation on the collective political and social memory of Singapore cannot be underestimated, and it has partly inspired Singapore's modern preoccupation with security.

Japanese rule was harsh. Yamashita had the Europeans and Allied POWs herded onto the Padang; from there they were marched away for internment. Many of them were taken to the

1877	1939	1942
Britain establishes Chinese Protectorate in each of the Straits Settlements in an effort to tackle the 'coolie trade', the exploitative labour market system run by Chinese secret societies.	Britain completes massive naval base in Singapore at a cost of around $500 million, boasting world's largest dry dock, heavy defences and enough fuel storage to run the British Navy for months. Dubbed 'Fortress Singapore'.	Fortress Singapore cruelly exposed when Japanese forces overrun the island from the north, preparation for northern invasion not having been completed properly. Allies surrender on 15 February.

infamous Changi Prison, while others were herded up to Siam (Thailand) to work on the even more horrific Death Railway.

The Japanese also launched Operation Sook Ching to eliminate Chinese opposition. Chinese Singaporeans were driven out of their homes, 'screened', then either given a 'chop' (a mark on the forehead meaning they had been cleared for release), or driven away to be imprisoned or executed (there's a memorial to one massacre at Changi Beach). Estimates of the number of Chinese killed vary – some sources put the number at 6000, others at more than 45,000.

Malays and Indians were also subject to systematic abuse.

The Japanese renamed the island 'Syonan' (Light of the South), changed signs into Japanese, put clocks forward to Tokyo time and introduced a Japanese currency (known by contemptuous locals as 'banana money'). As the war progressed, inflation skyrocketed and supplies of food, medicines and other essentials dwindled to the point that people were dying of malnutrition and disease.

The war ended suddenly with Japan's surrender on 14 August 1945, and Singapore was passed back into British control. While the returning British troops were welcomed, the occupation had eroded the innate trust in the empire's protective embrace. New political forces were at work and the road to independence had begun.

INTERNATIONAL RELATIONS

While the British laid the country's early foundations, and the Japanese forever affected its sense of security, Singapore's postindependence international relations have been equally crucial in shaping its present.

From the moment it was thrown out of the Malay Federation in 1965, Singapore has been acutely conscious of the giant neighbours enveloping it in all sides, a sense of vulnerability enhanced by almost continual squabbles with Malaysia and Indonesia over anything from water supplies and resource exports to land reclamation and territory.

As recently as 2007, Indonesia banned sand exports to Singapore (the ban was almost certainly linked to Singapore's reluctance to sign an extradition treaty with Indonesia), while in 2008 the International Court of Justice was called upon to settle the disputed ownership of a clutch of tiny islands, which Singapore calls Pedra Blanca and Middle Rocks, and Malaysia knows as Pulau Batu Puteh. The court divided them between the two nations.

From the outset, Lee Kuan Yew's solution to this vulnerability was to form a close alliance with the United States and pour billions into Singapore's military (with Israeli training assistance). Singapore hosts regular military exercises with Western powers and you can hardly spend a day in the city without seeing some form of military aircraft – Chinooks, fighter jets, or transport planes – flying overhead.

The formation of Asean (Association of Southeast Asian Nations) also helped reinforce Singapore's security, though many member countries are uncomfortable with the steady advance of Singapore's business interests in the region. Its substantial investments in Burma, effective takeover of former Thai Prime Minister Thaksin Shinawatra's communications giant Shin Corp – which sparked the mass protests that ultimately culminated in Thaksin's overthrow – and stakes in Indonesia's telecommunications industry have all caused recent controversy.

In recent years, the government has been at pains to develop close ties with China (and, less overtly, India), arresting Falun Gong protestors and ensuring the media do not print anything

1942–45	1945–59	1959
Singapore is renamed Syonan by Japanese. Chinese massacred and brutalised, Allied prisoners incarcerated at Changi or shipped off to the Death Railway. The economy collapses.	British resume control of Singapore, but anticolonial sentiments grow. Straits Settlements wound up in 1946 and until 1955 Singapore was run by partially elected legislative councils, then a semi-autonomous government.	First full legislative elections held. People's Action Party, led by young Cambridge graduate Lee Kuan Yew, win landslide. Aggressive economic development and social programs launched.

too critical of Beijing. Singapore is often compared to a corporation and tends to be most vocal on foreign-policy issues when there are economic implications.

THE LEE DYNASTY

If one person can be considered responsible for the position Singapore finds itself in today, it is Lee Kuan Yew.

Born on 16 September 1923, this third-generation Straits-born Chinese was named Harry Lee (he's known locally by two nicknames: Uncle Harry and The Old Man) and brought up to be, in his own words, 'the equal of any Englishman'. His education at the elite Raffles Institution and later Cambridge, from which he graduated in 1949 with a first-class honours degree in law, equipped him well to deal with both colonial power and political opposition when Singapore took control of its own destiny in the 1960s.

The early years were not easy. Fatal race riots in 1964 and ejection from the Malay Federation in 1965 made Lee's task look even harder, but he displayed extraordinary vision and single-mindedness in dragging this fraught, divided port city up by its pyjama bottoms. Perhaps only those who remember the Singapore of the 1960s can truly appreciate the mammoth changes the city has undergone in those four decades.

Lee used generous tax incentives and strict new labour laws to attract foreign investment. This, combined with huge resources poured into developing an English-language education system that churned out a competent workforce, saw Singapore's economy rapidly industrialise.

Under Lee's rigidly paternal control, his People's Action Party (PAP) also set about eliminating any viable political opposition, banning critical publications and moulding the city into a disciplined, functional society built along Confucian ideals, which value the maintenance of hierarchy and social order above all things. The island's small size made this hothouse experiment easier to manage, enabling the effective enforcement of Singapore's famous social regulations on everything from spitting to chewing gum to jaywalking.

Lee was successful at containing what he evidently saw as the anarchic tendencies of Singapore's citizens, inspiring ever more ambitious attempts at social engineering. For example, a (now defunct) matchmaking club was established to pair off suitable couples – one of the dating clubs was restricted to graduates.

Lee's rapid industrialisation filled government coffers and enabled the PAP to pursue massive infrastructure, defence, health, education, pension and housing schemes, giving Singaporeans a level of prosperity and security that remains the envy of many countries in the region and around the world (many foreign governments have studied and tried to copy 'the Singapore model').

Housing and urban renovation, in particular, have been the keys to the PAP's success. By the mid-1990s, Singapore had achieved the world's highest rate of home ownership.

Despite resigning as prime minister in 1990 after 31 years in the job, and handing over to the more avuncular but no less determined Goh Chok Tong, Minister Mentor Lee still keeps an eye on proceedings and his comments on various issues frequently flag future government policy.

'Even from my sickbed,' said Lee in 1988, 'even if you are going to lower me into the grave and I feel that something is wrong, I'll get up.'

1963	1964	1965
After strong campaigning from Lee Kuan Yew, Singapore joins Sabah and Sarawak in combining with Malaya to form the single state of Malaysia.	Two outbreaks of race rioting between Malays and Chinese see 36 people killed and more than 500 injured, fuelling the already testy relations between the PAP and the Malay ruling party UMNO.	Singapore expelled from federation after unanimous vote in Malaysian Parliament in Kuala Lumpur. Lee Kuan Yew cries as he announces the news. The Republic of Singapore is born.

No one can deny his extraordinary achievements, but many argue he should have let go a long time ago and allowed the country to progress naturally. The continued unbending suppression of critical or opposition views, many argue, is anachronistic, at odds with the stable, prosperous society Lee has built.

'If after four decades the society remains so volatile that one can't even discuss sensitive topics openly, the government must have failed in its duty to build a harmonious society', wrote the editor of the *Far Eastern Economic Review* in response to one of the many lawsuits the Lee family has filed against the foreign media.

Some argue that while modern Singapore's founding father retains such an influence, the government's belligerent approach to criticism can never change. But whether the government is being held back by him, or whether it still happily relies upon his stature to inspire fear and respect, is a question only time can answer.

RECENT PAST & IMPENDING FUTURE

Lee Kuan Yew's son, Lee Hsien Loong, who was deputy PM and Defence Minister under Goh Chok Tong, took over the top job unopposed in 2004. Goh took over the Senior Minister role from Lee Snr, who assumed the newly created title of Minister Mentor.

Lee Hsien Loong faces challenges as great as those his father dealt with, principally how to continue the momentum and maintain Singapore's astonishing success. The Asian financial crisis starting in 1997 and the SARS outbreak in 2003 both had a major impact on the country's economy and its sense of vulnerability to forces beyond its control. Though economically and financially Singapore is in a strong position, the migration of its manufacturing base to cheaper competitors like Vietnam and China has forced the government to embark on a radical makeover of the country as a whole in an attempt to turn it into a vibrant, modern metropolis.

The port, petrochemical-refining, shipbuilding, rig-manufacture and other key heavy industries will remain, but Singapore is also trying to remodel itself as a high-tech modern economy by attracting industries like biotechnology, 'new media' and financial services, as well as international higher-education institutions and medical services.

To bolster this effort, the government has been at pains (with sometimes painful results) to banish the country's parochial, insular, conservative image and recast it as fun, creative and hip, energetically promoting arts, entertainment and tourism. It is also urgently trying to overhaul the education system, having realised a touch belatedly that its rigid rote-learning methods, while generating accomplished exam results, are failing to produce the kind of independent, creative thinkers the country needs for its future.

These efforts have met with mixed success, but physically they are transforming the city beyond recognition. Apart from the two huge casinos (euphemistically called 'integrated resorts') at Marina Bay and Sentosa, there is the Singapore Flyer observation wheel, the new Marina Bay

1971	1975	1981
British forces withdraw from Singapore, sparking economic crisis. PAP uses withdrawal to mount election to win mandate for tough laws curbing unions, which succeed in luring wave of foreign investment, mostly from US.	Singapore becomes world's third-busiest port, after Rotterdam and New York, and third-largest oil refiner, as well as a rig and drilling-platform manufacturer and a huge oil-storage centre.	Changi Airport opens for business, replacing Paya Lebar airport, and handles eight million passengers in its first year. By 2004 passenger traffic hits 30 million and Changi regularly named world's best airport.

A SEISMIC SHIFT?

At the most recent general election in 2006, the PAP won the expected landslide majority, claiming 82 of the 84 seats in parliament. Only the constituencies of Hougang and Potong Pasir remained stubbornly in opposition hands.

There was rather more to the election than the *Straits Times,* or any other Singapore newspaper, led its readers to believe. Perhaps the most telling statistic was that fully one-third of the electorate voted against the government, though the electoral system ensures those numbers are not reflected proportionally in the House.

Even more striking were the enormous crowds that turned out to opposition rallies, twice filling local sports stadia (http://en.wikipedia.org/wiki/Image:Hougangwpcrowd.jpg), and the not altogether surprising fact that the newspapers failed to mention them.

It was the first time since 1988 that the PAP was not automatically returned to power on nomination day.

It's unlikely that this is indicative of a groundswell of opposition serious enough to threaten the PAP's grip on power (the electoral rules alone will see to that), but the fact that around 330,000 of the 1.01 million voters are unhappy with the state of things is not insignificant.

lifestyle, leisure and water-sports area, a second botanic gardens, the St James Power Station entertainment complex, a large new sports complex, the transformation of the city's drainage canals into waterfront leisure areas…the list keeps growing.

In 2008 Singapore planted itself on the world sports calendar twice, first by staging the first Formula One night race, on a street circuit around the Colonial District and Marina Bay, then by winning the bid to host the first Youth Olympics in 2010.

Like the decision to build the two enormous casino projects, the bid to host a Formula One race represented a surprising reversal of government policy. Singapore had previously held races, along a circuit that once wound along Old Upper Thomson Rd (Map pp48–9), but in the most zealous phase of his social-engineering project, Lee Kuan Yew had banned motor sports, arguing that a ban would discourage dangerous driving. (Five minutes on an expressway are enough to demonstrate that it may have been one of his least successful ideas!)

This radical makeover is aimed at more than tourism. By increasing the city's 'liveability' and its global profile, the government is trying to attract more companies to set up in Singapore, in the process adding the extra 2 million people to the population that it reckons it needs to keep the country competitive.

Of course, there is a flipside to this development. Except for all the new labourers, service staff and other low-wage workers needed to run this new economy, most of these extra people will be highly paid foreigners. With living costs rising rapidly, wages failing to keep up and the income gap becoming ever wider, the danger is that most of the people left behind by the New Singapore will be Singaporeans, among whom there is already an undercurrent of resentment.

It didn't help that, just as low-income Singaporeans were starting to feel the pinch, government ministers awarded themselves ample pay increases – the PM alone got a handsome 25% rise to a staggering $3.9 million (see p27). Local newspapers devoted hundreds of column inches to 'news' stories and editorials justifying the rises, a sign that the government knew just how unpopular it would be. The argument goes that the high salaries only mirror those of top corporations, and that they help maintain probity in high office by making ministers impervious to corruption.

1989	2004	2008
Lee Kuan Yew steps down as Prime Minister, handing over reins to Goh Chok Tong. Lee becomes Senior Minister and retains oversight of government policy.	Goh Chok Tong steps down as Prime Minister and is replaced by Lee Kuan Yew's son, Lee Hsien Loong, who announces decision to build two casinos, reversing decades of government policy on casino gambling.	Singapore stages Formula One grand prix.

An increase in private rents of more than 100% between 2006 and 2008 will have kept local landlords happy, but large numbers of Singaporeans are struggling to make ends meet, and this may have a long-term impact on the government's popularity, especially if its top-down economic policies fail to propel Singapore through the next few decades.

CULTURE

As prosperous Singapore forges ahead into the 21st century, it is keenly examining what it means to be a Singaporean. Is there such a thing as a Singaporean identity? The government is keen to promote one, but beyond the almost universal use of the Singlish dialect (see p41) and the obsession with food, it is questionable whether the different communities feel a deep, shared sense of Singaporeanness.

The Malay, Tamil and Chinese (and Peranakan – see below) communities retain strong individual religious, cultural and moral values. Despite the astonishing pace of change and the city's Westernised veneer, or maybe because of it, many traditional customs, festivals and ceremonies survive and even flourish.

If there is any shared sense of values, it is the neo-Confucian ideals espoused by the government. These ideals are based on subservience to family and authority, hard work, discipline and the desire to succeed. The sanctity of the extended family unit and respect for parents is reinforced both socially and through legislation.

It is not unusual for Singaporeans to continue living with their parents until they are well into their 30s, partly because of cultural mores, partly because housing legislation makes it next to impossible for young people to move out of home until they are married, unless they can afford a private house or condo. Single people cannot buy or rent Housing Development Board (HDB) flats until they are 35, and even then they have to apply together with another single person.

It is expected, in Chinese families particularly, that children care for ageing parents much as parents care for young children. By and large this is still the case, but there are signs of change,

THE PERANAKANS

'Peranakan' means half-caste in Malay, which is exactly what the Peranakans are: descendants of Chinese immigrants who from the 16th century onwards settled in Singapore, Melaka and Penang and married Malay women. The term does not in fact strictly denote Chinese – there were also Peranakan Yahud (Jews), Ceti Peranakan (Hindus from southern India) and Peranakan Yawi (Arabs).

The culture and language of the Chinese Peranakans is a fascinating melange of Chinese and Malay traditions. The Peranakans took the name and religion of their Chinese fathers, but the customs, language and dress of their Malay mothers. They also used the terms 'Straits-born' or 'Straits Chinese' to distinguish themselves from later arrivals from China, who they looked down upon (nowadays pretty much all Chinese Singaporeans look down on the mainlanders!).

Other names you may hear for these people are Babas or Nonyas, after the Peranakan words for male (baba) and female (nonya). The Peranakans were often wealthy traders and could afford to indulge their passion for sumptuous furnishings, jewellery and brocades. Their terrace houses were gaily painted, with patterned tiles embedded in the walls for extra decoration.

Peranakan dress was similarly ornate. Nonyas wore fabulously embroidered kasot manek (slippers) and kebaya (blouses worn over a sarong), tied with beautiful kerasong brooches, usually of fine filigree gold or silver. Babas, who assumed Western dress in the 19th century, reflecting their wealth and close association with the British, saved their finery for important occasions such as the wedding ceremony, a highly stylised and intricate ritual dictated by adat (Malay customary law).

The Peranakan patois is a Malay dialect containing many Hokkien words – so many that it is largely unintelligible to a Malay speaker. The Peranakans also included words and expressions of English and French. There are very few monolingual Peranakans left – and they are very old – and the culture has endured a long, slow decline.

In recent years, there have been vigorous efforts to keep this heritage alive. The Peranakan Association (☎ 6255 0704; www.peranakan.org.sg) reports growing interest in Peranakan traditions, the cuisine remains extremely popular, and the opening of the fabulous Peranakan Museum (p56) has cemented the community's importance to Singapore's history and culture.

IN PERFECT HARMONY?

In 1964, when Singapore was still part of the Malay Federation, the city was twice shaken by race riots between Malays and Chinese. The first took place in July, on Prophet Muhammad's birthday and subsequent days, during which more than 20 people were killed and around 450 injured.

Then, in September, a Malay man was found murdered – allegedly by a group of Chinese – in the traditional Malay district of Geylang Serai, sparking fresh riots that engulfed Geylang and Joo Chiat. A further 13 people were killed and more than 100 injured.

The riots inspired decades of government attempts to foster religious and racial tolerance, which continue unabated. Racial discrimination remains the country's second-most taboo subject, after criticising the government.

Religious instruction is not permitted in school, HDB flats must maintain strict quotas of racial mixing and there are harsh punishments for those who publicly air racist opinions in blogs or elsewhere.

Has it worked? Well, there haven't been any riots since, so in essence the answer is yes. Singapore has worked extremely hard at maintaining a multicultural society; its economic success has depended upon it. But it's also true that many Singaporeans are acutely mindful of racial differences – perhaps as a consequence of being continually reminded about race – and you don't have to dig too far beneath the surface to uncover lingering prejudice, though of course the same could be said of dozens of societies.

Surveys have indicated that there is very little interaction between races, despite the enforced mixing, and the evidence on the street seems to support that conclusion. Seeing mixed-race groups of friends is not particularly common, and mixed race couples draw stares.

Privately, many Indians and Malays say they believe pro-Chinese discrimination is universal, though you'll never see any such sentiments expressed in the media. While employment classifieds cannot specify a preferred race, many simply get around this by saying they require 'Mandarin speakers'.

While Singapore remains economically stable and successful, racial differences are likely to remain hidden, but as the experiences of countless countries show, if the hard times hit, ugly sentiments are the first to surface.

as newspaper stories about elderly people being abandoned in nursing homes periodically remind the population.

Until a recent abrupt reversal, the government education system sternly discouraged individuality and gave little merit or attention to most nonacademic pursuits. From a very young age, children are 'streamed' according to their academic abilities, and once placed in an academic stream it is difficult to break into a higher one. The system, now being reformed, was derided in the popular local movie *I Not Stupid*.

The value placed on order and conformity means that the familiar East–West cultural clashes found elsewhere in Asia are also common in Singapore. Westerners often complain that Singaporeans are process-driven, either unwilling or incapable of thinking laterally or creatively. Conversely, Singaporeans are often uncomfortable with Westerners' outspokenness and willingness to challenge authority or accepted norms, seeing it as brash, arrogant and disruptive. These differences can make themselves evident to the visitor in small ways, whether you're trying to get a coffee chain to serve breakfast two minutes after the allotted breakfast period has ended, or a bank clerk to perform an unfamiliar transaction. Foreigners trying to carry out any task in an unusual or nonprescribed manner often hit a logjam they find baffling, which also creates the potential for problems between expatriate workers and local staff.

However, you won't find many Westerners complaining about how safe Singapore is – unlike many cities in the West, you don't have to think twice about walking past groups of young men late at night.

But while the strong sense of discipline has engendered an often punishing lifestyle involving long hours and hard work, affluent citizens make full use of their leisure time. Singaporeans are keen travellers, whether popping off to Kuala Lumpur, Bangkok or Hong Kong for weekend shopping trips, to Genting Highlands for weekend gambling orgies, or to Australia, Europe and the US for long holidays. Likewise, younger Singaporeans are gradually becoming more interested in independent travel, while you'll find plenty of young Singaporeans educated overseas who have a radically different mindset from those who passed through the local education system.

ARTS

Singapore's art scene is flourishing like never before, and the city-state offers scores of galleries filled with works by both local and foreign artists, theatres featuring locally produced plays, and increasingly successful directors putting Singaporean scenes onto the big screen. The combination of diversity and stability that's made Singapore into a financial powerhouse has helped create a fairly vibrant arts scene.

There are, of course, some who say that the scene in Singapore is somewhat lacking in grit. Singapore's social stability and overall comfort level provides little to rebel against, and this in turn may have created an environment more sterile than perhaps Beijing or New York, cities with long histories of social rebellion. Singapore, lacking this tradition, produces art and artists somewhat less radical in nature.

In *The Wild One,* Marlon Brando, in response to the question 'What are you rebelling against?' answered 'What have you got?' Had this been a Singaporean film, his answer might well have been 'Against what am I permitted to rebel?'

This pretty well describes the complaint some critics level at the overall art scene in Singapore.

Still, from a strictly aesthetic perspective, Singapore produces beauty far more copious than its tiny size might suggest, all the while playing host to artists in all mediums from around the world. Visitors can reasonably expect to experience anything from Chinese opera and Indian classical dance to British Pantomime and stand-up comedians. The number of galleries hosting local and nonlocal artists has increased exponentially over the last decade, and of course Singapore is a major stopover for touring theatre companies from the West, and major international pop artists.

top picks

ART GALLERIES

- Singapore Art Museum (p56) Eclectic Asian.
- Gajah Gallery (p151) Chic Asian.
- Red Sea Gallery (Map pp52–3; 232 River Valley Rd) Well-priced Vietnamese.
- Utterly Art (p108) Modern local.
- Opera Gallery (Map pp74–5; Ngee Ann City 02-12, Orchard Rd) Expensive European.

Singapore's place in world cinema has never been stronger, and the city's annual international film festival offers both a venue for local and international filmmakers. Theatre, too, is blossoming. A number of local theatre groups have, over the last decade, pushed the boundaries of what's considered 'speakable discourse', and while Singapore still can't be considered a free-for-all artistic environment, nowadays shows are more likely to close because of poor ticket sales than government interference.

Shoppers looking to pick up local art and sculptures will find plenty to choose from, but the far better bargains can be had in Hanoi, Bangkok or Bali.

A mix of architectural styles makes wandering the streets an eclectic delight, with Indian temples in Chinatown, and the Foster & Partners–designed Supreme Court looming like a spaceship over the old colonial quarter. Art and architecture go hand in hand, as the spiky, endearing Esplanade shows, and many colonial buildings are reinventing themselves as arts venues, such as the Arts House at the Old Parliament House.

Music and dance performances, such as the Womad (World of Music and Dance) festival and Ballet under the Stars in Fort Canning Park, are often held in open spaces and shopping malls to appeal to a wider audience. The annual Arts Festival (June/July) ranges from larky street theatre to the impenetrably avant-garde.

Extensive listings for galleries, theatre groups and cinemas can be found in the Arts & Leisure chapter (p150).

PAINTING

The School of Singapore hasn't established itself in quite the same way as Indonesia, Vietnam or China – apart from the Nanyang School of the Sixties, which went on to found the Nanyang School of Fine Art. Among its founders, collagist Goh Beng Kwan is still working hard today. Artists Tan Swie Hian, Heman Chong and Francis Ng all took part in the Venice Biennale in 2003. Tan also became the first Singaporean to receive the World

Economic Forum Crystal Award in 2003. Ong Kim Seng is a well-regarded local watercolourist while Chua Ek Kay works beautifully in Chinese ink. Visiting local galleries (there are many, both older and newly opened) is a great way to learn about the local painting scene. Check out the Arts & Leisure chapter on p150 for gallery listings.

The MICA Building (Ministry of Information, Communication and the Arts) has a handful of galleries, while boutique galleries like Red Sea Gallery on River Valley Rd and Utterly Art on South Bridge Rd showcase art from the region.

The grand old man of pottery is Iskandar Jalil, who fell foul of the authorities when his ancient kiln turned out to flout planning regulations (though admirers gave him a newer, safer one).

THE SCULPTURE TRAIL

Start at Raffles Place (Map pp52–3) and tick off the following sculptures.

- Aw Tee Hong's boat-shaped *Struggle for Survival* at the south end of Raffles Place
- the Singapore streetscape *Progress & Advancement* by Yang Ying-Feng at the north end of Raffles Place
- Henry Moore's *Reclining Figure* in front of the OCBC Centre on Chulia St
- the surreal *Homage to Newton* by Salvador Dalì in the atrium of the UOB Plaza on Chulia St
- Fernando Botero's giant, fat *Bird* on the river in front of UOB Plaza
- the river-diving boys of *First Generation* by Chong Fat Cheong on the right-hand side of Cavenagh Bridge
- the family of tiny Kucinta cats on the left-hand side of Cavenagh Bridge

SCULPTURE & PUBLIC ART

Sculpture Square (Map pp52–3), on Middle Rd, was launched in 1999, and public art is springing up everywhere. While New York's Wall Street has the bull, Singapore's financial district has a chubby, somewhat whimsical sculpture called *Bird* by Colombian artist Fernando Botero. The area on both sides of the river is dotted with sculptural works, including a series entitled *The People of the River*. Showing scenes from Singapore's history, the series includes bronzes of little boys frozen in action jumping joyously into the river, pigtailed Chinese businessman negotiating with a 19th-century colonial over the price of a bale of cotton, and some rather curious (and undeniably cute) cats at the Fullerton Hotel end of the Cavenagh Bridge. Fans of surrealistic master Salvador Dali won't want to miss the sculpture *Homage to Newton,* a typically bizarre work that feels somewhat out of place in a city not known for its appreciation of the hallucinatory.

MUSIC & DANCE

The Singapore rock scene is surprisingly lively. Local rock band Electrico is still going strong, having just released its third album *We Satellites* in the summer of 2008. Other bands include Ugly in the Morning, Mi Lu Bang, the Observatory and the oddly named I Am David Sparkle (an electronica band whose sound has been compared to another oddly named group, Godspeed You Black Emperor!). Going lighter, pianist Jeremy Monteiro, his sister Clarissa, and others like guitarist Eugene Pao keep the Singapore flag flying proudly on the international jazz scene.

The superb Singapore Symphony Orchestra (SSO), set up in 1979, was Singapore's first professional orchestra and now performs over a hundred times per year at the Esplanade, while the well-respected Singapore Chinese Orchestra, set up in 1997, performs about 20 traditional and symphonic Chinese pieces each year, as well as Indian, Malay and Western pieces.

There are more than 30 dance companies and societies. Singapore's leading dance company, the Singapore Dance Theatre, puts on about 28 performances a year – the annual Ballet under the Stars season at Fort Canning Park draws an audience of 10,000. Odyssey Dance Theatre represented Singapore at the ASEAN Festival of Arts, while groups such as EcNad and Ah Hock & Peng Yu all add to a growing scene. The minority groups are well represented: Bhaskar's Arts Academy and the Nrityalaya Aesthetics Society for Indian dance, and Sri Warisan Som Said Performing Arts for contemporary and traditional Malay dance.

Chinese Opera

In Singapore, *wayang* (Chinese opera) is derived from the Cantonese opera, which is seen as a more music-hall mix of dialogue, music, song and dance. What the performances lack in literary nuance they make up for in garish costumes and crashing music. Scenery is virtually nonexistent, but action is all-important. Performances can go for an entire evening, with the audience drifting in and out, eating and chatting. It's usually easy for the uninitiated to follow the gist of the action. The acting is stylised, and the music searing to Western ears, but seeing a performance – or at least part of one – is worthwhile.

Street performances are held during important festivals such as Chinese New Year, the Festival of the Hungry Ghosts and the Festival of the Nine Emperor Gods – head to Chinatown for the best chance of seeing performances.

CINEMA

In 2008 the Singapore International Film Festival (SIFF) celebrated its 21st year as a major event on the Singapore arts calendar; whether this is indicative of the city-state's coming of age in the world of film is debatable, but Singaporean filmmakers seem to be producing films of increasingly mature subject matter.

Many explanations have been cited for Singaporean cinema's patchy achievements in the past – including lack of money, lack of interest, dearth of creative talent, lack of official encouragement – but now there is certainly no lack of money or official encouragement.

Recently, money has been poured into local movies, through the conduit of the Singapore Film Commission and local deep-pocket production houses like Mediacorp-owned Raintree Productions, with mixed success.

Probably the best local director is Eric Khoo, whose *12 Storeys, Mee Pok Man* and *Be with Me* are set in the island's 'heartlands' and have been well received. The latter two were hits at the Cannes Film Festival.

Jack Neo boasts Singapore's three highest-grossing local productions. *Money No Enough* focused on the dark side of the heartlands in the shape of the loan sharks who patrol these vast estates and feed on the impoverished. *I Not Stupid* is an amusing and biting look at Singapore society through its pushy hot-house education system, while sequel *I Not Stupid Too* was more successful commercially, though not as satirical.

Young director Royston Tan came to prominence in 2005, when his film *15: The Movie*, which dealt with drug abuse and wayward youth, was cut by the censors, winning at-

top picks

MOST IMPORTANT SINGAPOREAN FILMS

Representing the next generation of cinema in Singapore, filmmaker Wesley Wong, whose real-life concerns mirror those of his alter-ego 'ah-tan' in the short film *Zo Gang* (http://hosaywood.com/2007/12/05/zo-gang-online-now/), has been working in local independent film since graduating from film school in Perth. These are Wesley's picks for most important Singaporean films.

- **Bujang Lapok** (Confirmed Bachelor; 1957) The first comedy of P Ramlee, one of the most versatile and prolific artistes-turned-filmmaker. The film jumped-started a whole series of *Bachelor* comedies, simultaneously making Ramlee a household name, even today.
- **They Call Her...Cleopatra Wong** (1978) Singapore's take on the blaxploitation films of the '70s, the film proved to be a good formula to copy as it swept through the region and made it to cult status beyond the region.
- **Medium Rare** (1991) A real anomaly, this was both a good and bad thing for Singapore films. It marked the revival of locally made films, but it also became a report card to explain the dearth of local films and filmmaking. The unfortunate experiment will also forever be remembered, as a local magazine put it, as 'Tedium-rare'. Hardy Singaporean filmgoers bounced back from this, which led us to...
- **12 Storeys** (1997) Eric Khoo's name pops up more often than any other local filmmaker. His second feature is probably his most accessible and realistic portrayal of Singapore. It explores Singaporeans and their neighbours in public housing projects, which are, by now, world renowned.
- **Money No Enough** (1998) Directed by Jack Neo, one of the leading actors in *12 Storeys*, this soon became an all-time top-grossing locally made film. Its success was both boon and bane, much like *Medium Rare*. On the one hand, it made Singaporean film once again competitive; on the other, it became the unspoken template for maximising profit from locally made movie ventures.
- **Perth** (2004) Djinn Ong's sophomore feature is at once a homage to Scorsese's *Taxi Driver* and a critique of the typical Singaporean dream: to retire in a slower-paced city like Perth, Australia. It features excellent acting from the supporting cast along with a fairly over-the-top performance from a veteran lead who, some say, tried just a bit too hard to channel Travis Bickle. A very gritty film.

BACKGROUND ARTS

tention for both the film and Tan, who lampooned the censors in a musical sequence called *Cut* (watch it on YouTube).

Among the locally produced films presented in the festival's Singapore Panorama were Kan Lumé's *Dreams from the Third World* (concerning the spiritual journey of a man making a porno). Though tame by Western standards, it's worth noting that its doubtful the film would have been screened locally as recently as 10 years ago.

THEATRE

Singapore's theatre groups have been at the forefront of pushing the boundaries of what is and isn't 'permissible discourse', offering intellectually challenging plays with socially – and sometimes politically – taboo subject matter. Creative, inventive luna-id Theatre specialises in plays by overseas playwrights that 'contain universal relevance'. Producing cutting-edge works by resident playwright Haresh Sharma, Singapore's the Necessary Stage aims for 'challenging indigenous and innovative theatre that touches the heart and mind'. Other theatre companies include WildRice, Theatreworks and Action Theatre.

ARCHITECTURE

Like many cities around the world, Singapore endured its own architectural Dark Ages in the 1960s and '70s, when legions of city planners and architects decided the concrete box was the way of the future and sent the wrecking ball scything through acres of architectural heritage.

Fortunately sense prevailed before they got too far. Areas of Chinatown, Little India and Katong contain beautifully preserved or restored shophouses, and the city centre is a treasure trove of tropical colonial design, interspersed with some outstanding modern buildings (see p36).

Singapore's notable architecture can be divided into several broad categories.

COLONIAL

Irishman George Drumgoole Coleman, who became Singapore's town surveyor and superintendent of public works in 1826, is the pre-eminent colonial architect. He was a skilful adapter of the Palladian style (Doric columns, high ceilings, wide verandas) to suit the tropical climate. His buildings include the Armenian Church (Map pp52–3), Caldwell House in CHIJMES (Map pp52–3) and Old Parliament House (Map pp52–3); he was also responsible for the city's original central road network, which was drawn by Sir Stamford Raffles.

Other colonial buildings of note from the mid-1800s include St Andrew's Cathedral (Map pp52–3) and the Cathedral of the Good Shepherd (Map pp52–3), as well as the Thian Hock Keng Temple (p61) and the Hajjah Fatimah Mosque (p67).

SHOPHOUSES

Before HDB flats, the definitive Singaporean building was the shophouse, whose long, narrow design was also a distinctive feature of other port cities like Penang and Melaka.

They were designed to have a shop or business on the lower floor and accommodation upstairs. Often projecting over the footpath is a solid canopy, known as a five-foot way. The canopy was in use in Southern China and parts of Southeast Asia, and were mandated by Sir Stamford Raffles in 1822, when in a set of ordinances he stated that 'all houses constructed of brick or tiles have a common type of front each having an arcade of a certain depth open to all sides as a continuous and open passage…'

Raffles wanted to ensure pedestrians were protected from the sun and rain. But shopkeepers had other ideas and before long they all became extensions of the shops inside. Most five-foot ways are now clear of commerce, but walk along Buffalo Rd in Little India, or the northern end of Telok Ayer St in Chinatown, and you get an idea of how difficult it became for pedestrians to negotiate these passageways.

The load-bearing walls separating the buildings are heavy masonry, which was a departure from the traditional timber, and not only provided strength and privacy from neighbours, but also deterred the spread of fire.

PUSHING THE LIMITS OF DISCOURSE: THE NECESSARY STAGE

Mr Tan, I've heard it said that you're the mind, (resident playwright) Haresh is the heart, and the theatre itself is the body. How do you feel about this analogy? (Laughs) There's some truth to the analogy, but I don't know where to go with it! I guess I am a little more cerebral, while Haresh is somewhat more emotional.

How important is the social message component in the work you do? Very important. There are some artists who say our work is not 'art' enough because it is too much of a platform for social messages. But we are most concerned with creating works that have multiple dimensions, in putting paradox on stage.

When the play *Off Centre* came out in 1994, it was considered controversial. Why? There are two protagonists in the story, one of whom is a military officer who happens to be a bully. The Ministry of Health said you couldn't commission a play that puts another ministry in a bad light. Also, at the time we were accused of being Marxists, and the theatre was shut down in 1995. We were later vindicated as being idealists, not Marxists.

Fast forward to 2008, and the same play has been chosen by the Ministry of Education to be part of the high-school literature syllabus. This must be a great vindication. Very much so. Today, of course, we're doing things that are far more controversial, covering topics ranging from paedophilia to the death penalty, topics that would have been unthinkable in 1994.

Your latest play, *Good People*, also seems controversial, because of its dealing with the issue of medical marijuana. Could you even have done this play 15 years ago? No, of course not. In Singapore there is tangible, real relaxation. Right now Singapore is in a really interesting space.

Is one of the jobs of the Necessary Stage to define the limits of what can and can't be spoken about? We like to think that. How can we make visible what is usually swept under the rug? This is what we're talking about.

How do you feel about the current degree of artistic censorship in Singapore? I don't believe in censorship, but I do believe in regulations. If we all set our rules together, it's fine. But it isn't something that we worry about at this point. The Necessary Stage is no longer doing plays that challenge the government. Now we are doing plays that disturb the audience.

For over two decades, theatre group the Necessary Stage (www.necessary.org) has put on plays designed not merely to entertain, but also to enlighten and create greater discourse on important social issues. Along the way, the group has pushed the envelope of what is 'speakable discourse' in the normally conservative city. Alvin Tan is the artistic director at the Necessary Stage.

The first shophouses dating from 1840 are plain, squat, two-storey buildings. These Early shophouses, in the vernacular, were followed by First Transitional, Late, Second Transitional and Art Deco style. Classical elements such as columns are often used on the facades, along with beautiful tiles and bright paint – the Chinese, Peranakans and Malays all favoured lively colours.

Shophouses typically featured a central courtyard, which was often open to the skies, allowing natural light to penetrate the building and, in the early days, acting as a useful water collection method (the courtyards usually had open cisterns). In some designs, a high rear wall acted as a kind of wind deflector, diverting breezes downwards and channelling them through the house.

A peculiarly Singaporean variation was the 'chophouse' – recreated examples of which can be seen at the Chinatown Heritage Centre (p60). Built to the same basic design as the shophouse, they were constructed to hold many dozens – sometimes hundreds – of residents. Floors were divided into tiny, dark, miserable cubicles and the high concentration of people meant conditions were squalid in the extreme. A few chophouses remain in Little India, along Desker Rd, for example, but most of them were torn down.

BUNGALOWS

Not the single-storey retirement homes of the West, bungalows here are named after Bangalore-style houses and are usually two storeys high. Most were built in the style now locally known as 'black and whites', after the mock-Tudor exposed-beam style adopted from 1900 to the late 1930s, and are much sought after by expatriates chasing colonialism's glory days three generations ago. You'll find many black and whites lurking in the leafy residential areas off Orchard Rd, such as along Nassim Rd and the stretch of Scotts Rd near the Sheraton Towers hotel. They also cluster in the exclusive areas such as Alexandra Park and Ridley Park, where you can practically taste the gin-slings and elegantly discreet liaisons.

Down at Mountbatten Rd in Kallang (Map p80) are examples of both the highly decorative Victorian bungalow and the concrete Art Deco bungalows dating from the 1920s and '30s, typically with flat roofs, curved corners and a strong horizontal design.

HDB FLATS

Only in Singapore could you walk safely through a tower-block estate at night and find a cold-drinks vending machine full, working and unvandalised. While public high-rise housing estates are being torn down elsewhere, in Singapore they work. They have to: land is limited, so the government had little choice but to build upwards. The state-run Housing Development Board (HDB) is locked into a mammoth construction project, erecting areas of well-built, well-maintained and affordable housing. So far, they have built around a million units.

HDB 'towns' such as Toa Payoh, Pasir Ris and Tampines provide homes for nearly 84% of the population. HDB developments have markets, schools, playgrounds, shops and hawker centres hardwired into them; the older ones (from the 1960s and '70s) have mature trees keeping them shady and (relatively) attractive. Many blocks also have 'void decks', empty areas on the ground floor that allow a breeze to circulate, and where old men play chess in the shade.

The HDB is also locked into a continuous renovation and upgrading program, even though the majority of the flats are privately owned, making them perhaps unique among the world's public housing projects. Every few years, they get licks of paint and new features added. There is a huge project currently underway to install lifts on every floor of these blocks, where previously the lifts stopped every three floors, which could be a nightmare for the elderly.

The MRT system makes it simple to visit the HDB heartlands. Just jump on a train and pop up somewhere like Toa Payoh. You won't see stunning architecture, but you will get a glimpse of what life is like for most Singaporeans.

top picks

MODERN BUILDINGS

- **Supreme Court** (Map pp52–3) Foster & Partners' contributions to the Singapore skyline tend to involve large silver discs, which are prominent on both the Expo Station near Changi Airport, and now on the gleaming, ultramodern new Supreme Court, which opened in June 2005.
- **The Esplanade** (Map pp52–3) Designed by Briton Michael Wilford and affectionately known as the Durians, this bulbous, spiky double concert hall intends to be the iconic equivalent of Sydney's Opera House. It's a magnificent sight, particularly at night.
- **National Museum of Singapore** (Map pp52–3) A masterpiece of melding traditional and modern, the new annex sits behind the original classic Palladian 19th-century building. Bathed in natural light but kept cool by large natural air-conditioning vents, it features large double-skinned glass rotundas, a glass passage linking it to the old building and whimsical features like swinging chandeliers.
- **Parkview Square** (Map p68) A study in 1930s Art Deco kitsch, Parkview Square, designed by American James Adam, is a Gotham City–style throwback, with a cathedral-domed entryway, terraced courtyard, a phalanx of statues of notable men of history, plus eight bronzed colossi kneeling at the building's corners.
- **Gateway** (Map p68) The clean lines of the Gateway provide a stark contrast to the frivolity of Parkview Square. These sleek glass-and-steel twin towers, designed by IM Pei as identical parallelograms, appear two-dimensional at almost any angle you view them from.

MODERN

The area around Bras Basah, which links Orchard Rd and the Colonial District, is filling up with new educational establishments, all showcasing extraordinary design and pointing to the more experimental line Singapore is now taking with its cityscape – a process heralded by the outrageous Esplanade theatres.

The Singapore Management University (Map pp52–3) looks chunky and functional, but saves itself with frills of greenery, while the Lasalle-SIA College of the Arts (Map p80) is a remarkable, irregular, crystalline building, designed to look as if a block of ice has been dropped and shattered into six parts.

The National Library (Map pp52–3) is one of the government's showpiece eco-buildings, designed for minimal energy use and wastage. The new annex of the National Museum of Singapore (p56), meanwhile, brilliantly melds some daring and whimsical design features with the original Victorian structure.

In the central business district is a cluster of gleaming towers by famous Japanese architects including Kurokawa Kisho's 66-storey Republic Plaza, and Tange Kenzo's OUB Centre and UOB Plaza. Tange also designed the URA Centre in Chinatown (Map pp62–3), an interesting place to drop by if you want to find out more about the future of Singapore's built environment.

As in most cities, public opinion is fiercely divided over architecture but so far Singapore has been spared the more horrendous modern follies that blight other cities.

ENVIRONMENT

THE LAND

Singapore is very flat, very hot and often very wet.

The main island of Singapore is 42km long and 23km deep, and sits a degree above the equator. There are a further 63 outlying islands, some industrial, some military, some for pleasure and some little more than wave-washed rocks. Altogether, Singapore has a land mass of nearly 700 sq km, though land reclamation is making it ever larger (see below).

The other main islands are Pulau Tekong, which is a military area, the largely rural Pulau Ubin, and Sentosa, Singapore's rapidly developing pleasure isle. Around half the island is built up, and the rest is given over to parkland, reservoirs, some small farms, large military areas and a few remaining pockets of jungle. Altogether, less than 3% of the country is farmland.

The absence of significant hills makes Singapore easy for walking, though that is counteracted by the relentless heat and humidity. Bukit Timah (which means 'hill of tin' in Malay) is the highest point, at a dizzying 166m. The central area has most of Singapore's forest and open areas, but the entire city is sprinkled with large parks. The western part is a sedimentary area of low-lying hills and valleys, while the southeast is mostly flat and sandy. Singapore is connected to Peninsular Malaysia by a causeway in the north and a bridge in the west.

WILDLIFE

The tigers that roamed the forests have long since been shot into oblivion, and elephants no longer swim across to Pulau Ubin, but nature spotting is still possible in Singapore's remaining forests.

The animals you're most likely to spot on a walk through the Central Catchment Nature Reserve (p88) are long-tailed macaques, monitor lizards and squirrels. The forests are also home to flying lemurs, pythons, cobras and other snakes, bats and even anteaters, but these are difficult to spot.

THE GROWING ISLAND

It's a long time since Beach Rd was anywhere near the sea. The island state has increased its landmass from 581 sq km at independence in 1965 to 682.7 sq km today and plans to add a further 100 sq km to itself in the future – much to the disquiet of neighbours Malaysia and Indonesia. This is nothing new: Singapore's first land reclamation project was during Raffles' time, when earth was removed from a hill to fill a swamp.

Reclamation has drastically changed the geography around the city centre, particularly in the Marina Bay area, where more than 550 hectares have been added. In the Tanah Merah and Changi Airport area in the east, and Tuas in the west, land is creeping into the sea. Some reclamation projects have trodden on the toes of Malaysia next door.

One of the most ambitious projects was the joining up of seven islands to make Jurong Island, now the biggest island after Singapore itself. The new land is mainly used for oil storage.

Singapore has been recognised as an important node on the East Asia Flyway, inspiring the government to gazette the bird-rich Sungei Buloh Wetland Reserve as a protected area. A bird-watcher's paradise, the reserve is also home to otters, massive monitor lizards and even a few saltwater crocodiles. Other protected mangrove areas include Pasir Ris Park and Chek Jawa on Pulau Ubin.

Though constant vigilance has kept the island's urban mosquito population under reasonable control, Singapore has an astonishingly rich six- and eight-legged population. There are 935 species of insect, and new ones continue to be discovered.

Underwater, the magical 'forests of coral' described by traveller Isabella Bird in the 19th century have been largely destroyed, and whatever marine life flourished in the Singapore Strait has been pummelled by shipping, pollution and land reclamation. However, *kelong* (fishing platforms) still exist, especially off Pulau Ubin (though Singaporeans usually go to Malaysia for *kelong* fishing trips) and there are an estimated 451 species of crab and shrimp living in Singapore waters, including the prehistoric blue-blooded horseshoe crab.

FLORA

Singapore consisted of mangrove and lowland dipterocarp forest and freshwater swamp forest. Most of it is now gone, but pockets remain in Bukit Timah Nature Reserve, MacRitchie Nature Reserve (though this is secondary forest) and on Pulau Ubin.

Nevertheless, Singapore has earned its Garden City moniker, and few cities around the world can match it for the range, size and variety of its green spaces, from the smallest city parks like Telok Ayer Green in Chinatown to large pockets of urban forest like Labrador or Kent Ridge Parks to large suburban green oases like Pasir Ris or Bishan Parks, to the superb Botanic Gardens.

Not surprisingly, Singapore's hot, humid climate nurtures a bewildering variety of flora, to the extent that one botanist estimated the island contains more plant species than the whole of North America.

GREEN SINGAPORE

A 10-year blueprint for environmental sustainability, called the Singapore Green Plan 2012, was launched in 2002, focusing on waste management, clean air, water supply and ecology. Updated every few years, the plan aims to make this already spotless and well-organised island even cleaner and greener.

However, on the ground, attitudes have been slow to change. Potentially, Singapore is the ideal test-bed for green vehicles, but the government has been reluctant to introduce the kind of incentives that might encourage mass adoption of hybrid or electric cars, perhaps because of its status as the world's third-biggest oil refiner. While new emissions standards have been introduced, congestion on the city's roads has dramatically worsened in recent years.

Recycling has been slow to take off, which is surprising given the pressure waste disposal puts on Singapore's scarce land resources. Most stores still hand out mountains of plastic bags (though some global retailers such as Ikea are setting the pace and weaning customers off) and Singaporeans appear largely reluctant to give up the bag habit. Change, though, will come. You'll find recycling bins dotted around the city centre, particularly along Orchard Rd.

But while the island tries to tackle environmental issues at home, it has no control over its neighbours. From June to September, fires in Indonesia (mostly from massive plantations) can send a brown haze over the island, so that it smells heavily of wood smoke, a gloomy reminder of its environmentally vulnerable position in the region.

GOVERNMENT & POLITICS

In theory, Singapore has a democratically elected government based on the Westminster system. In practice, however, the electoral laws are biased in favour of the ruling PAP, to the extent that though 33% of the electorate voted for one of the three opposition parties at the 2006 general election, the government won all but two of the 84 seats up for grabs. Even so, most Singaporeans quietly accept the status quo, figuring that political freedom is a fair trade-off for the high standard of living they generally enjoy.

The current unicameral parliament has 84 elected members, with nine of the MPs from single-member constituencies and the 75 others from group representation constituencies, which are supposed to ensure the representation in parliament of members of the Malay, Indian and other minority communities. A side effect of having several MPs for a single seat is that it's harder for opposition parties to field enough candidates to contest the seat.

Voting in elections is compulsory and governments are elected for five years, but a ruling government can dissolve parliament and call an election at any time.

Singapore also has a popularly elected president, who at the time of writing is SR Nathan. The position is largely ceremonial.

The PAP argues that since it listens to all opinions and is happy to take on good ideas no matter where they originate from, there is less need for political plurality.

It also asserts that, relieved of the tiresome task of answering to a strident opposition in parliament, it has more time to focus on running the country, citing the chaotic democracies of countries like India, Thailand and Indonesia to (somewhat convincingly) support its case. TV news reports display punch-ups in the parliaments of South Korea and Taiwan with a certain satisfied relish.

top picks

POLITICAL BOOKS

Naturally, you won't find any books on the dark side of Singapore's politics inside the country, though they are available from online bookstores – and many shops in Malaysia happily sell these dissenting volumes.

- Singapore Story (Lee Kuan Yew) To get the official story on the Singapore Miracle, skip all the sycophantic tomes churned out by local hacks and go straight to the source – the man who masterminded the whole thing.
- Lee's Law (Chris Lydgate) A disturbing and sad account of the rise and systematic destruction of Singapore's most famous dissenter and most successful opposition politician, lawyer JB Jeyaretnam.
- No Man Is An Island (James Minchin) A broad critical study of Lee Kuan Yew.
- To Catch A Tartar & Beyond Suspicion? The Singapore Judiciary (Francis Seow) The first book by the former Law Society president tells how he was plunged into a nightmare of persecution and professional ruin after he began to openly oppose Lee Kuan Yew. The second book questions the independence of the country's legal system.

Vocal opposition does exist, but those who have chosen to follow that path, like Chee Soon Juan, JB Jeyaretnam and Francis Seow (see boxed text, above), have found themselves subject to vilification, legal harassment and ridicule, and ignored by the media, unless there is something

JBJ

JB Jeyaretnam is Singapore's most famous dissenting voice, and his experiences are burned into the country's collective unconscious as a kind of cautionary tale.

A lawyer by profession, JBJ led the Worker's Party in an effort to challenge the all-powerful PAP. In 1981 he became the first opposition candidate in 13 years to win a seat, taking the Anson constituency in a by-election.

He was re-elected in 1984, but shortly afterwards was dragged into court to face charges relating to the party's accounts. Found not-guilty on all but one charge, he was sentenced to three months in prison and fined $5000, enough to have him disqualified from elections for five years and disbarred from legal practice.

JBJ appealed to the British Privy Council, which overturned his disbarment (leading the government to change the law relating to such appeals). He then asked the President of Singapore to overturn his conviction, but was refused.

Banned from the 1988 election, he nevertheless campaigned for the Worker's Party, but uttered comments about Lee Kuan Yew that, with a little creative legal interpretation, enable the prime minister to sue him. Lee Kuan Yew was awarded $260,000. Another 1995 lawsuit saw him hit for $465,000 in damages. Then, after he was appointed to parliament as a 'nonconstituency MP' in 1997, a further 11 defamation suits were filed against him for referring to police reports made against PM Goh Chok Tong.

The judge said the PM had overstated his case, but nonetheless awarded him $20,000. On appeal, this was raised to $100,000 – and the judge was later dismissed.

JBJ resigned as party leader in 2001 and in his last days scratched a living selling his two books – *Make it Right for Singapore* and *The Hatchet Man of Singapore* – on the street. He died on 20 September 2008, a few weeks after launching a political comeback under his newly created Reform Party, and his passing was marked by tributes and obituaries in media around the globe. Even in death, he remained a thorn in the government's side.

negative to report. The government's favoured means of dealing with these intrepid souls is to run them through the courts and ruin them with lawsuits. This is a tidy means of removing them from the political process, since bankrupts are forbidden from running in elections.

The legal system is based on the British system and the judiciary's independence is enshrined in the constitution, but in practice many judges are appointed on short tenure and their renewal is subject to party approval. Rulings that have gone against the government have seen new laws enacted by parliament to ensure the government's victory.

Singapore's Internal Security Department keeps records of its citizens, and there is a widespread (albeit unverifiable) fear that criticising the authorities will cost people their jobs, promotional opportunities or contracts.

As elsewhere, the internet has effected a sea change in the area of political and social debate and there has been a minor explosion in blogs expressing dissent and criticism of the government (see below).

Singapore does have an extensive local council machinery, which organises public meetings to listen to ideas on various issues of neighbourhood concern and domestic policy. The massive 'e-government' network, which enables citizens to perform all sorts of transactions online – from booking football pitches to filing income tax – also has a channel through which people can express opinions on certain issues.

The most notable recent example was the year-long debate over the building of the two casino resorts, which involved ordinary citizens, religious and grassroots leaders, charities and social services. Though there was a widespread belief that the government had made its mind up well before the 'public consultation' period, it was marked by some surprisingly outspoken views.

MEDIA

In theory, the news media in Singapore is free to express its opinions, but in reality this is far from the case. Self-censorship combined with stern government oversight and complicit editors keeps dissent and damaging stories away from the pages of the local press. Any local journalist intent on breaching the unwritten boundaries known to the local media as 'OB markers' will not keep their job very long, as former *Today* columnist and current blogger mr brown (www.mrbrown.com) found out.

The largest media company is the giant Singapore Press Holdings (SPH), which has become exceedingly wealthy on decades of effective monopoly. It publishes the country's flagship paper, the dreary *Straits Times* broadsheet, which is effectively a branch of the civil service. Its coverage of Asia is not bad, but even that is heavily skewed when Singapore's national interests are involved. Indeed, so well-practised is it at conjuring the illusion of free media that, according to local academic sources, governments such as Burma and China have sent teams over to Singapore to study its model.

SPH also publishes the tabloid *New Paper*, which offers up a lurid and mildly entertaining platter of crime, scandal, sensation, moral outrage, English football and atrocious graphics.

SPEAKING OUT IN SINGAPORE

On the surface, Singaporeans enjoy a substantial level of social freedom. But, as opposition figures like JB Jeyaretnam (see boxed text, p39) and Chee Soon Juan have discovered, once you start making yourself a nuisance to the Singapore government, life can change dramatically. Both men were hauled through the courts and bankrupted by lawsuits and Chee was fired from his job as a university lecturer.

The government, keen to be seen as democratic, established Speaker's Corner (Map pp62–3) in Hong Lim Park in 2000, but imposed firm restrictions on the subjects speakers could cover. After an initial burst of enthusiasm, the novelty quickly wore off and, perpetually deserted, Speaker's Corner became a something of a local joke – though several hundred people did gather there in 2008 to express their dismay at having lost massive investments in the collapse of Lehman Brothers bank…Whether this outpouring of discontent emboldens more Singaporeans to openly challenge the status quo is another matter, but clearly the ground is shifting, and in the long-term this could have serious implications for the ruling PAP.

Starting in the late 1990s, the government briefly experimented with media competition between SPH and Mediacorp, both of which operated rival daily freesheet newspapers and TV stations for a few years, but it was a commercial failure. Mediacorp's surviving freesheet *Today* (pick it up at the MRT stations in the morning) is the most entertaining read of any of the dailies, but its reputation as a paper willing to confront uncomfortable issues has largely been lost since the appointment of more government-friendly senior editors.

International English-language publications such as *Time*, the *Economist* and *Newsweek* are readily available, but you won't find the *Far Eastern Economic Review*, which has been banned and sued by the government over a story it published on opposition leader, Chee Soon Juan.

While there is a gaping lack of 'serious' local media, bookstore shelves groan under the weight of lifestyle and special interest publications like *Her World, Expat Living* and *Tatler*. Men's and women's magazines like *Maxim, FHM* and *Cosmopolitan* are permitted to brandish their customarily sensational sex cover lines and soft porn, within limits.

For entertainment listings, see *8 Days, Time Out* or *I-S* magazines. See also p198.

Local TV, which is divided into English, Chinese, Tamil and Malay language stations, features a mixture of local and imported soaps and dramas (which are sometimes censored), magazine shows (many of them about food), reality TV and the ubiquitous talent contests. The quality, to be frank, leaves much to be desired.

Of all the media, radio is probably the biggest risk-taker and is certainly the medium that lands itself in hot water with the authorities most frequently. The music stations are still, though, dominated by bland, identikit DJs with American accents.

LANGUAGE

Having a population with a broad range of native languages naturally presented the country with a few problems. The answer, of course, was to have everyone know at least two languages, their mother tongue and a national lingua franca, which is of course English. All schoolchildren must study English and a 'mother tongue': Malay, Tamil or Mandarin.

Chinese dialects are still widely spoken, especially by older residents – the most common being Hokkien, Teochew, Cantonese, Hakka and Hainanese. And where once the government pestered its citizens to learn English, or speak it better, nowadays with the rapid growth of China there is an equally insistent campaign to get more Chinese Singaporeans learning Mandarin.

This rather inconsistent approach has left many Singaporeans in a kind of linguistic limbo, having mastered neither English nor Mandarin.

SINGLISH

Perhaps the first thing many visitors will notice, after the city's immaculate cleanliness, is that most Singaporeans speak English fluently, sometimes so fluently you can barely understand a word they are saying. This patois, which is basically English peppered with Malay, Hokkien and Tamil slang and spoken in a distinctive sing-song staccato manner, is proudly known as Singlish.

Singlish mortifies the government, which runs the sternly named Speak Good English campaign, and even once banned a song with Singlish lyrics, 'Fried Rice Paradise', from the radio.

It was akin to trying to ban Cockney or some other local dialect. In essence, Singlish is no different from the pidgin of Melanesia, or the creoles of the Caribbean, or any other dialect. Sure it is virtually unintelligible to most visitors, but it is also a vernacular in its own right, and language is the ultimate manifestation of the national identity the government is at pains to foster.

Happily, the government has quietly realised the sheer futility of fighting Singlish and given up. Besides, you'll find that many Singaporeans carry a kind of spare English speaking accent and can effortlessly swap between the baffling machine-gun assault of Singlish they use with their friends and a more understandable Standard English they use with foreigners.

Even so, you're unlikely to spend much time in Singapore without finding yourself at some point staring dumbly at someone, trying to work out what on earth they are on about. Unnecessary prepositions and pronouns are dropped, word order is flipped, phrases are clipped short, and stress and cadence are unconventional, to say the least.

There isn't a Singlish grammar as such, but there are definite characteristics, such as the long stress on the last syllable of phrases, so that the standard English '*gov*ernment' becomes 'guvva-*men*'. Words ending in consonants – particularly 'l', 'k' and 't' – are often syncopated and vowels are often distorted.

And of course no discussion of Singlish is complete without referring to those expressive, but ultimately meaningless, particles Singaporeans attach to the end of sentences for emphasis. The most well-known is 'lah', but you'll also hear 'mah', 'meh', 'lor', 'hor' and 'leh'.

These particles have created memorable phrases, such as the romantic overture we overheard passing from a young fellow to his beloved: 'I love you hor'.

For a list of slightly more common Singlish expressions, see the Language chapter (p202).

NEIGHBOURHOODS

top picks

NEIGHBOURHOODS

An ancient parable, so old its origins are lost in the mists of time, tells of a group of blind men who, after touching different parts of an elephant, offer completely different opinions about what an elephant really is. One touches the leg and pronounces the elephant 'like a pillar'. Another touches the tail, and says the animal is 'like a rope'. Another the tusk, another the ear, and so forth.

'The Lion City is far more than just the sum of its parts'

Modern Singapore is to travellers much as the proverbial elephant was to the blind men: it leaves vastly different images depending on which part one chooses to touch.

Business visitors passing through for a three-day conference will probably spend their time in the central business district (CBD), perhaps carving out a few hours of after-work R&R on the riverfront. 'A modern metropolis of gleaming steel and glass skyscrapers, with just enough surviving colonial splendour to give it a historical feel. Really quite Western!' this visitor may pronounce upon returning home, most likely adding that old chestnut often used to describe the Lion City '…and it's so clean and orderly'.

Other travellers, after choosing to spend time around Orchard Rd, might describe the city as 'A wall-to-wall fashion-junkie's paradise, and an expensive one at that, steeped in a peculiar West-meets-East culture, similar to some of the more fashionable neighbourhoods of Hong Kong, only cleaner and less chaotic'.

Backpackers (doing the obligatory two-day stopover on their way through Southeast Asia, most likely) may find themselves prowling the budget-friendly climes of Little India and Kampong Glam. They'll come away with tales of a cacophonous, curry-and-cumin-scented city of colourful, low-slung buildings and sari-clad women – and sari-clad men if they stray down certain alleys. Other backpackers will head to Geylang, where on some streets they may encounter a row of Buddhist shrines and temples, and on other streets a row of semilegal brothels and a veritable army of sex workers. (Whichever street they choose, their description of it afterwards promises to be colourful!)

And so it goes, from the sterility of Singapore's seemingly endless housing blocks (even these neighbourhoods aren't without surprises for those who take the time to explore) to the tropical lushness of farms, parks and patches of jungle found on the city's outskirts, and in places like the forest island of Pulau Ubin.

So which of these impressions best encompass the true essence of Singapore? Returning to the parable of the elephant, all of the blind men are equally correct and incorrect: the elephant is more than just what they're able to glean through a single experience. So it is with Singapore. Take the time to explore each neighbourhood individually, and you'll agree that the Lion City is far more than just the sum of its parts.

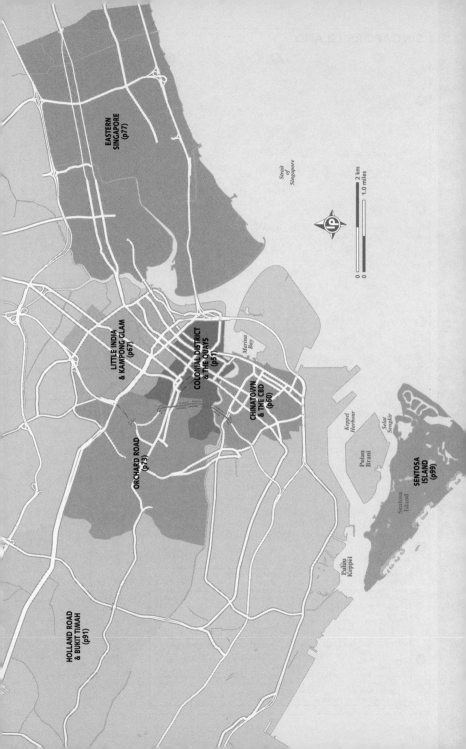

SINGAPORE ISLAND

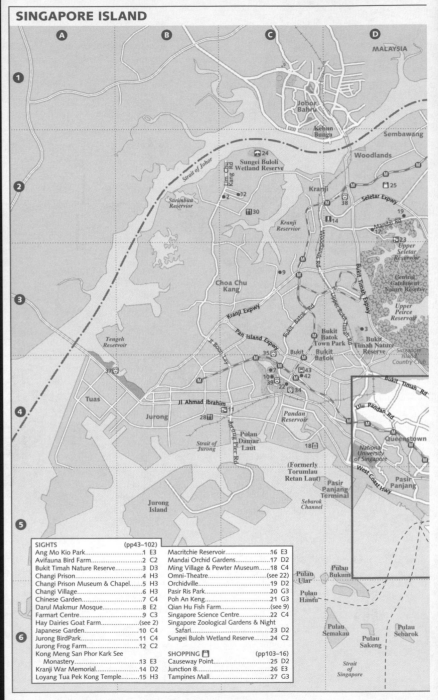

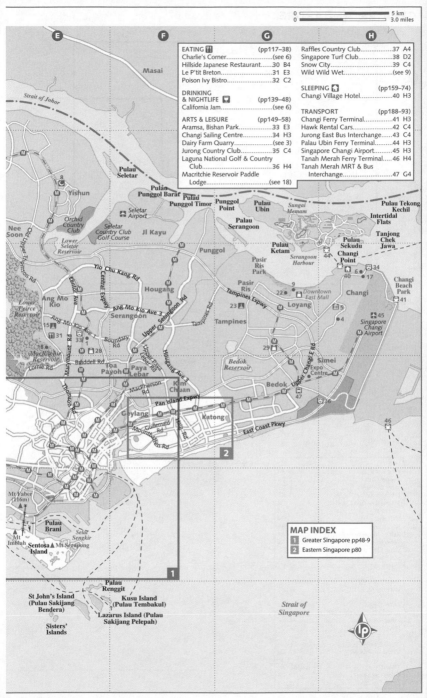

MAP INDEX
1 Greater Singapore pp48-9
2 Eastern Singapore p80

GREATER SINGAPORE

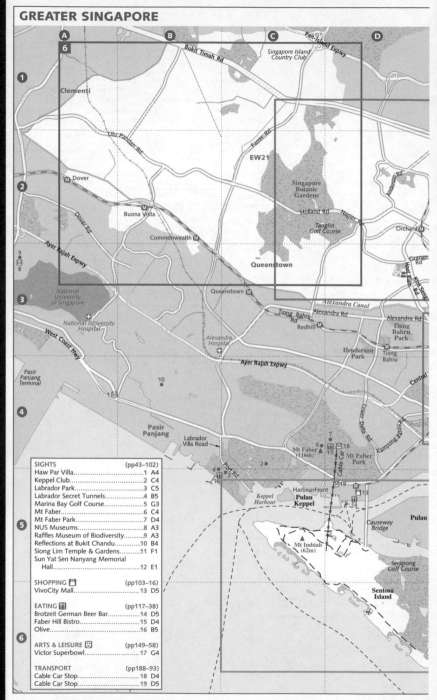

SIGHTS	(pp43–102)
Haw Par Villa	1 A4
Keppel Club	2 C4
Labrador Park	3 C5
Labrador Secret Tunnels	4 B5
Marina Bay Golf Course	5 G3
Mt Faber	6 C4
Mt Faber Park	7 D4
NUS Museums	8 A3
Raffles Museum of Biodiversity	9 A3
Reflections at Bukit Chandu	10 B4
Siong Lim Temple & Gardens	11 F1
Sun Yat Sen Nanyang Memorial Hall	12 E1

SHOPPING 🛍	(pp103–16)
VivoCity Mall	13 D5

EATING 🍴	(pp117–38)
Brotzeit German Beer Bar	14 D5
Faber Hill Bistro	15 D4
Olive	16 B5

ARTS & LEISURE 🎭	(pp149–58)
Victor Superbowl	17 G4

TRANSPORT	(pp188–93)
Cable Car Stop	18 D4
Cable Car Stop	19 D5

MAP INDEX

ITINERARY BUILDER

Singapore's an especially easy city to get around in, so you'll be able to take in plenty of indoor culture during the heat of the day, enjoy the city-state's spectacular outdoor offerings when the weather's a bit cooler, and still have some energy left for fantastic nightlife in the evening.

For the purpose of our Itinerary Builder, southern & western Singapore include Sentosa Island and Jurong & western Singapore neighbourhoods.

AREA	ACTIVITIES	Sights	Eating	Drinking & Nightlife
	Colonial District & the Quays	Peranakan Museum (p56) Singapore Art Museum (p56) Esplanade – Theatres on the Bay (opposite)	Chef Chan's Restaurant (p123) Hai Tien Lo (p124) Garibaldi (p124)	Brewerkz (p141) Butter Factory (p142) Crazy Elephant (p142)
	Chinatown & the CBD	Buddha Tooth Relic Temple (p61) Sri Mariamman Temple (p61) Chinese Heritage Centre & Pagoda St (p60) Sultan Mosque (p70)	Lau Pa Sat (p128) Saint Pierre (p126) Annalakshmi (p128)	Penny Black (p143) Play (p144) Tantric Bar (p144)
	Little India & Kampong Glam	Sakaya Muni Buddha Gaya Temple (p70) Haji Lane (p67)	Gayatri (p129) French Stall (p129) Tekka Centre (p130)	Night & Day (p145) Cafe Domus (p145) Blujaz Café (p144)
	Orchard Rd, Holland Road & Bukit Timah	Istana (p73) Bukit Timah Nature Reserve (p91) Singapore Botanic Gardens (p91)	Wasabi Tei (p132) Din Tai Fung (p131) Newton Circus Hawker Centre (p132)	Alley Bar (p145) Downunder Bar (p145) Wine Network (p147)
	Eastern Singapore	Small temples & lorongs of Geylang (p77) Sri Senpaga Vinayagar Temple (p78-9) Joo Chiat walking tour (p83)	Old Airport Road Food Centre (p125) Guan Hoe Soon (p133) 328 Katong Laksa (p134)	Artoholic (p147) California Jam (p147) Sunset Bay Garden Beach Bar (p148)
	Northern & central Singapore	Kong Meng San Phor Kark See Monastery (p86) Singapore Zoological Gardens & Night Safari (p87) Sungei Buloh Wetland Reserve (p88)	Au Jardin (p134) PS Café (p135) L'Estaminet (p136)	2am: Desert Bar (p147) Dempsey's Hut (p146) Wala Wala Cafe Bar (p147)
	Southern & western Singapore	Haw Par Villa (p96) Singapore Science Centre (p98) Reflections at Bukit Chandu (p95)	The Cliff (p137) Il Lido (p137) Hilltop Japanese Restaurant (p136)	St James Power Station (p147) KM8 (p148) Sunset Bay (p148)

COLONIAL DISTRICT & THE QUAYS

Drinking & Nightlife p140; Eating p123; Shopping p106; Sleeping p161

An urban treasure-trove of pristine colonial buildings, galleries, museums, massive shopping centres, parks and three riverside entertainment strips, this is the heart of Singapore. Nowhere else do you get as vivid a picture of Singapore as an organic city, where old courthouses and churches now welcome boozers and gluttons, men on trishaws offer you rides outside glassy megamalls and everywhere you look there is the loud echo of British rule.

The mark of Sir Stamford Raffles remains indelibly stamped on this district. His statue watches over the Singapore River and his house is still perched on a hill in the lush green oasis of Fort Canning Park. The edifices of colonialism still surround the Padang, where British high society once converged to play cricket and exchange gossip. It's here you'll find the famous Raffles Hotel, a string of old churches, the old and new parliament houses, the art and history museums and, dragging the area into the present, the dazzlingly contemporary 'durians', otherwise known as Esplanade – Theatres on the Bay.

top picks

- Walking along the river (p58)
- Esplanade – Theatres on the Bay (below)
- Fort Canning Park (p55)
- Peranakan Museum (p56)
- Singapore Art Museum (p56)

ASIAN CIVILISATIONS MUSEUM
Map pp52–3

☎ 6332 7798; 1 Empress Pl; adult/child $5/2.50; ☿ 1-7pm Mon, 9am-7pm Tue-Sun, to 9pm Fri; Ⓜ Raffles Place

Offering a plethora of exhibits on the civilisations and cultures of Asia, this museum is definitely the jewel in the crown of the National Heritage Board's bevy of museums. You enter through a series of images projected onto walls, floors and finally a slatted curtain, which you walk through to enter the galleries. The Hindu-Buddhist gallery is perhaps the highlight, with beautifully lit displays including a stunning 18th-century Burmese Buddha head and a large bronze drum. Elsewhere you'll find exquisite examples of porcelain, textiles, lacquerware, costumes and huge traditional procession statues. There are also regular touring and programmed exhibitions. Tours in English run at 11am and 2pm most days.

CIVIL DEFENCE HERITAGE GALLERY
Map pp52–3

☎ 6332 2995; 62 Hill St; admission free; ☿ 10am-5pm Tue-Sun; Ⓜ City Hall

The Civil Defence Heritage Gallery, which is devoted to fire fighting and civil defence in Singapore, will be of interest to few. This gallery is based in the handsome red-brick and white-plaster Central Fire Station, built in 1908, which is still in use today.

ESPLANADE – THEATRES ON THE BAY
Map pp52–3

☎ 6828 8222; www.esplanade.com; 1 Esplanade Dr; Ⓜ City Hall

Nicknamed, quite aptly, 'the durians' (after the pungent, spiky fruit), the twin silver hedgehog domes of this $600-million arts complex couldn't be more of a contrast to the colonial ensemble of the Padang. Love it or hate it, the Esplanade complex has become the poster child of contemporary Singapore, a shining example of the arty, creative side of the island state.

As well as twin auditoriums that are both visually and acoustically spectacular (they both rest on rubber pads to soak up external noise and vibrations), there are several decent eating options here. Also worth looking out for are the regular free performances outside, which are advertised either on the theatre's website or in the monthly what's-on guide. The Esplanade has a branch of the National Library where you can read or watch movies in a spectacular setting.

The building itself was the product of Singapore's recognition that it needed iconic buildings to keep pace with the competitive international tourist industry – a kind of Asian Sydney Opera House.

Despite their fruity nickname, the theatre complex's twin glass domes, covered in spiky metal sunshades, do not take their

COLONIAL DISTRICT & THE QUAYS

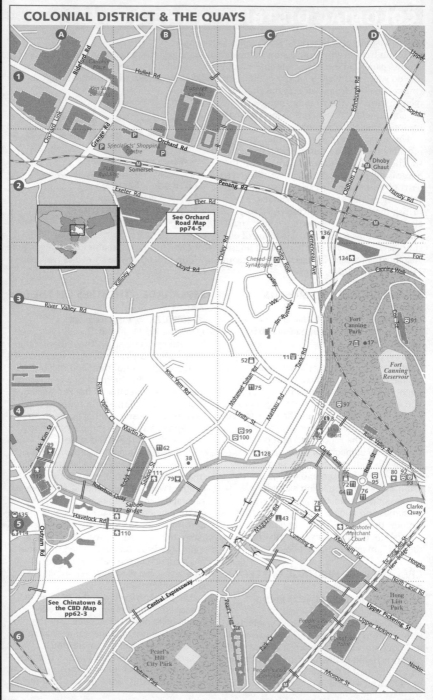

See Orchard
Road Map
pp74-5

See Chinatown &
the CBD Map
pp62-3

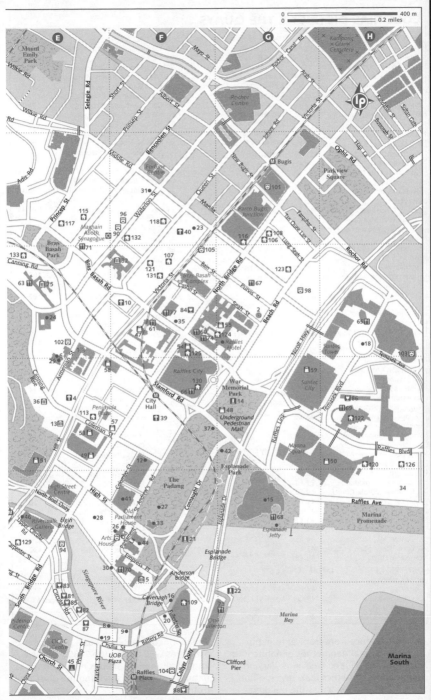

COLONIAL DISTRICT & THE QUAYS

design reference from tropical fruit, but from the natural geometries of nature and traditional Asian reed weavings. Varying angles and geometrics make the roofline morph and mutate across the building.

The distinctive exterior has a practical aspect as well in that the 7139 variously angled aluminium shades maximise the natural light while shielding the glass roof from the sun.

FORT CANNING PARK Map pp52-3
Ⓜ Dhoby Ghaut

This park has a shrine to Sultan Iskander Shah, the last ruler of the ancient Majapahit empire, which once ruled Singapore. In those days Fort Canning Park was known as Bukit Larangan (Forbidden Hill). These days the park is much more welcoming; the only natural high spot in the district, the park offers a wonderfully cool retreat from the hot streets below (even after climbing the exhausting steps leading up). Its little pathways and quiet corners mean that at times you'd hardly know you were in a city.

A couple of Gothic gateways lead into the pleasant park, where gravestones from the old Christian cemetery are also embedded in the brick walls. There's also a **spice garden** here, on the site of Raffles' original botanical garden, where hollowed-out coconut shells on sticks offer samples of various spices for tasting. These sampling bins are all labelled, as are many of the trees throughout the park. Inside the spice garden is an archaeological dig, where under a wooden roof you can see the Javanese artefacts from the 14th-century Majapahit empire that have been uncovered there.

Also on Fort Canning Hill is the **Battle Box** (☎ 6333 0510; 51 Canning Rise; adult/child $8/5; ☉ 10am-6pm Tue-Sun), Singapore's largest underground military operations complex during WWII. This warren of 26 rooms and tunnels now houses a fascinating hi-tech exhibition on the fall of Singapore in 1942. You can gaze through binocular-like lenses to view holographic figures tapping out Morse-code messages; the Japanese codes are still etched on the walls.

The park hosts several outdoor events each year including Womad and Ballet under the Stars and the occasional outdoor movie festival.

PADANG & AROUND Map pp52-3
Ⓜ City Hall

The open field of the Padang is where flannelled fools play cricket in the tropical heat, cheered on by members of the Singapore Cricket Club in the pavilion. At the opposite end of the field is the Singapore Recreation Club. Cricket is still played on the weekends.

This rather prosaic spot has darker historical significance, as it was here that the invading Japanese herded the European community together before marching them off to Changi prison. Apart from the reconstructed monstrosity that is the Singapore Recreation Club (it looks like something made from kids' building blocks), the Padang is flanked by a handsome collection of colonial buildings and assorted monuments, all of which can be taken in on a leisurely stroll (see p58).

At the Padang's southern end, the **Victoria Theatre & Concert Hall** (1862), once the town hall, is now used for cultural events. **Parliament House** (1827) is Singapore's oldest government building. Originally a private mansion, it became a courthouse, then the Assembly House of the colonial government and, finally, the Parliament House for independent Singapore.

Along St Andrew's Rd, the **Supreme Court**, built in 1939, is a relatively new addition and was the last classical building to be erected in Singapore. It replaced the Grand Hotel de L'Europe, which once outshone the Raffles as Singapore's premier hotel. Situated next door, and even newer, is the Foster & Partners–designed **Supreme Court** (p36), which opened in 2005.

TRANSPORT: COLONIAL DISTRICT & THE QUAYS

The grid layout of the district makes it easy to navigate. From City Hall MRT station underneath the towering Raffles City mall-hotel complex, the area to the south has most of the colonial treasures, including the Padang, St Andrew's Cathedral, City Hall, the Old Parliament House and Asian Civilisations Museum (which is actually closer to Raffles Place MRT). From there you can cross the elegant Cavenagh Bridge to Boat Quay and follow the river to Clarke Quay, then along to Robertson Quay or north to climb the steep steps up to Fort Canning Park.

Unless you're lucky enough to be staying in the pricey Colonial District, your point of reference will be City Hall MRT, which is an easy walk from all main attractions. If it's too hot to walk, the following buses can ease the pain. Bus 2 takes you down Victoria St and Hill St. Buses 51, 61, 63 and 80 go along North Bridge Rd. For Beach Rd, hop on bus 100, 107 or 961. Along Bras Basah Rd, get on bus 14, 16, 77 or 111. At night, the best guaranteed taxi spots are the Clarke Quay rank on River Valley Rd and at the Elgin Bridge next to the Jazz@Southbridge pub on South Bridge Rd. Elsewhere, it can be a lottery.

City Hall, with its classical facade of Corinthian columns, is located next to the Supreme Court and dates from 1929. It was here that Lord Louis Mountbatten announced Japanese surrender in 1945 and Lee Kwan Yew declared Singapore's independence in 1965. Completing the colonial trio is St Andrew's Cathedral.

PERANAKAN MUSEUM Map pp52–3
☎ 6332 7591; 39 Armenian St; adult/child $6/3;
🕓 1-7pm Mon, 9.30am-7pm Tue-Sun, to 9pm Fri;
Ⓜ City Hall

Singapore's newest museum stands as a testament to the Peranakan cultural revival in the Lion City. Opened in 2008, it has 10 galleries featuring over 1200 artefacts and a variety of multimedia exhibits designed to introduce visitors to historical and contemporary Peranakan culture.

In addition to featuring traditionally crafted, beaded Peranakan clothing and exquisitely carved antique furniture, the museum also has a number of interesting and interactive exhibits. Our favourite is the diorama displaying a traditional Peranakan home complete with two video-mounted portraits of elders who argue with each other about whether or not their descendents are leading culturally appropriate lives. This museum is a must-visit for anyone who wants to understand local culture.

RAFFLES HOTEL Map pp52–3
☎ 6337 1886; www.raffleshotel.com;
1 Beach Rd; Ⓜ City Hall

Viewing the regal edifice that stands today, it's hard to believe that Raffles Hotel started life as a 10-room bungalow. It was opened in December 1887 by the Sarkies brothers, immigrants from Armenia and proprietors of two other grand colonial hotels, the Strand in Yangon (Rangoon) and the Eastern & Oriental in Penang.

The hotel's heyday began in 1899 with the opening of the main building, the same one that guests stay in today. Raffles soon became a byword for oriental luxury ('A legendary symbol for all the fables of the Exotic East', went the publicity blurb) and was featured in novels by Joseph Conrad and Somerset Maugham. The famous Singapore sling was first concocted in the hotel's Long Bar in 1915.

The hotel lobby is open to the public, and is a popular tourist attraction. Dress standards apply; so no shorts or sandals.

Hidden away on the 3rd floor of the Raffles Hotel Arcade, the Raffles Hotel Museum (admission free; 🕓 10am-7pm) is worth hunting out. Here you'll find a fascinating collection of memorabilia including photographs and posters from bygone eras and a fine city map showing how Noel Coward could once sip his gin sling and stare out at the sea from the hotel verandah.

SINGAPORE ART MUSEUM Map pp52–3
☎ 6332 3222; www.nhb.gov.sg/sam;
71 Bras Basah Rd; adult/child $3/1.50; 🕓 noon-6pm Mon, 9am-6pm Tue-Thu, Sat & Sun, 9am-9pm Fri; Ⓜ City Hall or Dhoby Ghaut

Two blocks west of Raffles Hotel is this fine museum based in the former St Joseph's Institution, a Catholic boys' school that was relocated in 1987.

The reconstruction by local architect Wong Hooe Wai fuses historical charm with a strong contemporary feel. Features include Filipino artist Ramon Orlina's abstract-glass window in the former school chapel and US artist Dale Chihuly's sea anemone–like blown-glass installations, which incidentally can also be seen at the Chihuly Lounge (p142) at the Ritz-Carlton Millenia hotel.

The 13 galleries focus on Singaporean and regional artists, with exhibitions ranging from classical Chinese calligraphy to contemporary works examining issues of Asian identity and the modern Singaporean experience, as well as temporary overseas exhibitions. Afterwards, it's worth stopping for coffee in the museum's genteel cafe, Dôme. Admission to the museum is free from noon-2pm on weekdays.

NATIONAL MUSEUM OF SINGAPORE Map pp52–3
☎ 6332 3659; www.nationalmuseum.sg;
93 Stamford Rd; Ⓜ Dhoby Ghaut

The grand dame of Singapore's museum scene, NSM is located in the history-drenched neoclassical 19th-century building that once housed the former Raffles Museum and Library. Perhaps the most magnificent feature of the building itself is the recently restored rotunda, which includes 50 carefully crafted pieces of stained glass. At once modern and classical, NSM features a wide variety of multimedia exhibits focused primarily on – naturally – Singapore's history, culture and overall glory.

QUAYS OF THE CITY

The stretch of riverfront that separates the Colonial District from the CBD is known as the Quays.

Boat Quay

Closest to the harbour, Boat Quay was once Singapore's centre of commerce, and remained an important economic area into the 1960s. By the mid-1980s, many of the shophouses were in ruins, business having shifted to hi-tech cargo centres elsewhere on the island. Declared a conservation zone by the government, the area has since become a major entertainment district filled with colourful restaurants, bars and shops.

It's on Boat Quay that you'll find riverfront restaurants serving all manner of Singaporean delicacies, though many find the restaurant touts a bit on the aggressive side.

Clarke Quay

This quay, named after Singapore's second colonial governor, Sir Andrew Clarke, was developed like Boat Quay into a dining and shopping precinct in the early 1990s. Its unique design has cemented its status as one of Singapore's most popular night haunts in the first decade of the 21st century.

How much time you spend in Clarke Quay really depends upon your personal sense of aesthetics, for it's on this stretch of riverfront that Singapore's most whimsical designers have been given carte blanche to bring their dreams to life. Among the high (or low) lights: gumdrop railings done out in kids' paintbox colours, lilypad umbrellas straight out of a Dr Seuss colouring book, and many once-dignified shophouses now painted in shades that might be a tad too bright for some eyes. A hip hangout for some, Jellybean Town for others.

Robertson Quay

At the furthest reach of the river, Robertson Quay was once used for the storage of goods. Now some of the old *godown* (warehouses) have been tarted up into flash party places and bars, though it's quieter and more low-key than its counterparts downriver. You'll also find several good hotels and restaurants clustered around here.

SINGAPORE PHILATELIC MUSEUM
Map pp52–3

☎ 6337 3888; www.spm.org.sg; 23B Coleman St; adult/child $5/4; ☺ 9am-7pm Tue-Sun, 1-7pm Mon; Ⓜ City Hall

Housed in the attractive former Methodist Book Room Building dating from around 1895, this museum holds a well-presented collection of rare and not-so-rare stamps from Singapore and around the world. While some of the artwork and design is impressive, the museum is a must-visit for stamp collectors only.

CHETTIAR HINDU TEMPLE Map pp52–3

☎ 6737 9393; 15 Tank Rd; ☺ 8am-noon & 5.30-8.30pm; Ⓜ Clarke Quay or Dhoby Ghaut

Completed in 1984 and replacing a much earlier temple built by Indian *chettiars* (moneylenders), this Shaivite temple is dedicated to the six-headed Lord Subramaniam. If you can, come during the festival of Thaipusam (p16), whose procession ends here.

TAN SI CHONG SU TEMPLE Map pp52–3

15 Magazine Rd; Ⓜ Clarke Quay

With its decorative roof, guardian dragons and lions, and painted wooden doors, this

is a particularly fine example of temple design. Built in 1876, much of the material used to make this temple arrived in Singapore as shipping ballast.

SINGAPORE TYLER PRINT INSTITUTE
Map pp52–3

☎ 6336 3663; www.stpi.com.sg; 41 Robertson Quay; admission free; ☺ 1-5pm Sun & Mon, 9.30am-6pm Tue-Sat; ⊟ 54 from Ⓜ Clarke Quay

Established by the American printmaker Kenneth E Tyler, the institute features a gallery holding exhibitions on various aspects of printmaking, as well as a paper mill and an educational facility.

YEO SWEE HUAT Map pp52–3

☎ 6533 4288; 15 Upper Circular Rd; ☺ 8.30am-5.30pm, closed Sun; Ⓜ Clarke Quay

Superstitious locals may give this shop a wide berth, but travellers with an interest in Eastern religious rites will be fascinated by this family-owned workshop which, for three generations, has handcrafted paper effigies and accessories for Buddhist and Taoist funerals. The Yeo family also creates all manner of auspicious paper items, which make excellent gifts.

RIVERSIDE HERITAGE TOUR
Walking Tour

1 Esplanade – Theatres on the Bay Our tour begins here at Esplanade – Theatres on the Bay (p51), the world's largest and most expensive sculptural homage to the durian, king of all fruits. Climb up to the roof for some excellent shots of the surrounding area, and to get your last dose of air conditioning for a while.

2 War Memorial Park Crossing Esplanade Dr takes you into War Memorial Park, in which you'll find the Cenotaph, Singapore's best-known war memorial. Initially built to commemorate soldiers of WWI, a second dedication was added to commemorate Singaporeans who made the ultimate sacrifice during WWII. The foundation stone for this monument was laid by former colonial governor Sir Lawrence Nunns Guillemard. In and around the area of this park are a number of other notable sculptures, including the Lim Bo Seng Memorial, built in honour of a WWII hero, the Indian National Army Monument and the Victorian-style Tan Kim Seng Fountain. Across Stamford

Rd is the Civilian War Memorial, locally known as 'the chopsticks' – it's not difficult to see why.

3 St Andrew's Rd Heading through the park and across Connaught Dr takes you past the Singapore Recreation Club and Singapore Cricket Club; across St Andrew's Rd is where you'll find the magnificent St Andrew's Cathedral. Hanging a left on St Andrew's Rd takes you past City Hall and the old Supreme Court. Located right next to the old court is the brand new Foster & Partners–designed Supreme Court, with its unmistakable spaceship design. You can go all the way to the top, but you can't snap any photos (all cameras are checked at the door).

WALK FACTS

Start Esplanade – Theatres on the Bay
End Merlion Park
Distance 3km
Time Two hours
Exertion Easy
Fuel stop Boat Quay

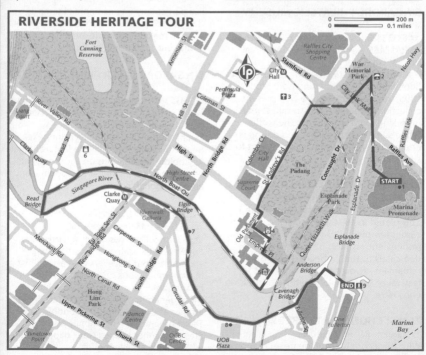

RIVERSIDE HERITAGE TOUR

4 Victoria Theatre & Concert Hall Below where St Andrew's Rd curves to the left you'll find a group of colonial-era buildings including the Victoria Theatre & Concert Hall, in front of which you'll see the original Raffles statue, which once stood at the Padang.

5 Asian Civilisations Museum If you have time, explore the extremely impressive Asian Civilisations Museum (p51), which sits on the North bank of the river on Empress Pl. If you don't have time (or are short on funds), at least take the time to visit the free Singapore River Gallery on the 1st floor.

6 Clarke Quay The walk along the northern bank of the Singapore River is a pretty one, offering some of the best opportunities for photographs of downtown Singapore. The rather picturesque building with the multi-coloured window frames, on the corner of Hill St overlooking the river, is the old Hill Street police station, which currently houses the Ministry of Communication and the Arts (MICA). Past this, still on the north side of the river, is Clarke Quay (p57), where you'll find the G-max reverse bungee (which some find exciting and others find nauseating) and Clarke Quay Pavilion (which provokes similarly varied reactions).

7 Boat Quay From Clarke Quay, head across the river over Read Bridge. Built in 1881, the pedestrian and bicycle bridge links Clarke Quay to the Swisshotel Merchant Court. Hang a left

at the hotel and walk along the southern side of the river. This stretch is mostly filled with bars and restaurants more modern and a good deal less gaudy than those over on Clarke Quay. Past Coleman Bridge on the riverbank is where many of the river's sculptures begin, starting with the bronze statues of river-swimming children caught mid-jump.

8 Sculpture Walk On the south side of the river past Boat Quay (p57) is where you'll find some of Singapore's finest outdoor sculpture. Some, like Fernando Botero's Bird (a gigantic pudgy bird squatting on a marble podium) are whimsical. Others tell clear stories, like Aw Tee Hong's The River Merchants, which displays three bronze merchants (one Chinese, one Malay, and one Caucasian) engaged in negotiation. Salvador Dali's Homage to Newton is more difficult to describe. There are several others spread around the riverbank for those who care to look.

9 Merlion Having had your fill of culture and sculpture, end your tour with a leisurely stroll along the river, stopping at whichever pub or restaurant strikes your fancy. Libations consumed, you'll be ready to complete the circuit by following the river further east to the point where it reaches Marina Bay. It's here where you'll find stairs leading into the bay, on top of which, staring out into the sea, you'll come face to face with the famous Merlion (p101) statue, Singapore's most famous icon.

CHINATOWN & THE CBD

Drinking & Nightlife p143; Eating p126; Shopping p108; Sleeping p165

That a primarily Chinese city like Singapore has a neighbourhood designated as 'Chinatown' might seem a bit odd to some, so let's clarify the distinction. Once upon a time, in a much smaller Lion City, this was the area where the new immigrants – mostly, but not entirely, from China – would sleep and eat, working primarily on the shores of the nearby Singapore River where most commerce occurred. Hence, to the mostly-Anglo captains of industry (who lived in fancier neighbourhoods), the area came to be known as 'Chinatown', and now, generations later, the name has stuck.

Nowadays, Chinatown is mostly known as a tourist destination for those looking to take in Singapore on the quick, and as such much of the neighbourhood has taken on a distinctly Disneyland vibe. In between temples, parks and other culturally edifying spots are plenty of restaurants, shops and endless street-stalls selling the same trinkets you'll find in Chinatowns throughout the world.

top picks

- Buddha Tooth Relic Temple (opposite)
- Nei Xue Tang (opposite)
- People's Park (p109)
- Chinatown Heritage Centre (left)
- Sri Mariamman Temple (opposite)

Between Chinatown and the Singapore River is the central business district (CBD), the financial pulse of the city. Once the city's vibrant heart, Raffles Place is now a rare patch of grass above the MRT station, surrounded by the gleaming towers of commerce. The CBD is a short walk across the Cavenagh Bridge from the Colonial District. There are some interesting sculptures here and along the nearby Singapore River (see p32), including the latest incarnation of the island's much-hyped Merlion, which is in Merlion Park.

Chinatown is roughly bounded by the Singapore River to the north, New Bridge Rd to the west, Maxwell and Kreta Ayer Rds to the south and Cecil St to the east. The principal centres of visitor attention and activity are clustered between New Bridge Rd and South Bridge Rd, where you'll find the Chinatown Complex, the Pagoda and Trengganu St pedestrian strips (or tourist traps) and the temples, while the Club St bar area lies just to the east of South Bridge Rd.

CHINATOWN HERITAGE CENTRE

Map pp62–3

☎ 6325 2878; www.chinatownheritage.com.sg; 48 Pagoda St; adult/child $9.80/6.30; ☼ 9am-8pm; Ⓜ Chinatown

A reflection of the oft-frenetic atmosphere of Chinatown itself, this museum is crammed to the rafters with imaginative, interactive displays on the area's history. Three restored shophouses have been combined to make the three-storey centre, part of which recreates very evocatively and accurately the cramped and miserable living quarters that many Chinese immigrants once endured.

The fascinating oral and video histories of local people describe what life was like in the days when Singapore was less than immaculate, from the old woman who survived through unspeakable suffering to the stories of the Triad-style secret societies that patrolled and terrorised the neighbourhoods.

Andrew Yip, owner of the nearby Service World Backpackers Hostel (p166) sells and displays the works of his late father, famed Singaporean photographer Yip Cheong-Fun, in front of the centre.

EU YAN SANG MEDICAL HALL

Map pp62–3

☎ 6223 6333; 269A South Bridge Rd; ☼ 8.30am-6pm Mon-Sat; Ⓜ Chinatown

First opened in the early 20th century and now very tastefully refurbished, this is Singapore's most famous Chinese medicine centre and has spawned branches across the country.

A nearby spot of a similar medical vein worth checking out is the People's Park Complex (p109), where you'll find endless stalls offering all manner of Asian health gadgets and treatments, from herbal tinctures and arthritis-curing marble hand-balls to massage and footbaths with tiny fish that suck the dead skin off your feet.

BUDDHA TOOTH RELIC TEMPLE
Map pp62–3

☎ 6220 0220; www.btrts.org.sg; 288 South Bridge Rd; ◷ 4.30am-9pm; Ⓜ Chinatown
Opened with much fanfare in 2008, this magnificent five-storey southern Chinese–style Buddhist temple is quickly altering Chinatown's gravity by becoming the number-one attraction for both tourists and local worshippers alike. The temple, as you may have guessed from the name, houses what is believed to be the sacred tooth of the Buddha. The magnificent relic stupa is composed of 420kg of gold donated by worshippers. This is also the only temple that – to our knowledge – has its own underground parking garage.

NEI XUE TANG Map pp62–3

☎ 6220 0220; 235 Cantonment Rd; adult/child $5/3; ◷ 10am-5pm; Ⓜ Outram Park
This museum offers the largest collection of Buddhist artefacts in the city, including relics from China, Tibet, India, Japan, Burma and beyond. Pieces range from statues and jewellery to assorted esoteric devotional items.

SENG WONG BEO TEMPLE
Map pp62–3

113 Peck Seah St; Ⓜ Tanjong Pagar
Tucked behind red gates next to the Tanjong Pagar MRT station, this temple, seldom visited by tourists, is dedicated to the Chinese City God, who is not only responsible for the well-being of the city but also for guiding the souls of the dead to the underworld. It's also notable as the only temple in Singapore that still performs ghost marriages.

SRI MARIAMMAN TEMPLE
Map pp62–3

☎ 6223 4064; 244 South Bridge Rd; ◷ 7.30-11.30am & 5.30-8.30pm; Ⓜ Chinatown
This South Indian Dravidian-style temple is Singapore's oldest Hindu temple, built originally built in 1827 by Nariana Pillay, who arrived in Singapore on the same ship as Sir Stamford Raffles. Its present form dates back to 1843; the distinctive, colourful *gopuram* (tower), crowded with deities, soldiers and floral decoration over the entrance gate, dominates the street.

TRANSPORT: CHINATOWN & THE CBD

The centre of any trip to Chinatown will be Chinatown MRT station. Exit A from the station lands you right on Pagoda St. Coming from the Colonial District, hop on bus 61, 145 or 166, which takes you from North Bridge Rd to South Bridge Rd. From Hill St, buses 2, 12 and 147 run you down New Bridge Rd. It's possible to walk from the CBD to Chinatown, but from Raffles Quay, bus 608 goes to South Bridge Rd, or take bus C2 from Clifford Pier.

Inside are a series of shrines. The main one, straight ahead after you walk through the gate, belongs to the healing goddess Mariamman. Another shrine is devoted to Periyachi Amman, who is supposed to protect children.

In late October/early November each year, the temple is the scene for the Thimithi festival, during which devotees walk barefoot over burning coals – supposedly feeling no pain, although spectators report that quite a few hot-foot it for the final few steps!

THIAN HOCK KENG TEMPLE
Map pp62–3

☎ 6423 4626; 158 Telok Ayer St; Ⓜ Raffles Place or Chinatown
Its name translates as Temple of Heavenly Bliss, which is entirely apt given the gorgeous decoration of this, the oldest and most important Hokkien temple in Singapore. It was built between 1839 and 1842 on the site of the shrine to the goddess of the sea, Ma-Chu-Po, which was once the favourite landing point of Chinese sailors, back when Telok Ayer St ran along the shoreline. All the materials came from China except, interestingly, the gates (which came all the way from Scotland) and the tiles (from Holland). The temple was magnificently restored in 2000.

As you wander through the courtyards of the temple, look for the rooftop dragons, the intricately decorated beams, the gold-leaf panels and, best of all, the beautifully painted doors. During the restoration, a calligraphic panel from 1907 and from the emperor of China, Guang Xu of the Qing dynasty, was discovered above the central altar.

CHINATOWN & THE CBD

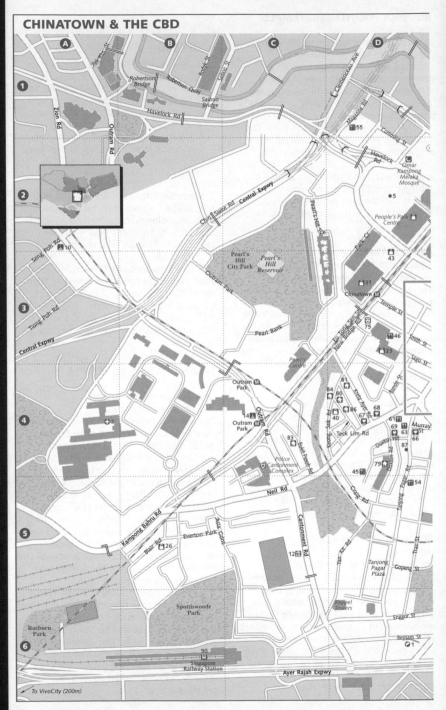

To VivoCity (200m)

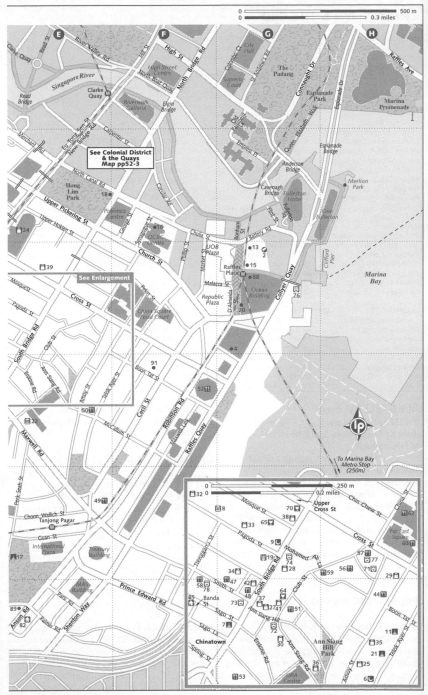

CHINATOWN & THE CBD

URA GALLERY Map pp62–3

☎ 6321 8321; www.ura.gov.sg; 45 Maxwell Rd; admission free; ⏰ 9am-5pm Mon-Sat; Ⓜ Tanjong Pagar

To understand how Singapore's urban environment has changed over recent decades and how it will change further in the future (especially with regards to the amazing development happening around Marina Bay), pop into the URA Gallery. This showcase of the Urban Redevelopment Authority (URA) includes video shows, interactive exhibits and a huge scale-model of the island state with its own six-minute sound-and-light show.

WAK HAI CHENG BIO TEMPLE
Map pp62–3

cnr Phillip & Church Sts; Ⓜ Raffles Place

On the CBD edge of Chinatown, this Taoist temple is also known as the Yueh Hai Ching Temple, which translates as Calm Sea Temple. Dating from 1826, it's an atmospheric place, with giant incense coils smok-

ing over its empty courtyard, and a whole village of tiny plaster figures populating its roof.

CHINATOWN WALK
Walking Tour

1 Wak Hai Cheng Bio Temple Take a moment as you emerge at Raffles Pl to consider how much the surrounding CBD has changed over the last century. A graceful note amid the gleaming towers are the Mass Rapid Transport (MRT) entrances, scaled-down copies of the facade of the long-gone John Little department store that once stood here. Head west along Chulia St and turn south down Phillip St to the Wak Hai Cheng Bio Temple (left).

2 Fuk Tak Ch'i Museum Cross over Church St to Telok Ayer St – the name means 'bay water', for this street once ran alongside the bay. On your right, practically swallowed up into the Far East Sq dining precinct, is the small Fuk Tak Ch'i Museum. Further along is

Ying Fo Fui Kun, a two-storey building established in 1822 for the Ying Fo Clan Association, which services Hakka Chinese.

3 Nagore Durgha Shrine At the junction with Boon Tat St is the Nagore Durgha Shrine, a mosque built between 1828 and 1830 by Chulia Muslims from South India's Coromandel Coast. A little further down is the beautifully restored Thian Hock Keng Temple (p61), Singapore's most impressive Chinese temple. If you continue along Telok Ayer St, you'll encounter the Al-Abrar Mosque, which was built between 1850 and 1855.

4 Siang Cho Keong Temple By the Amoy St hawker centre, turn right into Amoy St, where at No 66 you'll see the Siang Cho Keong Temple, built between 1867 and 1869. Left of the entrance is a small 'dragon well' into which you can drop a coin and make a wish.

5 Anglo-Chinese School At the junction of Amoy and McCallum Sts you'll see a small brown archway next to the temple marked Ann Siang Hill Park. Go through here, then follow the walkways and wooden steps upwards to what is Chinatown's highest point.

Climbing up past the historical site of the old Anglo-Chinese School, and up a wrought-iron spiral staircase, follow the charming back street downhill, emerging on Club St.

6 Club St After a rest, head up Club St. The highly decorated terraces here once housed Chinese guilds and clubs, but now it's almost all trendy bars and restaurants. You'll want to return for libations after dark, and you'll want to look your best. Why not head over to Mohamed Ali Lane, where you can get a haircut in an antique barber chair for $6.

7 Jinriksha Station On the corner of Neil and Tanjong Pagar Rds is the triangular Jinriksha station, once the depot for hand-pulled rickshaws, but now a restaurant. Take a quick

WALK FACTS

Start Raffles Place MRT station
End South Bridge Rd
Distance 2km
Time 2½ hours
Ease Moderate
Fuel stops Smith St hawker stalls

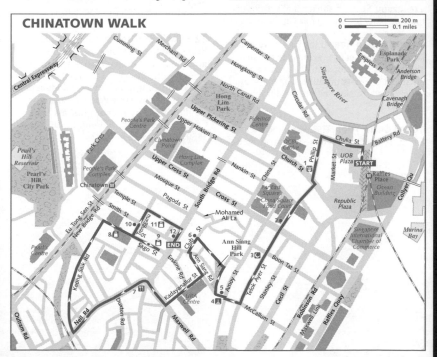
CHINATOWN WALK

COMING SOON IN SINGAPORE: MORE!

'...Seriously folks, I love Singapore. I can't wait to see what it looks like when they finish building it.'

With that line, Singapore-based comedian Jonathan Atherton describes succinctly the endless drive for expansion that in Singapore borders on mania. The area just southwest of the CBD, known as Marina Bay, once a mere gleam in the eyes of city planners, now sits as a shining example of land reclamation, boasting wide, palm-lined boulevards ringed with high-class condominiums, bars and restaurants. In autumn of 2008, Singapore's first Formula One Grand Prix tore through a street circuit in Marina Bay in what could become a yearly event. So what's next?

For a glance at the future, hop on bus 30 (a double-decker that offers lovely views) for a trip along the East Coast Parkway as it runs south of the CBD. Just a few years back, the view southward would have been sea and cargo ships. At the time this book was being researched, water and freight had been replaced by reclaimed land covered by a forest of building cranes. If all goes according to plan, by the time you read this the vast construction site will be transformed into what the Singapore government euphemistically refers to as the 'Integrated Resort', one of two proposed casinos to be built in Singapore (the second is slated to be built on Sentosa Island) before 2012.

walk southwest along Neil Rd to Keong Saik Rd, a curving street of old terraces with coffee shops, clan houses, clubs and small hotels. At the junction with Kreta Ayer Rd is the small Indian Layar Sithi Vinygar Temple.

8 Chinatown Complex Heading into the heart of Chinatown along Keong Siak Rd, you'll hit the back of the Chinatown Complex (p110). If you're hungry, stop for a cheap bite; there's a fascinating wet market and a bustling food centre. Outside, facing the corner of Sago and Trengganu Sts, is a square that's a popular meeting place for the old folks in the evening.

9 Fong Moon Kee At the back of Fong Moon Kee (16 Sago St), an elderly gentleman still makes and mends traditional rattan using an antique sewing machine. The mats, once widely used for sleeping on, are durable and absorbent.

10 Lai Chun Yuen The next three streets – Smith, Temple and Pagoda – all run off Treng-

ganu St and are the heart of tourist Chinatown. Consequently they are packed with shops, restaurants and outdoor stalls. On the corner of Smith and Trengganu Sts is a former Cantonese opera house, Lai Chun Yuen, designed by the same architect responsible for Raffles Hotel and the Victoria Theatre.

11 Temple St In days gone by, Temple St used to have tinsmiths down one side and ceramics shops on the other. Today the tradition lingers in places such as Bao Yuan Trading at No 15 and Sia Huat (p109) from No 9 to 11.

12 South Bridge Rd Along nearby South Bridge Rd there are also the traditional Chinese medicine shops. Also worth stopping by on South Bridge Rd are the Sri Mariamman Temple (p61), Singapore's oldest Hindu temple, and the nearby Jamae Mosque (also known as Chulia), built by Indian Muslims from the Coromandel Coast of Tamil Nadu between 1830 and 1855.

LITTLE INDIA & KAMPONG GLAM

Drinking & Nightlife p144; Eating p128; Shopping p110; Sleeping p166

Abandon all thoughts of sterile Singapore; this colourful enclave of the Indian community is anything but organised and clean. Fruit and vegetable shops crowd the grubby five-foot ways with their boxes of eggplants, okra and tomatoes, jostling for space with the goldsmiths and raucous stores selling electronics and cheap CDs from India. And everywhere is the smell of incense and spices, wafting from the merchants' shops and countless eateries offering amazing Indian cuisine.

It's a fascinating area to wander around, shopping, browsing, eating and, in traditional Indian style, being stared at by groups of men (if you're female). For shopping there probably isn't anywhere in Singapore to match the 24-hour Mustafa Centre for sheer chaotic variety.

A 15-minute walk southeast brings you to Kampong Glam, (called by tourists, but not locals, 'the Arab quarter'). By day the area is a great place for visiting mosques and shops selling clothing, raw cloth and other dry goods. At night it becomes a focal point for a strange social mix of the Middle Eastern community and the city's trendy, alternative youth, who come here to smoke sheesha. Behind Arab St, the narrow back street of Haji Lane has developed a scene of its own, with alternative record shops, offbeat boutiques and some more Middle Eastern cafes.

top picks

- Haji Lane (left)
- Arab Street (left)
- Sultan Mosque (p70)
- Museum of Shanghai Toys (p70)
- Sakaya Muni Buddha Gaya Temple (p70)

ARAB STREET Map p68
Ⓜ **Bugis**
This is the traditional textile district, where you'll find several caneware shops near the junction with Baghdad St. Stop here for a well-deserved rest and some bread, dips and grilled lamb at the area's best Muslim restaurant, Café Le Caire (p130), also known as Al Majlis.

HAJI LANE Map p68
Ⓜ **Bugis**
A picturesque, narrow lane (the narrowest in Singapore, some say) running parallel to Arab St with fascinating shops, including three places selling non-mainstream CDs, books and DVDs. There are also several shops selling sheesha pipes. Kazura (☎ 6293 1757; 51 Haji Lane; ⏲ 10am-5pm Mon-Sat) is a traditional perfume business with rows of decanters containing perfumes, such as Ramadan, for the faithful. For more on shopping in Haji Lane, see p112.

HAJJAH FATIMAH MOSQUE Map p68
☎ 6297 2774; 4001 Beach Rd; Ⓜ **Lavender or Bugis**
Constructed in 1846, the mosque is named after a Malakan-born Malay woman, Hajjah Fatimah; the site was once her home. It has two unusual features. First is its architecture, which is British influenced, rather than traditional Middle Eastern. The second is its leaning minaret, which leans about six degrees off-centre.

MALAY HERITAGE CENTRE Map p68
☎ 6391 0450; www.malayheritage.org.sg; 85 Sultan Gate; adult/child $3/2; ⏲ 10am-6pm Tue-Sun, 1-6pm Mon
The Kampong Glam area is the historic seat of the Malay royalty, resident here before the arrival of Raffles, and the *istana* (palace) on the site was the built for the last sultan of Singapore, Ali Iskander Shah, between 1836 and 1843. An agreement allowed the palace to belong to the sultan's family as long as they continued to live there. Even though this was repealed in 1897, the family stayed on for over a century and the palace gradually slid into ruin.

In 1999 the family moved out and a long period of renovation ended in 2004 with the opening of the Malay Heritage Centre. The building and grounds are a delight and the museum itself is a sparse but interesting account of Singapore's Malay people, featuring an reconstructed Kampong house upstairs.

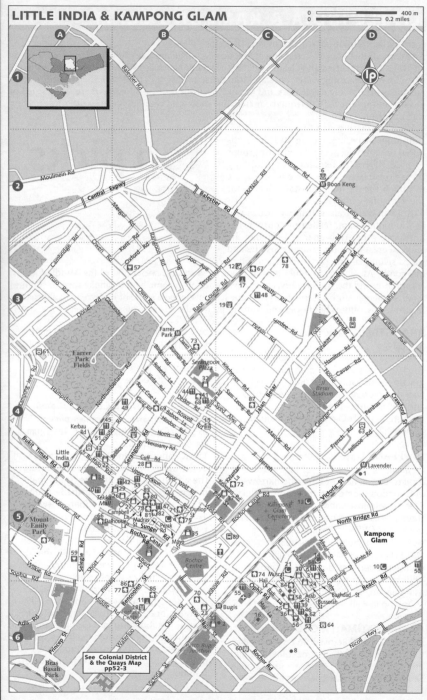

LITTLE INDIA & KAMPONG GLAM

0 — 400 m
0 — 0.2 miles

See Colonial District
& the Quays Map
pp52-3

LITTLE INDIA & KAMPONG GLAM

KUAN IM THONG HOOD CHO TEMPLE
Map p68
178 Waterloo St; Ⓜ Bugis
Dedicated to Kuan Yin (Guan Yin; goddess of mercy), one of the most popular deities, this temple attracts a daily crowd of devotees seeking divine intervention. Flower sellers can always be found outside the temple, which is particularly busy on the eve of Chinese New Year, when it stays open right through the night. Just up from the temple, near the South-East Asia Hotel, is a large money god, with a polished belly where the faithful rub their hands for good luck.

Next door is the recently renovated and even more polychromatic Sri Krishnan Temple, which also attracts worshippers from the Kuan Yin temple, who show a great deal of religious pragmatism by also burning joss sticks and offering prayers at this Hindu temple.

LEONG SAN SEE TEMPLE Map p68
☎ 6298 9371; 371 Race Course Rd; ⏰ 6am-6pm; Ⓜ Farrer Park
Across the road from the Sakaya Muni Buddha Gaya Temple (p70) is this less gaudy Taoist place of worship (dating from 1917 and dedicated to Kuan Yin). The name translates as Dragon Mountain Temple and it's beautifully decorated with timber beams carved with chimera, dragons, flowers and human figures.

MALABAR MUSLIM JAMA-ATH MOSQUE Map p68
☎ 6294 3862; 471 Victoria St; Ⓜ Lavender
The blue-tiled Malabar Muslim Jama-Ath Mosque, the only one on the island dedicated to Malabar Muslims from the South Indian state of Kerala, is one of the most distinctive in Singapore, but it didn't always look this way. Work on the building started in 1956, but it wasn't officially opened until 1963 due to cash-flow problems.

TRANSPORT: LITTLE INDIA & KAMPONG GLAM

Little India MRT station is the starting point for most visits, and lands you at the end of the bustling Buffalo Rd food market. Bus 65 runs from Orchard Rd to Serangoon Rd (the spine of Little India, off which many narrow streets branch, offering myriad interesting exploration opportunities). From the Colonial District, catch bus 131 or 147 on Stamford Rd to Serangoon Rd. Little India's borders are roughly marked by Lavender St to the north, Bukit Timah and Sungei Rds to the south, Race Course Rd to the west and Jalan Besar to the east. Following Serangoon Rd south, you will eventually hit the eastern end of Orchard Rd.

For Kampong Glam, get off at Bugis MRT station – it's a 10-minute walk to Arab and Bussorah Sts. If the walk from Little India is too much, there are no direct bus services, but a cab will cost about $4. From Orchard Rd, catch bus 7 to Victoria St and get off at the Stamford School, just past Arab St. From the Colonial District, buses 130, 133, 145 and 197 head up Victoria St and buses 100 and 107 run along Beach Rd from the Raffles Hotel to the end of Bussorah St.

The magnificent tiling on the mosque was only finished in 1995!

MUSEUM OF SHANGHAI TOYS
Map p68

☎ 6294 7742; www.most.com.sg; 83 Rowell Rd; ☿ 10am-8pm; Ⓜ Little India

Who knew that toys played such an integral role in 20th-century Chinese history? Marvin Chan, founder and curator of the Museum of Shanghai Toys, certainly did, and his expertise shows in the impressive assortment of antique toys in this renovated three-storey shophouse in Little India. You can shop for contemporary toys on the 1st floor after visiting the collection on the second. Don't forget to chat with Marvin, who'll be able to explain the cultural and historical importance of various items.

SAKAYA MUNI BUDDHA GAYA TEMPLE
Map p68

Temple of 1000 Lights; ☎ 6294 0714; 366 Race Course Rd; ☿ 8am-4.45pm; Ⓜ Farrer Park

In 1927 a Thai monk founded this Buddhist temple, popularly known as the Temple of 1000 Lights. It's dominated by a brightly painted 15m-high, 300-tonne Buddha that sits alongside an eclectic range of deities, including Kuan Yin, the Chinese goddess of mercy, as well as Brahma and Ganesh (both Hindu deities).

Flanking the entrance to the temple are yellow tigers, symbolising protection and vitality. On your left as you enter the temple is a huge mother-of-pearl footprint, complete with the 108 auspicious marks that distinguish a Buddha foot from any other 2m-long foot. It's said to be a replica of the footprint on top of Adam's Peak in Sri Lanka.

SRI SRINIVASA PERUMAL TEMPLE
Map p68

☎ 6298 5771; 397 Serangoon Rd; ☿ 6.30am-noon & 6-9pm; Ⓜ Farrer Park

This large complex, dedicated to Vishnu, dates from 1855 but the 20m-tall *gopuram* is a relatively recent addition, built in 1966 for $300,000. Inside the temple you will find a statue of Perumal, or Vishnu, his consorts Lakshmi and Andal, and his bird-mount, Garuda. This temple is the starting point for devotees who make the walk to the Chettiar Hindu Temple during the Thaipusam festival.

SRI VEERAMAKALIAMMAN TEMPLE
Map p68

☎ 6293 4634; 141 Serangoon Rd; ☿ 8am-12.30pm & 4-8.30pm; Ⓜ Little India

This Shaivite temple, dedicated to Kali, is one of the most colourful and bustling in Little India. Kali, bloodthirsty consort of Shiva, has always been popular in Bengal, the birthplace of the labourers who built this temple in 1881. Images of Kali within the temple show her wearing a garland of skulls and ripping out the insides of her victims, and sharing more peaceful family moments with her sons Ganesh and Murugan.

SULTAN MOSQUE Map p68

☎ 6293 4405; 3 Muscat St; ☿ 5am-8.30pm; Ⓜ Bugis

Singapore's biggest mosque is the golden-domed focal point of Kampong Glam. It was originally built in 1825 with the aid of a grant from Raffles and the East India Company, as a result of Raffles' treaty with the Sultan of Singapore that allowed him to retain sovereignty over the area. A hundred years later in 1928, the original mosque was replaced by the present magnificent building, which, interestingly, was designed by an architect who was from Ireland and worked for the same company that designed the Raffles Hotel.

The building follows classic Turkish, Persian and Moorish style. Inside the huge prayer hall, which can accommodate around 5000 people, the mosaic-tiled walls bear inscriptions from the Koran calling the faithful to prayer. The luscious rug on the floor was donated to the mosque by a Saudi Prince, whose emblem is woven into it. You might also notice a number of incongruous-looking digital clocks, which were installed so that prayer times could be accurately observed.

Bear in mind that this is a functioning mosque and only go inside if there isn't a prayer session going on. Non-Muslims are asked to refrain from entering the prayer hall at any time, and all visitors are expected to be dressed appropriately. Pointing cameras at people during prayer time is never appropriate.

LITTLE INDIA WALK
Walking Tour

1 Tekka Centre Beginning at the Little India MRT station, walk to the corner of Serangoon and Buffalo Rd; the famous Tekka Centre (p111 and p130) is currently under renovation, but many of the stalls have moved to a temporary location one block north on Race Course Rd. Buffalo Rd is a fun street to explore, as is Kerbau Rd (*kerbau* means 'buffalo' in Malay) one block east.

2 Tan House Note the fine two-storey Tan House, a Peranakan-style building constructed in 1905. Head southeast along Kerbau Rd (a pedestrian strip designated an 'arts village'), which is given over to shops and galleries specialising in Indian clothes, artwork and beauty treatments, including henna designs for the hands and feet – and a beer garden. Turn left at Serangoon Rd, which has numerous gold shops with glittering window displays.

3 Khan Mohamed Bhoy & Sons Walk 50m, then turn right down Cuff Rd, where you can get a glimpse of Singapore's past at one of the island's last spice-grinding shops, Khan Mohamed Bhoy & Sons (p111).

4 Kampong Kapor Methodist Church At the end of Cuff Rd, turn left along Kampong Kapor Rd and pass the Kampong Kapor Methodist Church, built in 1929. Hang a left

up Veerasamy Rd, bringing you back up to Serangoon Rd and the bustling, polychromatic Sri Veeramakaliamman Temple (opposite).

5 Mustafa Centre Around 500m further along Serangoon Rd is the thoroughly Indian shopping complex the Mustafa Centre (p111) – a great place for well-priced electrical goods, luggage and all manner of household items. It's open 24 hours a day and always seems to be seething with bargain-hungry shoppers. In this area, in the alleyways off Desker Rd, the brothels are successors to the long-demolished ones in old Bugis St.

6 Sri Srinivasa Perumal Temple A block north of the Mustafa Centre along Serangoon Rd, the Sri Srinivasa Perumal Temple (opposite) is a large, ornately decorated complex dedicated to Vishnu.

7 Sakaya Muni Buddha Gaya Temple Cut through the pedestrian alley, next to the temple, to Race Course Rd, where you'll find the glitzy, Thai-influenced Sakaya Muni Buddha Gaya Temple (opposite), better known as the Temple of 1000 Lights. Head across the road to the Leong San See Temple (p69) considered by some to be even more beautiful than its striking neighbour.

8 Shophouses Head back to Serangoon Rd and walk southwest, turning left onto Petain Rd, noting the beautifully restored block of shophouses on the corner of Surdee Rd. When you reach Jalan Besar turn right and head south along this grimy, busy main road lined with hardware and lighting shops. The Indian influence wanes here, but there are still some fine old pastel-coloured terraces with intricate stucco and tiles. If you're feeling a bit worn out, turn left at the end of Petain Rd, cross over Jalan Besar to the bus stop, hop on a bus (64, 65, 130, 139 or 147) and get off at the third stop, before Sim Lim Tower.

9 Sungei Rd Thieves Market Near the end of Jalan Besar duck into the Sungei Rd Thieves Market (p112) next to Sim Lim Tower, an arresting jumble of wares sold by anybody from fashionable students, gnarled old Hokkien 'uncles' and some of Singapore's homeless.

10 Abdul Gaffoor Mosque Back on Jalan Besar, turn right on to Mayo St to view the Abdul Gaffoor Mosque. An intriguing blend of Arab and Victorian architecture, it was declared a national monument in 1979.

LITTLE INDIA WALK

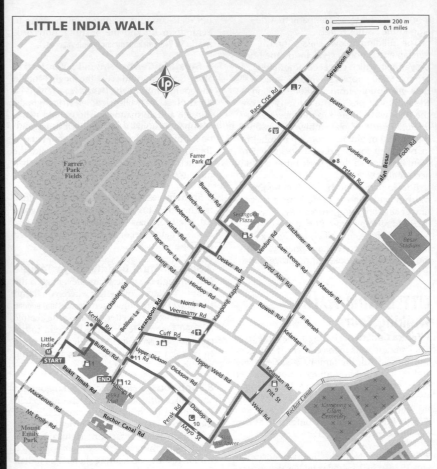

11 Fortune-tellers From here, spend some time exploring the atmospheric back streets, which bear the names of imperial India, such as Clive, Hastings and Campbell. This is the beating heart of Little India, with all manner of colourful shops and street life. At the Serangoon Rd end of Dunlop St you'll find fortune-tellers, who use birds to pick your fortune (though bear in mind that some people say these birds are not treated well). Campbell St is something of a tourist strip, lined with shops selling souvenirs, crafts and 'antiques'. You will also find a few garland-makers scenting the air with their jasmine flowers.

WALK FACTS

Start Little India MRT station
End Little India MRT station
Distance 2.5km
Time Two hours
Ease Moderate
Fuel stops Tekka Centre or Dunlop St

12 Little India Arcade Finish up at the Little India Arcade, a block of renovated shophouses containing various shops selling spices, Ayurvedic remedies, textiles, tapes, brassware, homeware and souvenirs.

ORCHARD ROAD

Drinking & Nightlife p145; Eating p130; Shopping p112; Sleeping p169

Singapore's wall-to-wall consumerist nirvana is an assault on your senses – and your wallet. Faced with this immense stretch of towering malls, some will scream with delight, others will run screaming. From quirky, rundown Lucky Plaza to the imposing chocolate-coloured marble edifice of Ngee Ann City and the chic, exclusive grey of Paragon, it's possible to spend days here and never visit the same mall twice. Trees that shade the ever-present crowds are almost the only reminder that this area was, in the 19th century, an orchard lined with nutmeg and pepper plantations. However, between the five-star hotels and hulking shrines to materialism, a few architectural relics from this time remain.

When you've had your fill of the shops and chilly air-conditioning, escape is close to hand with the serene Singapore Botanic Gardens a short bus ride from the west end of the road.

CUPPAGE TERRACE & EMERALD HILL Map pp74–5

Cuppage Rd; Ⓜ Somerset

Named after William Cuppage, who was the 19th-century owner of the nutmeg estate here, Cuppage Tce, a renovated terrace of Peranakan-style shophouses dating from the 1920s, is overwhelmed by the surrounding shopping malls and hotels. Most of the terrace is given over to bars and restaurants, as is the Orchard Rd end of Emerald Hill.

Take some time out, though, to wander up from pedestrianised Peranakan Pl to Emerald Hill Rd, where some fine terrace houses remain; the quiet atmosphere feels a million miles from bustling Orchard Rd. Check out Nos 39 to 45, built in 1903 with an unusually wide frontage and a grand Chinese-style entrance gate, and the art deco–style houses Nos 121 to 129, dating from 1925.

ISTANA Map pp74–5

☎ 6737 5522; www.istana.gov.sg; Ⓜ Dhoby Ghaut

Home of Singapore's president, the Istana was built between 1867 and 1869 as Government House, a neoclassical monument to British rule. Public works were never a high priority in laissez-faire colonial Singapore, but the need to impress the visiting Duke of Edinburgh convinced the island's Legislative Council to approve the building's huge budget. The actual construction – stone-masonry, plumbing, carpentry, painting and stone-cutting – was done by Indian convicts transported from Bencoolen on Sumatra.

The Istana is situated approximately 750m back from the road in beautifully maintained grounds including a nine-hole golf course and terraced garden. Most of the time the closest you are likely to get to it are the well-guarded gates on Orchard Rd, it's open to the public on selected public holidays – call or check the website for details. If you are lucky enough to be in Singapore on one of these occasions,

THE KING & 'EYESORE'

It's a question many visitors to the blissfully quiet and efficient Royal Thai Embassy on Orchard Rd quietly ask themselves. What on earth is it doing here? An ageing house that some consider an eyesore (we love it), surrounded by a lush compound on a prime spot on one of the most expensive real estate strips in Singapore? And why hasn't the Thai government sold the plot for the fortune it's undoubtedly worth?

The answer lies in history. The plot was bought for Thailand in 1893 for $9000 by the revered King Chulalongkorn (King Rama V), whose picture, as most visitors to Thailand will know, is hung in virtually every house and building in the country.

There has been talk of developing the embassy site for decades. The Thai government was reportedly offered $139 million for the plot in the late '90s, but turned the offer down. Thai prime minister Thaksin Shinawatra revived the idea of developing the site in 2003, but nothing has happened as yet, and since selling the plot would be seen as an affront to the great monarch's memory, it's likely to remain a delightful peculiarity for some time to come.

ORCHARD ROAD

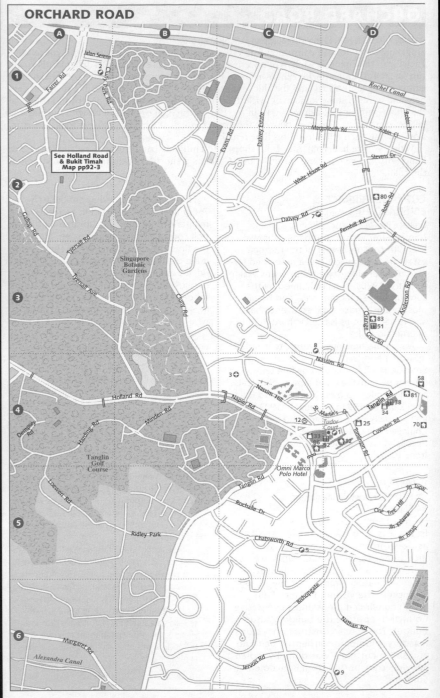

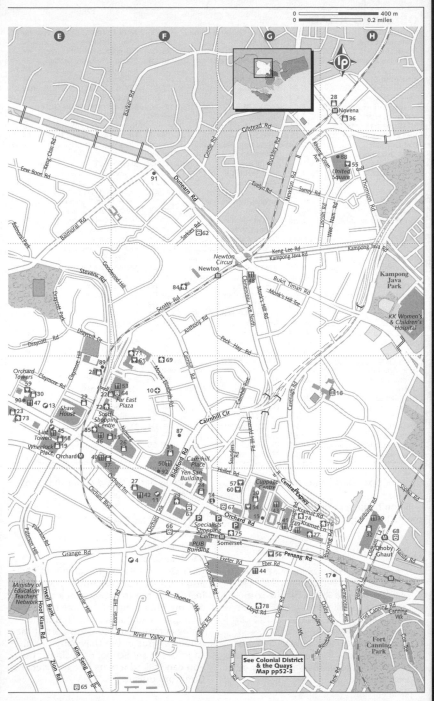

See Colonial District
& the Quays
Map pp52-3

ORCHARD ROAD

take your passport and join the queues to get in.

If you happen to be in the area on the first Sunday of any given month, the Changing of the Guard parade happens in the evening on this day.

TRANSPORT: ORCHARD ROAD

Orchard Rd is important enough to have three MRT stations: Orchard MRT at the western end, Somerset in the centre and Dhoby Ghaut at the eastern end. (Believe it or not, some Singaporeans do take the train between them rather than walk.) Dhoby Ghaut is an important MRT junction, from which trains fan off to City Hall and Raffles Pl (Colonial District), Little India, Clarke Quay and Chinatown. Buses from Orchard Rd and Scotts Rd also fan out across the island.

TAN YEOK NEE HOUSE

Map pp74–5

207 Clemenceau Ave;
Ⓜ **Dhoby Ghaut**

Near Orchard Rd, on the corner of Penang Rd, Tan Yeok Nee House was built in 1885 as the townhouse of a prosperous merchant, and is the sole surviving example in Singapore of a traditional Chinese mansion. Today it's part of the Asian campus of the University of Chicago Graduate School of Business, but you can still admire its fine roof decoration from outside.

Drinking & Nightlife p147; Eating p132; Shopping p115; Sleeping p171

Though comprising a fair swath of the island, the neighbourhoods of the east receive far less attention from tourists than do those of the city centre. It's a shame, really, because whereas Chinatown is becoming a Disney-esque parody – existing mostly as a museum piece for tourists – the neighbourhoods of the east are vibrant, alive and, on the whole, more reflective of Singapore culture, both today and of days past.

Eastern Singapore is where you'll find the Geylang district (at once notorious and spiritual); Katong (also known as Joo Chiat), a picturesque neighbourhood of multicoloured shophouses that, in recent years, has come into its own as the spiritual heartland of Singapore's Peranakan people; and Changi, the city's easternmost region.

Stretching for several kilometres along the seafront, from the city right up to Tanah Merah, is East Coast Park, whose well-paved waterfront paths offer many kilometres of skating and bicycling, as well as numerous spots for eating and drinking.

GEYLANG

Though the very name Geylang is synonymous in Singapore with the flesh trade, there's more to this neighbourhood than meets the eye. Yes, what you may have heard about this district being an open-air meat market filled with a Dante-esque assortment of brothels, girlie bars, cheap hotels and alley after alley lined with prostitutes from all over Southeast Asia is all true. Yet strange as it may seem, the area is also one of the Lion City's spiritual hubs, with huge temples and mosques, and picturesque alleys dotted with religious schools, shrines and temples.

Geylang borders the Katong/Joo Chiat district, with Paya Leber Rd being the marker.

AMITABHA BUDDHIST CENTRE
Map p80

☎ 6745 8547; www.fpmtabc.org; 44 Lorong 25A; ⊗ 10am-9pm; Ⓜ Aljunied

This seven-storey Tibetan Buddhist centre holds classes on dharma and meditation (check its website for the schedule), as well as events during religious festivals. The upstairs meditation hall, swathed in red-and-

gold cloth, is open to the public and filled with beautiful statues and other objects of devotion. In addition to being involved with community outreach, the centre also operates a store selling religious and spiritual items such as prayer flags, spinning wheels, and other items associated with Tibetan Buddhism.

Around the corner from Amitaba over a large fruit-stand selling durians is the Sakyamuni Dharma Centre (☎ 6745 5900; Level 3, 270-B Sims Ave; ⊗ 10am-9pm). Much smaller than Amitaba, this centre has a meditation hall, and welcomes people wishing to learn about Tibetan Buddhism.

PU JI SI BUDDHIST RESEARCH CENTRE
Map p80

☎ 6746 6211; www.pujisi.org.sg; 39 Lorong 12; Ⓜ Aljunied

Inside this fantastic four-storey building, which is part educational facility, part house of worship, visitors will find meditation halls, Buddhist libraries filled with books and scripture, and a seeming endless well of serenity. Take the elevator up for a sit by the fountain in the rooftop statue

THE LURE & LORE OF GEYLANG'S LORONGS

True enough, Geylang is known as a red-light district; still, the vast majority of Geylang's unsavoury trade takes place west of Aljunied Rd. A daytime stroll through the *lorongs* (alleys) that run north to south between Sims Ave and Geylang road offers surprising charm for those who take the time to look.

Several pretty side-streets well worth checking out include tree-lined Lorong 27, a small street chock-a-block with colourful shrines and temples. Picturesque Lorong 24A is lined with renovated shophouses, from which the sounds of chanting often emerge; this is because many of these houses have actually been taken over by numerous smaller Buddhist associations in the area. Gorgeous Lorong 34 boasts both restored and unrestored shophouses painted in varying hues, as well as a number of colourful shrines and braziers for burning incense. One house on the street even boasts a street-side bamboo garden.

TRANSPORT: EASTERN SINGAPORE

Compared to the city centre, eastern Singapore isn't particularly well served by the MRT network; Aljunied is the closest MRT station to Geylang, and Paya Lebar takes you into the northern end of Joo Chiat. For this reason, buses can be a better bet.

Buses 33 and 16 run into the centre of Joo Chiat after passing through Geylang, while 14 goes from Orchard Rd to East Coast Rd. To and from the Colonial District, buses 12 and 32 head into the city along North Bridge Rd.

To get to East Coast Park, you can get bus 401 from Bedok MRT station, but only on weekends. At other times, you'll be forced to take a taxi (an increasingly expensive proposition, especially at night), or walk from East Coast Rd.

garden. Breathe in the air of serenity while pondering the eternal. Across the street from the centre sits a nameless jungle park for postmeditation contemplation.

KATONG/JOO CHIAT

The heart of Singapore's re-emerging Peranakan culture, the Joo Chiat area runs roughly southeast from the Paya Leber MRT station over to Still Rd in the west and East Coast Park to the south. The heart of the neighbourhood is Joo Chiat Rd, which has a host of restaurants, daytime businesses, clubs and bars. What makes the neighbourhood truly worth exploring are the myriad renovated Peranakan-style terrace shophouses, which exist on both Joo Chiat Rd and on side-streets throughout the neighbourhood, as well as a number of temples (Chinese and Indian), mosques, and other landmarks that will give visitors a taste of old Singapore. Joo Chiat is also home to the Geylang Serai wet market.

Joo Chiat Rd runs into East Coast Rd, also noted for its Peranakan influence, mostly because of the opportunity to sample Peranakan food (also known as Nonya cuisine). The alleyways to the west of Joo Chiat along East Coast Rd are particularly good for exploration. Joo Chiat Rd itself has something of a red-light reputation, but this is felt primarily only at night, and only on the stretch containing bars between Koon Seng Rd and Joo Chiat Pl.

GEYLANG SERAI WET MARKET
Map p80
Geylang Serai; M Paya Lebar
Hidden behind some older-style housing blocks on Geylang Rd, this is a bustling and traditional Southeast Asian market, crammed with stalls selling food, fabrics and other wares. Some say that its continued existence defies the odds: as

real-estate prices in the area skyrocket the trend seems to lean towards tearing down older shopping areas and replacing them with more 'Disney-esque' areas such as the nearby (and thoroughly avoidable) Malay Cultural Village. The market reaches its peak of activity during Ramadan, when the whole area is alive with evening market stalls. Just north of the market is a strip of park (next to the elevated MRT) where you can eat your durian in peace.

CHURCH OF THE HOLY FAMILY
Map p80
6 Chapel Rd; M Eunos
With its gracefully curving roof, stained glass and gleaming white edifice, this Catholic church displays an interesting mixture of Western and Asian architecture. Though not the original building (the original chapel on this spot was built in 1923, though the origins of the congregation go back further), the edifice is worth a look. Keep an eye out for the unusual stained-glass window featuring the image of a 16-pointed star over the altar.

KATONG ANTIQUE HOUSE
Map p80
☎ 6345 8544; 208 East Coast Rd; M Eunos
Part shop, part museum, the Katong Antique House is a labour of love for Peter Wee. A lifelong resident of the area, Peter displays (and occasionally sells) Peranakan antiques, artefacts, and other *objects d'art*. A noted repository of Peranakan history and culture, Peter will happily regale you with tales as you browse.

SRI SENPAGA VINAYAGAR TEMPLE
Map p80
19 Ceylon Rd; M Paya Lebar
Easily among the most beautiful Hindu temples in Singapore, Sri Senpaga

Vinayagar is also probably the most visitor-friendly as well, thanks to the efforts of staff and volunteers who've made sure that all of the temple's devotional art is labelled in a number of languages. The temple has a number of unique features that make it well worth a visit even if you weren't in the neighbourhood already, especially the *kamalapaatham,* a specially sculptured granite foot-stone found in certain ancient Hindu temples. The roof of the inner sanctum sanctorum is covered in gold.

KUAN IM TING TEMPLE Map p80
cnr Tembeling Rd & Joo Chiat Lane; Ⓜ Paya Lebar
A beautiful temple dedicated to Kuan Yin, goddess of mercy, this Buddhist temple is home to many festivals throughout the year. Of particular interest to temple-lovers is the ornate roof ridges, adorned with dancing dragons and other symbols important to worshippers of the goddess.

PERANAKAN TERRACE HOUSES
Map p80
Koon Seng Rd; Ⓜ Paya Lebar
Just off Joo Chiat Rd you'll find some of the finest Peranakan terrace houses in Singapore. Exhibiting the typical Peranakan love of ornate design, they are decorated with stucco dragons, birds, crabs and brilliantly glazed tiles. *Pintu pagar* (swinging doors) at the front of the houses are another typical feature, allowing in breezes while retaining privacy. (For background information on the Peranakan people, see p29.)

EAST COAST PARK
This 11km stretch of seafront park is where Singaporeans come to swim, windsurf, kayak, picnic, bicycle, rollerblade and, of course, eat. The whole park has been superbly designed so that the many leisure facilities don't crowd the green space. In this single, narrow strip, there are several bird sanctuaries, patches of unmanaged bushland, golf driving ranges, tennis courts, a resort, Playground@Big Splash (not a water park, but a family-themed playground), several ponds and a lagoon, sea sports clubs, hawker centres, and some excellent bars and restaurants.

Renting a bicycle or rollerblades and gently pedalling from one end to the other, enjoying the sea breezes, watching the veritable city of container ships out in the strait and capping it off with a meal and a few beachfront beers is one of the most pleasant ways to spend a Singapore afternoon.

The East Coast Park starts at the end of Tanjong Katong Rd in Katong and ends at the National Sailing Centre in Bedok, which is actually near the Tanah Merah MRT station. At the western end of the park, the bicycle track continues right through to Geylang, ending at the Kalang River.

MARINE COVE RECREATION CENTRE
Map p80
East Coast Park Service Rd; 🚌 401 from Ⓜ Bedok (weekends only), taxi from Ⓜ Bedok ($4-5) or the city ($8) on weekdays
Midway along the park, near the end of Still Rd South, this outdoor leisure complex has tenpin bowling, squash, crazy golf and a large selection of restaurants, food stalls and bars, plus a McDonald's (Singapore's only one with a skate-through window). On the beach side of the complex there are a couple of bicycle and rollerblade rental stations and a kayak and sailboat rental place on the beach itself.

CHANGI & PASIR RIS
These 'remote' neighbourhoods at the extreme east of the island were once dominated by Malay kampong (villages). While the stilted houses are long gone, replaced by modern housing estates and reclamation projects, the area, particularly Pasir Ris, still has a pleasant atmosphere, with manicured lawns, Ma-and-Pa stores and attractive seafront parks. Here's where you'll find the moving Changi Prison Museum & Chapel site, a

---

TRANSPORT: CHANGI & PASIR RIS

Pasir Ris is easily reachable by MRT — it's at the end of the East West Line. From the station, all the attractions are within easy walking distance. To get to Changi, get off the train at Tanah Merah MRT station and hop on bus 2, which will take you to both the Changi Chapel and Changi Village, which is the end of the line.

A taxi from the city to either area costs approximately $15.

EASTERN SINGAPORE

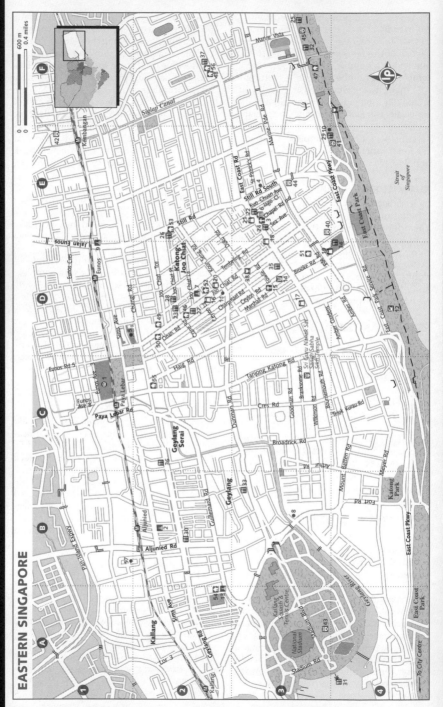

EASTERN SINGAPORE

few resorts and theme parks for the kids, a sprinkling of malls and the giant space-age Expo centre.

At Changi Village you'll also find the ferry terminal for bumboats to Pulau Ubin (p176) and Johor in Malaysia.

CHANGI PRISON MUSEUM & CHAPEL
Map pp46–7

☎ 6214 2451; www.changimuseum.com; 1000 Upper Changi Rd North; admission free; ⏱ 9.30am-5pm; 🚌 2

A steady stream of visitors makes its way to this quiet, moving museum commemorating the Allied POWs who were captured and imprisoned and suffered horrific treatment at the hands of the invading Japanese forces during WWII. It was shifted from the original Changi prison site in 2001 when Singapore Prisons reclaimed the land to expand its operations.

Former POWs, veterans and historians will feel the loss of the actual site most keenly, but to the architects' credit the understated design of the new building is well suited to its dual role as a shrine and history museum. The square white facade is reminiscent of a concrete bunker, yet the greenery hints at healing and renewal. The gaping entrance and open plan suggest accessibility. The museum's centrepiece is a replica of the original Changi Chapel built by inmates as a focus

for worship and presumably as a sign of solidarity. Tucked into the walls beside the altar, with its cross made of ammunitions casings, are little mementos left by visitors – white crosses, red poppies, fresh flowers and handwritten notes. Services are held on Sundays (at 9.30am and 5.30pm), but the shadeless courtyard heats up like an oven.

Bus 2 from Victoria St or Tanah Merah MRT station will take you past the entrance. Get off at bus stop B09, just after the Changi Heights condominium. The bus terminates at Changi Village.

LOYANG TUA PEK KONG TEMPLE
Map pp46–7

20 Loyang Way; admission free; 🚌 9 from Ⓜ Bedok

The embodiment of the Singaporean approach to spirituality, this temple hosts three religions, Hinduism, Buddhism and Taoism, under one vast roof. There's even a shrine devoted to Datuk Kung, a saint of Malay mysticism and Chinese Taoist practices. This temple is new and grand with large handcrafted wooden cravings, swirling dragons on large granite pillars and hundreds of colourful effigies of deities, gods and saints. It's a bit off the beaten path, but worth the trip. Get off bus 9 at the Loyang Valley condominium.

CHANGI VILLAGE Map pp46–7

🚌 2

On the far northeast coast of Singapore, Changi Village is an escape from the hub-bub of central Singapore. The buildings are modern (although there are some interesting old 'black-and-white' bunga-lows along Loyang Ave), but there's still a village atmosphere, with the lively and quite renowned hawker centre next to the bus terminus being a focal point. There's a small, attractive beachfront camp site across the Changi Creek from the bus terminal, where you can watch the planes gliding into Changi airport while relax-ing on the imported sand. It's popular on weekends but almost deserted during the week. You might want to avoid swimming here, though. Changi's beach is where thousands of Singaporean civilians were executed by the Japanese during WWII. A memorial marks the site.

Next to the bus terminal is the Changi Point Ferry Terminal, where you can catch bumboats to Pulau Ubin (p176) or Johor (p180).

PASIR RIS PARK Map pp46–7

Pasir Ris Dr 3; Ⓜ Pasir Ris

Stretching along a couple of kilometres of the northeast coast, a short walk from

---

TO BE PERANAKAN MEANS TO BE ACCEPTED AS A LOCAL Peter Wee

The word Peranakan originated during British colonial times, around 1825, when settlement began in Malacca, Penang and Singapore. To understand what the term Peranakan means, you need to start with the Straits Chinese. Peranakan culture is really the interfusion between local people and Chinese traders. When the traders of China first came to Malacca in 1500, they came down to trade and intermingled with local inhabitants, forming communities of sorts. It was these Chinese traders, through intermingling with the local inhabitants, that gave birth to a new culture, the Peranakan.

Peranakan culture isn't found only in Singapore. Throughout coastal Indonesia and Malaysia you'll find other pockets of Peranakan culture. To some, Peranakan culture may seem very similar to traditional Chinese culture, which makes sense, as our culture is about 80% derived from Chinese culture. However, there are subtle differences, certainly in our traditions, the way we speak and, of course, in our culinary traditions. Many of these differences come from a combination of time and the other cultures that make up the Peranakan, both local Straits inhabitants and colonial – especially British – influence.

Increasingly, there seems to be an awakening cultural awareness among members of the younger generation in Singapore. One recent event sticks out. A young couple came to my shop while planning their wedding. The bride-to-be was shopping for a *kebaya*, a beautiful hand-embroidered outfit traditionally worn by Peranakan women. This struck me as odd, and I assumed that the choice of dress had been made by the parents. So I was surprised to learn that, in fact, the parents objected. They wanted to have a more modern wedding. But it was the young people themselves that chose to get married wearing the clothing of their past.

Most Peranakan tend to be Christian because of the influence of early missionaries – French, Dutch, Portuguese, and finally English – in the area. But Peranakan culture crosses religious boundaries. In 2008, there are Peranakans who are Muslims, others who maintain Buddhist traditions. The way we speak is itself unique, not quite a language in and of itself, but more like a *patois*, a mixture of Hokkien, Malay, English, with a tinge of Dutch, and even Portuguese. It's very unique to Malacca, Penang and Singapore, only found around here.

The Joo Chiat district derives its name from a famous Peranakan family. The main street is named after Chew Joo Chiat, who was a philanthropist in the late 19th century. Many of the original families have left, for various reasons, but some are returning. There is a lot of nostalgia for the area. We are trying to put it back together again, so that Joo Chiat can become what it once was.

Visitors to Singapore should take the time to visit the area to see the truly unique architecture that exists, especially the art deco shophouses of Koon Seng and Tembeling Rd. And of course, Joo Chiat is the place in Singapore to sample Peranakan cuisine. I always take friends out to try our *mee siam* (white thin noodles in a sourish and sweet gravy made with tamarind), laksa, and our traditional Peranakan dumplings. One Peranakan specialty is the *buah keluak*, a creamy, almost cacao like nut found in Indonesia.

There are Peranakan Indian, Peranakan Chinese, Peranakan Hokkien. Even Peranakan Eurasians. My great-great grandfather came from Malacca, but he traced his ancestry back to Xiamen (in China), and I am a Singaporean-born Peranakan. To be Peranakan means to be accepted as a local.

Peter Wee, 62, is the owner and curator of the Katong Antique House in Joo Chiat, the heart of Singapore's Peranakan cultural renaissance. His shop, which is open only by invitation, offers a unique collection of textiles, porcelain, Peranakan furniture and spices. The shop also doubles as a kind of 'living museum' of local culture. Under the gaze of the portraits of four generations of Straits Peranakan, Peter spoke about Joo Chiat's renaissance, and Peranakan culture and identity.

Pasir Ris MRT station, this peaceful place is the third-largest park in Singapore and certainly among the best. There's a surprising variety of attractions here, including a maze garden, adventure playground and sea fishing for kids; fish ponds; bicycle, rollerblade and kayak rentals; and a pristine 5-hectare mangrove swamp, complete with boardwalks and signboards describing the ecology of the area, and a large observation tower for bird-watchers.

JOO CHIAT WALK
Walking Tour
1 Geylang Serai From Paya Leber MRT, head south by southwest to and through the bustling Geylang Serai Wet Market (p78), an excellent hawker centre and wet market with an accent on Malay food. Towards the back are a number of stalls selling clothing and surprising objets d'art. From the market, head down Joo Chiat Rd; if you aren't already full, sample snacks at any one of the many small restaurants that line the road.

2 Kuan Im Ting Temple Hang a left at Joo Chiat Lane and walk to the corner of Tembeling Rd, where you'll find the beautiful Kuan Im Ting Temple (p79). The heart of Joo Chiat's Buddhist community, the temple features an ornate facade, including traditional circular windows surrounded by the symbols of the eight immortals. Check out the central prayer hall, dedicated to Kuan Yin, goddess of mercy.

3 Koon Seng Road Shophouses Walk south a block to Koon Seng Rd; while the whole street is filled with beautiful examples of Peranakan-style shophouses (p79), you'll find the most ornate of these on the strip between Tembeling and Joo Chiat Rd. You may notice a subtle difference in style between houses on either side of the street, with one side affecting a slightly more art deco facade; according to

WALK FACTS
Start Paya Lebar MRT station
End East Coast Park
Distance 4km
Time Three hours
Ease Moderate
Fuel stops Nonya laksa stalls

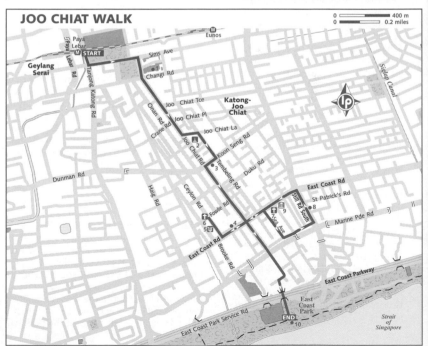

JOO CHIAT WALK

top picks

MUST-TRY TOURS

- When it comes to selecting a guide to show you the sights and sounds of the Lion City, you won't find anyone more idiosyncratic than Jeffery Tan (☎ 9784 6848; http://jefflimo.tripod.com /jefflimo.htm). Known as 'Singapore's Singing Cabbie', Tan can croon in nine languages, and will happily serenade you in the language of your choice while showing you the city's attractions. A native Singaporean, Tan's tours include any sights that you'd like; he also does a food tour, ensuring that all your senses are stimulated. If you feel like singing along, Jeff can accommodate you: the limo is equipped with the latest in video karaoke systems.
- Operated by the amazing Tony Tan, owner of the Betel Box Hostel and expert on all things Singapore, a Real Singapore Tour (☎ 6247 7340; www.betelbox.com) is one you won't soon forget. His food tours, a Singapore must-experience, generally start each Friday evening around six. Tony takes his charges on a veritable gastronomic odyssey through the historical Joo Chiat neighbourhood, where they sample over 20 authentic dishes from all over Southeast Asia. Other tours include walking or cycling trips focusing on history, nature and culture. Tony also leads an amazing pub crawl. Prices start at $50 including food, equipment and the services of one of the most knowledgeable tour guides in Singapore.
- Geraldene Lowe-Ahmad (☎ 6737 5250; geraldenestours@hotmail.com) and Diane Chua (☎ 9489 1999; dianachua1999@yahoo.com.sg) are the venerable dynamic duo of the Singapore guide scene, offering a wide variety of tours to suit all interests. Geraldine's knowledge of Singapore's history, cuisine, architecture, botany, ethnic diversity, religions and festivals is second to none. She also does amazing WWII tours, popular among veterans. Diane, in addition to cultural and historical tours, also specialises in more esoteric areas, such as excursions examining Singaporean feng shui, cemeteries and other less-examined facets of the Lion City. Both offer time-specific tours, taking advantage of various religious and cultural festivities. Tours can be conducted in English, Malay, Chinese, Italian or French.

locals, this reflects the style that happened to be in vogue during restoration.

4 East Coast Road Head south down Joo Chiat Rd and hang a right at East Coast Rd; this stretch is known for its great restaurants, particularly the Nonya laksa stalls on the corner of East Coast and Ceylon Rds. There are also some more fine shophouses along this stretch.

5 Sri Senpaga Vinayagar Temple Hang a left on Ceylon Rd. See that fantastically ornate Hindu Temple on the corner? That's the Sri Senpaga Vinayagar Temple (p78-9), and with multi-coloured scenes of Hindu myth and legend carved into the ceilings, it's even more beautiful on the inside. The temple is also a hub of activity, especially on weekdays. Volunteers will be glad to walk you through and explain the meaning behind the temple's overwhelming devotional art.

6 St Hilda's Anglican Church Right across Fowlie Rd from the temple sits St Hilda's Anglican Church; with its sloped, red-tiled roof and white walls, the church is as quaint as any you might find in the British Isles. The serene garden is a particularly nice spot to catch your breath.

7 Church of the Holy Family Head back south to East Coast Rd and turn left, crossing Joo Chiat Rd once more. Take a right at the next alley takes you down a pleasant cul-de-sac with a number of traditional terrace houses in various states of restoration. One block past this, in between Sea Ave and Chapel Rd, is the Church of the Holy Family (p78). A unique mixture of East and West, the Catholic church boasts a gracefully curving roof and an edifice so white it almost hurts the eyes. Of particular note is the stained-glass window featuring the image of a 16-pointed star over the altar.

8 Former Grand Hotel From the Church of the Holy Family, heading directly south will take you into a small park filled with trees, kids and folks walking their dogs. On the north end of the park you'll see a few bungalows, which, once upon a time, all had sea views (prior to the land reclamation that pushed the ocean south nearly half a mile). Hanging a left through the park will take you to both wings of the Former Grand Hotel, built in 1917 and split in two with the creation of Still Rd. Though there are plans to renovate at least one wing of this Singaporean Grand Dame, currently both are vacant.

9 Katong Antique House Continue north on Still Rd and hang a left on East Coast Rd. On the south side of the street you'll find the Katong Antique House (p78), whose owner, Peter Wee, welcomes visitors who are interested in local culture. See the interview with Peter on p82.

10 East Coast Park From Peter's shop, you can head north on Joo Chiat Rd for some more wandering through Joo Chiat before heading back to the MRT at either Paya Leber or Eunos (both east of Geylang Serai). Heading south on Joo Chiat Rd takes you past Marine Parade Rd, south of which you'll find the lovely East Coast Park (p80), an excellent spot from which to watch the sun go down.

NORTHERN & CENTRAL SINGAPORE

A short drive through the central and northern areas of the island is enough to dispel any notion of Singapore as a purely urban city. Yes, there is never-ending construction and land reclamation, but Singapore also has an astonishing variety of green spaces, from the many delightful city parks to large nature reserves and forests. Apart from Rio de Janeiro, it is the only city in the world that retains an area of primary rainforest, in the form of Bukit Timah Nature Reserve. Just 15 minutes from Orchard Rd, you could be standing next to a centuries-old tree surrounded by macaque monkeys and monitor lizards, with not a mall or high-rise apartment building in sight.

CENTRAL CATCHMENT NATURE RESERVE Map pp46–7

🚍 162

Encompassing the MacRitchie and Lower and Upper Peirce Reservoir parks, this 2000-hectare area is Singapore's largest nature reserve. The area is criss-crossed by a series of trails, ranging from short boardwalks around the reservoirs to long treks through the forest. The most popular entry point to this precious wilderness is the MacRitchie Reservoir, a delightful, partly manicured park wrapped around the water's edge, where you can rent a kayak (see p157) and get a bite to eat at the small hilltop food centre overlooking the water and a bizarre zigzagging pontoon bridge. It's also the starting point for some fairly arduous forest walks (see p88). To get here, take bus 162 from Orchard Blvd or Scotts Rd, and or bus 157 from Toa Payoh MRT station, and get off at the reservoir entrance at the top of Thomson Rd.

KONG MENG SAN PHOR KARK SEE MONASTERY Map pp46–7

☎ 6453 4046; http://kmspks.org; 88 Bright Hill Dr; ⏰ 7am-6pm; 🚍 410

A fascinating couple of hours can be had exploring this monastery and temple complex, Singapore's largest. Founded in 1921, the monastery's main function is as a

crematorium, which is huge. There are also several monumental halls housing various guises of the Buddha. A highlight is the Pagoda of 10,000 Buddhas, with its golden cone-shaped stupa lined on the inside with 9999 Buddha images – the 10,000th Buddha is the giant one inside the pagoda.

For a few weeks every year during April's Qing Ming festival (p17), the monastery swarms with Chinese families paying respect to their ancestors and cleaning their tombs.

Call in advance if you want to arrange a guided tour of the complex.

Free vegetarian meals are served in the refectory, but they are supposed to be for the needy, not tourists. On the 27th of each month an informal flea market is held in the monastery's grounds.

Opposite the monastery is Singapore's largest park, Bishan Park, the northern section of which is a beautiful, quiet spot with a series of linked ponds spanned by small wooden Japanese-style bridges, immaculately kept gardens and a delightful ornamental lily pond. An outdoor cafe called Explorer Zone is next to the park entrance north of the temple and is a perfect spot for a pond-side lunch or dinner.

Bus 410 runs here from behind the Junction 8 shopping centre above Bishan MRT station.

KRANJI WAR MEMORIAL Map pp46–7

☎ 6269 6158; 9 Woodlands Rd; admission free; ⏰ 24hr; Ⓜ Kranji or 🚍 170

Near the Causeway off Woodlands Rd, the Kranji War Memorial includes the graves of thousands of Allied troops who died in the region during WWII. The walls are inscribed with the names of 24,346 men and women, and registers, stored inside unlocked, weatherproof stands, are available for inspection. The memorial can be reached by bus 170 from Rochor Rd, or it's about 10 minutes' walk from Kranji MRT station.

TRANSPORT: NORTHERN & CENTRAL SINGAPORE

Central Singapore is encircled by the North South Line of the MRT network and while none of the stops are particularly close to any of the nature reserves, they'll get you close enough to limit your taxi costs. The area is also threaded with expressways, which means getting there by taxi from the city is only a matter of minutes.

MANDAI ORCHID GARDENS Map pp46-7

☎ 6269 1036; www.mandai.com.sg; 200 Mandai Lake Rd; adult/child $2/0.50; ⏰ 8.30am-5.30pm; 🚌 138 from Ⓜ Ang Mo Kio

Singapore has a major business in cultivating orchids, and with four solid hectares of orchids, the Mandai Orchid Gardens, a short walk from the zoo (or one stop on bus 138), is one of the best places to see them, though nonenthusiasts might find there's little to hold their attention. You can arrange to have a gift box of fresh orchids flown to just about anywhere in the world. It's next to the Singapore Zoo (below).

SINGAPORE ZOOLOGICAL GARDENS & NIGHT SAFARI Map pp46-7

☎ 6269 3411; www.zoo.com.sg; 80 Mandai Lake Rd; adult/child $16.50/8.50; ⏰ 8.30am-6pm; 🚌 138 from Ⓜ Ang Mo Kio

In the far north of the island, Singapore's world-class zoo has 3600 animals, representing 410 species including endangered white rhino, Bengal white tigers and even polar bears. Wherever possible, moats replace bars, and the zoo is beautifully spread out over 28 hectares of lush greenery beside the Upper Seletar Reservoir. As far as zoos go, this is one of the best. Some of the animal shows might be a little circuslike, such as the elephant rides and the sea lion performance, but most are magnificent – particularly the white tiger, elephant, crocodile and, best of all, baboon enclosures. Feeding times are well staggered to allow you to catch most of them as you walk around. There are trams (adult/child $5/3) that can shuttle you around if it's too hot, or you're too lazy.

Next door, but completely separate from the zoo, is the acclaimed Night Safari (☎ 7269 3412; www.nightsafari.com.sg; adult/child $22/11; ⏰ 7.30pm-midnight), which many people count as the highlight of their trip to Singapore. This 40-hectare forested park allows you to view 120 different species of animals, including tigers, lions and leopards. In the darkness the moats and other barriers seem to melt away and it actually looks like these creatures could walk over and take a bite out of you. The atmosphere is heightened even further by the herds of strolling antelope, which often pass within inches of the electric trams that are available to take you around. For an even creepier experience, walk through the enclosed Mangrove

Walk, where bats flap around your head and dangle from trees a few feet above your head.

You are asked not to use a flash on your camera since it disturbs the animals and annoys fellow visitors.

top picks

FOR KIDS

Few Asian metropolises are as kid-friendly. There's so much for kids to do in Singapore that at the end of your trip you may have to drag the little ones screaming to the airport – unless, that is, it's the kids who are dragging you from Orchard Rd. The city packs in a huge number of family-friendly activities, with enough variety to please children of every temperament, as long as they can cope with the heat.

- **Singapore Zoological Gardens & Night Safari** (left) Hands-down the best zoo in Asia. Have breakfast with an orang-utan at the zoo, or combine a zoo visit and night safari trip.
- **Haw Par Villa** (p96) Though the graphic depictions of Buddhist hell might scare the little ones, this colourful and wonderfully weird theme park of Chinese culture scores high on both the educational and gross-out scale.
- **Singapore Science Centre** (p98) An amazing hands-on science museum; watch hydrogen balloons being blown up by lightning generated from a Tesla coil.
- **Singapore Flyer** (p156) Come on, how could the world's largest Ferris wheel fail to excite young and old alike?
- **East Coast Park** (p80) Rollerblade or bicycle along the lovely stretch of coastline that wraps around the island's southeast flank, stopping for sustenance with an ocean view in one of the park's restaurants, bars or food stalls.
- **Orchard Road malls** (p112) Check out the fabulous Christmas light displays from November to the end of December.
- **Singapore DUCK Tour** (p198) Board the amphibious craft that tours the city streets before plunging into the harbour. Go on, you know you want to.
- **Bukit Timah** (p91), **MacRitchie Reservoir** (p88) **or Sungei Buloh** (p88) Introduce the kids to a bit of tropical nature at one of Singapore's reserves, where they can see cavorting monkeys and, if you're lucky, huge monitor lizards that'll scare them witless.
- **Dolphin Lagoon** (p102) Get up close to the impossibly cute pink dolphins.

As well as exploring the park on foot, it is worth taking the night-safari tram tour (adult/child $6/3), which lasts about 45 minutes and also has a live commentary. Expect queues; it's very popular.

You can save a bit of money with a combined zoo and night safari ticket (adult/child $30/15), but specify when you buy this whether you want to view both parks on the same day or different days. Both parks have plenty of decent food outlets (plus the usual junk) and the zoo boasts award-winning, clean and creatively designed 'outdoor' toilets!

When returning from the night safari you should catch a bus at around 10.45pm to ensure you make the last train leaving Ang Mo Kio at 11.28pm. A taxi to or from the city centre costs around $15; there is a taxi stand at the zoo entrance, though queues are often long and taxis can be maddeningly infrequent.

SIONG LIM TEMPLE & GARDENS
Map pp48–9

☎ 6259 6924; 184E Jalan Toa Payoh; ⏰ 7am-5pm; Ⓜ Toa Payoh or 🚌 238

Nestled in a corner of the Toa Payoh HDB estate is Siong Lim Temple, also known as Lian Shan Shuang Lin Monastery (Twin Groves of the Lotus Mountain). The original buildings date from 1912 and the main hall is wonderfully atmospheric – a towering space stained by decades of incense smoke and perpetually buzzing with visitors. The adjoining complex of newer temples is also beautifully decorated and surrounded by neatly clipped bonsai. Sadly the ambience is disrupted by traffic thundering by on the expressway.

You can walk to the temple – it's about 1km east of Toa Payoh MRT station – or take one of several buses for three stops from Toa Payoh bus interchange.

SUN YAT SEN NANYANG
MEMORIAL HALL Map pp48–9

☎ 6256 7377; www.wanqingyuan.com.sg/english; 12 Tai Gin Rd; admission $3; ⏰ 9am-5pm Tue-Sun, to 6pm Sat; Ⓜ Toa Payoh or 🚌 145

This national monument, built in the 1880s, was the headquarters of Dr Sun Yat Sen's Chinese Revolutionary Alliance in Southeast Asia, which led to the overthrow of the Qing dynasty and the creation of the first Chinese republic. Dr Sun Yat Sen briefly stayed in the house, which was donated to the Alliance by a wealthy Chinese businessman, while tour-

ing Asia to whip up support for the cause. It's a fine example of a colonial Victorian villa and houses a museum with items pertaining to Dr Sun's life and work. A magnificent 60m-long bronze relief depicting the defining moments in Singapore's history runs the length of one wall in the garden.

Next door is the Sasanaramsi Burmese Buddhist Temple (14 Tai Gin Rd; ⏰ 6.30am-9pm), a towering building guarded by two *chinthes* (lionlike figures).

Bus 145 from the Toa Payoh bus interchange stops on Balestier Rd near the villa and temple.

SUNGEI BULOH WETLAND RESERVE
Map pp46–7

☎ 6794 1401; www.sbwr.org.sg; 301 Neo Tiew Cres; adult/child $1/0.50; ⏰ 7.30am-7pm Mon-Fri, 7am-7pm Sat & Sun; 🚌 925 TIBS from Ⓜ Kranji

This 87-hectare wetland nature reserve, situated in the far northwest of the island overlooking the Strait of Johor, is home to 140 species of birds, most of which are migratory. It has been formally declared a nature reserve by the government and recognised as a migratory bird sanctuary of international importance. From the visitor centre, with its well-presented displays, trails lead around ponds and mangrove swamps to small hides, where you can observe the birds and, sometimes, massive monitor lizards. The birdlife, rather than the walks, is the main reason to visit (the best time for viewing them is before 10am).

Free guided tours begin at 9am, 10am, 3pm and 4pm on Saturday. On other days, tours have to be pre-booked and cost $50 per group, though it's claimed you need to book a month in advance. Audiovisual shows on the park's flora and fauna are held at 9am, 11am, 1pm, 3pm and 5pm (hourly between 9am and 5pm on Sunday). Allow yourself three hours to do the park justice.

On weekdays, the bus stops at the carpark a 15-minute walk from the park. On weekends, the bus goes right to the park entrance.

MACRITCHIE RESERVOIR NATURE WALK
Walking Tour

1 Lornie Rd bus stop Take bus 157 from Toa Payoh MRT station, or bus 162 from Scotts Rd. Start at the bus stop on Lornie Rd and walk up to the edge of the reservoir. Head right (anticlockwise) around the reservoir, past the kayak rental station until you reach a boardwalk going off to your left and a track going straight ahead. Take the track, which leads you on to the MacRitchie Nature Trail, or follow the boardwalk along the water's edge – looking out for terrapins or, if you're very lucky, a massive monitor lizard zipping through the water at remarkable speed. At various points along the boardwalk, you'll come across signs pointing you towards the nature trail; take one of these. If you haven't encountered them already, you'll see plenty of long-tailed macaques as you follow the 3km-long stretch along the northeast side of the reservoir. (Watch out: if you have food they can sometimes be aggressive, but generally they just ignore you. Don't look them in the eye!)

2 Singapore Island Country Club After about 3km of uninterrupted jungle, you'll emerge at the Singapore Island Country Club. Turn left and follow the signs to the Treetop Walk, which takes you alongside the huge, heavily protected tanks of the Kallang Service Reservoir.

3 Ranger Station After some twists and turns you'll eventually come to the Ranger Station and interpretation centre.

4 Treetop Walk From here it's a short walk to the wooden steps leading down to the Treetop Walk, a narrow 250m suspension bridge through the upper levels of the jungle canopy, affording excellent views (and apparently the odd snake encounter). Closed on Monday.

5 Petaling Trail On the other side, a boardwalk and a long series of steps up and down through some dense forest – known as the Petaling Trail – brings you out to a rest hut. (To shorten your walk to about 7km, turning left

WALK FACTS

Start MacRitchie Reservoir Park
End MacRitchie Reservoir Park
Distance 12km
Time Four hours
Ease Difficult
Fuel stop Le P'tit Breton

MACRITCHIE RESERVOIR NATURE WALK

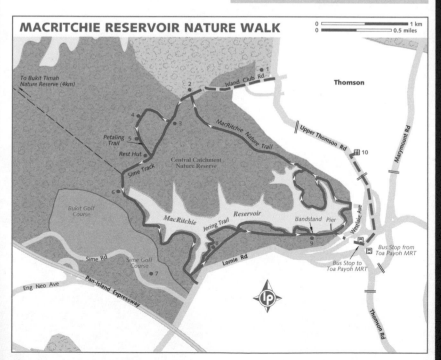

from here will take you back to the Country Club, from where it's a 25-minute walk along Island Club Rd to Upper Thompson Rd.)

6 Jelutong Tower Turn right and follow the Sime Track, then Golf Link to the Jelutong Tower, an observation deck providing a good view over the trees to the reservoir.

7 Sime Golf Course After this you hit another boardwalk running downhill through jungle and alongside the Sime Golf Course, coming to a slightly unnerving and surreal sign describing the differences between crocodiles and monitor lizards. (In the event of a crocodile confrontation, we don't think there would be much doubt, but in any case be wary of any swishing in the water just beneath the boards!)

8 Tombstone After diverting away from the golf course and hugging the edge of the reservoir for about 1km, you'll hit the fairways again for another 1km before reaching a junction. Follow the Jering Trail boardwalk left along the water's edge, looking out for a lone Chinese tombstone near the water's edge. It dates from 1876, but apparently no record exists of who is buried there. Not surprisingly, there are rumours of a 'water ghost' that haunts this area, dragging unsuspecting walkers to their doom.

9 Zigzag bridge Winding along the boardwalk, you'll emerge, finally, back into civilisation. Cross the bizarre zigzag bridge that adjoins the bandstand, where concerts are sometimes held at the weekend, and reward yourself with a drink and something to eat at the hilltop food centre.

10 Le P'tit Breton Or, if you still have energy, catch bus 162 one stop to Upper Thompson Rd and head to Le P'tit Breton for a French crêpe feast.

HOLLAND ROAD & BUKIT TIMAH

Drinking & Nightlife (p146); Eating (p134); Shopping (p116)

Primarily residential, and overwhelmingly affluent, these two areas to the immediate west of the city centre are book-ended by two of Singapore's best-loved green spaces: the astoundingly beautiful Singapore Botanic Gardens and the Bukit Timah Nature Reserve. The latter is a tiny patch of jungle offering a chance to see tropical birds, monkeys and other exotic wildlife (look, but don't touch, and for their sake and that of your bank account, don't feed the monkeys – fines for feeding them approaches the yearly GNPs of some emerging nations). Both of these places are absolute must-sees. After spending an afternoon strolling through manicured gardens or primary rainforest, take some time to visit some of the area's upscale restaurant strips like Holland Village, Greenwood Ave and Dempsey Rd, which, also known as Tanglin Village, offers great shopping, eating and drinking opportunities, and is pretty swank considering the site is a converted former army barracks. Holland Village has long been a favourite nightspot for Singapore's expatriate community, offering a number of excellent restaurants, bars and clubs. An evening out in any of these eating areas, not often visited by casual tourists, is a good way to get a real taste of Singapore.

SINGAPORE BOTANIC GARDENS

Map pp92–3

☎ 6471 7361; www.sbg.org.sg; 1 Cluny Park Rd; admission free; ☽ 5am–midnight; Ⓜ Orchard, then 🚌 7, 77, 123 or 174 from Orchard Blvd

You can't beat the botanic gardens as a spot to recover from your jet lag, have a picnic or just lie around forgetting you're in a large metropolis. Established around 1860 and covering 52 hectares, the gardens originally acted as a test ground for botanical research and potential cash crops, such as rubber. Today they still host a herbarium housing more than 600,000 botanical specimens and a library with archival materials dating back to the 16th century.

Visitors can enjoy manicured garden beds or explore a 4-hectare patch of 'original Singaporean jungle', a sample of the kind of forest that once covered the entire island – though Bukit Timah Nature Reserve (right) and MacRitchie Reservoir (p88) give a more accurate picture of that. Still, it's worth taking one of the rainforest tours. They usually cost $15 for a group of up to 15 people, but call ahead because there are free tours at certain times.

Also don't miss the extraordinary National Orchid Garden (adult/child $5/free; ☽ 8.30am–7pm), one of the world's largest orchid displays featuring over 60,000 of these delicate-looking but incredibly hardy plants, including the Vanda Miss Joaquim. This hybrid orchid, Singapore's national flower, was discovered in 1893 by Agnes Joaquim in her garden.

BUKIT TIMAH NATURE RESERVE

Map pp46–7

☎ 1800 468 5736; www.nparks.gov.sg; ☽ 8.30am–6pm; 🚌 65, 75, 170 or 171

The only area of primary forest remaining in Singapore, this 164-hectare nature reserve offers a range of nature walks, testing jungle treks and even mountain-bike trails. It's a haven for plants (one naturalist estimated there are more species here than in the whole of North America) and 160 species of animals. It also boasts the highest point on the island, Bukit Timah (163m), though the dense foliage doesn't afford much of a view.

The most popular and easiest walk in the park is along a paved road to the top of Bukit Timah. Even during the week it attracts a number of walkers, but few venture off the pavement to explore the side trails, which are more interesting. For a distinctly out-of-Singapore experience, try the North View, South View or Fern Valley paths.

TRANSPORT: HOLLAND ROAD & BUKIT TIMAH

The area is poorly serviced by the MRT, the closest station to Holland Village being Buona Vista. Bus 174 runs from Eu Tong Sen St in Chinatown, along Orchard Rd and past the Botanic Gardens and Dempsey Rd, then turns off Holland Rd and runs the length of Bukit Timah Rd. Bus 170 runs from Little India all the way to Bukit Timah Nature Reserve.

For Holland Rd, catch bus 7 from behind the Orchard MRT.

HOLLAND ROAD & BUKIT TIMAH

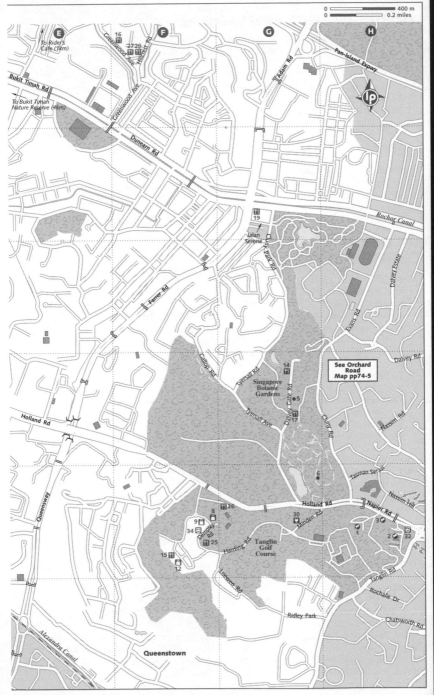

0   400 m
0   0.2 miles

To Rider's
Cafe (1km)

Greenwood Ave

16

27 29

Hill Crt Rd

Bukit Timah Rd

To Bukit Timah
Nature Reserve (4km)

Adam Rd

Pan-Island Expwy

Dunearn Rd

Rochor Canal

Dalvey Estate

19

Jalan
Serene

Cluny Park Rd

Evans Rd

Dalvey Rd

Farrer Rd

14

See Orchard
Road
Map pp74-5

Dalvey Gate Rd

5

17

Singapore
Botanic
Gardens

Tyersall Rd

Cluny Rd

Nassim Rd

Holland Rd

Cluny Rd

Tyersall Ave

6

Tasman Series

Nassim Hill

Holland Rd

Napier Rd

3

26

8

30

Minden Rd

1

9

Dempsey
Rd

34

25

Harding Rd

Tanglin
Golf
Course

2

32

15

12

Loewen Rd

Tanglin Rd

Rochalie Dr

Queensway

Ridley Park

Chatsworth Rd

Alexandra Canal

Queenstown

CHINESE TEMPLE FESTIVALS OF SINGAPORE

Anyone's trip to Singapore should include a visit to some of the Lion City's vibrant Chinese temples. Should your journey coincide with a temple festival, you'll be in for an amazing display indeed – not to mention the possibility of a free vegetarian meal.

Festivals are based on the Chinese Lunar Calendar, so you'll need to convert the dates into their Western-calendar equivalents using an online Western-to-Chinese date calculator. A good one is available at www.chinesetools .eu/tools/chinesecalendar.

- **Chinese New Year's Eve** Held on the 29th or 30th day of the 12th month, depending on the year. This is perhaps the most important Chinese holiday (think of Christmas in the West). Expect to breathe in temple air filled with incense burned to welcome in the lunar New Year. Some excellent spots to join the revelry include **Thian Hock Keng** (p61) on Telok Ayer St, **Wak Hai Cheng Bio** (p64) on Philip St and the **Kuan Im Thong Hood Cho** (Goddess of Mercy Temple; p69) on Waterloo St.
- **Birthday of the Monkey God** Held on the 15th or 16th day of the first month. Beloved by many in Singapore, this religious celebration honours the birthday of T'se Tien Tai Seng Yeh, the Monkey God, who cures the sick and frees the hopeless. During the ceremony, mediums called Tan Kees perform miraculous feats, going into trances, piercing their cheeks and tongues with skewers and writing out charms in their own blood. This festival is celebrated at many temples throughout the city, including **Qi Tian Gong** (Monkey God Temple; Map pp62–3) in Tiong Bahru and **Poh An Keng** (Map pp46–7) on Tampines Rd.
- **Birthday of Matsu** Held on the 23rd day of the third month. The birthday of the goddess of the sea, Matsu (sometimes spelled 'Mazu'), is a major cause for celebration for Taoists, especially those who live by the ocean. Expect processions, incense and celebrations galore. **Thian Hock Keng** (p61) on Telok Ayer St and **Wak Hai Cheng Beo** (p64) on Philip St both play host to worshippers on the goddess' birthday.
- **Vesak Day** Held on the first full moon of the fourth lunar month. This important holiday celebrates three important events in the life of the Buddha: his birth, his enlightenment, and his attainment of nirvana. The flavour of this holiday will differ depending on which sect is celebrating it. The **Amitabha Buddhist Centre** (p77) in Geylang sponsors a huge tent festival in the park across the street; expect the air to be filled with incense and Tibetan chanting. Free vegetarian meals are also served.
- **Hungry Ghost Festival** Held on the seventh lunar month. An important festival that incorporates various prayers and activities all over the island. The Chinese believe that during this month, the gates of hell are opened to free the hungry ghosts who then wander to seek food on Earth. If you're feeling spooked, remember that offering food to the deceased is believed to appease the spirits and ward off bad luck.
- **Nine Emperor Gods Festivals** Held from the first to the ninth day of the ninth month. This is celebrated at many of the Taoist temples devoted to the nine Emperor Gods. During this festival, many temples of the nine Emperor Gods will be celebrating by going to the river or sea to welcome the gods on the eve of the first day and at a grand sending off on the night of the ninth day. In between, they do processions visiting fellow temples.

Special thanks to local author and noted scholar of Chinese culture and religion Victor Yue, who was gracious enough to share his expertise on the Chinese temple festivals of Singapore. Victor recommends Margaret Chan's book Ritual Is Theatre, Theatre Is Ritual *to anyone interested in gaining a deeper understanding of local Chinese popular religion. Victor's blog can be found at http://chinesetemples.blogspot.com.*

These involve some scrambling over rocks and tree roots and can be quite testing in parts.

Pick up a map of the park's trails from the visitor centre, where an exhibition details the various flora and fauna that can be found in the reserve. A small shop here sells drinks, snacks, guidebooks and the all-important mosquito repellent.

Bukit Timah has two tough mountain-bike trails, 6km in all, running around the edge of the nature reserve between Chestnut Ave and Rifle Range Rd. The trails cut though jungle and abandoned quarry sites and are hilly in parts. There's also a bike trail running through the neighbouring Central Catchment Nature Reserve to the MacRitchie Reservoir, 6km east.

Several buses run close to the park, including buses 65 and 170 from Newton MRT, bus 75 from the CBD and Chinatown, and bus 171 from the YMCA on Orchard Rd or from Scotts Rd. Get off at the Bukit Timah Shopping Centre; the entrance to the park is about 1km north along Hindhede Dr.

SOUTHWEST SINGAPORE

Eating (p136)

On the face of it, there's little to draw the visitor to this corner southwest of the city centre, bisected by the roaring Ayer-Rajah Expressway and flanked by Singapore's vast ports. Look a little closer, however, and you'll see several peaceful hilltop parks harbouring areas of historical interest, some unusual museums, the magnificently tasteless Haw Par Villa, plus the city's largest shopping mall VivoCity and newest entertainment centre, Golden Village Cinema.

MT FABER PARK Map pp48–9

cable car from Ⓜ HarbourFront

Off Kampong Bahru Rd, 116m-high Mt Faber forms the centrepiece of Mt Faber Park, one of the oldest parks in Singapore. The hillside slopes, covered with secondary rainforest, offer some fine views over the harbour and central Singapore, and on the hike up here you'll catch glimpses of colonial-era black-and-white bungalows and the strikingly stripy Danish Seaman's Mission built in 1909. It's a steep, sweaty walk to the top, so if this sounds unappealing, the cable car (☎ 6270 8855; adult/child $8.90/3.90; ☽ 8.30am-9pm) might be a better option. It connects the World Trade Centre, next to HarbourFront MRT station, with the summit and Sentosa Island.

At and around the summit are a number of red-brick paths through manicured gardens, pavilions, look-out points and, beside the distinctly tacky souvenir shop, a cafeteria with fantastic views over the Singapore Strait and onward to the Indonesian Riau Islands. The Jewel Box, a glass-fronted dining and entertainment centre boasting a ballroom, look-out points and chairlifts is a particularly classy touch; even the toilets boast harbour views.

NUS MUSEUMS Map pp48–9

☎ 6874 4616; www.nus.edu.sg/museum/;
50 Kent Ridge Cres; admission free; ☽ 9am-5pm
Mon-Sat; ▣ 95 from Ⓜ Buona Vista

On the campus of the National University of Singapore (NUS), these three small but exquisite art museums all hold fine collections. On the ground floor is the Lee Kong Chian Art Museum with works spanning 7000 years of Chinese culture, from ancient ceramics to modern paintings done in traditional style.

The concourse level houses the South & Southeast Asian Gallery, showing a mixture of art from across the region, including textiles and sculptures. On the top level is the Ng Eng Teng Gallery, which displays the

TRANSPORT: SOUTHWEST SINGAPORE

Bus 408 from Harbourfront MRT runs along the main artery through the area.

paintings, drawings and sculptures of Ng Eng Teng (1934–2001), one of Singapore's foremost artists specialising in imaginative, sometimes surreal, depictions of the body.

While you're in the area, make time for the nearby Raffles Museum of Biodiversity Research (☎ 6516 5082; http://rmbr.nus.edu.sg; admission free; ☽ 9am-5pm Mon-Fri), a small on-campus museum with top-notch exhibits on flora and fauna. There are stuffed and preserved examples of some rare and locally extinct creatures, including a tiger, a leopard, a huge elephant's leg bone, a slightly creepy preserved banded leaf monkey, a huge king cobra that, a few years back, made the mistake of slithering into the Singapore Country Club, a crocodile skull and a massive, frankly terrifying, Japanese spider crab.

REFLECTIONS AT BUKIT CHANDU

Map pp48–9

☎ 6375 2510; www.s1942.org.sg; 31K Pepys Rd;
admission $2; ☽ 9am-5pm Tue-Sun; ▣ 10, 30,
51 or 143

Atop Bukit Chandu (Opium Hill) in Kent Ridge Park, this 'WWII interpretive centre' based in an old renovated villa is a worthwhile and moving memorial. Its focus is the brave sacrifice made by the 1st and 2nd Battalions of the Malay Regiment defending the hill in the Battle of Pasir Panjang when the Japanese invaded in 1942. The battalion was all but wiped out when, facing 13,000 Japanese soldiers, they decided to make a stand. Hi-tech displays, using films from the period and audio effects to transport you to the scene of the battle, are all quite evocative. It's also possible to hold the kind of rifles and wear the heavy iron helmets those soldiers wore in the 'Hands-On' room.

The nearest bus stops are on Pasir Panjang Rd, from where it's a steep hike up the hill. A taxi from the nearest MRT station at Queenstown shouldn't cost more than $6.

LABRADOR SECRET TUNNELS
Map pp48–9

☎ 6339 6833; Labrador Villa Rd, Labrador Nature Reserve; adult/child $8/5; ☉ 10am-7pm; Ⓜ HarbourFront, then 🚍 408 Sat & Sun, taxi other days

This series of storage and armament bunkers built by the British in the 1880s remained undiscovered for 50 years after WWII, until it was unearthed when work began on turning Labrador Park into a nature reserve. There are small but fascinating displays of artefacts left behind when the British abandoned the tunnels in 1942, as well as the buckled and caved-in walls from a direct hit from a Japanese bomb.

HAW PAR VILLA Map pp48–9

☎ 6872 2780; 262 Pasir Panjang Rd; admission free; ☉ 9am-7pm; 🚍 200 from Ⓜ Buona Vista, 🚍 10, 30 or 188 from Ⓜ HarbourFront

Originally known as the Tiger Balm Gardens, this wonderfully weird (some might call it tacky) theme park was originally built by Aw Boon Par and Aw Boon Haw (the original creators of the medicinal salve Tiger Balm) as a venue for teaching visitors about Chinese mythology. But how do you cram thousands of years of mythology into a mere theme-park? With statues, over a thousand of 'em, laid out lovingly (though sometimes chaotically) throughout the grounds.

The result is a visual barrage of folklore and fable, with dioramas depicting scenes from the Romance of the Three Kingdoms, Confucianism, and – everybody's favourite – a walk-through exhibit depicting the myriad gruesome torments that await sinners in the underworld. Called 'The Ten Courts of Hell', this last exhibit goes into great detail, visually cataloguing which afterlife punishments (impaling, freezing, being cast into fiery lakes) fit which crimes. The Ten Courts might scare the little ones; best leave them by the food court with a guardian, or perhaps beneath the watchful gaze of the nearby laughing Buddha.

Located on a hill on the grounds of the park, Hua Song Museum (☎ 6872 2780; adult/child $8.50/5.40; ☉ 9am-6pm) offers visitors a glimpse into the lives, enterprises and adventures of Chinese migrants around the world. This indoor museum features beautifully laid out historical and cultural exhibits done in a more studious fashion than those in Haw Par Villa (which may account for its admission fee). Well worth it for those enchanted by Chinese history.

Western Singapore is a mass of contradictions. It's the engine room of the country's economic success and home to the huge, if slowly declining, manufacturing industry. At the same time, it's also full of greenery. It boasts an entire island devoted to heavy industry, yet another island nearby, Sentosa, is Singapore's centrepiece tourist attraction. And though the area bristles with Housing Board tower blocks and industrial estates, it has the largest number of specialised attractions for kids of any district in Singapore.

Hence, not far from the unnerving spires of the Jurong Island chemical plants and oil refineries, you have the magnificent Jurong BirdPark, Snow City (p155) and Singapore Science Centre.

CHINESE & JAPANESE GARDENS

Map pp46–7

☎ 6261 3632; 1 Chinese Garden Rd; admission free; ◷ 6am-10pm Mon-Fri, 6am-11pm Sat & Sun; Ⓜ Chinese Garden

These spacious gardens, which occupy 13.5 hectares in the vicinity of Jurong Lake, are a very pleasant place for an afternoon stroll, though by themselves they are not worth the trek from the city.

The Chinese Garden is actually an island containing a number of Chinese-style pavilions and a seven-storey pagoda providing a great view. Apart from the pavilions, there is an extensive and impressive *penjing* (Chinese bonsai) display, as well as some more of those spectacularly clean 'outdoor' public toilets that seem to be catching on all over Singapore.

Inside the large compound near the bonsai display is an unusual Live Turtle & Tortoise Museum (adult/child $5/3; ◷ 10am-7pm), where, among other things, you can see a live two-headed, six-legged turtle – one of the few in the world ever to have survived – and a large pond literally teeming with the little, one-headed fellows.

The gardens are a five-minute walk on a pedestrian path from Chinese Garden MRT station.

TRANSPORT: JURONG & WESTERN SINGAPORE

Most of the attractions in western Singapore are within easy reach of Jurong East MRT station, which lies near the western end of the East West Line. A cab ride out here from the city will cost around $12. Alternatively, take bus 502 from Orchard Blvd (behind Orchard MRT). Sentosa is easily reached via the HarbourFront MRT station, from where you can get the Sentosa bus, or the cable car.

JURONG BIRDPARK Map pp46–7

☎ 6265 0022; www.birdpark.com.sg; 2 Jurong Hill; adult/child $18/9; ◷ 8am-6pm; 🚌 194 or 251 from Ⓜ Boon Lay

Over 8000 birds representing around 600 species can be seen at this beautifully landscaped 20-hectare park. Highlights include the new Birds 'n' Buddies show; a walk-through Waterfall Aviary (with its 30m-high custom-made waterfall, the highest in Southeast Asia); the Penguin Parade, which simulates a slice of Antarctica; a lake with pink flamingos; the fascinating Pelican Cove enclosure featuring some massive specimens; and an underwater viewing gallery where you can watch the birds catch fish. There's also the World of Darkness, in which day and night have been reversed to allow visitors a look at nocturnal birds doing something other than sleeping. A monorail (adult/child $4/2) will transport you around it all.

As with the zoo (which is run by the same management), there are bird shows at various times during the day, kicking off with the Breakfast with the Birds show (adult/child $18/12, from 9am to 10.30am) and including the Birds of Prey show, starting at 10am.

If you're planning to visit the Singapore Zoo and Night Safari as well (and you should be), you can buy an all-inclusive ticket that gets you entrance to all three (adult/child $40/20); you don't need to do all three in one day, however.

MING VILLAGE & PEWTER MUSEUM

Map pp46–7

☎ 6265 7711; 32 Pandan Rd; admission free; ◷ 9am-5.30pm; free shuttle service from Ⓜ Clementi

Reproduction Ming and Qing dynasty pottery is made in this workshop, where you can watch the craftspeople at work.

NEIGHBOURHOODS JURONG & WESTERN SINGAPORE

DOWN ON THE FARM

First-time visitors are usually surprised to learn that the tiny island-state, far from being an endless urban canyon, actually contains a fair bit of jungle, parkland, and even farms. These are some of the most interesting:

- **Avifauna Bird Farm** (Map pp46–7; ☎ 6793 7461; avifauna@signet.com.sg; 2 Lim Chu Kang Lane; admission $3.50; ☼ 10am-4.30pm Sun) One of the largest exotic bird breeding and research farms in Southeast Asia, the farm was recently re-opened after being closed by the bird flu scare. Take bus 175 from Choa Chu Kang MRT.
- **Farmart Centre** (Map pp46–7; ☎ 6767 0070; www.farmart.com.sg; 67 Sungei Tangah Rd; ☼ 10am-7pm) Established by Uncle William, 'the quail man of Lim Chu Kang', this is a one-stop showcase of small farms, including bees, goats, quails, ornamental fish, herbs and frogs. Take the free shuttle bus from Choa Chu Kang MRT. Various tour packages range from $5 to $10.
- **Hay Dairies Goat Farm** (Map pp46–7; ☎ 6792 0931; www.haydairies.com.sg; 3 Lim Chu Kang Lane 4; ☼ 9am-4pm) Goats bred for milking. Demonstrations and tours take place in the morning and cost $3, including a free bottle of goat's milk. Take bus 175 from Choa Chu Kang MRT and get off at Lim Chu Kang Lane 4. It's a three-minute walk from there.
- **Jurong Frog Farm** (Map pp46–7; ☎ 6791 7229; www.jurongfrogfarm.com.sg; 56 Lim Chu Kang Lane 6; ☼ 7am-6pm) Breeding station for bullfrogs, sold for their meat and medicinal value; more fun than you'd think. A taxi from Choa Chu Kang MRT should cost around $4.
- **Orchidville** (Map pp46–7; ☎ 6552 5246; www.orchidville.com; Lot MD1A Lorong Lada Hitam; ☼ 8am-6pm) Massive orchid farm with more than two million specimens for sale. Education programs also available. Take bus 138 from Ang Mo Kio MRT and get off at Stop B13 on Mandai Rd.
- **Qian Hu Fish Farm** (Map pp46–7; ☎ 6766 7087; 71 Jalan Lekar; admission free; ☼ 9am-6pm Mon-Thu, 9am-7pm Fri-Sun) A very modern farm breeding more than 200 species of exotic ornamental fish for sale, with an attached cafe. Take bus 172 or 175 from Choa Chu Kang and walk from the junction of Old Choa Chu Kang Rd and Jalan Lekar.

The complete production process is done on the premises and guided tours are available.

Ming Village is owned by Royal Selangor Pewter, whose products are sold at Orchard Rd's Centrepoint and Takashimaya department stores. There's also a small pewter museum here with some interesting pieces. The pewter is made in Malaysia, but the polishing and hand-beaten designs are demonstrated at the village. The showroom sells an extensive selection of pewter and porcelain.

The company runs a free shuttle service from Orchard, Mandarin, Raffles and Pan Pacific Hotels from 9.20am; enquire with the hotel concierges.

OMNI-THEATRE Map pp46–7

☎ 6425 2500; adult/child $10/5; Ⓜ Jurong East
An essential part of any trip to the Science Centre, this vast domed cinema is an unforgettable experience, showing short 15- to 20-minute movies on anything from African wildlife to space exploration and simulated thrill rides, on a huge screen that envelopes you on your reclining seat. The sound quality is magnificent. It's also worth taking a moment to examine the bizarrely complex

Sputnik-like device that projects the images onto the screen.

SINGAPORE SCIENCE CENTRE
Map pp46–7

☎ 6425 2500; www.sci-ctr.edu.sg; 15 Science Centre Rd; adult/child $6/3; ☼ 10am-6pm Tue-Sun; Ⓜ Jurong East
With multiple levels of interactive displays (nearly 900 of them in all) covering subjects like the human body, aviation, optical illusions, ecosystems, the universe and robotics, this museum is at once educational and thoroughly absorbing. Our favourite exhibit is the gigantic spark-shooting Tesla-coil on the first level. The outdoor kinetic garden, featuring movable, interactive sculpture, is also great fun.

The Science Centre is a very popular item on the school-trip calendar and you can often find yourself overwhelmed by hordes of jostling, wild, uniformed scamps eager to prevent you from trying out the exhibits.

Travellers with children might want to consider spending a full day to take in the Science Centre and the next-door Omni-Theatre (left), perhaps with a visit to nearby Snow City (p155) to top things off.

SENTOSA ISLAND

Drinking & Nightlife p148; Eating p137; Sleeping p173

Five hundred metres off the south coast of Singapore sits Sentosa Island (☎ 1800 736 8672; www.sentosa .com.sg; admission $2), the city's favourite resort getaway. An almost entirely synthetic attraction, Sentosa is a tropical Disneyland where Singaporeans come to frolic on beaches of imported sand as half the world's container-ship traffic passes within shouting distance. Sentosa is in the midst of a major US$3.6 billion renovation; if all goes according to plan, by 2010 the island will boast a Universal Studios theme-park, a casino to rival Macau, an enclosed 24/7 waterfront walkway, and even more resorts and spas.

Even without the new additions, Sentosa still has plenty to draw locals and tourists alike, including decent museums, a fine aquarium and plenty of outdoor activities including cycling and golf. There are also some lovely hotels and resorts on the island, as well as places to get massages and lounge in mud baths.

Along Sentosa's southern coast are three beaches: Siloso at the western end, Palawan in the middle and Tanjong Beach at the eastern end. As a beach paradise, Sentosa has a long way to go to match the islands of Malaysia or Indonesia, but the imported sand and planted coconut palms do lend it a tropical ambience even if the muddy Singapore Strait and the towering industrial chimneys of Jurong Island in the distance might make you think twice about swimming.

BUTTERFLY PARK & INSECT KINGDOM
Map p100

☎ 6275 0013; www.butterflypark.com.sg; adult/ child $10/6; ☾ 9am-6.30pm

Just next to the cable-car station, the Butterfly Park is tropical rainforest in miniature; the caretakers of this park have created a lovely environment for more than 50 species of butterflies. many of these species are endangered and nearly all have been bred in the park itself. In the Insect Kingdom museum there are thousands of mounted butterflies, rhino beetles, Hercules beetles (the world's largest beetles) and scorpions, among others. Children, especially, should be entranced for hours.

FORT SILOSO Map p100
adult/child $8/5; ☾ 10am-6pm

This fascinating slice of the past presents the island's history, dating from the time it was called Pulau Blakang Mati (Malay for 'island behind which lies death', thought to be a reference to a deadly malaria outbreak that killed hundreds of villagers).

Fort Siloso itself was built in the 1880s as a military base to protect, with a series of gun emplacements linked by underground tunnels, Britain's valuable colonial port. Designed to repel a maritime assault, the guns had to be turned around when the Japanese invaded from Malaya in WWII. The fort was later used by the Japanese as a POW camp.

TRANSPORT: SENTOSA ISLAND

The highly frightening (huge, mazelike and nigh-inescapable) VivoCity Mall is, for all intents and purposes, the gateway to Sentosa. You can catch a shuttle-bus to the island from in front of it ($3, including the $2 admission), take the monorail from inside it (same price as shuttle) or even walk to it over the footbridge behind it (free, but at the time of research the bridge was closed). The mall is located on top of the HarbourFront MRT station.

For a more memorable trip with some spectacular views, there is the cable car, which runs from the top of Mt Faber or from the Cable Car Towers adjacent to the World Trade Centre (standard cabins return $13.90/8.50 adult/child). For $20/13, you can take the distinctly unsettling glass-bottom cabins, which afford a relaxing view of the sea 60m below your feet. It operates between 8.30am and 9pm. The cable-car ride is one of the best parts of a visit to Sentosa. If the weather is fine, take it at least one way.

All the transport on the island is covered in the admission price. The monorail that once took visitors on a slow loop around the island's attractions has been shut down, but it's easy to get around using the four colour-coded bus routes linking the island's attractions.

The Sentosa Island Guide, a free pamphlet available all over the island, has good maps and transport guides.

You can also hire bicycles and roller blades for between $5 and $10 per hour at Siloso and Palawan Beaches or at the Ferry Terminal, which on weekends in particular is a tempting way to avoid the long queues at some of the bus stops.

SENTOSA ISLAND

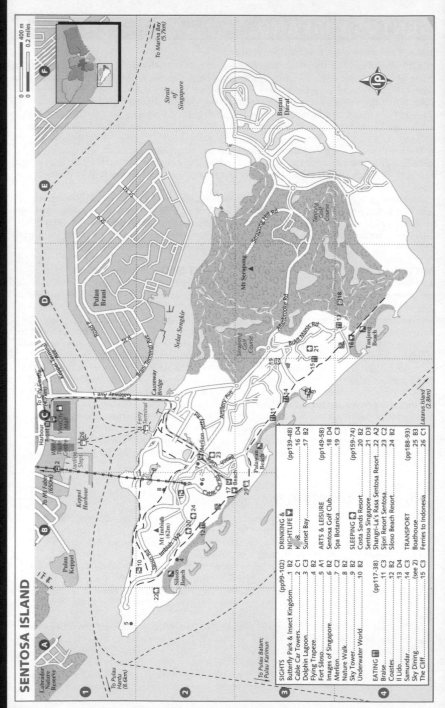

SIGHTS (pp99–102)
Butterfly Park & Insect Kingdom.....1 B2
Cable Car Towers.....2 C1
Dolphin Lagoon.....3 C3
Flying Trapeze.....4 B2
Fort Siloso.....5 A1
Images of Singapore.....6 B2
Merlion.....7 C2
Nature Walk.....8 B2
Sky Tower.....9 B2
Underwater World.....10 B2

EATING (pp117–38)
Braise.....11 C3
Coastes.....12 B2
Il Lido.....13 D4
Samundar.....14 C3
Sky Dining.....(see 2)
The Cliff.....15 C3

DRINKING & NIGHTLIFE (pp139–48)
KM8.....16 D4
Sunset Bay.....17 B2

ARTS & LEISURE (pp149–58)
Sentosa Golf Club.....18 D4
Spa Botanica.....19 C3

SLEEPING (pp159–74)
Costa Sands Resort.....20 B2
Sentosa Singapore.....21 D3
Shangri-La's Rasa Sentosa Resort.....22 A2
Sijori Resort Sentosa.....23 C2
Siloso Beach Resort.....24 B2

TRANSPORT (pp188–93)
Boathouse.....25 B3
Ferries to Indonesia.....26 C1

The path around the fort leads to the gun emplacements, tunnels and buildings, with jolly wax re-creations and voice-overs about life in a colonial barracks. There's also a small obstacle course on which to try out your army skills.

The tunnel networks have been upgraded with trendily designed information posters and a short historical documentary film about the defence of Singapore.

IMAGES OF SINGAPORE Map p100
adult/child $10/7; ⏰ **9am-7pm**
This diverting historical and cultural museum starts with Singapore as a Malay sultanate and takes you through its establishment as a busy port and trading centre, its trials during WWII, and the subsequent Japanese surrender. Scenes are re-created using lifelike wax dummies, film footage and dramatic light and sound effects.

MERLION Map p100
adult/child $8/5; ⏰ **10am-8pm**
Half-lion, half-fish, all 'symbol of Singapore'. This is one of Sentosa's more kitschy of attractions, but the 37m-tall statue does offer a nice view. If you've already been to Raffles and had a Singapore sling, well, a trip up the Merlion is the next logical step.

SKY TOWER Map p100
adult/child $12/8; ⏰ **9am-9pm; shuttle bus from** Ⓜ **HarbourFront**
A revolving air-conditioned cabin that lifts you up a 110m pole for panoramic views over the city and the southern islands; who says you can't get high in Singapore?

FLYING TRAPEZE Map p100
Siloso Beach; per swing $10, 3 swings $20; ⏰ **4-6pm Tue-Fri, 4-7pm Sat, Sun & holidays**
Set up on the beach is this flying trapeze on which children (above four) can fly through the air with the greatest of ease. Guaranteed to either cure or cause a lifelong fear of heights.

UNDERWATER WORLD Map p100
☎ **6275 0030; www.underwaterworld.com.sg; adult/child $19.90/12.70;** ⏰ **9am-9pm**
This spectacular aquarium is deservedly one of Sentosa's most popular attractions. The star attraction is the 'travellator', an

OFF THE RAILS IN SINGAPORE

The Lion City is blessed with one of the greatest mass-transit systems on the planet, and one of the best ways to experience the real Singapore is by hopping on the MRT and exploring the neighbourhoods surrounding stations in the outer districts. A trip through these districts, seldom visited by casual tourists, offers far more to intrepid trekkers than a chance to check out the seemingly endless housing blocks that over 85% of Singapore calls home. A few suggestions for some off-the-beaten-tourist-path mini-adventures:

- Strange Neighbours in Commonwealth (Green Line) Head through the food court directly south of the station and walk 250m east down the first street you see. This takes you to a spiritual, architectural scene the like of which you'll only see in Singapore: rising like a gigantic crystalline outcropping, the near-cubist design of the Catholic Church of the Blessed Sacrament (Map pp92–3) offers a stark contrast to its nearest neighbour, the traditionally designed Sri Muneeswaran Hindu Temple (Map pp92–3).
- Classic Chinese Splendour in Chinese Gardens (Green Line) Hop off the train and head south into the Chinese Gardens (Map pp46–7), a park replete with pagodas, arches and traditional Chinese structures that might make you think you've stepped into a classical Chinese painting.
- Suburban Mosque of Yishun Station (Red Line) When you get off the train at Yishun, head west until you get to the Darul Makmur Mosque (Map pp46–7). It's a large and modern looking black-and-white mosque with a particularly fetching onion-dome tower, somewhat different from the more traditional mosques of the inner city. There are also a number of smaller temples in the neighbourhood worth checking out.
- The Nature of Landscaping in Ang Mo Kio (Red Line) An excellent example of the Singaporean fetish for landscaping perfection, Ang Mo Kio Park (Map pp46–7), just across from the station, is one of those magnificently manicured neighbourhood parks in which every tree seems to have been planted equidistant from the last. One stop away is Yio Chu Kang, home of Nanyang Polytechnic, a good place to meet Singapore's next generation of intelligentsia.
- Shrines and Temples of Eunos (Green Line) Though not as chock-a-block with temples, shrines and other random spiritual spots as Geylang, the blocks south of the Eunos MRT station offer some interesting surprises for those who care to wander. Especially beautiful are the Malay-style mosques in the area, and the very colourful Mangara Vihara (Shrine of Blessing; Map p80) on Jalan Eunos, just a block south of the station.

acrylic tunnel with a moving walkway that takes spectators through the main tanks. There is nothing quite like the sight of 60kg giant groupers, brown stingrays and sharks swimming overhead. The aquarium also offers a dive-with-sharks package. Check the website for more details.

Your ticket to the aquarium also includes entry to the specially constructed Dolphin Lagoon (10.30am-5.30pm) at Palawan Beach. Here you can see the Indo-Pacific hump-back dolphins, commonly known as pink dolphins, perform in shows at 1.30pm, 3.30pm and 5.30pm daily with an extra 11am session on the weekends, when you can find yourself fighting for seats. It's possible to get in the water to feed and touch the dolphins, too.

For $120, kids can go on a one-hour Swim with the Dolphins session, which takes place at 9.45am every day.

top picks

- Orchard Road (p112)
- Haji Lane (p112)
- Little India (p110)
- Holland Road Shopping Centre (p116)
- Dempsey Road (p116)
- VivoCity (p110)

SHOPPING

Singapore's mania for shopping almost rivals its obsession with food, and barely a year goes by without some vast new retail monolith flinging open its doors to the slavering hordes.

Among visitors, the city's reputation as a bargain-hunters' paradise has lingered, though in price terms Singapore is no match for neighbouring Malaysia or Thailand. Though prices are closer to Western levels, Singapore does beat its neighbours for sheer convenience and familiarity. There's no urban chaos to negotiate, it's easy to get around, you don't need to haggle (though it's possible) or worry too much about rip-offs, and the choice and quality are generally excellent.

Electronics and computers are no longer the steal they once were, but they can be cheaper provided you do your homework and shop around. Clothes and CDs are cheaper than in most Western countries, and you can pick up reasonably priced Asian antiques provided you know what you're doing.

Once a year, for around six weeks between late May and early July, the city lays on the Great Singapore Sale (www.greatsingaporesale.com.sg), a showpiece retail event aimed at dragging in the tourists and keeping its 'shopping Mecca' image alive. Opinions on the sale vary, but it's true that most of the best bargains are grabbed in the first week or two.

SHOPPING STRIPS

Everybody's heard of Orchard Rd, Singapore's shopping mecca, which used to be lined with plantations of the natural kind, and now seems to grow new malls every few years.

If you're after art or antiques, it pays to know your original piece from your cheap copy. While there are many dedicated art galleries and antique shops throughout Singapore, there is a fair degree of overlap between them and craft shops. For Asian antiques, the best places to head are Chinatown (p108), Dempsey Rd (p116) or Tanglin Shopping Centre (p112). There's also a decent collection of contemporary art galleries at the Ministry of Information, Culture and the Arts (MICA; p106) building next to Clarke Quay.

For fabrics and textiles, head to Little India and the Arab Quarter.

If you're buying electronics, computer equipment and peripherals, the latest hi-tech stuff can be found all over Singapore, much of it at very competitive prices. It pays to do a little research into makes and models before you arrive. When you buy, make sure your guarantees are worldwide, your receipts are properly dated and stamped, and your goods are compatible with electricity supplies and systems in your country of origin.

Lucky Plaza (p114), Sim Lim Square (p110) and the Mustafa Centre (p111) are all good places to scout for cheap electronics and computer equipment, but you have to shop around and be prepared to bargain. If you just want a no-nonsense experience and more reliable quality, head for the Funan The IT Mall (Funan DigitalLife Mall; p106).

Otherwise, global chains like Best Denki (Map pp74–5) and Harvey Norman (Map pp52–3) can be found at malls all over the city – every major mall has at least one audiovisual store.

Fashion stores abound, and although clothes and shoes are not as cheap as other countries in the region, the range of styles and quality is hard to beat. The annual Singapore Fashion Festival (www.fashion-festival.com) in March showcases international and local designers.

For clubbing fashions the best places to scope are the Heeren Mall (p114), Far East Plaza (p113) and Parco Bugis Junction (p111), all of which have sections packed with fun boutiques and stalls. For local boutique designers, head to Haji Lane (p112) or Stamford House (p107).

For books and CDs, you should head to Orchard Rd, which houses huge chain shops – like Borders (p112) and Kinokuniya (p112) for books and HMV (Map pp74–5) for music – as well as smaller but equally good CD shops like That CD Shop and Gramophone.

Most of Singapore's outlying and 'heartlands' areas now have their own malls, where you can often find the same shops selling the same items at lower prices than in the city centre (because the rents are lower). Try Causeway Point (Map pp46–7) next to Woodlands MRT station, Junction 8 next to Bishan MRT, or Novena Square (Map pp74–5) and sports specialist Velocity@Novena next to Novena MRT station.

BUYER BEWARE

Singapore has stringent consumer laws and promotes itself as a safe place to shop. However, you should still be wary when buying. This is particularly true in smaller shops where a salesperson may match your low price but short-change you by not giving you an international guarantee or the usual accessories. Guarantees are an important consideration if you're buying electronic gear, watches or cameras. Make sure it's international and that it is filled out correctly, with the shop's name and the serial number of the item written down.

Make sure you get exactly what you want before you leave the shop. For example, check for the right voltage and cycle when you buy electrical goods. Singapore, Australia, New Zealand, Hong Kong and the UK use 220V to 240V at 50 cycles, while the USA, Canada and Japan use 110V to 120V at 60 cycles. Most shops will also attach the correct plug for your country. Also note that there are two main types of video systems: PAL in Australia and Europe, and NTSC in the USA and Japan – video equipment must be compatible with your system.

When buying antiques, ask for a certificate of antiquity, which is required in many countries to avoid paying customs duty.

Singapore enforces international copyright laws, so being palmed off with pirated goods is not likely to happen. If you do run into trouble, take your purchases back to the shop. If you fail to get satisfaction, contact the Small Claims Tribunal (Map pp62–3; ☎ 6241 3575; www.smallclaims.gov.sg/SCT-General_Info.html; 2 Havelock Rd; ☑ 8.30am-1pm Mon-Sat, 2-5pm Mon-Fri) or any of the visitor centres (see p200). Tourist complaints are usually heard within two or three days.

SERVICE

Singapore has a large and enduring problem with good service – in restaurants, bars, hotels and shops. Staff are frequently not very helpful, friendly, knowledgeable or interested in the products they sell, though they're a long way behind Hong Kong shop assistants when it comes to out-and-out rudeness.

Despite endless government-run courtesy campaigns and the enticement of generous awards for good service handed out by the Singapore Tourism Board, many places continue to hire disinterested kids, presumably because they're cheap (restaurants, bars and big coffee chains are notable offenders). However, at places such as department stores Robinsons and Tangs, which tend to favour hiring older staff, the service can be fantastic.

OPENING HOURS

Wet markets aside, Singapore is not an early bird's shopping destination. In fact, most big shopping centres will be as quiet as churches until around 11am, so take your time and have a leisurely breakfast. Most shops are open from 10am or 11am through until 9pm and 10pm, and the quietest and most enjoyable time to look around can be that small window of calm between around 10am and 11am, when you can even sometimes hear the birds twittering along Orchard Rd.

TAXES & REFUNDS

Visitors leaving from the airport (not land or sea) can get a refund of the 7% GST on their purchases, under the following conditions.
- To qualify, you must spend a minimum of $100 at the same retailer on the same day for not more than three purchases.
- Get a copy of the GST refund form from the shop (they aren't available at customs).
- Present the refund form, items and receipts to customs at the airport. They stamp the form, then you can claim the refund, which is processed here.

AUNTIES FROM HELL

It's a common scenario at shops and stalls. You're standing there, clutching your purchase or waiting to ask for something when a middle-aged or elderly lady comes bustling up demanding – and getting – service.

These apparently harmless creatures are Satan's Aunties. They routinely jump bus queues, shop queues, food court queues and do anything and everything to get in front, get ahead or get an advantage.

The temptation is to accept this as a cultural quirk, but most Singaporeans don't like it either. Here's a (culturally incorrect) tip from someone who got ignored once too often: bark loudly, get annoyed, tell them off and they back off as fast as lightning, usually muttering about rude foreigners in the process! In fact, you won't be offending anybody but them, and even bystanders don't say anything. Most of them will be secretly applauding you.

ALL THAT GLITTERS...

Gold shops are all over town, but you'll find a concentration in Little India along Serangoon Rd (Map p68) – where the shops teem with Indians from all over the diaspora stocking up on jewellery, often for weddings and other special events – and in People's Park Complex (p109) in Chinatown. Here 22- and 24-carat gold is sold by weight.

The concentration of gold shops in these areas reflects its importance in Chinese and Indian cultures, in which it is not only an overt symbol of prosperity but also, for the Chinese particularly, a good-luck symbol usually given at births, weddings and Chinese New Year.

Singapore is also a good place to buy pearls and gemstones, but you really need to know the market. Jade is a Chinese favourite, but there's lots of imitation jade around waiting for a mug to buy it. The broad and multiple definitions of the word jade in the Chinese language – *yu* – don't help matters (the *yu* character is used in words for a variety of ornamental rocks, so a dealer who sells an almost worthless lump of green rock for an exorbitant price can legitimately claim he wasn't lying when he advertised it as jade!).

Jade comes in many colours, green being the most well-known and popular. As a rule of thumb, visit dealers in the more upmarket parts of town and look for semitransparent, uniformly coloured, highly polished items (nephrite is cheaper than jadeite and, being softer, can't be polished as intensely). If you detect any flaws or cracks, leave it alone.

BARGAINING

Prices are usually fixed in all shops, except at markets and in some shops in touristy areas. If you do have to haggle, stay good-humoured and don't get petty – this causes everyone to lose face. Name a realistic price, smile a lot, and if you don't get what you want from the shopowner, making a polite move towards the door can often spark a sudden change of heart.

COLONIAL DISTRICT & THE QUAYS

The cluster of protected architecture around the Colonial District means it has been spared the consumerist blitzkrieg that consumed Orchard, but the area still has its fancy malls, among them Suntec City, Raffles City and City Link Mall, as well as historical curiosities such as Stamford House. For computers and electronics, Funan is the place to go, while along the Quays the focus is on entertainment, rather than retail.

MICA BUILDING Map pp52–3   Art
140 Hill St; M Clarke Quay
Among the several galleries in the brightly coloured colonial MITA Building is Art-2 Gallery (www.art2.com.sg) and Gajah Gallery (www.gajahgallery.com), which both specialise in contemporary Southeast Asian work. Soobin Art Gallery (www.soobinart.com.sg) displays a lot of work from the region, plus avant-garde artists from China. Artmosaic (www.artmosiac .com.sg), meanwhile, specialises in Indian art.

CHIJMES Map pp52–3   Art & Antiques
30 Victoria St; M City Hall
Hugging the northerly rim of the Chijmes compound is a collection of small shops selling art, curios, decorative objects, fabrics and clothes, all with a strong Southeast Asian focus. Outlets come and go, but among the most appealing are Olathe and the rather disorderly Empress Myanmar.

FUNAN – THE IT MALL
Map pp52–3   Computers & Electronics
☎ 6337 4235; 109 North Bridge Rd; M City Hall
The principal computer centre, Funan is the place for brand-name goods, and a better bet than Sim Lim Square if you don't know exactly what you're doing. There are dozens of computer and electronics shops on the upper floors, as well as a large Challenger Superstore (☎ 6336 8327), where you can find pretty much everything.

ROYAL SELANGOR Map pp52–3   Gifts
☎ 6268 9600; 01-01 Clarke Quay; M Clarke Quay
Malaysia's pewter specialists aren't high on the hip list – think the kind of personalised tankards your uncle uses for his real ale – but recently a few items of jewellery have crept into the showroom that might not embarrass even the most painfully fashionable teen.

SPELLBOUND Map pp52–3   Gifts
☎ 6337 8005; www.getzspellbound.com; No 211 Peninsula Plaza, 11 North Bridge Rd; M City Hall
This is possibly the only Western-style magic shop in Singapore. High priest Adrian's services include tarot readings, consultations, spell casting and other magical consultations. He also has an absorbing

stock of arcane goods such as talismans, incense and magical powders.

CITYLINK MALL Map pp52–3   Mall
☎ 6238 1121; 1 Raffles Link; Ⓜ City Hall
The first underground mall in Singapore, designed by Kohn Pederson Fox from New York, this seemingly endless tunnel of retail links City Hall MRT station with Suntec City and the Esplanade. It's a tempting means of escaping searing sun or teeming rain, and a comfortable way of getting into the city from the Marina Bay hotels. It's a bit disorienting, but there's a full range of fashion, books, music and food down here.

ESPLANADE MALL Map pp52–3   Mall
☎ 6828 8399; 8 Raffles Ave; Ⓜ City Hall
With more than 8000 sq metres to cover, it's not hard to spend several hours browsing here. There are speciality violin and guitar shops, a make-your-own-teddy-bear shop (great for kids), a clutch of classy gift shops and an overwhelming array of eating options. Human traffic tends to be light in the daytime, so turnover can be high among the retail outlets.

MARINA SQUARE Map pp52–3   Mall
☎ 6339 8787; www.marinasquare.com.sg; 6 Raffles Blvd; 🚌 36, 111, 502
It looks dowdy, but 225 outlets, including brands such as Calvin Klein, Levis and Esprit, pack into this massive shopping space. It's centrally located in the Marina Centre area with easy access to and from CityLink Mall, Suntec City, Millenia Walk and the Esplanade.

PENINSULA EXCELSIOR
Map pp52–3   Mall
5 Coleman St; Ⓜ City Hall
The shopping centre that props up the Peninsula Excelsior Hotel has definitely seen better days, but it's one of the best hunting grounds in Singapore for sporting goods. Among the tennis rackets, bowling balls, cricket bats and football shirts are also plenty of unexpected and eccentric little shops, from guitar repairmen to what appears to be a death-metal specialist.

SUNTEC CITY Map pp52–3   Mall
☎ 6821 3668; www.sunteccity.com.sg; 3 Temasek Blvd; 🚌 36, 111, 502
Vast and bewildering – and often frustratingly inaccessible – Suntec has everything

under the sun, plus 60 restaurants, cafes and a food court. One of the biggest crowd-pullers is the Fountain of Wealth, which was once accorded the status of World's Largest Fountain (though not, you'll observe, Most Attractive) in the *Guinness Book of Records*. Scan the media for one of Suntec's regular themed 'fairs', where you can pick up substantially discounted items such as cameras, electronics and computer gear.

RAFFLES CITY Map pp52–3   Mall
☎ 6338 7766; www.rafflescity.com; 252 North Bridge Rd; Ⓜ City Hall
The name and the soaring atrium give the impression of expensive exclusivity, but Raffles City is one of Singapore's best malls. There's a three-level branch of the excellent Robinsons department store, a Marks & Spencer, global fashion brands, a top floor specialising in children's clothes and toys, the Ode to Art gallery, New York's Metropolitan Museum of Art gift shop and a clutch of handbag boutiques on the ground floor, plus a top-floor food court and several basement restaurants. Check out the deli counters at the basement Marketplace supermarket for gourmet snacks.

RAFFLES HOTEL ARCADE
Map pp52–3   Mall
328 North Bridge Rd; Ⓜ City Hall
Part of the hotel complex, stylish Raffles Hotel Arcade is firmly upmarket, with designer clothes and accessories, watchmakers, the Thos SB Raffles gourmet shop, galleries, wine-sellers and similarly refined places gently tempting you into credit-card wantonness.

STAMFORD HOUSE Map pp52–3   Mall
cnr Stamford Rd & Hill St; Ⓜ City Hall
The oldest, most elegant and distinctive shopping centre in the city, Stamford House was built in 1904 and mercifully conserved (a similar old building across the road was destroyed to make way for Stamford Court). Its wooden floors, ornate ironwork and plasterwork and aura of hushed refinement remain, and the tenants – art galleries, hair and beauty salons, local designer boutiques and spas – generally treat the place with the respect it deserves.

CHINATOWN & THE CBD

For a fine Asian antique, statuette or magnificent wardrobe, modern hip homewares or just a cheap souvenir, Chinatown is the place to come. Pagoda St and its immediate surroundings have become a byword for tourist tat, but behind and beyond the stalls crammed with 'Fine City' T-shirts and two-minute calligraphers, there are small shops selling everything from modern Asian homewares to old furniture, though it pays to know your Khmer antique from your Javanese sweatshop knock-off. The area is also famous for its Chinese medicine centres, if you're feeling a little unhealthy.

Up on Club St, the hip restaurants and bars are now being joined by equally hip homeware, design and clothes shops.

FAR EAST LEGEND Map pp62–3   Antiques
☎ 6323 5365; 233 South Bridge Rd; Ⓜ Chinatown
A small warrenlike shop – the kind you tiptoe around for fear of knocking something over – selling an excellent collection of furniture, lamps, handicrafts, statues and screens from Korea, Thailand, Burma and China. The owner is happy to engage in some gentle, polite bargaining. Keep smiling.

SHANG'S ANTIQUE GALLERY
Map pp62–3   Antiques
☎ 6224 4332; 24A-26 Pagoda St; Ⓜ Chinatown
Stuffed as it is with a fine collection of genuine Southeast Asian religious antiques (including some huge ones in the outdoor area) and furniture, Shang's must be mortified that it has to share Pagoda St with all the tourist stalls. A diamond among the dross.

YONG GALLERY Map pp62–3   Antiques
☎ 6226 1718; 260 South Bridge Rd; Ⓜ Chinatown
Specialising in Chinese antiques, old jade, calligraphy and wood carvings. If you're shopping for jade, which is so often a lottery in Asia, you can be assured of the real stuff here.

UTTERLY ART Map pp62–3   Art
☎ 6226 2605; 229A South Bridge Rd; Ⓜ Chinatown
One of the more interesting pure art galleries, this is a small, welcoming exhibition space for local and international artists and a good place in which to get a flavour of the local art scene.

WHATEVER Map pp62–3   Books
☎ 6224 0300; www.whatever.com.sg; 20, 29A & 31 Keong Saik Rd; Ⓨ 9am-late; Ⓜ Chinatown
It's beatific smiles and inspirational titles all round at one of Singapore's leading proponents of wellness, aimed at the affluent and stressed. Along with books, CDs and DVDs, you can also sign up for classes in yoga, massage, meditation and the more esoteric healing disciplines. At the back of the bookshop is an excellent vegetarian cafe.

EU YAN SANG MEDICAL HALL
Map pp62–3   Chinese Medicine
☎ 6223 6333; 269A South Bridge Rd; Ⓜ Chinatown
The venerable Eu Yan Sang is one of the stalwarts of the Chinese medicine industry, which has been given a boost in recent years by overt government support and promotion. Looking like a modern Western chemist, the goods on the shelves are anything but familiar to Western eyes. Pick up some Monkey Bezoar powder to relieve excess phlegm, or Liu Jun Zi pills to dispel dampness – or just stop guessing and ask the resident herbalist.

SIN BEE TRADING COFFEE POWDER
Map pp62–3   Coffee
☎ 6223 0832; 42 Amoy St; Ⓜ Tanjong Pagar
One of the few remaining traditional coffee grinders in Singapore. The smell, the tins of beans and the ancient grinding machine offer a glimpse into Chinatown's almost forgotten past. The owner's son is friendly and will describe the various grades and blends on offer (including the staple kopitiam blend, mixed with margarine!). Hopefully soaring rents and gentrification in the area won't force it out.

EM GALLERY Map pp62–3   Crafts
☎ 6475 6941; www.emtradedesign.com; 5 Blair Rd; Ⓜ Outram Park
An exquisite collection of silks, ceramics, lacquerwork, art and homewares from around Southeast Asia, though if you're travelling elsewhere in the region, you can pick up this stuff for much less in the countries of origin.

RED PEACH GALLERY Map pp62–3   Crafts
☎ 6222 2215; 68 Pagoda St; Ⓜ Chinatown
An upmarket decorative homeware shop selling large, expensive couches, silk cushions and jewellery. It also houses a 'boutique

spa' done out Ming dynasty–style with lanterns, wooden floors and fancy furniture.

YUE HWA CHINESE PRODUCTS
Map pp62–3   Department Store
☎ 6538 4222; 70 Eu Tong Sen St; Ⓜ Chinatown
This department store, in an old six-storey building with echoes of Shanghai, specialises in products from the motherland. Downstairs you'll find Chinese medicine and herbs, as well as clothes and cushions. Moving up to Level 5, you'll pass through silks, food and Chinese tea, arts and crafts, and household goods, before ending up at the large (though unattractively lit) furniture section.

PATISSIER Map pp62–3   Food
☎ 6220 5565; 18 Ann Siang Rd; Ⓜ Chinatown
Tucked behind a rather grand doorway, this modest little shop produces masterpieces of cake-design sold whole or by the slice, attracting streams of office women, who line up and coo over the display cabinet. It's closed on Saturday and Sunday, but the Mohamed Sultan Rd branch (Map pp52–3) is open weekends if the cravings get too strong.

TONG HENG PASTRIES Map pp62–3   Food
☎ 6223 3649; 285 South Bridge Rd; Ⓜ Chinatown
Going strong for more than 70 years, Tong Heng is arguably Singapore's most popular place for egg tarts and other tempting cakes and cookies.

WANG SAN YANG Map pp62–3   Food
☎ 6532 2707; www.wystm.com; 01-61, Block 531 Hong Lim Complex, 535 Upper Cross St; ⏰ 10am-9pm; Ⓜ Chinatown
An elegant speciality tea merchant, which looks slightly out of place among the rough and ready bustle of the Hong Lim Complex, but has a feeling of authenticity lacking in Chinatown's more tourist-friendly teahouses. Tea demonstrations are supplied on demand (see p127).

WILD CHILD Map pp62–3   Gifts
☎ 9617 8248; 94 Club St; Ⓜ Chinatown
A refreshing antidote to the overbearing Kidz'R'Uz world of mass production. Parents-to-be and baby-shower shoppers of a more traditional bent will love this collection of cribs, toys and other Victorian-style nursery decorations.

DAHLIA HOME Map pp62–3   Homeware
☎ 6327 9685; 47 Amoy St; ⏰ 11am-7pm Mon-Fri, 11am-6pm Sat, noon-5pm Sun; Ⓜ Chinatown
Beautifully designed beds, couches, lamps and other homewares brought in from Thailand, much of it made from specially treated rattan. There's enough great stuff in here to kit out an entire flat.

STYLE:NORDIC Map pp62–3   Homeware
☎ 6423 9114; 39 Ann Siang Rd; ⏰ noon-8pm Mon-Sat, noon-5pm Sun; Ⓜ Chinatown
Distinctively Scandinavian kitchenware, dining sets, furniture and racks of clothes set in a (now unrecognisable) old clan building – lots of clean, bright colours crying out for a hip modern professional to take care of them.

KITCHEN HABITS Map pp62–3   Kitchenware
☎ 6227 2012; 102 Amoy St; Ⓜ Tanjong Pagar
Top-of-the-range kitchen supplier, stocking quality brands like Alussi, Brandt and De Dietrich. Pans, glasses, squeezers, mills, crushers and grinders…it's a paradise of stainless steel, cast iron and glass for the food fetishist.

SIA HUAT Map pp62–3   Kitchenware
☎ 6223 1732; 9-11 Temple St; Ⓜ Chinatown
Singaporean chefs and amateur enthusiasts flock to Sia Huat, which stocks all manner of high-end and midrange pots, pans and utensils for the kitchen. A place for the serious foodie.

CHINATOWN POINT Map pp62–3   Mall
133 New Bridge Rd; Ⓜ Chinatown
A good option to hunt down handicrafts, souvenirs, clothes and Chinese products, though the centre is ageing and a little unpleasant inside. You'll need to browse, but there are some good bargains to be found. For Chinese products you're better off heading across the road to Yue Hwa (p109).

PEOPLE'S PARK COMPLEX
Map pp62–3   Mall
1 Park Rd; Ⓜ Chinatown
An interesting mall to wander around if you're after some decent quality Chinese souvenirs and don't feel like bargaining too hard for them, or some traditional herbal remedies. It even has fish that'll nibble the dead skin off your feet.

VIVOCITY

With its vast size, distinctive wavy shape, odd Flintstones-style facade and waterfront location facing Sentosa Island, VivoCity was unveiled as the new poster child of Singapore retail – the mall that would lure the city's shoppers away from the madness of Orchard Rd. To help achieve that, planners cunningly inserted the new Sentosa Monorail into the building, forcing people into the mall.

It hasn't quite achieved the intended iconic status, but there's no denying it's a pleasant place to shop, with lots of open space, an outdoor kids' playground on Level 2, a rooftop 'skypark' where the little ones can splash about in the paddling pools and a large Golden Village cineplex.

With more than 90,000 sq metres of space, it also crams in just about every category of purchasable item known to humanity, and once you're done shopping there's a range of restaurants and bars with outdoor seating where you can sit and soak up the sea breeze.

To get there, take the MRT to HarbourFront.

CHINATOWN COMPLEX
Map pp62–3   Market
11 New Bridge Rd; M Chinatown
Once famously rundown and grungy, Chinatown Complex was inevitably closed for upgrading at the time of writing. Hopefully, when it reopens, the singular charms of its wet market, barking stallholders and famous hawker centre will not be lost – but we have our doubts.

LITTLE INDIA & KAMPONG GLAM

A world apart from the gleaming malls of Orchard and the tourist tat of Chinatown, Little India's streets are a browser's delight. The ramshackle streets are a treasure trove of art, antiques, textiles, food and music, while the infamous 24-hour Mustafa Centre department store is an experience in itself. Keen bargainers might find the cut-price electronics that were once abundant in Singapore, while computer enthusiasts will make a beeline for Sim Lim Square. Heading down to Kampong Glam, you'll find handicrafts, textiles and boutiques and, sandwiched between the two areas, the thoroughly un-Singaporean 'thieves' market'. A short walk away is the old neighbourhood of Bugis, which, while strictly located neither in Little India or Kampong Glam, has something of the atmosphere of both.

ANSA STORE Map p68   Art
6295 6605; 29 Kerbau Rd; M Little India
This is the place to come if you want a frame, freshly carved to your specifications, for that painting you bought in Vietnam. This gaudy shop also sells wildly coloured posters and extravagant pictures of religious icons.

SIM LIM SQUARE Map p68   Computers
6332 5839; 1 Rochor Canal Rd; M Bugis
A byword for all that is cut-price and geeky, Sim Lim is not for those uninitiated in the world of SIM, RAM, motherboards, soundcards and other matters. If you know what you're doing, there are real bargains to be had, but the untutored are more likely to be taken for a ride. Hard bargaining is essential.

INDIAN HANDICRAFT CENTRE
Map p68   Crafts
6392 0769; 2 Dalhousie Lane; M Little India
Cushions, fabrics, screens, statuettes, cabinets, furniture – anything Indian you can put in a house can be found here. The shop is too small to accommodate everything they have, so if you're after something specific, ask the owners.

GRANDFATHER'S COLLECTIONS
Map p68   Curios
6299 4530; 42 Bussorah St, Arab Quarter; M Bugis
A wonderful, dusty bric-a-brac shop that does indeed look like your grandfather's attic, with pre-WWII radios, clocks and

BUSSORAH STREET

While the government's plans to turn this area into an 'alternative lifestyle hub' never quite took off, attractively pedestrianised Bussorah St, lined with trees and bookended by the Sultan Mosque, is still one of the most pleasant places in the city to hang out. The nature of the street has changed recently, as the original quirky, arty shops have given way to more tacky souvenirs, but a few gems like Grandfather's Collections (above), Little Shophouse (opposite) and Melor's Curios (Map p68) remain.

typewriters, old Coke bottles, Ovaltine and Horlicks tins, and vinyl records. It's a true oddity that is worth supporting, even if it means buying an old John Denver LP.

MUSTAFA CENTRE Map p68 Department Store
☎ 6295 5855; 145 Syed Alwi Rd; ☺ 24hr; Ⓜ Farrer Park
The bustling 24-hour Mustafa Centre in Little India is a magnet for budget shoppers, most of them from the subcontinent. This place has just about everything (electronics, jewellery, household items, shoes, bags, CDs), all at bargain rates. Forget about presentation or service, price is king here. There's also a large supermarket with a superb range of Indian foodstuffs. Avoid the evenings at weekends, when seemingly the entire subcontinental male migrant-worker population descends on the area.

SIM LIM TOWER Map p68 Electronics
☎ 6295 4361; 10 Jalan Besar; Ⓜ Bugis
A big electronic centre with everything from capacitors to audio and video gear – not far removed from Sim Lim Square. Again, arm yourself with knowledge and be prepared to bargain hard.

EDGE Map p68 Fashion
☎ 6557 6557; 03 Parco Bugis Junction, 200 Victoria St; Ⓜ Bugis
This corner of the generally mainstream Bugis Junction mall is one of the best places to check out what small local designers are turning out at the moment. Shops come and go with dizzying speed, so if you see something you like, grab it, because the shop may have gone when you come back.

HOUSE OF JAPAN Map p68 Fashion
6396 6657; 55 Haji Lane; Ⓜ Bugis
Like a hip Salvation Army store, this rather dank shop sells very cheap, fashionable secondhand clothes straight from Japan. Hopefully it'll help sharpen up Singaporean teenagers somewhat.

TEKKA CENTRE Map p68 Fashion
cnr Serangoon & Buffalo Rds; Ⓜ Little India
Once you've fought your way through the hawker centre (p130) and the rather lurid wet market (best avoided if you don't like severed sheep's heads), there's a whole floor of textile and sari shops on the first level – the cheapest place to pick up an Indian outfit. Prices are labelled, but bargaining is possible.

GOLDEN MILE COMPLEX
Map p68 Food
Beach Rd; Ⓜ Lavender
The whole panoply of Thai cuisine is laid out here, from the essential leaves, herbs and roots to the sauces and pastes and the challengingly pungent butchery products, plus all the snacks that soothe homesick Thai workers. This could be Bangkok, except for the fact that you have space to walk, and there are no motorbike taxis nipping at your heels. Stay for a bite to eat (see p130) once you've done your shopping.

KHAN MOHAMED BHOY & SONS
Map p68 Food
☎ 6293 6191; 20 Cuff Rd; Ⓜ Little India
Follow your nose to what may be the last traditional spice-grinding shop in Singapore. Bins full of dried bell-chillies crowd the doorway, while inside you can take away big scoops of turmeric, cumin and fennel or order them freshly ground – though standing around and staring and not buying anything is not appreciated.

LITTLE SHOPHOUSE Map p68 Gifts
☎ 6295 2328; 43 Bussorah St; Ⓜ Bugis
Traditional Peranakan beadwork is a dying art, but it's kept very alive in this little shop. Whatever you think of the gaudy colours and elaborate patterns of Peranakan fashion, you can't deny the handiwork is exquisite.

PARCO BUGIS JUNCTION Map p68 Mall
200 Victoria St; Ⓜ Bugis
One of Singapore's more distinctive malls, featuring two streets of recreated shophouses, covered with a glass ceiling and air-conditioned. Levels 1 and 2 are fashion central, stuffed with big local names, major midrange international brands, and a host of smaller local designers. On the top floor you'll find the large Shaw Bugis cineplex.

BUGIS STREET MARKET Map p68 Market
Victoria St; Ⓜ Bugis
Lock up your teens. A far cry from its seedy past as Singapore's most notorious red-light area, the Bugis St market is now a teeming three-level hive of stalls selling

HAJI LANE

Blink and you'd walk right past this narrow back-alley without a second thought, but Haji Lane is a place of pilgrimage for Singapore's hipsters and fashionistas, who insist on wearing originals from shops that don't use capital letters in their names. Boutiques come and go rapidly, but try dulcetfig for retro dresses, dion de cruz and Victoria JoMo for street chic, salad for home accessories or the long-standing House of Japan for secondhand Japanese fashion. There was even a secondhand kimono store, but how long that can last is anyone's guess. For more on Haji Lane, see p67.

clothes, shoes and accessories, plus a few manicurists and nail bars, food stalls and, in a nod to the area's past, a sex shop.

SUNGEI ROAD THIEVES MARKET

Map p68   Market

Sungei Rd, Weld Rd, Pasar Lane & Pitt St; ☽ daily; Ⓜ Little India or Bugis

How and why the authorities allow this kerbside jumble sale to exist is a mystery, but happily it remains, spread out across four streets around a patch of open ground. The array of old geezers hawking random collections of used items makes it an interesting place to wander around, mingle with Singapore's impoverished underbelly and perhaps throw them a few dollars for some of their wares.

INDIAN CLASSICAL MUSIC CENTRE

Map p68   Music

☎ 6291 0187; 26 Clive St; Ⓜ Little India

Despite the drily formal name, this place looks unpromisingly dilapidated from the outside, but it's well stocked with every instrument in the Indian musical firmament, the quality of which is geared towards playing rather than hanging on the wall. Enthusiasts can sign up for lessons.

STRAITS RECORDS Map p68   Music

☎ 9341 1572; 22 Bali Lane; ☽ 3-11pm Mon-Fri, to midnight Sat & Sun; Ⓜ Bugis

Probably the only alternative music store in Singapore, Straits stocks alternative, hip-hop, hardcore and reggae CDs, as well as some old vinyl LPs, T-shirts and books. Opening hours tend to be erratic, so don't be surprised to find it shut when the sign on the door suggests it's open.

ORCHARD ROAD

Orchard Rd inspires awe and horror in equal measure. The sheer scale of this retail onslaught is overwhelming, and it's only getting bigger. As if there weren't enough malls already, at the time of writing two more giants – Ion at Orchard Turn and Orchard Central at Somerset – are under construction, obliterating two of the last empty spaces on the road. You have two options: dive in, or run screaming.

ANTIQUES OF THE ORIENT

Map pp74–5   Antiques

☎ 6734 9351; www.aoto.com.sg; 02/40 Tanglin Shopping Centre, 19 Tanglin Rd; Ⓜ Orchard

Call us nerdy if you like, but poring over the wonderful collection of antique and reproduction maps, prints and photos in this pleasantly bookish, unpretentious shop can swallow up hours. A hidden gem.

THE LOFT Map pp74–5   Antiques & Homeware

☎ 6738 7687; 04-05 Centrepoint, 176 Orchard Rd; Ⓜ Somerset

Offers a wide and wonderful range of old clocks and also stocks a diverse range of antique (or at least antique-style) furnishings, art, lamps and other homey objects.

TANGLIN SHOPPING CENTRE

Map pp74–5   Art & Antiques

☎ 6732 8751; 19 Tanglin Rd; Ⓜ Orchard

Although dim and unappealing inside, this relic contains the best collection of antiques and art galleries in Singapore, including Antiques of the Orient (above) and several Middle Eastern and South Asian carpet shops. There's also the superb Select Books (opposite).

BORDERS Map pp74–5   Books

☎ 6235 7146; 01-00 Wheelock Pl; Ⓜ Orchard

Singapore may be one of the few places where you can see a bookshop as crowded as a pub on a Saturday night (someone we know was even approached by a prostitute in here!). Not as vast or as refined as Kinokuniya, but still a great bookshop.

KINOKUNIYA Map pp74–5   Books

03-10/15 Ngee Ann City; 391 Orchard Rd; Ⓜ Orchard

Claims to be Southeast Asia's biggest bookshop, and who are we to argue? This is a bibliophile's paradise. Spend hours browsing, or use the electronic book locater inside the entrance, which finds the title of your choice and prints a map telling you where to find it. In a shop this size, you probably need it.

SELECT BOOKS Map pp74–5   Bookshop
☎ 6732 1515; www.selectbooks.com.sg; 03-15 Tanglin Shopping Centre; 19 Tanglin Rd; Ⓜ Orchard
For nearly 30 years, Select has been Singapore's Asian-book specialist, carrying amazing numbers of academic and special-interest titles on anything from Tibetan furniture and Japanese history to Singaporean fiction.

SUNNY BOOKS Map pp74–5   Bookshop
☎ 6733 1583; 03-58/59 Far East Plaza, 14 Scotts Rd; Ⓜ Orchard
One of the few secondhand bookshops and book exchanges in Singapore, Sunny stocks a fantastic range, including the latest hit novels and travel guides, plus old comics. The owner is quite a character.

APPLE CENTRE Map pp74–5   Computer
☎ 6238 9378; www.apple.com.sg; 02-07/08 Wheelock Pl, 501 Orchard Rd; Ⓜ Orchard
Apple's flagship Singapore store, stuffed to the brim with all the products and accessories that cause acolytes to glaze over and reach for their credit cards. Prices are a little higher than the US, but substantially lower than Australia or Europe, particularly after the GST rebate.

TANGS Map pp74–5   Department Store
☎ 6737 5500; 320 Orchard Rd; Ⓜ Orchard
Since opening its doors more than 70 years ago, Tangs has become a Singaporean institution. This five-floor department store is popular with all generations, selling business suits, formal evening attire and streetwear in the huge clothes section, electronics, shoes and some of the best homeware in town.

PAGODA HOUSE Map pp74–5   Furniture
☎ 6732 2177; www.pagodahouse.com; Tudor Court, 143/145 Tanglin Rd; Ⓜ Orchard
An exquisitely designed shop selling restored antique and modern furniture of the highest quality. The styles range from colonial gentleman's club to modern penthouse to Asian boutique, but each piece exudes class and sophistication. One of the best in town.

CENTREPOINT Map pp74–5   Mall
☎ 6737 9000; 176 Orchard Rd; Ⓜ Somerset
This spacious, practical, no-nonsense midrange shopping centre has long been a favourite with Singaporeans. The biggest draw is anchor tenant Robinsons department store, which was established in 1858, and has some of the best service in Singapore (one of the assistants even measured us for a shirt). Also has Harvey Norman, midrange fashion stores like Mango and Lacoste and a curio shop, the Loft (opposite).

DFS GALLERIA Map pp74–5   Mall
☎ 6229 8100; 25 Scotts Rd; Ⓜ Orchard
With its distinctive bright-red exterior and ground-floor replica shophouse selling Singapore-themed souvenirs, DFS is of course squarely aimed at tourists. Ride the huge escalator to explore three floors of exclusive brand names above.

FAR EAST PLAZA Map pp74–5   Mall
☎ 6732 6266; 14 Scotts Rd; Ⓜ Orchard
Renowned as a teenage hangout, principally because of its large range of cheap boutiques, shoe shops and salons. It's also notable for its tailors, Sunny Books (p113), the

CLOTHING SIZES

Women's clothing

Aus/UK	8	10	12	14	16	18
Europe	36	38	40	42	44	46
Japan	5	7	9	11	13	15
USA	6	8	10	12	14	16

Women's shoes

Aus/USA	5	6	7	8	9	10
Europe	35	36	37	38	39	40
France only	35	36	38	39	40	42
Japan	22	23	24	25	26	27
UK	3½	4½	5½	6½	7½	8½

Men's clothing

Aus	92	96	100	104	108	112
Europe	46	48	50	52	54	56
Japan	S		M	M		L
UK/USA	35	36	37	38	39	40

Men's shirts (collar sizes)

Aus/Japan	38	39	40	41	42	43
Europe	38	39	40	41	42	43
UK/USA	15	15½	16	16½	17	17½

Men's shoes

Aus/UK	7	8	9	10	11	12
Europe	41	42	43	44½	46	47
Japan	26	27	27½	28	29	30
USA	7½	8½	9½	10½	11½	12½

Measurements approximate only; try before you buy

Wasabi Tei (p132) eatery and its tattoo parlours (see p154). Bargaining is possible with most retailers here.

FORUM – THE SHOPPING MALL
Map pp74–5   Mall

☎ 6732 2479; 583 Orchard Rd; Ⓜ Orchard
One for the kids, Forum is dominated by children's fashion and toy retail outlets, including a large Toys'R'Us outlet occupying most of the top floor. Strangely, it's often very quiet.

HEEREN Map pp74–5   Mall
☎ 6733 4725; www.heeren.com.sg; 260 Orchard Rd; Ⓜ Somerset
Like Far East Plaza, except with more money, Heeren is another magnet for the young and hip, boasting big names like Converse, Adidas and Levis, plus a host of small local designer boutiques and anchor tenant HMV.

LUCKY PLAZA Map pp74–5   Mall
☎ 6235 3294; 304 Orchard Rd; Ⓜ Orchard
One of the few remaining dingy old malls along the snazzy Western end of Orchard, Lucky Plaza has a bit of everything, from clothes to joke shops to tailors to massage parlours and a sex shop, but is notable for its basement hive of electronics and mobile phone stores (haggling essential). Packed with Filipina maids enjoying their day off on Sundays.

NGEE ANN CITY Map pp74–5   Mall
☎ 6739 9323; 391 Orchard Rd; Ⓜ Orchard
You could easily spend a day in this monolithic, chocolate milkshake–coloured marble behemoth, which dominates the streetscape like a fortress. Anchor tenant Takashimaya dominates the eastern wing, while the rest of its mazelike interior is peppered with exclusive names like Louis Vuitton, Chanel and Burberry, though there are less expensive clothing options like Spanish chain Zara. Others will make a beeline for giant bookstore Kinokuniya (p112).

PACIFIC PLAZA Map pp74–5   Mall
☎ 6733 5655; 9 Scotts Rd; Ⓜ Orchard
Another mall popular with teenagers (aren't they all, you might ask?), Pacific is targeted at the affluent, more mainstream adolescent, boasting a vintage Adidas shop (which looks more like a gallery) and Nike Originals store, plus a large outlet of the excellent That CD Shop.

BAG BOYS

In your wanderings around Orchard and other shopping sanctums, you may be a little puzzled to see young men walking around carrying handbags. No, this is not some new craze imported from Japan. Singapore's infamously demanding females consider it a mark of devotion if their men offer to play mule for the afternoon, and many, evidently, are happy to oblige.

PALAIS RENAISSANCE Map pp74–5   Mall
☎ 6737 6933; 390 Orchard Rd; Ⓜ Orchard
Another monument to designer opulence housing both international and local designer label boutiques. A must if you're aiming for the exclusive shopping scene with labels such as DKNY, Valentino and Jim Thompson Thai silks. Very popular with wealthy locals and expatriates. The Marmalade Pantry, located in basement 1, is a favourite lounging spot for ladies who shop.

PARAGON Map pp74–5   Mall
☎ 6738 5535; 290 Orchard Rd; Ⓜ Orchard
There is no shortage of upmarket malls in Singapore, but Paragon screams exclusivity. Prada, Gucci and Salvatore Ferragamo try to out-dazzle each other while local streetwear favourite ProjectShop pulls in the teens and keeps everyone fed (see p131). It also has a spa and a large Toys'R'Us on the upper floors, and food and wine galore in the basement.

PLAZA SINGAPURA Map pp74–5   Mall
☎ 6332 9298; 68 Orchard Rd; Ⓜ Dhoby Ghaut
Located on top of Dhoby Ghaut MRT station, Plaza Singapura was Singapore's first multistorey mall and remains as popular as it is vast, featuring a 10-screen Golden Village cineplex, Carrefour hypermarket, Spotlight homeware, Bose and the Barang Barang Asian-themed furniture chain, as well as countless varieties of store and multiple eating options.

SHOPPING GALLERY AT HILTON
Map pp74–5   Mall

☎ 6737 2233; 581 Orchard Rd; Ⓜ Orchard
One of the most exclusive shopping spots in Singapore, housing a series of elegant boutiques like Gucci, Donna Karan, Missoni, Giorgio Armani, Paul Smith and Louis Vuitton, to name just a few. The Four Seasons Hotel is linked to the Hilton Gallery and offers fine art.

TANGLIN MALL Map pp74–5   Mall
☎ 6736 4922; 163 Tanglin Rd; 🚌 7, 123, 174 from Ⓜ Orchard

A favourite among the hordes of expatriate wives, who gather here by the dozen at Caffé Beviamo in the middle of the mall to compare maid woes. Aside from its excellent Marketplace gourmet supermarket, That CD Shop branch and midrange clothes retailers like British India, the offerings here are surprisingly modest, but there is a notable collection of shops catering to mothers (kids' clothes, party essentials etc).

WISMA ATRIA Map pp74–5   Mall
☎ 6235 2103; 435 Orchard Rd; Ⓜ Orchard

You can't miss Wisma – fronted by a huge, boastful sign and a flashy glass exterior, its central circular aquarium is a popular meeting spot. Specialises in midrange fashion names such as Gap, Levis and French Connection, as well as local names like Daniel Yam and ProjectShop. The anchor tenant is the large Japanese department store Isetan.

EASTERN SINGAPORE

The narrow lanes of shophouses and affluent residential suburbs of eastern Singapore are more renowned for their food than their shopping, and rightly so. Indeed, some of the better shopping options in the area are food related, though there are a couple of decent malls and knick-knack shops to divert the mind from its culinary pursuits.

CHANGI VILLAGE Map pp46–7   Market
☎ 6788 8370; 4 Tampines Central 5; 🚌 2

A wander around Changi Village offers a window into a more relaxed side of Singapore, where vests, bermudas and flip-flops (the quintessential heartlander uniform) is the look, and people are slightly less accustomed to seeing *ang moh* (Europeans) in their midst. The atmosphere is almost village-like and a browse around the area will turn up cheap clothes, batik, Indian textiles and electronics. For a different kind of Singapore day, combine a few hours here with a trip to Pulau Ubin (p176) and round the day off with a meal at the famous hawker centre, then a few beers at Charlie's Corner (p133).

HOME'S FAVOURITE COOKIES & DURIAN Map p80   Food
☎ 6272 2028; www.homesfavourite.com; 266 Joo Chiat Rd; 🚌 10 & 14

If the flavour and smell of durian has bewitched you (and admittedly that's a sizeable 'if'), then this little bakery will be heaven for you. Durian cookies, durian pastries, durian cheesecake…as the name suggests, this is the home of all things sweet and smelly.

KIM CHOO KUEH CHANG Map p80   Food
☎ 6486 0375; 109 East Coast Rd; 🚌 10 & 14

Joo Chiat is stuffed with bakeries and desserts, but Kim Choo retains that old-world atmosphere, selling its traditional pineapple tarts and other gaudy Peranakan desserts from a wooden counter that looks more like an apothecary's shop.

SCANTEAK Map p80   Furniture
☎ 6342 5718; 341 Joo Chiat Rd; Ⓜ Eunos, then 🚌 155

Looking conspicuously modern along Joo Chiat Rd, this furniture shop boasts modern, elegantly functional Scandinavian-style teak furniture, with prices to match. Some of the designs may be a little conservative for certain tastes, but the quality is top notch.

THE GALLERY HOUSE Map p80   Furniture
☎ 6440 5123; 181 East Coast Rd; 🚌 10 & 14

A tiny but appealing shophouse selling attractive wooden outdoor furniture and a curious range of carved animals. If you're in the market for a sunbed and a wooden chicken, this is the place.

KATONG SHOPPING CENTRE
Map p80   Mall
865 Mountbatten Rd; 🚌 10 & 14

Not a great deal of outstanding retail (unless you like model cars and suchlike), but an insight into Singaporean life. This ageing mall is full of 'maid agencies' – the people who source and place Indonesian, Filipina, Burmese and Indian maids with employers, taking a huge cut of their pay in the process – and lots of women coming and going, or waiting around for work. There's also lots of 'enrichment centres' for parents worried that their kids might get left behind. An interesting but mildly depressing place.

PARKWAY PARADE Map p80   Mall
☎ 6344 1242; www.parkwayparade.com.sg; Marine Pde; 🚌 15, 31, 36, 76

The most modern mall in the east, Parkway houses anchor tenants like Borders bookstore,

A PARADE OF ANTIQUES

Dempsey Rd (Map pp92–3), southwest of Singapore Botanic Gardens off Holland Rd, has boomed in recent years, as more and more of the former British Army barrack buildings have been turned into high-end restaurants and bars.

Happily, the art and antique shops that populated the area before the boom have survived, and during the daytime it's a peaceful, almost rustic area to wander around, perusing anything from Kashmiri carpets and teak furniture to landscaping ornaments and antiques.

Try Shang Antiques (☎ 6388 8838; No 16), which specialises in Southeast Asian antiques, some of them around 2000 years old, with price tags to match. Red House Antiques (☎ 6474 6980; No 26) is one of the best of the city's dealers in Chinese antiques, in both original and restored condition.

Pasardina Fine Living (☎ 6472 0228; No 13) has just about everything decorative and Asian for the home, while Asiatique (☎ 6471 3146; No 14) stocks Indonesian furniture made from recycled wood. Eastern Discoveries (☎ 6475 1814; Block 26, 01-04) has a superb range of antiques from around the region.

Isetan department store, Best Denki and Harvey Norman electronics, plus a large range of fashion retailers and the customary on-slaught of food outlets.

TAMPINES MALL Map pp46–7   Mall
☎ 6788 8370; 4 Tampines Central 5; Ⓜ Tampines
One of Singapore's largest suburban shopping centres, conveniently located right at the Tampines MRT station. Aimed at the middle-class heartlanders, you'll find a branch of the Isetan department store, a Golden Village cinema and several bookshops inside this bottle-green monster.

HOLLAND ROAD & BUKIT TIMAH

These largely residential suburbs are speckled with the kind of shops that appeal to affluent residents: antiques, gourmet foods, chic homewares, furniture and decor, 'wellness' centres, ethnic curios and the like. The New Age heart of the area is the Holland Road Shopping Centre, an ageing mall packed with everything the Asiaphile shopper could desire.

GASTRONOMIE Map pp92–3   Food
☎ 6475 1323; 43 Jalan Merah Saga; 🚍 7
If you're on a wander around the Holland Village expat enclave, there's no better place than this to fuel up. Pre-made salads, breads, dips, pizzas by the slice, cakes – everything you could want for a gourmet lunch. If you're lucky, one of the bench tables along the street will be a free and you can spread out and have an urban picnic.

JONES THE GROCER Map pp92–3   Food
☎ 6476 1512; www.jonesthegrocer.com; Block 9, Dempsey Rd; 🚍 7, then walk
While we noted with some outrage that this Australian posh-nosh store had brazenly imposed huge mark-ups on items readily available in local supermarkets, we were appeased by the wonderful (and wonderfully pungent) cheese room.

HOLLAND ROAD SHOPPING CENTRE
Map pp92–3   Gifts
211 Holland Ave; 🚍 7
It's anyone's guess whether this ageing shopping centre will survive Singapore's mania for redevelopment, but if it does, this magnet for expats and fashionable Singaporeans is a great place for art, handicrafts, gifts, homeware and offbeat fashion. Lim's Arts & Living (Shop 01, Level 2) is a virtual encyclopaedia of home furnishing, Island & Archipelago (Shop 05, Level 2) offers retro, beachy dresses, while EMF (Shop 24, Level 2) has a large selection of secondhand books for sale, rent or trade. Framing Angie (Shop 02, Level 3) is a gallery that'll also frame pictures. On Level 3 there's a series of massage and reflexology shops to soothe shop-weary limbs.

PANTRY MAGIC Map pp92–3   Kitchenware
☎ 6471 0566; www.pantry-magic.com, 43 Jalan Merah Saga; 🚍 7
You got that Nigella book for Christmas, now it's time to splash out on cast-iron pots, stainless-steel grinders, knuckle-slicing graters and other shiny kitchen knick-knacks. And if you didn't get a Nigella book, they have those too.

EATING

top picks

- Au Jardin (p134)
- Chef Chan's (p123)
- Din Tai Fung (p131)
- Hai Tien Lo (p124)
- Il Lido (p137)
- Saint Pierre (p126)
- The Cliff (p137)
- Wasabi Tei (p132)

EATING

Singaporeans live to eat, and while you're here you might as well join them.

For Singaporeans, what's on the plate is far more important than the quality of the china (or plastic) it's served on. The smartest-dressed businessman is as comfortable sitting down on a cheap plastic chair at a plastic table and wading into a $3 plastic plate of *char kway teow* (Hokkien dish of broad noodles, clams and eggs fried in chilli and black-bean sauce) as he is eating $50 crabs in an air-conditioned restaurant. Combine this unpretentiousness with infinite variety, high standards of hygiene and the prevalence of the English language, and you have some of the best and most accessible eating opportunities in Southeast Asia.

The city has every imaginable cuisine, for every imaginable budget. Not surprisingly, Chinese food in its many varieties dominates, but there are significant pockets of North and South Indian food, particularly in the area of Serangoon Rd, which, along with Kampong Glam, is also home to a large number of Muslim eateries.

In the Colonial District and the Quays area, expensive restaurants hold sway. Here, and in affluent neighbourhoods around Holland Rd and Bukit Timah, you'll find the greatest concentration of Western food. Eastern Singapore is well known for its seafood and Peranakan restaurants – the rich, sour-and-spicy cuisine developed by the mixed Malay-Chinese people.

But everywhere, from the city to the heartlands, you will find countless hawker centres and food courts, where the majority of ordinary Singaporeans spend an extraordinary amount of time.

HISTORY

Step into any large hawker centre and you'll see the history of Singapore laid before you in edible form: fish-head curry from South India, *nasi biryani* (saffron rice flavoured with spices and garnished with cashew nuts, almonds and raisins) or *rendang* (curried meat in coconut marinade) from Malaysia, chicken rice from Hainan, Hokkien *char kway teow*, Cantonese crispy pork, Teochew rice porridge, Peranakan *popiah* (similar to a spring roll but not fried), or those Western 'mixed grills' that most Westerners find unrecognisable.

As each ethnic group and subgroup came to Singapore, it brought its own cuisine along. They remain largely undiluted to this day, but as often happens when cultures are transplanted far from home, local variations and customs have crept in. Just as the people of Singapore developed their own characteristics the longer they were separated from their homelands, the character of dishes such as fish-head curry, chilli crab and *yu sheng* (raw fish salad eaten at Chinese New Year) have all evolved from traditional favourites.

ETIQUETTE

Visitors to Singapore often say that hawker centres are among the most memorable parts of their trip. Food courts located in malls are easy, but for the first-timer the older hawker centres can be a little daunting, so it's worth brushing up on some etiquette before plunging in.

When you arrive, bag a seat first, especially if it's busy. You can either do this by placing a member of your group at a table, or do it Singaporean style and lay a packet of tissues on a seat. Don't worry if there are no free tables; it's quite normal to share with a complete stranger.

You're then free to wander off in search of food. Signboards list the stall's specialities, and you can buy any number of dishes from any number of stalls. Sometimes the stall will have a sign saying 'self service', which means you have to carry the food to the table yourself, not dish up your own food. Otherwise, the vendor brings your food to you (which is why you should get a table first, or they won't know where you are).

Generally, you pay when you order, but some hawkers take money when they deliver.

In most older hawker centres and *kopitiam* (coffeeshops), someone will come to your table and take your drinks order. You pay them when they deliver the drinks. In the modern food courts in malls, you have to go and order from the drinks stalls.

Some hawker centres, notably Newton Circus – the one most popular with visitors – have wandering touts who try to grab you when you arrive, sit you down and plonk menus in front of you. You are not obliged to order from them and in fact it's illegal for stalls to tout at all, which you might like to point out to any persistent pests.

Singapore's amalgam of cultures has largely made strict eating etiquette redundant. Each ethnic group still follows its own eating code for its own food, but often ignores the codes of other cuisines. You'll see Chinese eating *roti prata* (fried Indian flat bread) with a spoon and fork, Indians eating Chinese food with a spoon, Malays attacking a pizza with a knife and fork... In other words, don't feel obliged to follow any rules.

SPECIALITIES
Chinese
With Chinese food, the more people you can muster for a meal the better, because dishes are traditionally shared. A Chinese meal should be balanced; a yin (cooling) dish such as vegetables, most fruits and clear soups, should be matched by a yang (heating) dish such as starchy foods and meat.

The best-known and most popular style of Chinese cooking is Cantonese, despite the majority of Singaporean Chinese not being of Cantonese descent. Cantonese food is usually stir-fried with just a touch of oil to ensure that the result is crisp and fresh. Typical dishes include *won ton* (dumpling filled with spiced minced pork) soup and *mee* (noodles). At the expensive end of the spectrum is shark's-fin and bird's-nest dishes.

One of the most famous Cantonese specialities is dim sum (also known as yum cha); small snack-type dishes usually eaten at lunchtime or as a Sunday brunch in large, noisy restaurants where the dishes are whisked around the tables on trolleys or carts; take what you like as they come by.

The most popular Hainanese dish is chicken rice: steamed fowl, rice cooked in chicken stock, a clear soup and slices of cucumber. It's practically the national dish and the ultimate Singaporean comfort food. Eaten with dips (ginger and chilli, and soy), it's light but surprisingly filling. Another popular Hainanese dish is steamboat, which features a boiling stockpot in the middle of the table, into which you dip pieces of meat, seafood or vegetables.

Many of Singapore's Chinese are Hokkien, from southern China, infamously coarse-tongued folk whose hearty noodle dishes like *char kway teow*, *bak chor mee* (noodles with pork, meat balls and fried scallops) and *hokkien mee* (yellow Hokkien noodles with prawn) are a fast-food favourite.

If you're looking for something more fiery, try Sichuan (aka Szechuan) food – garlic and chillies play their part in dishes such as diced chicken and hot-and-sour soup. Beijing cuisine also has more robust flavours and is usually eaten with noodles or steamed buns.

From the area around Shantou in China, Teochew is a style noted for its delicacy and natural flavours (many say it's bland). Seafood is a speciality – fish *maw* (a fish's swim bladder) crops up alarmingly often. The classic Teochew comfort food is rice porridge, served with fish, pork or frog (the latter being a Geylang favourite).

Indian
Essentially, Indian cuisine can be classified into two broad categories: south and north. South Indian food dominates, as most Indian Singaporeans and migrant workers originate from the south, but North Indian restaurants are becoming much more widespread, thanks to the growing number of North Indian professionals and tourists in Singapore.

South Indian food tends to be hot, with the emphasis on vegetarian dishes. The typical South Indian dish is a thali (rice plate), often served on a large banana leaf. On this leaf is placed a large mound of rice, then various vegetable curries, *rasam* (hot, sour soup) and a dessert. South Indian food is traditionally eaten with the right hand, not utensils – though spoons are always available.

The most popular Indian dish among local Chinese is *roti prata* – a heavy flat bread cooked with oil on a hotplate and served with a curry sauce. Pratha restaurants usually list dozens of varieties, both sweet and savoury.

Other South Indian vegetarian dishes include *masala dosa*, a thin pancake that, rolled around spiced vegetables with some chutney and *rasam* on the side, makes a cheap light meal. An equivalent snack meal in Indian halal (Muslim) restaurants is *murtabak*, made from paper-thin dough filled with egg and minced mutton and lightly grilled with oil.

Another favourite Indian halal dish is biryani, which is different from the North Indian version. Ordering a chicken biryani will get you a mound of spiced, saffron-coloured rice, a piece of deep-fried chicken, a bowl of curry

EATING SPECIALITIES

THE INVENTION OF CHILLI CRAB

In 1956, Mr and Mrs Lim opened a seafood restaurant called the Palm Beach. It was here that Mrs Lim first concocted the now-famous tomato, chilli and egg sauce that makes the quintessential Singapore chilli crab. At least that's the story according to her son Roland, who is the proprietor of the eponymous Roland Restaurant (p134). Singaporean food outlets love their rags-to-riches tales.

The Lims emigrated to New Zealand in the 1960s, but Roland returned to Singapore to find his mum's dish a huge hit. He opened his own restaurant in 1985, and since moving to its present location along Marine Pde in 2000, the 1300-seater place has built up a solid reputation – so much so that former prime minister Goh Chok Tong dines here on National Day.

sauce and a small mound of salad (often with a squirt of sweet chilli sauce on top).

North Indian cuisine is more familiar to Westerners, and most commonly associated with heavier, slightly less spicy, dishes, eaten with breads like naan (leavened bread baked inside a clay oven) and chapati (griddle-fried whole-wheat bread).

Malay & Indonesian

The cuisines of Malaysia and Indonesia are similar. Satay – tiny kebabs of chicken, mutton or beef dipped in a spicy peanut sauce – is ubiquitous. Other common dishes include *tahu goreng* (fried soya bean curd and bean sprouts in a peanut sauce), *ikan bilis* (anchovies fried whole), *ikan assam* (fried fish in a sour tamarind curry) and *sambal udang* (fiery curried prawns).

Both *ayam goreng* (fried chicken) and *rendang* are popular staples. *Nasi goreng* (fried rice) is widely available, but it is as much a Chinese and Indian dish as Malay, and each style has its own flavours. *Nasi lemak* is coconut rice served with fried *ikan bilis*, peanuts and a curry dish.

The Sumatran style of Indonesian food bends much more towards curries and chillies. *Nasi padang*, from the Minangkabau region of West Sumatra, consists of a wide variety of hot curries served with rice. *Mee rebus* (noodles in a rich soya-based sauce) is a Javanese dish that is also widely available in food centres.

Peranakan

As descendants of early Chinese immigrants who married Malay women, the Peranakans developed a unique cuisine that blends Chinese ingredients with Malay sauces and spices. It is commonly flavoured with shallots, chillies, *belacan* (Malay fermented prawn paste), peanuts, preserved soybeans and galangal (a ginger-like root). Thick coconut milk is used

to create the sauce that flavours the prime ingredients.

In the past decade there has been a resurgence of interest in Peranakan cuisine, which was once confined to the home, and there are numerous excellent Peranakan restaurants, like Chilli Padi (p133) and Guan Hoe Soon (p133).

Typical dishes include *otak-otak* (a delicious sausage-like blend of fish, coconut milk, chilli paste, galangal and herbs, wrapped and cooked in a banana leaf) and *ayam buah keluak* (chicken stewed with dark nuts imported from Indonesia to produce a rich sauce – the black, paste-like nut filling, eaten in small amounts with each mouthful, has an unusual, earthy flavour).

Also don't miss out on slurping the distinctive Peranakan laksa (noodles in a savoury coconut-milk gravy with fried tofu and bean sprouts).

Desserts

The lurid mini-volcanoes you'll often see at food centres are *ais kacang* (ice ka-*chan*), a combination of a mound of shaved ice, syrups, evaporated milk, fruit, beans and jellies. *Cendol* is similar, consisting of coconut milk with brown sugar syrup and green jelly strips topped with shaved ice. Both taste terrific – or at least a lot better than they look. Also worth trying is *ah balling*, glutinous rice balls filled with a sweet paste of peanut, black sesame or red bean and usually served in a peanut- or ginger-flavoured soup.

Head to Little India to experiment with Indian sweets: *burfi, ladoo, gulab jamun, gelabi, jangiri, kesari* and *halwa*, to name a few, are made with ingredients that include condensed milk, sesame and syrups.

Nonya (Peranakan) desserts are typified by *kueh* (colourful rice cakes often flavoured with coconut and palm sugar) and sweet, sticky delicacies such as miniature pineapple tarts

EATING SPECIALTIES

that are sold everywhere in small plastic tubs with red lids. The magnificent *kueh lapis*, a laborious layer cake that involves prodigious numbers of eggs, is a must-try.

One notable popular Singaporean oddity is the ice-cream sandwich, dished out by mobile ice-cream vendors and enjoyed by young and old alike. This consists of a thick slab of ice cream folded into a slice of bread, though sometimes it's served between the more traditional wafer slices.

WHERE TO EAT

Aside from the standard Western-style restaurants and cafes, Singapore has several local species of eating venue: hawker centre, *kopitiam*, food court, food centre, canteen…all of them feature open dining areas, around which are clustered anything from a handful to a hundred stalls. The subtle distinctions between these places are often a mystery to foreigners, but Singaporeans insist they are different.

The term 'hawker' was once used to describe food vendors who moved their wares around in mobile carts, stopping and setting up their burners wherever there were customers. Of course, such itinerant behaviour was unacceptable in modern Singapore and virtually all of them are now stockaded into hawker centres. Admittedly, it makes life easier for everyone.

Hawker centres are usually stand alone, open-air (or at least open-sided), large and old. There are usually a wide variety of different local cuisines on offer and the atmosphere is often raucous. However, the food is uniformly good. If it isn't, stalls go out of business very quickly.

Food courts are indoor dining areas, often found in air-conditioned shopping malls. There's usually a wider variation of cuisines and prices are marginally higher. Some very swanky food courts are springing up, like

Wisma Atria's Food Republic (p132), where the food is fancier and the prices a little higher still.

Coffeeshops, also called *kopitiam* (*tiam* is Hokkien for 'shop'), are another Singaporean institution. These are open shopfront cafes, usually with a handful of stalls inside, patrolled by an 'auntie' or 'uncle' who takes your drinks order after you've got your food.

Hawker centres and food courts are scrupulously inspected for hygiene. Look for the 'ABC' signs, representing an annually awarded grading based on excellence in cleanliness and food hygiene ('A' is the highest award, which some local wags say stands for Absolutely Tasteless). Some also have special stickers indicating that they offer healthier dishes low in oil, salt, lard and other life-threatening substances.

VEGETARIANS & VEGANS

The predominance of the Buddhist and Hindu religions in Singapore means finding a vegetarian restaurant, stall or cafe is usually not difficult. Little India in particular teems with vegetarian food, but food courts and hawker centres all over the island often feature a vegetarian stall, or have some vegetarian options.

One thing to be aware of is that interpretations of dishes among Chinese and Malays can be slightly different. We have encountered 'vegetable soup' that contains both chicken and prawn (the reasoning being that because it contains vegetables, it's a vegetable soup!) The solution is to be highly specific when ordering food – don't just say 'vegetarian', but stress that you eat 'no meat, no seafood' and make sure you've been understood.

Vegans are likely to find life a little more difficult, but since the consumption of dairy and other animal by-products is relatively limited, usually all you have to do is ensure there are no eggs.

WATCH YOUR QUEUES

It's a common sight in all hawker centres and food courts: a collection of dozens of stalls, some devoid of customers, some with a handful, then one stall with a line of 10, 20 or sometimes more people patiently waiting to place an order.

It's thoroughly baffling to most foreigners, but Singaporeans are so manic about food that they are quite happy to spend half an hour or more in line to get a dish that's new, popular, or famous. According to local wisdom, if you want the best food, join the longest queue.

Stalls go in and out of favour very quickly, but if you want to witness or join in with this phenomenon, you can find sure-fire mammoth queues for black-pepper crab at Eng Seng Coffeeshop (p133) in Joo Chiat or for *satay bee hoon* (peanut sauce–flavoured noodles) at East Coast Lagoon Food Village (p134).

top picks

VEGETARIAN RESTAURANTS

Indian

- **Ananda Bhavan** (p129) Top-notch informal eatery, with three branches.
- **Annalakshmi** (p128) Magnificent pay-what-you-like buffet lunches.
- **Madras New Woodlands** (p130) Excellent thalis and *dosai* (South India savoury pancake), away from the Komala Vilas tourist crowd.
- **Bombay Woodlands** (p131) Superb, affordable North Indian food just off Orchard Rd.

Chinese

- **Lingzhi Vegetarian** (p132) Excellent traditional and modern Chinese food on Orchard Rd and Novena Sq.
- **Ci Yan Organic Vegetarian Health Food** (p128) It's 100% organic, onion and garlic-free, and surrounded by spiritual books.

Other

- **Original Sin** (p135) Stylish Mediterranean fare in the Holland Village expat enclave.
- **Whatever** (p108) New Age bookstore at the front, superb veggie food at the back.

For a complete list of vegetarian restaurants, check out www.vegetarian-restaurants.net/Asia/Singapore.

COOKING COURSES

Whether you want to know how to whip up your own laksa (no, not out of a jar) or finally learn what the hell *jus* is, there are a number of courses available.

At-Sunrice (Map pp52–3; ☎ 6336 3307; www.at-sunrice.com; Fort Canning Centre) In Fort Canning Park. Pay $35 for a walk around the spice garden and a tea reception, then an extra $100 for a half-day class, where you can learn five dishes of your choice (three hands-on, two demo), followed by lunch. More-serious amateur chefs can sign up for a course, taking place on eight consecutive Saturdays and costing $2100.

Cookery Magic (☎ 6348 9667; www.cookerymagic.com) Perhaps the best classes of all are offered by Cookery Magic, run by the wonderful Ruqxana, who teaches a huge range of popular Indian, Malay, Indonesian, Chinese and Singaporean classics to small groups in her own home, or on field trips. Classes cost from $50 to $75 per person.

Shermay's Cooking School (Map pp92–3; ☎ 6479 8442; www.shermay.com; 03-64 Block 43, Jalan Merah Saga, Chip Bee Gardens, Holland Village) Slightly more formal are these hands-on and demo courses, costing from $69 to $139. The dessert classes are particularly popular (how often do you get the chance to attend a cupcake workshop?) and there are also courses in European and Asian cuisines.

Raffles Culinary Academy (Map pp52–3; ☎ 6412 1256; www.raffleshotel.com/culinaryclass.html) On the second level of the Raffles Hotel Arcade, the academy offers a wide variety of one-day cookery classes for groups of up to 20 people, costing from $65 to $130 per person. Very few are hands-on, but you will get lunch or dinner at the end.

Coriander Leaf (Map pp52–3; ☎ 6732 3354; www.corianderleaf.com; 02-03, 3A Merchant Court, Clarke Quay) This Asian fusion restaurant also runs regular classes in anything from Italian and French to Thai and Vietnamese. Each lasts three-and-a-half hours, covers around eight recipes (which seems a little rushed) and costs $120 to $130.

PRACTICALITIES

Opening Hours

Generally, the fancier the restaurant, the shorter the opening hours. Top restaurants usually open from noon to 2.30pm, then from around 6pm to 11pm (we've listed the hours where they differ). Food courts, coffeeshops and hawker centres operate throughout the day – sometimes 24 hours a day – and usually close down sometime between 10pm and 1am. Midrange restaurants often stay open throughout the day, while chain cafes such as Coffee Bean stay open as late as 1am.

How Much?

You can spend as much or as little as you like on food in Singapore and still find a good meal – the mark of a great eating city. At a hawker centre or coffeeshop, a meal with coffee, tea or juice will set you back as little as $4.50, while a food court might cost you an extra $2. A hearty meal for two in a midrange restaurant with a couple of beers will cost around $40 or $50. Top-end restaurants will set you back at least $100 a head, and if you're drinking wine, a decent bottle will cost a minimum of $40.

Bear in mind that most menu prices will have a hefty 18% added to them at the end: 10% for service charge, 7% for GST and 1% government tax.

PRICE GUIDE

The following price guide is based on dinner for two, with a couple of drinks.

$$$	over $75
$$	$20-75
$	under $20

Booking Tables

Generally, the more expensive the restaurant, the likelier it is you'll have to make a reservation. As a rule of thumb, always book ahead for a top-end restaurant. For midrange restaurants, make bookings for Friday, Saturday and Sunday nights.

Tipping

Tipping is usually unnecessary in Singapore, as most restaurants impose a 10% service charge – and nobody ever tips in hawker centres. It's worth checking your bill, though, as a number of bars and restaurants are now opting to withdraw the 10% charge and let customers decide whether or not to leave a tip, presumably in an effort to improve the notoriously poor standard of Singaporean service.

Self-Catering

Food markets like those at Tekka Market, Chinatown Complex and Geylang Serai are pretty thin on the ground in Singapore, but supermarkets are everywhere. Two decent local chains dominate the scene: NTUC Fair-Price and Cold Storage (Map pp92-3), which has earned a reputation for being slightly more upmarket – it's certainly more consistent than FairPrice – but in reality there's little to choose between them.

Other popular retailers include French *hypermarché* empire Carrefour (Plaza Singapura and Suntec City), where you'll find a much wider choice and better quality produce, and high-end grocers Jason's Market Place (Raffles City, Orchard Towers, Paragon and Tanglin Mall).

Singapore's relative wealth, large expat population and obsession with food has also spawned a thriving industry in gourmet food and wine retail. Shops like Gastronomie (p116), Swiss Butchery and Jones the Grocer (p116), sprinkled around the city centre and wealthy residential areas like Holland Village, do a roaring trade.

The online store at www.greengrocer.com .sg offers a wide range of fairly high-priced gourmet imports.

COLONIAL DISTRICT & THE QUAYS

Eating around the Colonial District and the three quays is a fancy affair – budget options are pretty thin on the ground in this part of town. The range of international restaurants, from sophisticated French, such as Saint Pierre, to shameless raunch, like Clarke Quay's Hooters, is so staggering it would take a year or more just to eat your way through the Quays. A few hawker centres, ideal for a quick lunch or cheap dinner, remain and all the main shopping malls have their obligatory food courts.

BOBBY'S TAPROOM & GRILL

Map pp52–3   American $$$

☎ 6337 5477; www.bobbys.com.sg; B1-03 Chijmes, 30 Victoria St; mains from $20; ☯ noon-midnight Sun-Tue, noon-2am Wed-Sat; Ⓜ City Hall; ☝

A completely refurbished high-end American barbecue and sports bar specialising in steaks, chops, ribs and all things meaty. It's particularly well-known for its baby back pork ribs, but the steaks are also excellent. Veggie options available.

CHEF CHAN'S RESTAURANT

Map pp52–3   Chinese $$$

☎ 6333 0073; 01-06 National Museum, 93 Stamford Rd; set menu $88; Ⓜ Dhoby Ghaut

Staking a very strong claim to be Singapore's top Chinese restaurant, everything about Chef Chan's is outstanding, from the glorious location buried in a hard-to-find nook of the National Museum to the genuine antique Chinese decor and the magnificent, classic set menu (featuring his famous crispy roast chicken, complete with head). Reservations only.

DOC CHENG'S Map pp52–3   International $$$

☎ 6412 1264; level 2, Raffles Hotel Arcade, 1 Beach Rd; mains from $20; Ⓜ City Hall

Decked out with curtained booths, high ceilings, soft lighting and chequered tiles, Doc Cheng's has a discreetly colonial air. The food, however, is decidedly modern fusion. 'Son-in-law' egg starter is surprisingly successful, as are dishes like the tandoori trout.

EQUINOX Map pp52–3   International $$$
☎ 6431 5669; level 70, Swissôtel, 2 Stamford Rd; mains $30

Seventy floors up, with the city sprawled below, you'll wonder what brought you – the view or the food. The former is better than the latter, but it's still an unforgettable experience. Tastefully decorated with plush red carpets, hanging Chinese screens, subdued lighting, Equinox is a must-visit. Retire for a drink at the New Asia Bar or City Space afterwards.

GARIBALDI Map pp52–3   Italian $$$
☎ 6837 1468; 36 Purvis St; mains $26-48; Ⓜ Bugis

One of the most accomplished Italian restaurants in Singapore – and there's no shortage of competition – Garibaldi's is the perfect spot for a romantic occasion, offering rich, hearty country food. Expect to come out at least $150 lighter if you have wine.

HAI TIEN LO Map pp52–3   Chinese $$$
☎ 6826 8338; 37th fl, Pan Pacific Hotel, 7 Raffles Blvd; mains from $20; 🚇 N1-N7

In preparation for a superb meal, savour the spectacular views while riding the external lift up to the 37th floor. A large range of nearly 30 set menus tailored to different tastes and requirements takes the headache out of ordering and allows you to concentrate on the scene outside.

INDOCHINE WATERFRONT
Map pp52–3   Southeast Asian $$$
☎ 6339 1720; 1 Empress Pl; mains from $20; Ⓜ Raffles Place; 🔌

This is boutique dining at its peak, surrounded by Buddha statues and with a superb view across the Singapore River to the CBD and the Fullerton Hotel. It's often packed, but the food (if you can forget that you're paying top dollar for what are essentially Lao, Khmer or Vietnamese street dishes) is generally very good, particularly the Cambodian tiger prawns. Next door is the equally trendy Bar Opiume.

MY HUMBLE HOUSE
Map pp52–3   Chinese $$$
☎ 6423 1881; 02-27/29 Esplanade Mall; mains $15-20; Ⓜ City Hall

With an outlandish interior designed by Chinese artist Zhang Jin Jie, the name of this restaurant cannot be anything but ironic.

The menu doesn't hold back either, with set lunches named 'The Wind Wafts Above the Shoulder' and suchlike. Eating here is an experience you're unlikely to forget.

PEONY JADE Map pp52–3   Chinese $$$
☎ 6338 0305; 02-02 Clarke Quay; mains from $15; Ⓜ Clarke Quay

Boasting a picturesque riverside location, Peony offers Szechuan and Cantonese food, often with a twist – everyone raves about the prawn with curry leaves, but it's also known for its smoked duck and baked cod.

PIERSIDE KITCHEN & BAR
Map pp52–3   Fusion Seafood $$$
☎ 6438 0400; 01-01 One Fullerton, 1 Fullerton Rd; Ⓜ Raffles Place

Completely refurbished and reborn to exploit its superb bayside location to full advantage, Pierside promises outdoor dining with a fantastic view. Ideal spot for a breezy romantic meal – provided you're both into seafood.

ROYAL CHINA Map pp52–3   Chinese $$$
☎ 6338 3363; 03-09 Raffles Hotel, Beach Rd; Ⓜ City Hall

Raffles does most things superbly, and its signature Chinese restaurant is no exception. Dress in your best summer casuals and pop in for afternoon dim sum. The scallop dumplings are magnificent, as is the crispy duck. Worth skipping breakfast for.

TIFFIN ROOM Map pp52–3   Indian $$$
☎ 6431 6156; lobby, Raffles Hotel, 1 Beach Rd; lunch/dinner buffet $48/52; Ⓜ City Hall

A Raffles institution to rank with the Long Bar and Bar & Billiard Room, this priceless dining room, complete with lazy ceiling fans, takes our prize for best buffet in town. The largely North Indian food is superb and the temptation to overeat almost irresistible. The tourist-friendly reduced chilli content is the only disappointment.

AH TENG'S BAKERY Map pp52–3   Café $$
☎ 6337 1886; Raffles Hotel Arcade, 1 Beach Rd; 🕑 7.30am-5.30pm; Ⓜ City Hall; 🔌

A great place for breakfast pastries or *dim sum* and just about the only part of Raffles Hotel you can enter without your wallet trying to make a run for it. With its genteel wooden chairs and marble-top tables, it has the same colonial air, but it's more reasonably priced.

BOOK CAFÉ Map pp52–3
Cafe $$

☎ 6887 5430; 01-02 Seng Kee Bldg, 20 Martin Rd; mains $10-15; ⏱ 8.30am-10.30pm Sun-Thu, 8.30am-midnight Fri & Sat; 🚌 33, 54, 139, 195; ♿
At the river end of Mohamed Sultan Rd, Book Café is a convivial bistro with large, comfy sofas and a good selection of old books, magazines and foreign newspapers to browse through while you lounge around enjoying breakfast or a coffee.

CORIANDER LEAF
Map pp52–3
Asian Fusion $$

☎ 6732 3354; www.corianderleaf.com; 02-03, 3A Merchant Court, Clarke Quay; mains $15-25; Ⓜ Clarke Quay
A fusion of European, Middle Eastern and Southeast Asian menus, Coriander Leaf offers a wide selection of dishes, some a little jarring, most excellent. There's also a small deli and a demo kitchen offering cooking courses (see p122).

SAGE Map pp52–3
European $$

☎ 6333 8726; 7 Mohamed Sultan Rd; mains from $28; 🚌 33, 54, 139, 195
Set in a tiny converted shophouse on the Mohamed Sultan bar strip, Sage is one of the best restaurants in the Quays area. Intimate and relaxed, the service is immaculate and the food, from the prawn and escargot risotto starter to the mushroom soup and the beef cheek main, is superb. The only potential downside is the noise, if a big group happens to be sharing the small space with you. Booking is essential.

TAPAS TREE Map pp52–3
Spanish $$

☎ 6837 2938; 01-08, Block 3D, Clarke Quay; tapas from $5; Ⓜ Clarke Quay
Among the most popular of the recent Clarke Quay arrivals, this eatery boasts a huge range of classic tapas, a riverside location (though there's comfy seating inside) and great music (the flamenco trio are fun, though inevitably they're Filipino). Booking at weekends is essential.

WAH LOK Map pp52–3
Chinese $$

☎ 6311 8188; 2nd level, Carlton Hotel, 76 Bras Basah Rd; mains over $20; Ⓜ City Hall
The rotunda hall with the high dome ceiling, floor-to-ceiling glass windows, bright interior and warm ambience of this Cantonese place don't quite prepare you for the entertainingly brusque service, but

top picks

HAWKER CENTRES & FOOD COURTS

Hawker centres are one Singaporean institution you simply should not miss. Be prepared for a noisy, crowded, hot (unless you're in a mall) and wonderful time. These are among the best hawker and food centres in Singapore:

- **Smith Street Hawker Centre** (Map pp62–3) At night, Smith St is closed off and the road is filled with tables and diners munching seafood and drinking beer. One of our favourites.
- **East Coast Lagoon Food Village** (p134) Soak up the sea breezes by the beach while wolfing down satay and seafood.
- **Tekka Centre** (p130) The grimy, bustling heart of Little India, where you'll find dozens of Indian and Muslim stalls, wrapped in the noise and smells from the wet market.
- **Golden Mile Complex** (p130) Popular with Thai workers, this is the spot to get a *tom yum* (spicy and sour soup) and a *som tam* (green papaya salad) just like they make in the Land of Smiles.
- **Newton Circus Hawker Centre** (p132) OK, it's a well-worn stop on the tourist trail, but the food and the atmosphere are still memorable.
- **Old Airport Road Food Centre** (Map p80) Refurbished but not sanitised, this old Geylang favourite houses some legendary hawkers.
- **Kopitiam** (p126) A 24-hour food court perfect for post-drinking munchies, if you can stand the blazing lights.
- **Maxwell Road Hawker Centre** (p128) A throwback to the old days in the heart of Chinatown: noisy and chaotic.
- **Lau Pa Sat** (p128) Dating back to 1822, it's been substantially modernised, but still pulls in the crowds, and even tour buses.
- **Food Republic** (p132) One of a new breed of fancy food centres, with great views of Orchard Rd below.

the food is great. Wah Lok well known for its excellent tofu; the roast meats are also a highlight.

GLUTTONS BAY Map pp52–3
Hawker Centre $

☎ 6336 7025; 01-15 Esplanade Mall; mains $10-20; ⏱ 6pm-3am; Ⓜ City Hall; ♿
Selected by the Makansutra food guide (see p126), this bayside collection of the best hawkers (or street-food masters, as they call them)

GOURMET GUIDES

Of the annual restaurant guides available from most bookstores, *Singapore Tatler* magazine's *Best Restaurants* guide focuses on the best top-end establishments in town, while KF Seetoh, the founder of the superb *Makansutra* (the bible of hawker centre food), has attained guru status. *I-S* magazine produces free annual eating and drinking guides, but unless you're in town at the time they're published they're hard to get hold of.

The reviews in *Time Out* and *I-S* are a good source of news on Singapore's ever-changing restaurant scene. Check out these websites too:

www.makansutra.com The website of the TV food show, *Makansutra*, is lively, but apart from the Top 10, you have to purchase the book to read its reviews.

www.makantime.com Covering hawker centres, budget eateries and restaurants, this website has lots of local feedback, but is dated.

www.sbestfood.com An excellent site for hunting down hawker food, with listings arranged by type of food and by location. Reviews, though, are scant.

www.singaporehalaldirectory.com List of halal-certified companies and outlets in Singapore.

is a great place to start your exploration of the island's food culture. Everyone has their own favourites – we like the BBQ seafood stall.

KOPITIAM Map pp52–3   Coffeeshop $
cnr Bencoolen St & Bras Basah Rd; ☯ 24hr; Ⓜ City Hall
One of the top spots in the district for a late-night feed, this branch of the Kopitiam chain is brisk and blindingly bright, so if it's a late boozy night grab a table outside, where the light is more friendly. The food is uniformly good and you won't pay much more than $6 for a meal.

CHINATOWN & THE CBD

Combining the narrow lanes of olde Singapore with the bewildering variety of a truly 21st-century metropolis, Chinatown is probably the best food district in the city and has something for everyone: from the hip, sophisticated eateries of Club St and Ann Siang Rd to the tiny teahouses of Tanjong Pagar, to the jovial bustle of the Chinatown Food St and the rough-and-ready Maxwell Rd hawker centre and everything in between.

L'ANGELUS Map pp62–3   French $$$
☎ 6225 6897; 85 Club St; mains from $16; Ⓜ Chinatown
Cosy, friendly, traditional French restaurant run by a couple of attentive French expats, who also own the excellent bar Le Carillon de L'Angelus (☎ 6423 0353; 24 Ann Siang Rd; ☯ 5pm–

2am Mon-Sat, 5pm-1am Sun), further up on Ann Siang Rd. The escargot are a speciality, but we like the cassoulet, an incredibly filling, hearty bean and meat stew.

OSO RISTORANTE
Map pp62–3   Italian $$$
☎ 6327 8378; 27 Tanjong Pagar Rd; mains from $22; Ⓜ Tanjong Pagar
Slightly out of place among the mild sleaze of Tanjong Pagar Rd, Oso specialises in refined but hearty Tuscan food, with sauces that feature wild boar and rabbit, plus excellent cheeses and wines. Highly recommended.

SAINT PIERRE Map pp62–3   French $$$
☎ 6438 0887; 01-01 Central Mall, 3 Magazine Rd; mains from $50; Ⓜ Clarke Quay
While many are naturally sceptical of self-styled 'celebrity' chefs, the peroxide blond Mr Stroobant has earned his fame. The modern French menu is often inspired and though the six types of pate foie gras might test the patience of animal lovers, it pulls in the crowds. Easily one of the top restaurants in town.

SENSO Map pp62–3   Italian $$$
☎ 6224 3534; 21 Club St; Ⓜ Chinatown
Senso oozes class, from the understated chic of the bar at the front to the intimate courtyard – once the playground of the school that occupied the building. It's the perfect spot for a romantic evening under the stars, the food and the service are immaculate and the wines (a sommelier is on hand to make suggestions) are superb.

SPRING JUCHUNYUAN

Map pp62–3   Chinese $$$

☎ 6536 2655; www.juchunyuan.com.sg;
01-01 Far East Sq; dishes from $15;
Ⓜ Raffles Place

In terms of atmosphere, this must be the most irresistibly romantic Chinese restaurant in Singapore. Done up like a 19th-century house, it specialises in Fuzhou classics like Buddha Jumps Over The Wall. Save for a special occasion.

BROTH Map pp62–3   International $$

☎ 6323 3353; 21 Duxton Hill; mains $15-25;
Ⓜ Tanjong Pagar

Broth has a great location on a cobbled dead-end street closed to cars, as long as you don't mind walking past the Duxton Rd KTV bars to get there. It's a small, cosy, beautifully converted shophouse, with an appealing Western bistro-style menu, popular among the local office crowd.

CHUAN JIANG HAO ZI

Map pp62–3   Steamboat $$

☎ 6225 1518; 12 Smith St; steamboats from $25;
Ⓜ Chinatown

Delicious, traditional, impossibly fiery Sichuan steamboat, the eating of which involves strict etiquette (helpfully described in signs on the walls). The special octagonal pots, imported from China, have two chambers, so that two stocks can be used simultaneously, and some of the ingredients are unique to Sichuan steamboat, like duck gizzard, sweet potato and pork trotters. For hardy chilli lovers only.

CORK CELLAR KITCHEN

Map pp62–3   Western $$

☎ 6327 9169; 01-08 Capital Tower, 168 Robinson Rd;
mains from $20; ◷ Mon-Fri; Ⓜ Tanjong Pagar

This stretch of the CBD is a bit of a culinary vacuum, so it's not surprising this wood-and-glass bistro gets packed with businesspeople during lunchtimes, when the chatter echoing off the minimalist walls can be deafening. Instead, go in the evening, when the excellent food and wine list can be enjoyed in peace.

SEVEN ON CLUB

Map pp62–3   Mediterranean $$

☎ 6327 9663; 7 Club St; mains from $18;
Ⓜ Chinatown

One of the newer Club St restaurants, Seven exudes class and has been attracting the area's affluent professionals in droves. The alfresco area is a bit too close to the main road for comfort during early evening peak hour, so head inside or wait til the traffic dies down. The Mediterranean dishes, like swordfish belly, are excellent and its set lunches and dinners are good value.

SPIZZA Map pp62–3   Pizza $$

☎ 6224 2525; 29 Club St; pizzas from $15;
Ⓜ Chinatown

Easygoing, friendly pizzeria – one of the most relaxed options on Club St. The wood-fired thin-crust pizzas are perfect, not too heavy on the toppings – and unlike many pizzerias in Singapore they're happy to load on the anchovies if you ask nicely. Deservedly popular.

THE ART OF TEA APPRECIATION

Taking time out in a teahouse is a pleasant way to relax and learn about the finer points of many kinds of tea available and how to appreciate them. The best place to start is Yixing Xuan Teahouse (Map pp62–3; ☎ 6224 6961; www .yixingxuan-teahouse.com; 30/32 Tanjong Pagar Rd; ◷ 11am-11pm), where former banker Vincent Low explains all you need to know about sampling different types of tea. The demonstration with tastings lasts around an hour ($20 or $30).

Once you know your green tea from your oolong, nip around the corner to Tea Chapter (Map pp62–3; ☎ 6226 1175; www.tea-chapter.com.sg; 9-11 Neil Rd; ◷ 10am-11pm), where Queen Elizabeth and Prince Philip dropped by for a cuppa in 1989. There are several different areas in which to sit, but choose carefully: the more private incur a higher surcharge. If you don't know the drill, the waiter will give you a brief demonstration of how to make tea.

Wang San Yang (Map pp62–3; ☎ 6532 2707; www.wystm.com; 01-61, Block 531 Hong Lim Complex ◷ 10am-9pm) is an oasis of elegance amid the bustle of the Hong Lim Complex, and stocks a large range of teaware and does demonstrations on request.

ANNALAKSHMI

Map pp62–3   Indian Vegetarian $

☎ 6223 0809; www.annalakshmi.com.sg; 104 Amoy St; ⏱ 11am-3pm Mon-Sat; Ⓜ Tanjong Pagar

This Indian eatery is an institution in more ways than one: first, because of the outstanding quality of the vegetarian food, second, because it's a charity organisation staffed by volunteers. Eat your fill, then pay what you think it deserves at the cashier – $5 to $10 is appropriate, because the money goes to charity. There are other branches at Lau Pa Sat (below) and Chinatown Point (p109), and one in Johor Bahru (p180) across the Causeway.

CI YAN ORGANIC VEGETARIAN HEALTH FOOD

Map pp62–3   Chinese $

☎ 6225 9026; 2 Smith St; mains $10; ⏱ noon-10pm; Ⓜ Chinatown

Detox at Ci Yan Organic Vegetarian Health Food, where the food is organic, 100% vegetarian and contains no garlic or onion. The tiny wooden tables and chairs and the spiritual book selection give this place a schoolhouse atmosphere to complement your rising sense of worthiness.

HONG HU EXPRESS

Map pp62–3   Coffeeshop $

cnr Telok Ayer & McCallum St; ⏱ 24hr; Ⓜ Tanjong Pagar

This part of Chinatown is almost completely comatose at night (except for the gay cruising activity), but if you're spilling out of a club on the other side of Ann Siang Hill at 4am with a severe case of the munchies, the 24-hour Hong Hu might just be a lifesaver.

LAU PA SAT Map pp62–3   Hawker Centre $

18 Raffles Quay; ⏱ 11am-3am; Ⓜ Raffles Place

Lau pa sat means 'old market' in Hokkien, which is appropriate since the handsome iron structure shipped out from Glasgow in 1894 remains intact. A recent renovation has sapped some of the 'old Asia' atmosphere away, but everyone should come here at least once, if only to sit and down a few Tigers in the corner beer garden.

MAXWELL ROAD HAWKER CENTRE

Map pp62–3   Hawker Centre $

cnr South Bridge & Maxwell Rds; Ⓜ Chinatown

One of Chinatown's iconic hawker centres, Maxwell Rd is best viewed at lunchtime,

when it's heaving with people, though that might not be the best time to be a foreigner wandering bewildered among the hundreds of stalls. Its most famous resident is the Tian Tian chicken rice stall (No 10).

YA KUN KAYA TOAST

Map pp62–3   Coffeeshop $

☎ 6438 3638; 01-01 Far East Sq, 18 China St; ⏱ 7.30am-7pm Mon-Fri, 9am-5pm Sat & Sun; Ⓜ Raffles Place

Though a large chain of Ya Kun outlets has spread across the island, this is by far the most atmospheric and the closest to the original. It's packed with office workers during the week; try to get an inside table to watch the brusque staff in action. Polite they are not, but at least they won't tell you to have a nice day, or ask if you want fries with that.

LITTLE INDIA & KAMPONG GLAM

Obviously you don't come here looking for escargot (with one exception). This is curry paradise, with inexpensive food from almost every part of India. And because most restaurants cater primarily to Indian clientele, you know the food hasn't been adjusted for foreign palates.

Along Race Course Rd are the more upmarket restaurants, which cater to more foreigners, while the lanes off Serangoon Rd are worth exploring.

To the east is Kampong Glam, where a clutch of Middle Eastern restaurants play host to a low-key and mildly trendy night scene. Across Beach Rd is the Golden Mile Complex, spiritual home to thousands of Thai migrant workers, where you can find the most authentic Thai food in town.

AL-TAZZAG Map p68   Egyptian $$

☎ 6295 5024; 24 Haji Lane, Kampong Glam; mains from $8; ⏱ 11.30am-4am Mon-Sat, 4pm-4am Sun; Ⓜ Bugis

A small, colourfully painted Egyptian cafe in quiet Haji Lane, with leather cushions on the bench seats and a backlit display of sheesha pipes. At night it spreads out, putting up tables under the five-foot ways. It's quieter, more relaxed and far more atmospheric than Café Le Caire on Arab St, though the food isn't quite as good. Still, the dips, kebabs and sheesha pipes are top notch.

FRENCH STALL Map p68 French $$

☎ 6299 3544; 544 Serangoon Rd, Little India; mains $10-20; ⊙ 6-10pm Tue-Sun; Ⓜ Farrer Park

It's cash only at the French Stall, a charming Gallic cafe owned and run by a two-star Michelin chef all the way from Brittany, who embarked on a mission to show that great French food doesn't need to be expensive. His mission has been highly successful.

GAYATRI Map p68 Indian $$

☎ 6291 1011; www.gayatrirestaurant.com; 122 Race Course Rd; dishes from $6; Ⓜ Little India

Fame is a mysterious thing. While Banana Leaf Apolo 100m away is perpetually packed, Gayatri has much better service, better food (well, its fish-head curry is almost on par) and a far more pleasant ambience, yet it's much quieter and almost free of tourists. It deserves to be much more popular.

KASHMIR Map p68 Indian $$

☎ 6293 6003; 52 Race Course Rd; dishes from $8; Ⓜ Little India

From the moment a waiter brings a bowl of warm water and a towel to your table for you to wash your hands, you suspect you might be in for a good meal and excellent service – and you are! Stick with the Kashmiri specialities (marked with a maple leaf) and you'll walk out a very happy person.

KOREAN HOT STONE BBQ

Map p68 Korean $$

☎ 6299 3866; 249 Beach Rd; dishes from $12; 🚌 48

A popular alternative to the area's ubiquitous Middle Eastern fare, this no-frills shophouse joint is nearly always packed at night with Singaporean diners, clustered hungrily around the tables, feasting on *bibimbap* (rice with pickled vegetables and chilli sauce), hotpot and other Korean classics.

TEPAK SIREH Map p68 Malay $$

☎ 6396 4373; 73 Sultan Gate, Kampong Glam; buffet $16; Ⓜ Bugis

One of the most atmospheric Malay restaurants in the city, next to the former Sultan's palace (now Malay Heritage Cen-

tre, see p67) and inside the former 'Prime Minister's' house. The buffet spread is a virtual encyclopaedia of Malay specialities, though slopped into bain-marie trays it's not so appealingly presented. Tepak Sireh often caters for functions, so call ahead, or you might get swallowed up by a wedding reception.

ANANDA BHAVAN

Map p68 Indian Vegetarian $

☎ 6297 9522; 58 Serangoon Rd; ⊙ 7.30am-10.30pm; Ⓜ Little India

Far better than its rival, the Komala Vilas chain. Fill yourself up here with outstanding *idli* (steamed rice cakes with chutney) and *masala thosai* (savoury pancake filled with curried vegetables) or the enormous 'mini' set meal, all washed down with sublime ginger tea. There are also takeaway snacks and a tempting range of Indian sweets. There are other branches outside the Tekka Centre (221 Selegie Rd) and opposite the Mustafa Centre (☎ 6297 9522; 95 Syed Alwi Rd).

ANDHRA CURRY Map p68 Indian $

☎ 6296 3935; 41 Kerbau Rd; meals from $7; Ⓜ Little India

No fancy decor and no ceremony, but the food here, from the South Indian state of Andhra Pradesh, is superb and the service quick and functional. Particularly good is the Hyderabadi biryani (traditionally cooked in a dough-sealed pot) and the large vegetarian thalis.

ANJAPPAR Map p68 Indian $

☎ 6392 5545; www.anjappar.com.sg; 102 Syed Alwi Rd; meals from $8; Ⓜ Farrer Park

Originally from Chennai, this restaurant dynasty has spread to Singapore and proved extremely popular for its outstanding Chettinad cuisine, from the deep south of India. Our favourites are the mutton *uppu kari* (a dry, spicy mutton curry) and the chicken *nattu koli masala* (chicken in a spicy gravy), the latter guaranteed to have you bathing in a sweat of chilli bliss. The flagship branch is on Race Course Rd.

BANANA LEAF APOLO Map p68 Indian $

☎ 6293 8682; www.bananaleafapolo.com; 54-58 Race Course Rd; dishes from $6, fish-head curries from $18; Ⓜ Little India

A popular stop on the tourist route, but nevertheless the Apolo continues to attract a wide range of customers and has never compromised on the quality or spiciness of its famous fish-head curry, or any other dish it serves up on wide banana leaves. Like many places that get lots of tourists, though, the service can be a little grumpy and slow.

CAFÉ LE CAIRE (AL MAJLIS)
Map p68   Middle Eastern $
☎ 6292 0979; 39 Arab St, Kampong Glam; dishes under $10; ✆ 10am-2am; Ⓜ Bugis
Highly informal, Egyptian hole-in-the-wall cafe attracting a multinational crowd, run by a former accountant who went on a quest to preserve Arab culture in Singapore. In the daytime you'd hardly notice it, but at night it spreads its tables and rugs along both sides of the street, serving up superb dips, breads and kebabs, plus sheesha pipes. Best Middle Eastern food in the area.

COUNTRYSIDE CAFE
Map p68   Western/Indian $
☎ 6297 6964; 71 Dunlop St; ✆ 10am-midnight Tue-Sun, 5pm-midnight Mon; mains $6-12; Ⓜ Little India
A relaxed, friendly and cosy shophouse eatery ostensibly aimed at the local backpacker crowd, but attracting a broad range of people with its well-priced Western and Indian food (excellent veggie burgers), eager service and cheap beers ($6.50 for a pint of Tiger – about half the price of a city pub!). The Countryside's smart interior design, with its bookshelves and small wine collection, add a touch of charm not usually found in your average traveller joint.

GOLDEN MILE COMPLEX Map p68   Thai $
5001 Beach Rd; 🚌 48
This is Singapore's mini-Thailand, full of Thai shops, grocers, butchers and eateries. The signs are in Thai, the customers are mostly Thai and the food, clustered on the ground floor, is 100% magnificent like-mother-makes Thai. The atmosphere is often boisterous and drunken and a little rough-house for some. The Isan (northeast) food is best – try the Nong Khai Food & Beer Garden on the ground floor (with the orange sign in Thai and tiny lettering in English), then once you're fed and boozed up, head for Thai Disco 1 or 2 to complete the evening.

MADRAS NEW WOODLANDS
Map p68   Indian Vegetarian $
☎ 6297 1594; 12-14 Upper Dickson Rd; ✆ 7.30am-11.30pm; mains $5-10; Ⓜ Little India
Another excellent vegetarian joint dishing up some huge portions (if you ever wondered how vegetarians get fat, here's your answer) on banana leaves. The thalis are vast and truly magnificent, and need at least half an hour to finish, if you can finish them at all. The service is friendlier and more accommodating towards confused foreigners than many of the Little India eateries.

TEKKA CENTRE Map p68   Hawker Centre $
cnr Serangoon & Buffalo Rds; dishes $3-5; Ⓜ Little India
Like most of Little India, this is the perfect antidote to any notions of 'sterile Singapore'. Wrapped around the hacked bones, sloshed guts and pungent odours of the wet market, the Tekka hawker centre serves up excellent Indian and Muslim food at between $3 and $5 a dish.

ORCHARD ROAD

Like the Colonial District, Orchard Rd is dominated by fancier places to eat. The malls are studded with midrange to top-end restaurants, many of which are busy most evenings and weekends. Most malls also have their own food courts, however, where it's easy to find a good lunch or dinner for a few dollars.

BLU Map pp74–5   Western $$$
☎ 6213 4598; 24th fl, Shangri-La Hotel, 22 Orange Grove Rd; mains from $30; ✆ 7-10.30pm Mon-Sat; Ⓜ Orchard
Top-notch sophisticated Western cuisine against a backdrop of posh condominiums, all bathed in a seductive low blue light and serenaded by some decent lounge jazz make this a good option for the fashionably minded. The tables are well-spaced to give a feeling of privacy and the service is notably excellent.

NOGAWA Map pp74–5   Japanese $$$
☎ 6732 2911; 03-25 Le Meridien Singapore, 100 Orchard Rd; mains from $30; Ⓜ Somerset
This is not the place for a mid-shopping-trip light lunch, because you're liable to keep ordering once you get going on the sushi here. Plonk yourself at the counter

for a chefside view. At $35, the set lunches are a good deal, considering the quality of the food.

GORDON GRILL

Map pp74–5   International $$$

☎ 6730 1744; Goodwood Park Hotel, 22 Scotts Rd; mains from $30; Ⓜ Orchard

With its old military club atmosphere, complete with 'family' portraits, and its famed steaks, the Gordon Grill is an olde worlde oasis in the middle of ultramodern Orchard Rd. It's as much an experience as it is a meal, so it's worth splashing out on the wagyu, ordered by weight.

SHANG PALACE Map pp74–5   Chinese $$$

☎ 6213 4473; ground fl, Shangri-La Hotel, 22 Orange Grove Rd; mains from $20; Ⓜ Orchard, then taxi

Definitely on the A-list of Singapore's Chinese restaurants, Shang's Cantonese seafood and classics such as Peking Duck are well known – and the interior more than matches the food. To sample the ambience without distressing your bank manager, order from the dim sum menu. Book in advance.

PROJECTSHOP CAFÉ Map pp74–5   Cafe $$

☎ 6735 6765; 02-20/21 the Paragon, 290 Orchard Rd; dishes from $12; ⊙ 10am-8.30pm; Ⓜ Orchard; ♿

Dessert heaven. Pick a table in the middle of the mall for a view of the well-heeled shoppers, or head inside so that you and your banana cream pie can enjoy a private moment. The main courses here are pretty good too, but the real reason to come is for dessert and coffee.

BOMBAY WOODLANDS RESTAURANT

Map pp74–5   Indian Vegetarian $$

☎ 6235 2712; B1-01/02 Tanglin Shopping Centre, 19 Tanglin Rd; mains $5-7; Ⓜ Orchard; ♿

Tucked away below street level in the Tanglin Shopping Centre, Bombay Woodlands is the sort of place you'd pass by without a glance. Don't. The food is magnificent and cheap; go for the lunchtime buffet, or go à la carte and order the *idli* with terrific mint chutney, excellent *dosai* (try the Mysore Masala) or *bhindi* (okra), washed down with *lassi* (yoghurt-based drink). With its attentive white-shirted waiters, it has a charm not easily found in the Orchard Rd vicinity.

CRYSTAL JADE STEAMBOAT KITCHEN

Map pp74–5   Chinese $$

☎ 6336 2833; 02-32 Plaza Singapura, Orchard Rd; mains from $6; Ⓜ Dhoby Ghaut; ♿

Crystal Jade is the king of delicious, reliable and affordable Chinese food in Singapore, which is why it's nearly always packed. On offer here are excellent dim sum and rice porridges. As always, the best plan of attack is to get a group together and order up big.

DIN TAI FUNG Map pp74–5   Chinese $$

☎ 6836 8336; B1-03 Paragon, 290 Orchard Rd; dishes from $7; Ⓜ Orchard; ♿

One of the best restaurants in the country, Din Tai Fung is the first Singapore branch of Taiwan's oldest dumpling and noodle chain. The food here, carefully prepared by the large team of chefs visible through the full-length glass of the kitchen, is nothing short of unbelievable. Among the highlights, and worth savouring, is the simple pork and shrimp dumpling soup in a delicate broth, while the fried rice, delicately flavoured with spring onion, is superb. A must visit.

IMPERIAL TREASURE NAN BEI KITCHEN Map pp74–5   Chinese $$

☎ 6738 1238; 05-12 Ngee Ann City, 391 Orchard Rd; dishes from $8; Ⓜ Orchard

Superb midrange Cantonese and Shanghainese food. The *xiao long bao* (soup dumplings) here rival those of Din Tai Fung (above) for best in town, while its roast meats (goose and pork) are also excellent and its soups (which change daily) extremely tasty. Perfect way to end a shopping trip.

IZAKAYA NIJUMARU

Map pp74–5   Japanese $$

☎ 6235 4857; 02-10 Cuppage Plaza, 5 Koek Rd; mains from $12; Ⓜ Somerset; ♿

Modelled on the Japanese *izakaya* (drinking restaurant), the emphasis here is as much on boozing as it is eating – and the Japanese businessmen who come here like their booze. Sit down, order some sake and endless rounds of skewered meat, and kiss the evening goodbye. Cuppage Plaza is extremely popular with expatriate Japanese, so don't be surprised to find yourself in a minority of one.

NO RESTAURANT FOR DILETTANTES

The line at Wasabi Tei (Map pp74–5; 05-70 Far East Plaza, 14 Scotts Rd; dishes $5-15; ☺ noon-3pm & 5.30-9.30pm Mon-Fri, noon-4.30pm & 5.30-9.30pm Sat; Ⓜ Orchard) begins at the front door and often extends a dozen or more people down the corridor. Reserved seating is not permitted (it has no telephone), so be prepared to wait.

Once inside, order promptly, and only once. Your hostess – the chef's wife – will politely ignore any post-order amendments. Such are the rules laid out by the chef himself. Remember the Soup Nazi in Seinfeld? Well, here's the Singapore equivalent.

He works silently, fluidly, each movement efficient and solemn. The final gesture in each dish's preparation blends seamlessly into the next, its delivery. Neither asking nor offering acknowledgment, he's already begun work on the next by the time the last has even been tasted.

The diners eat quietly, reverently; most are well aware that, in a different world, the chef would be preparing sushi (and what sushi!) for royalty rather than serving a grateful public at a 20-seat mom-and-pop sushi bar in a mall off Orchard Rd.

Long before your meal is finished you'll understand why so many call this somewhat austere sushi bar Singapore's finest. But when your plate is clean, thank the hostess and pay your bill; post-meal dallying is not encouraged.

LINGZHI VEGETARIAN
Map pp74–5   Chinese $$
☎ 6734 3788; 05-01/02 Liat Towers, 541 Orchard Rd; mains $12-20; Ⓜ Orchard

The service here can be a bit variable (better to go in the evenings, when staff seem to be less grumpy), but the food is consistently excellent, with a creative menu, using ingredients many may not have encountered before. Another outlet at Novena Square (Map pp74–5; ☎ 6538 2992; 03-09, Velocity@Novena Square) is open for lunch only.

FOOD REPUBLIC Map pp74–5   Food Court $
level 4, Wisma Atria, 435 Orchard Rd; ☺ 11am-10.30pm; Ⓜ Orchard; ♿

One of the new breed of more upmarket food courts springing up around Singapore, Food Republic offers traditional hawker classics, as well as Thai, Indian, Japanese and other cuisines. It's survival of the quickest when it comes to grabbing a table at weekends and weekday lunchtimes, but some stalls have private seating areas, where you pay a little more for the food.

LUCKY PRATA Map pp74–5   Indian $
☎ 6235 5223; 01-42 Lucky Plaza, 304 Orchard Rd; dishes from $4; Ⓜ Orchard

From the outside, in seedy Lucky Plaza, it looks completely uninviting, but the difficulty in getting a table at lunchtime is a pretty good indicator of the food quality. Pick what you want from the counter at the front, or order à la carte. The fish-head curry is very popular.

NEWTON CIRCUS HAWKER CENTRE
Map pp74–5   Hawker Centre $
Scotts Rd; Ⓜ Newton

Near Newton MRT, and best visited late in the evening when the atmosphere is liveliest, this is one of Singapore's iconic hawker centres and a longtime favourite with tourists. This popularity has of course led to some un-Singaporean practices by the stall owners, like accosting you as you arrive and trying to direct you to a particular stall, but once you shrug them off it's one of the best hawker centres in the city for eating. Famous stalls include Boon Tat BBQ seafood, Hup Kee oyster omelette (stall 65) and, next door, Singapore's most beloved fish-ball noodles.

EASTERN SINGAPORE

Few visitors spend a great deal of time in Eastern Singapore, but we're hoping that will change, because the area is not only rich in history, culture and architecture, but also is home to some exceptional food, from the Peranakan delights of Katong and Joo Chiat to the superb seafood along East Coast. Hardier souls might brave the nightly sleaze of Geylang, where some great food lurks among the prostitutes and punters.

SIN HUAT EATING HOUSE
Map p80   Seafood $$$
☎ 6744 9755; Lorong 35, Geylang Rd; ☺ 11am-late; Ⓜ Paya Lebar then walk; ♿ fair

The best seafood in Singapore, or a victim of its own fame? Famous food writers have come here in legions and declared

Chef Danny's crab *bee hoon* to be one of the greatest dishes on earth. Inevitably, it's very expensive, usually busy, and service notoriously rude, but as much as you're itching to criticise it, the food is fantastic.

CHARLIE'S CORNER Map pp46–7 Western $$
☎ 6542 0867; 01-08 Changi Village Hawker Centre; dishes $10; Ⓜ Tanah Merah then 🚌 2
Charlie's Corner is something of an institution, run by an old fella who's been a fixture here for years. The endless varieties of beer and the fish and chips are the main draws, attracting people from far afield. The prices are a little high for a hawker-centre stall, but after a few beers you won't notice. Pop in if you're heading to or from the ferry terminal for Pulau Ubin (see p176) or Sungei Rengit (see p183).

CHILLI PADI Map p80 Peranakan $$
☎ 6275 1002; 11 Joo Chiat Pl; dishes from $6; Ⓜ Eunos then 🚌 155
Outstanding Peranakan food in its spiritual home of Joo Chiat – and so popular it's spawned a range of home-cook pastes. Try the sour *assam* fish head and or sambal *sotong* (squid), and don't miss the *kueh pie ti* (flour cups filled with prawn and turnip).

ENG SENG COFFEESHOP
Map p80 Hawker Centre $$
247/249 Joo Chiat Pl; 🕐 5-9pm; Ⓜ Eunos then bus 155
People start queuing up at this hawker centre, well known far and wide for its black-pepper crab, before it opens, so be prepared for a long wait. If you haven't yet acquired the bottomless Singaporean patience for a good meal, then try the BBQ seafood stall here, which is also excellent.

GUAN HOE SOON Map p80 Peranakan $$
☎ 6344 2761; 214 Joo Chiat Rd; mains under $20; 🕐 closed Tue; Ⓜ Eunos
Famously, this is Lee Kuan Yew's favourite Peranakan restaurant, but even boasts like that don't cut much ice with picky Singaporeans if the food doesn't match up. Fortunately, its fame hasn't inspired complacency and the Baba-Nonya food here is top notch.

JIA WEI Map p80 Chinese $$
☎ 6340 5678; 2nd fl, Grand Mercure Roxy Hotel, 50 East Coast Rd; mains from $15; 🚌 10, 14
Top spot in the East Coast area for dim sum, popular with business lunchers. Don't be put off by the remarkable ugliness of the hotel building – the service and the food here is excellent and there are some splendid views over the sea. If you've acquired a taste for durian, try the fried ice-cream for dessert.

JUST GREENS VEGETARIAN
Map p80 Vegetarian $$
☎ 6345 0069; 49/51 Joo Chiat Pl; dishes from $4; 🕐 8am-10pm; Ⓜ Eunos
You know you've found a good veggie place when meat eaters and monks are prominent among its happy customers. The lunchtime buffet is worth checking out, but you can also order à la carte – the dishes are clearly made with love and the service is generally friendly.

MANGO TREE Map p80 Indian $$
☎ 6442 8655; 1000 East Coast Parkway; mains $10-25; Ⓜ Bedok then taxi or 🚌 401 from Ⓜ Bedok, weekends only
An oasis of sophistication among the general Marine Cove brashness in East Coast Park, Mango Tree is a small, stylish beachfront eatery specialising in coastal Indian food, mainly from Goa and Kerala. The outside tables are nice if it's breezy, but the ambience can be spoiled a little by the nearby bars, so it's better to head inside.

NO SIGNBOARD SEAFOOD
Map p80 Seafood $$
☎ 6842 3415; 414 Geylang Rd; dishes from $15; 🕐 noon-2am; Ⓜ Aljunied
Madam Ong Kim Hoi famously started out with an unnamed hawker stall (hence 'No Signboard'), but the popularity of her seafood made her a rich woman, with five restaurants and counting. Principally famous for its white pepper crab, No Signboard also dishes up delightful lobster, abalone and less familiar dishes like bullfrog and deer. Other branches are at East Coast Seafood Centre (Map p80; ☎ 6448 9959), Kallang (Map p80; ☎ 6344 9959; Stadium Blvd), Esplanade (Map pp52–3; ☎ 6336 9959) and VivoCity (Map p100; ☎ 6376 9959).

ROLAND RESTAURANT
Map p80   Seafood $$

☎ 6440 8205; Block 89, 06-750 Marine Parade Central; crabs from $14; 🚍 10, 14; ♿
Located on top of a car park, but don't let that put you off. If the chilli crab and USA duck (see p120) in this giant restaurant are good enough for the prime minister, they're good enough for us, though eating in huge dining rooms is a little impersonal.

WERNER'S OVEN BAKERY & RESTAURANT Map p80   German $$

☎ 6442 3897; 6 Upper East Coast Rd; mains $18; 🚍 10, 14; ♿
It lacks the ostentatiously Teutonic decor of other German restaurants in town – in fact, it's downright plain-looking – but the food here is robust and tasty. Ignore the spaghetti and burgers, and plunge into a rich oxtail stew, a bratwurst, bockwurst or splendid wild garlic sausage (all served with a fine sauerkraut and mashed potatoes), some crispy pork knuckle or German meatloaf, washed down with some Paulaner beer. There are some superb breads in the bakery and the breakfasts are very good value.

328 KATONG LAKSA Map p80   Peranakan $
216 East Coast Rd; laksa $5; 🚍 10, 14
As controversial food subjects go, the source of the original, authentic Katong laksa is one of the most emotive. Several laksa stalls along this stretch have been engaged in Singapore's infamous 'Laksa Wars' for years, bickering over who was first. Decide for yourself. You won't go wrong at any of them, but this is, commercially at least, the most successful.

SERANGOON SALT-BAKED CHICKEN
Map p80   Peranakan $

☎ 6348 2282; 97 East Coast Rd; 🚍 10, 14
In typically Singaporean fashion, Serangoon Salt-Baked Chicken is found nowhere near Serangoon. Also in typically Singaporean fashion, people will travel across town whenever a craving for the wonderfully toothsome takeaway fowl takes hold. Rip it apart with your fingers and devour.

CHIN MEE CHIN CONFECTIONERY
Map p80   Dessert $

☎ 6345 0419; 204 East Coast Rd; dishes from $4; 🚍 10, 14

Kaya (jam made from coconut and egg) toast like grandma used to make. A nostalgia trip for many older Singaporeans, old-style bakeries like Chin Mee Chin are a dying breed, with their mosaic tile floors, wooden chairs and strong steaming coffee. One of the few Singaporean breakfast joints that still makes its own *kaya*, apparently.

EAST COAST LAGOON FOOD VILLAGE
Map p80   Hawker Centre $

East Coast Park Service Rd; ⏰ 10.30am-11pm; Ⓜ Bedok then taxi, 🚍 401 from Ⓜ Bedok, weekends only
Perfect for a cheap outdoor lunch and a beer or two after a stroll, cycle or rollerblade through East Coast Park, this hawker centre gets packed at weekends, but there's usually enough space to bag yourself a table – try to get one closer to the sea to catch any breeze. Well-known for its satay hawkers, BBQ seafood and the *satay bee hoon* stall (just look for the long queue).

HOLLAND ROAD & BUKIT TIMAH

The two long arteries of Holland Rd and Bukit Timah Rd, running east–west from the city centre, border some of Singapore's most affluent residential neighbourhoods, and they also host some fine eating. Infamously overrun with expatriates, Holland Village is one of the few places outside the Quays where locals are outnumbered, but explore further afield and you'll find neighbourhood bar-and-restaurant strips like Greenwood Avenue, and the excellent Rider's Café (opposite).

AU JARDIN Map pp92–3   French $$$

☎ 6466 8812; EHJ Corner House, Singapore Botanic Gardens, Cluny Rd; mains from $70; taxi
Set in a refurbished colonial mansion and surrounded by the extravagant lushness of the Botanic Gardens, there can hardly be a more charming restaurant in Singapore. It comes at a price, but in terms of both food and experience, it's hard to beat. Dress up, forget the bill and have a romantic promenade through the gardens afterwards.

SEBASTIEN'S BISTROT

Map pp92–3   French $$$

☎ 6465 1980; 12 Greenwood Ave; mains from $27;
🚌 66, 67, 174

Part of the Les Amis group (which also runs
Au Jardin), Sebastien's serves classic French
fare (soufflés, terrines, onion soup, escargot, *boeuf bourguignon,* coq au vin etc) in
a sophisticated but relaxed country-style
atmosphere, patrolled by the genial and
portly eponymous manager. If you have
room left, the cheese platter is outstanding and the desserts (profiteroles, rhubarb
crumble, lemon tart) are exceptional.

HALIA

Map pp92–3   Modern Asian $$$

☎ 6476 6711; Singapore Botanic Gardens, 1 Cluny Rd;
mains from $20; taxi; ♿

The outdoor deck at Halia is a magical spot.
Surrounded by the Botanic Gardens' ginger
plants and twittering birds, it's perfect for a
lazy breakfast, a light lunch, or a romantic
dinner. From 3pm to 5pm every day except
Sunday, there's an English Tea, with scones,
jam and sandwiches.

MICHELANGELO'S

Map pp92–3   Italian $$

☎ 6475 9069; 44 Jalan Merah Saga 01-60;
mains from $25; ☽ closed lunch Sat; 🚌 7

Along peaceful, upmarket Jalan Merah
Saga, Michelangelo's is definitely a place
for the hungry. Ignore the cheesy reproduction artwork and dive into the epic portions
of mussels, lamb shanks and pastas. There's
also an impressive wine list.

NORTH BORDER BAR & GRILL

Map pp92–3   American $$

☎ 6777 6618; 2 Rochester Park; mains $25-69;
Ⓜ Buona Vista

Part of the hip Rochester Park scene, the
North Border makes the most of its colonial
bungalow setting, offering southwestern
American food with the occasional modern
twist in a relaxed alfresco setting. The flavours are bold and hearty and the emphasis is firmly on flesh: grain-fed steaks; grilled
prawns, baby back ribs, chops.

ORIGINAL SIN

Map pp92–3   Vegetarian $$

☎ 6475 5605; 43 Jalan Merah Saga 01-62;
mains $20-30; 🚌 7

The food at this friendly and relaxed place
is exceptional and is accompanied by one
of the best wine lists in the city. Try the
stuffed portobello mushrooms ($15), ricotta
cake ($20) or Moroccan eggplant ($22)
washed down with a Portuguese port and
try to forget that it looks like you're in a
fancy Australian suburb. Fantastic.

PS CAFÉ

Map pp92–3   International $$

☎ 6479 3343; 28B Harding Rd; mains from $20;
🚌 7, 123, 174

One of the better results of the Dempsey
Rd restaurant explosion, PS Café is the
sister of the ProjectShop Café (p131) on Orchard
Rd. It's renowned for its desserts, but when
ordering mains it's best to stick to the classics. Some of the fusion offerings, like the
duck *rendang,* don't work and some of the
staff are too cool for school (or a restaurant,
apparently).

GREENWOOD FISH MARKET & BISTRO

Map pp92–3   Seafood $$

☎ 6467 4950; 34 Greenwood Ave; mains from $15;
🚌 170

When your meal is lying on a bed of ice, or
swimming around in a tank by your ankles,
you can be pretty sure it's fresh. Order up
the well-known fish and chips, or try one of
the more sophisticated offerings, or go on
Tuesday, when oysters are $1 each. You can
also buy fish to take home.

MONSTER MASH

Mapp pp92–3   British $$

☎ 8161 0967; www.monstermashcafe.co.uk;
26A Lorong Mambong; entrees from $12; 🚌 7

What can we say about a restaurant that
serves vegetarian haggis? That depends, of
course, on the quality of said haggis, which
in the case of Monster Mash is excellent:
savoury, warm, filled with wholegrain
goodness. Monster Mash also serves a wide
variety of traditional British foods, including puddings, sausage and mash and, of
course, outstanding fish and chips. It also
has a fine selection of wine, beer and ale.

RIDER'S CAFÉ

Map pp92–3   Western $$

☎ 6466 9819; www.riderscafe.sg; 51 Fairways Drive;
mains from $15; taxi

Our pick for the best breakfast spot in
Singapore. Part of the Bukit Timah Saddle
Club, it's set in an old colonial bungalow,
where you can sit on the veranda with a
coffee and pancakes. You're surrounded by
nothing but greenery (not a big building
in sight) and can watch the horses being

groomed, washed or put through their paces. You'd hardly believe you were 10 minutes from the city.

L'ESTAMINET Map pp92–3   European $$
☎ 6465 1911; 4 Greenwood Ave; mains from $15; 🚌 66, 67, 174; 👶

Done up like a rustic Belgian pub, L'Estaminet is heavily stocked with a wide selection of Belgian beers – including those potent monastery brews. It also has a selection of excellent wood-fired pizzas, which makes it worth coming for dinner, as well as drinks. The seating areas out the back and on the left are kid-friendly. Head to Sebastien's Bistrot (p135) for dessert afterwards.

SAMY'S CURRY RESTAURANT
Map pp92–3   Indian $$
☎ 6472 2080; Civil Service Club, Block 25, Dempsey Rd; mains from $5; 🚌 7, 123, 174

How things change. Once this was a charming, raffish old military canteen dishing up outstanding curries and cheap beer. The curries are still outstanding (though beware, they always offer you the most expensive ones first) and Samy's is still a Singapore institution, but now the building is hemmed in by two large restaurants and much of the atmosphere has been lost.

CA*CALIFORNIA Map pp92–3   American $$
☎ 6473 3231; 8B Dempsey Rd; dishes from $6; 🚌 7, 123, 174; 👶

A cool, rough brick interior, wooden bench tables, ceiling fans, leather couches, a man noodling on an acoustic guitar, this family-friendly restaurant (incorporating a Ben & Jerry's ice-cream outlet) has just about got everything right, serving up tasty sandwiches, salads, burgers and

other American fare. The special kids' area makes it ideal for parents, though things can get noisy.

HOLLAND VILLAGE MARKET & FOOD CENTRE Map pp92–3   Hawker Centre $
Lorong Mambong; ⏰ 10am-late; 🚌 7

Probably the only hawker centre in Singapore that has a signboard outside describing the local dishes and the etiquette of ordering – but then, this is Expat Central. Strangely, despite the dramatically lower prices, most foreigners seem to steer clear of the place, which is a mistake, because all the classics are here, from BBQ seafood to Katong laksa to fried *kway teow*.

ISLAND CREAMERY
Map pp92–3   Dessert $
☎ 6468 8859; 01-03 Serene Centre, 10 Jalan Serene; ⏰ 11am-10pm; 🚌 174; 👶

Small and nondescript, with only a handful of tables, Island Creamery serves ice creams and sorbets that are the stuff of legend. Local flavours are a speciality, including *teh tarik* (Indian spiced tea), *cendol* and the refreshing Tiger Beer sorbet. Others, like burnt caramel, black forest, Horlicks and berry are just plain superb. Be prepared to eat standing up.

SOUTHWEST SINGAPORE

Largely industrial and often overlooked, this area hides a few delights, tucked away in small hilltop parks and inside the monumental VivoCity shopping centre, which acts as the gateway to Sentosa. Getting around this area requires a little effort and some extra expense due to the limited public transport, but it's worth it to get away from the crowds.

THE OLIVE Map pp48–9   Italian $$$
☎ 6479 2989; Labrador Villa Rd, Labrador Park; Ⓜ HarbourFront then 🚌 408 Sat & Sun, or taxi other days

Tucked away on a hill inside thickly forested Labrador Park with the city lights peeping through the trees, the Olive cries out for a romantic, candlelit occasion. The food, like the location, is excellent – it's worth a bit of extra effort to get up here for a peaceful evening away from the city bustle.

FOOD ON THE FLY

If you've spent the day at the Jurong Bid Park, make a night of it and head up the hill to Hilltop Japanese Restaurant (Map pp46–7; ☎ 6266 3522; 2 Jurong Hill; dishes from $10; Ⓜ Jurong East then 🚌 194 or 251), an unusual restaurant. Boasting a perhaps unique Japanese-Indonesian menu, its location inside the observation tower is pretty memorable too. Climb the tower after dinner for a great view over the industrial sprawl.

BROTZEIT GERMAN BIER BAR

Map pp48–9   German $$

☎ 6272 8815; 01-149 VivoCity, 1 Harbourfront Walk; dishes from $15; M HarbourFront

Sausages, pork knuckle and German beers galore, with soothing views over Sentosa and the harbour. The sausages are superb (the knoblauchwurst was a favourite, and not just for the name) and the draft Paulaners are dangerously easy on the palate. Service swings wildly from outstanding to hopeless, depending on your luck.

FABER HILL BISTRO

Map pp48–9   Western $$

☎ 6377 9688; 101 Mt Faber Rd; mains from $12; ◔ 9am-1am Sun-Tue, 9am-2am Wed-Sat; M HarbourFront then 🚌 409 Sat & Sun, or cable car

Boasting magnificent views over the sea and the CBD, you'd expect prices to be sky-high, but the steaks, pastas and other bistro staples are fairly cheap, though not outstanding. Get here just before sunset and try to bag a table at the edge, then head to Altivo, a few metres up the hill, for an even more spectacular drink after dinner.

SENTOSA ISLAND

Once the management realised it wasn't against the law to provide something other than junk food at a tourist attraction (a lesson many tourist attractions could learn), eating on Sentosa underwent something of a renaissance. Combining decent beachfront eateries, fine hotel restaurants and some top-notch fine-dining institutions, Sentosa has planted its flag proudly on the city's culinary map. Some of the places double as bars in the evenings, catering mainly to the bikini-clad club crowd (see p148).

BRAISE Map p100   French $$$

☎ 6271 1929; Palawan Beach; mains from $38; M HarbourFront then monorail or shuttle bus

Braise typifies the new Sentosa, serving up refined nouvelle cuisine in a minimalist interior (sorry, *space*), with white walls, high vaulted ceilings, bare brick and full-length glass maximising the beachfront views. Seafood monopolises the starter menu, while meat dominates the mains. Don't come in your beach gear.

FARM FRESH

Set in the wonderfully peaceful Bollywood Veggies organic farm, Poison Ivy Bistro (Map pp46–7; ☎ 6898 5001; 100 Neo Tiew Cres; dishes from $4; ◔ 9am-6pm Wed-Sun; taxi) is the perfect place to stop after a visit to the other farms in the area, or Sungei Buloh Wetland Reserve (p88). The food, using veggies from the farm, is nothing to write home about, but the rural location makes it special.

IL LIDO Map p100   Italian $$$

☎ 6866 1977; www.il-lido.com; Sentosa Golf Club, Bukit Manis Rd; set menus $90-180, mains from $40; M HarbourFront then monorail or shuttle bus

With stunning views over the Strait of Singapore and the lights of Indonesia beyond, Il Lido does the vista justice with its food. Choose from modern, classic and vegetarian menus or, if you have a spare $3000 lying around, you can book the yacht for an evening of private dining.

SKY DINING Map p100   European $$$

☎ 6377 9633; www.mountfaber.com.sg; meals $98-168; ◔ 6.30-8.30pm Tue-Sun; M HarbourFront

We can't quite decide if this is inspired, or just plain silly, but the idea of eating a meal travelling along in a cable car 70m up in the air holds an undeniable appeal. The novelty might wear thin by dessert, but gliding from Mount Faber to Sentosa taking in the sunset cityscape is a stunning way to spend a romantic evening – though the cars are too small to contemplate anything indecent. Book at least two days in advance.

THE CLIFF Map p100   Seafood $$$

☎ 6275 0331; www.thesentosa.com; 2 Bukit Manis Rd ◔ 6.30-11pm (last order 9.30pm); M HarbourFront then monorail or shuttle bus; & good

Sitting on a clifftop, The Cliff has become a byword for 'special occasion', partly because of its location, partly its great service, but mostly because of its seafood. Take the pain out of it and order the set menu, then sit back as plate after plate of marine masterpiece files past you. Book one of the junior suites, and the evening will be complete.

COASTES Map p100 — International $$

☎ 6338 8832; Siloso Beach; snacks & mains $7-25;
Ⓜ HarbourFront then monorail or shuttle bus; ♿

The pick of Sentosa's beach eats, Coastes' atmosphere is relaxed and friendly. While it draws blatant inspiration from Ibiza, it's also the kind of place you can bring the kids without being made to feel like you're ruining the vibe. Pick a wooden bench, or recline on a lounger and order your wood-fired pizza while you sun-fire your body.

SAMUNDAR Map p100 — Indian $$

☎ 6276 8891; 85 Palawan Beach Walk; mains from $12; Ⓜ HarbourFront then monorail or shuttle bus

It boasts one of those vast menus that can drive you mad with indecision, but stick with the tandoor menu and you won't go wrong (unless you're vegetarian – but even then you have 15 choices). Order three days in advance for the special *sikandari raan* (marinated leg of lamb) – a snip at $84.

DRINKING & NIGHTLIFE

top picks

Step aside, New York City. Once-boring Singapore has stolen your 'city-that-never-sleeps' mantle. From small, poorly lit watering holes where characters straight out of Tom Waits ballads might meet to exchange tales over whiskey sours to thumping all-night clubs where fashionistas gather to dance until the birds are twittering, this city has something to offer people of every taste and inclination seven nights a week.

WHERE TO DRINK

In Singapore, what's hot and what's not changes as regularly as the seasons (if Singapore actually had seasons) meaning that this month's happening club may well be next month's old news. That and the sharply rising price-per-square-metre of commercial space mean that a club can open, gain and lose hipster status, and close down in a span of time slightly less than the career of your average boy-band. Neighbourhoods, for the most part, tend to retain their character for a bit longer, and for this reason we've gone ahead and expanded our listings to include a bit more verbiage about the streets and alleys surrounding the bars and clubs, which might still be hot (or even there) by the time this book goes to press.

PRACTICALITIES

How Much?

Barring Brunei, Singapore is probably the most expensive place in Southeast Asia for drinking and nightlife. A combination of liberal licensing laws and free-market economics breeds high prices, especially in some of the city's trendier joints, where an evening's libations can set even a casual drinker back a hefty sum. Those who are looking for spirits on the cheap, and don't mind plastic tables and fluorescent lights, can hang out at hawker centres and coffeeshops, drinking $6 bottles of Tiger to their hearts' content. A beer at most city bars can set you back between $10 and $15, ditto for mixed drinks, and many of the more upscale clubs have entrance fees of $20 or more (though these will usually include a drink).

If you're looking to save on libations, hit the bars early to take advantage of the happy hours; these typically stretch from around 5pm to 8pm, sometimes later. At these times you'll generally get two of most drinks for the price of one and cheaper 'housepours', which

are the bar's selections of spirits or wine. On Wednesday or Thursday night, some bars offer cheaper (sometimes free) drinks to women, presumably on the assumption that drunk women attract paying men. Of course, if you're really tight, you can always drink $5 beers in your hostel.

Opening Hours

While the government maintains tight controls on many aspects of life in the Lion City, Singapore's licensing laws are positively laissez-faire, and many bars and clubs stay open until the early hours, some right through to breakfast. Generally speaking, expect most clubs to open around 5pm, and stay open until 1am or 2am from Sunday to Thursday, and until about 3am on Friday and Saturday. We've made note of bars and clubs that keep hours vastly different from this.

COLONIAL DISTRICT & THE QUAYS

In a metropolis that practically straddles the equator, it only makes sense that the trendiest bar and club scene is found along the river; after all, this is where the coolest breezes tend to be found. Though the area is a bit too popular with tourists (say some in the know), and too yuppified (claim others), the three Quays (Clark, Boat and Robertson) and further west along the Singapore River is where you'll find some of the most up-and-coming (and priciest) clubs and watering holes in Singapore.

BAR OPIUME Map pp52–3   Bar

☎ 6339 1720; www.indochine-group.com; 1 Empress Pl; ⏱ 5pm-2am Mon-Thu, 5pm-3am Fri & Sat, 5pm-1am Sun; Ⓜ Raffles Place

Very posey, Bar Opiume is next to its sibling restaurant Indochine Waterfront (p124), facing Boat Quay. The expensive, slightly mismatched decor features a huge chan-

SCOOPING THE CITY WITH DAWN Dawn Mok

Besides the weather, change is the only other constant in Singapore. Us locals are always trying to find ways to beat the heat, keep up with the trends and be the first to tell our friends, 'Sorry I didn't reply to your SMS, I was at (fill in spunky name of spanking new place) – so fun! You haven't been? Must go lah!'

To accomplish all this, you need to head for the trees, the rooftops or the river. Sure, the city's concrete gems will continue to razzle and dazzle the masses but more discerning denizens will prefer to snuggle up to Mother Nature and admire her still-ample offerings while enjoying the buzz and excitement of city life.

The green, black and white Wessex Village Square (5B Portsdown Rd) is a tranquil creative suburb by day and an inviting bohemian hangout by night. Get a taste of Tuscany at family-run Italian restaurant, Pietrasanta, before moseying over to Klee, a retro-rustic saloon-style bar that serves an impressive array of freshly muddled cocktails (made with the best stuff on earth: real fruit juice and premium alcohol!).

If you dig the colonial vibe but prefer to posh things up a notch, head to 'lifestyle hub' Rochester Park. Here, housed in beautiful pre-war bungalows are top-class restaurants as well as a gourmet bakery, a modern gastrobar and a Russian caviar and vodka bar. Not far from here is yet another hub – HortPark (33 Hyderabad Rd), also touted as 'Southeast Asia's first gardening and lifestyle hub'. It's a surprising yet fitting location for Kha, a modern Thai restaurant with a swanky chill-out deck overlooking splendid trees and a water feature.

For more great views and al-fresco fun, go on and hit the roof. There's the ever-popular Loof (p142) at Odeon Towers and newish kid on the block Helipad (with 6000 sq feet of party space) over at the Central. If you prefer more intimate views and lounging options, check out The Screening Room's rooftop terrace with Chinatown as its backdrop. Or get closer to the stars via Moon Ladder Bar and Bistro nestled atop Labrador Nature Reserve.

The Singapore River – heart of the city – now pulsates to different rhythms. You can opt for the pump and grind of Clarke Quay or follow the river towards Robertson Quay to find authentic Japanese bars and eateries. At the Gallery Hotel (1 Nanson Rd), settle yourself under the trees with a chilled brew at eM by the River. For a giggle, head upstairs to Bar 84 and let the resident bartender-magician wow you with a selection of 300 whiskeys and illusionary tricks. On the other side of the river, between Clarke Quay and Boat Quay, you'll find the unpretentious Home Club, and a thriving alternative music scene. Make nice and attempt to chat with the ones who smile back at you. You can always read up about the latest cool hangout in Singapore, but if you want the real deal – talk to the locals.

Co-creator of Singapore CityScoops (www.cityscoops.com), the (semi) annual hip hiker's guide to hot spots and hidden finds throughout the city, Dawn Mok is the woman to ask about where to draw the up-and-coming dots on Singapore's cool map.

---

delier and large standing Buddhas. Not surprisingly for a location like this, the drink prices might have you sipping slowly, but the quiet spot next to the river is priceless. Check out the website for links to other Indochine Group–managed properties, all of which are worth a visit for the ambience alone.

BREWERKZ Map pp52–3   Bar
☎ 6438 7438; 01-05 Riverside Point Centre, 30 Merchant Rd; ☺ noon-midnight Sun-Thu, noon-1am Fri & Sat; Ⓜ Clarke Quay
One of Singapore's gems, this sprawling microbrewery and restaurant offers a variety of superb beers brewed on site and varying in strength from 4.5% to 6%. The India Pale Ale is apparently the most popular, but the dark beer and the Golden Ale are also excellent. Those with adventurous palates will want to try the fruit beers, brewed from whatever happens to be in season at the time.

ESKI Map pp52–3   Bar
☎ 6327 3662; 46 Circular Rd; ☺ 2pm-1am Sun-Thu, 2pm-3am Fri & Sat; Ⓜ Clarke Quay
The name is derived from the word 'Eskimo', and with good reason; Eski is Singapore's first sub-zero bar, complete with a solid ice bar for downing frozen shots of – what else – vodka. Singapore visitors foolish enough to have forgotten to pack ski parkas needn't worry, though; loaner winter clothing is available, and a good thing too, as temperatures here plummet to a testicle-shrinking -10°C.

HARRY'S Map pp52–3   Bar
☎ 6538 3029; www.harrys-bar.com.sg; 28 Boat Quay; ☺ 11am-1am Sun-Thu, 11am-2am Fri & Sat; Ⓜ Raffles Place
Loaded with history for those interested in doomed finance, Harry's is the one-time hangout of Barings' bank-breaker Nick Leeson. It's still a city-slickers' favourite,

with the suits flocking here for happy hour until 8pm. Later it turns into a good jazz venue (9.30pm to 12.30am from Tuesday to Saturday). The upstairs lounge is quieter and a comfortable place to contemplate busting a bank. It has a free pool table.

HIDEOUT Map pp52–3 — Bar
☎ 6536 9445; 31B Circular Rd; ☺ 7pm–midnight Wed & Thu, 7pm–3am Fri & Sat; Ⓜ Clarke Quay or Raffles Place
The walk up three floors might put you off, but this tiny, ultratrendy place is worth a little legwork, with its deep red walls, hotch-potch furniture and indie and hip-hop playlist. A little cliquey, so dress your coolest.

LOOF Map pp52–3 — Bar
☎ 6338 8035; 331 North Bridge Rd; ☺ 5.30pm–2am; Ⓜ City Hall
What's the name all about? We'll give you a clue – Loof is a rooftop bar, and they don't serve 'flied lice'. The view is superb and the space itself is ultracool, with secluded alcoves perfect for your more intimate moments. Happy hour lasts from 5.30pm to 8.30pm each weekday evening.

RAFFLES HOTEL Map pp52–3 — Bar
1 Beach Rd; Ⓜ City Hall
Yup, it's a cliché, but still, few visit Singapore without at least stopping off for drinks at one of the several bars in the famous Raffles Hotel. Bar & Billiard Room features live jazz and has a nice veranda for chilling out, Raj style. It was underneath this bar that a guest shot a tiger in his pyjamas in 1904 (how the tiger got in his pyjamas, he never did find out). The courtyard is where you'll find the Gazebo Bar, which also boasts live music in the evening. The most popular bar with tourists is the plantation-style Long Bar on the Arcade's second level, where you can throw peanut shells on the floor and enjoy a Singapore Sling for $16 (or $25 with a souvenir glass).

CHIHULY LOUNGE Map pp52–3 — Bar/Club
☎ 6434 5288; 3rd fl, Ritz-Carlton Millenia Singapore, 7 Raffles Ave; ☺ 8am–1am; Ⓜ City Hall
With its distinctive blue arched roof and amazing Daly Chihuly glass sculpture on the wall (his work is also on display at the Singapore Art Museum, p56), this refined hotel lounge deserves a bit of sartorial effort

and is worth a visit for an early-evening loosener or a late-night wind-down cocktail.

CRAZY ELEPHANT Map pp52–3 — Bar/Live Music
☎ 6537 7859; www.crazyelephant.com; 3E River Valley Rd, 01-03/04 Clarke Quay; ☺ 5pm–1am Sun-Thu, 3pm–2am Fri & Sat; Ⓜ Clarke Quay
The more things change, the more they stay the same at this Clarke Quay stalwart, which has remained consistently cool since it first opened a dozen years back (in the days pre-dating the area's trendy reincarnation). The walls are still covered with graffiti, the music is still loud, and heavy on the blues and rock, and the stage is still made of wood. For this reason and others, Crazy Elephant is popular with tourists and locals alike. If the live music gets too loud, outdoor seating is available for pints in relative peace.

ATTICA Map pp52–3 — Club
☎ 6333 9973; www.attica.com.sg; 3A River Valley Rd, 01-03 Clarke Quay; ☺ 5pm–3am Mon-Thu, 11pm–late Fri & Sat; Ⓜ Clarke Quay
One of the swankest clubs in town, Attica is where the bold and beautiful meet to dazzle and be dazzled. When it gets too hot inside, cool down in the chic courtyard and ogle the eye-candy. There's usually a line to get in, always a sign of pedigree in Singapore's club world.

BUTTER FACTORY Map pp52–3 — Club
☎ 6333 8243; www.thebutterfactory.com; 01-03 Robertson Quay 48; Ⓜ Clarke Quay
Where whimsy meets chic, the Butter Factory's interior is covered with cartoon graphics provided by ultra-hip Phunk Studio of Singapore; you'll feel like you've stepped into the pages of an underground comic book (the kind your parents used to confiscate). The front room features a bar and comfy leather couches, both milk-white, and the darker back room has a dance floor and bar of its own. The weekend cover charge (cheaper for ladies) includes a free drink.

MINISTRY OF SOUND
Map pp52–3 — Club/Live Music
☎ 6333 9368; www.ministryofsound.com.sg; 01-07 Block C Clarke Quay; men $15-25, women free-$20; ☺ 9pm–3am Wed-Sat; Ⓜ Clarke Quay; ♿ fair
Seven rooms, superb digital sound and

light, a chequered dance-floor and a 20ft water curtain, not to mention hordes of the nation's youth. Those all-conquering Brits have challenged the supremacy of Zouk (p146) and done a pretty good job of it, though the older beautiful crowd still prefer the latter. Women get in free on Wednesdays.

PAULANER BRAUHAUS
Map pp52–3   German Beer House

☎ 6883 2572; 01-01 Times Square@Millenia Walk, 9 Raffles Blvd; ⏰ 11.30am-1am Sun-Thu, 11.30am-2am Fri & Sat; Ⓜ City Hall

A three-storey wood-and-brass German microbrewery bar and restaurant serving up its excellent signature Munich lager and Munich dark brews. There are also special seasonal brews like Salvator Beer (March), Mailbock Beer (May) and Oktoberfest Beer (October). Beers are served in either 300mL, 500mL or 1L mugs! Tours of the brewery are available for $40, but you have to book well in advance.

MOLLY MALONE'S Map pp52–3   Irish Pub

☎ 6536 2029; 53-56 Circular Rd; Ⓜ Raffles Place

Just behind Boat Quay on Circular Rd, Molly Malone's has moved from its old location to larger premises just down the road. Well-travelled drinkers will have seen the mock-Irish interior and the genuine Irish stew and fish-and-chip menu a hundred times before, but that doesn't make it any less cosy or welcoming.

PENNY BLACK Map pp52–3   Pub

☎ 6538 2300; 26/27 Boat Quay; ⏰ 11am-1am Mon-Thu, 11am-2am Fri & Sat, 11am-midnight Sun; Ⓜ Raffles Place

Fitted out like a 'Victorian' London pub (without the tuberculosis and dodgy gin), the Penny Black's interior was actually built in London and shipped to Singapore, so it has some claim to authenticity. Specialises in hard-to-find English ales for the swathes of expat Brits that work in the area. The upstairs bar is particularly inviting.

RED LANTERN BEER GARDEN
Map pp52–3   Bar/Live Music

50 Collyer Quay; Ⓜ Raffles Place

For a taste of old Singapore, head to the seedy, bayside Red Lantern Beer Garden where bands often play, cheap meals are served, and you can get a reasonably

priced beer. It can get pretty rowdy late at night. There are so many bars, most with outdoor tables, that you can just wander along until one takes your fancy.

CHINATOWN & THE CBD

When the sun goes down, the blocks just south of Chinatown and the central business district (CBD) emerge like a butterfly from their daytime slumber, transforming into a centre of beautiful debauchery. Just south of Maxwell Rd, the area's main artery, South Bride Rd, forks off into Neil Rd and Tanjong Pagar Rd, an area referred to by those in the know as 'the Pink Triangle'; if Singapore has a 'gay district', this would be it.

BAR SÁ VANH Map pp62–3   Bar

☎ 6323 0145; 49 Club St; ⏰ 5pm-1am Mon-Thu, 5pm-3am Fri & Sat; Ⓜ Chinatown

If you're after more than just a drink, this is one of those 'do you remember…' places. The main attraction is a large waterfall cascading into a tranquil *koi* (ornamental carp) pond, surrounded by large Buddha statues, wafting incense and teak furniture. The music is mostly alternative, fusion style, which does not drown out conversation. Drinks are expensive, but it's worth having at least one.

BARRIO CHINO Map pp62–3   Bar

☎ 6324 3245; 60 Club St; ⏰ 4pm-midnight Mon-Thu, 4pm-2am Fri, 4pm-1am Sat; Ⓜ Chinatown

This cosy Spanish bar boasts great frozen margaritas, a large wine selection and some tasty tapas. Either sit out on the five-foot-way or enjoy the intimate set-up inside. Good Latin music sets the mood.

COWS & COOLIES KARAOKE PUB
Map pp62–3   Bar

☎ 6221 1239; 30 Mosque St; Ⓜ Chinatown

Smoke-filled (despite a city-wide ban on smoking) and often loud, C&C is a throwback to the good old days when a neighbourhood bar was a place you came to drown your sorrows in loud music, cigarettes and booze. Though it doesn't bill itself as a gay bar per se, the bar is very popular with both the gay and lesbian crowd.

POST BAR Map pp62–3   Bar
☎ 6733 8388; Fullerton Hotel; ⏰ noon–2am; Ⓜ Raffles Place

Named the Post Bar, as it retains the original ceiling of the General Post Office, this classy lounge bar within the glorious Fullerton Hotel lobby is way upmarket, without being snobbish. It also serves the best mojitos this side of Havana.

THE ROOFTOP Map pp62–3   Bar
6536 0456; rooftopbar@lycos.com; Level 4, 114C Neil Rd; Ⓜ Outram Park

This diminutive and lovely rooftop bar in the pink triangle district offers a secluded respite from the thumping music and crowds of the surrounding area. The bar itself, which barely seats six, serves fine, reasonably priced wine, beer and cocktails. And the outdoor patio, with just enough room for an additional dozen, offers panoramic views of Singapore's night sky.

TANTRIC BAR Map pp62–3   Bar
☎ 6423 9232; 78 Neil Rd; ⏰ 8pm–3am; Ⓜ Outram Park

A peaceful spot to relax among the fountains, palm trees and Arabian chic in the courtyard, this gay bar is a pleasant antidote, or warm up, to the queues and pounding music elsewhere.

VINCENT'S Map pp62–3   Bar
☎ 6736 1360; 15 Duxton Rd; ⏰ closes 2am; Ⓜ Outram Park

Singapore's first gay bar spent years in Lucky Plaza on Orchard Rd before moving to bigger, better premises to take advantage of what was at the time the developing gay ghetto around Tanjong Pagar. It's a popular starting-out point and offers a free gay guide to Singapore.

XPOSÉ Map pp62–3   Bar
☎ 6323 2466; 208 South Bridge Rd; ⏰ 6pm–midnight Mon–Wed, 6pm–1am Thu & Sun, 6pm–2am Fri & Sat; Ⓜ Chinatown

Another more relaxed gay bar, which also serves up some excellent Thai and Vietnamese food, though karaoke-phobes might want to stay away until after midnight, when the mic is turned off.

PLAY Map pp62–3   Club
☎ 6227 7400; www.playclub.com.sg; 21 Tanjong Pagar Rd; Ⓜ Tanjong Pagar

Flashing lights, loud music and boys galore all adds up to Play, one of the most popular and happening gay (though all are very welcome) bars in the city. Play features loud techno music, a big dance floor, and probably the most over-the-top (we mean this in the best way possible) 'F*** the world, it's time to play!' attitude you'll find anywhere in Southeast Asia. International DJs, mixed drinks, and more fellas than you can shake a stick at.

LITTLE INDIA & KAMPONG GLAM

A backpacker hub, Little India has its share of cheapish pubs and bars catering to the 'Singapore on a shoestring' crowd. Some of the hostels in Little India double as pubs, so if you're in need of a quick pint, check out the Sleeping options on p166 for leads.

PRINCE OF WALES Map p68   Bar
☎ 6299 0310; 101 Dunlop St; ⏰ 9am–1am; Ⓜ Little India

A rough at the edges, knockabout Australian pub, which doubles as a backpacker hostel (p168). With friendly, laconic bar staff, live music on most nights and a small beer garden, it's one of the few bars in Little India – and a little surreal on Sunday nights, when the streets are packed with migrant workers from the subcontinent enjoying their off-day.

BLUJAZ CAFÉ Map p68   Bar/Live Music
☎ 6292 3800; 11 Bali Lane; ⏰ noon–midnight Mon–Thu, noon–2am Fri, 4pm–2am Sat; Ⓜ Bugis; ♿ outside

Decorated in a decidedly eccentric fashion and located next to an artists' studio that spills its works into the laneway, this is as close as you'll get to a bohemian hangout in Singapore, though it attracts a diverse crowd. There's live jazz downstairs on Mondays, Fridays and Saturdays, and a funky lounge upstairs.

NIGHT & DAY Map p68 — Bar/Live Music
☎ 6884 5523; www.nightandday.sg; 139 Selegie Rd; Ⓜ Little India or Farrer Park
Art-school cool meets techno-groove chic at this three-storey bar, gallery and happening space located in a 1950s art deco building, smack in the centre of Singapore's burgeoning art-student district. The space has a 2nd-floor bar featuring drinks and live music (from grunge and heavy metal to more esoteric stuff), and the 3rd floor has an art-space where local students show their latest work. The second storey is taken up by the architecture studio of co-owner Randy Chan.

CAFE DOMUS Map p68 — Bar/Lounge
☎ 6392 5652; 124 Owen Rd; Ⓜ Farrer Park
This fantastic chill-out space is located on a seldom-traversed (by tourists) street just around the corner from Little India's 'curry belt'. Bare wooden ceilings, peony-painted walls and an opulent Tiffany chandelier are just some of the quirkier decorations of this café-bar frequented by artists, architects and other young professionals in creative industries. The backyard bamboo garden (complete with a narrow platform perch, accessible by spiral staircase) is a particularly intimate touch.

ORCHARD ROAD

By day it's Singapore's Grand Canyon of Shopping. But after the sun sets, Orchard Rd becomes Entertainment Avenue, replete with movie theatres, high-class hotel bars, and trendy pubs and clubs. The area is also where you'll find Orchard Towers – the infamous 'four floors of whores' – a multistorey commercial property, the first four floors of which are honeycombed with bars, clubs and massage parlours, all catering to men with more on their mind than mere libation.

3-MONKEYS Map pp74–5 — Bar/Nightclub
☎ 6735 3707; Orchard Tower 1, Backside; ⏱ 11am-5am; Ⓜ Orchard
Tiger on Tap, cocktails, and yes, Kumar too. 3-Monkeys is the playground of Singapore's

famed transvestite comic, whose riotous review is featured from 11pm until 1am every Friday and Saturday evening. Decor is an eclectic mix of Americana and Asian, and if you get bored waiting for Kumar, you can always stroll upstairs through the famed 'four floors of whores', where plenty of other (though probably not as humorous) transvestites loiter.

ALLEY BAR Map pp74–5 — Bar
☎ 6732 6966; 2 Emerald Hill, 180 Orchard Rd; ⏱ 5pm-2am Sun-Thu, 5pm-3am Fri & Sat; Ⓜ Somerset
Emerald Hill Rd has a collection of bars in the renovated terraces just up from Orchard Rd that formerly housed many Peranakan families. The focal point of Alley Bar has to be the large gilded mirror hanging at the far end of the room, while the decor reflects the name of the bar, which has been done up to look like a street, with fake shopfronts, parking meters and street signs.

BRAUHAUS RESTAURANT & PUB
Map pp74–5 — German Beer House
☎ 6250 3116; brauhaus@signet.com; Basement, United Square, 101 Thompson Rd; Ⓜ Novena
The brick walls and dark wooden furniture in this basement pub, a hidden favourite for over 20 years, give it a distinctly Teutonic vibe. But what really makes the Brauhaus a slice of basement Bavaria is the vast selection of beers from all over the world, 150-plus including obscure names like Old Peculiar Stout, König Ludwig and Strong Suffolk Vintage Ale. Easily the most well-stocked beer house in the area, Brauhaus also boasts live bands from Monday to Saturday from about 8pm until 2am. It also boasts an outdoor pool table and a good menu featuring continental fare.

DOWNUNDER BAR Map pp74–5 — Pub/Bar
☎ 6238 8492; downunder_connection@yahoo.com.sg; 400 Orchard Rd, 04-24 Orchard Towers; Ⓜ Orchard
Located inside the famous (or infamous) Orchard Towers, Downunder is probably one of the few pubs in the building that isn't specifically a cheap clip joint for picking up. This Australian pub has beer on tap, a pool table and a dart board, making it a nice oasis from the building's usual climate and clientele.

DUBLINERS Map pp74–5   Irish Pub
☎ 6735 2220; 165 Penang Rd; 🕑 11.30am-1am Sun-Thu, 11.30am-2am Fri & Sat; Ⓜ Somerset
In a quieter section of Orchard Rd, Dubliners is one of the friendliest Irish pubs in Singapore, with the usual range of Irish beers at reasonable prices and an outstanding menu (go in hungry; the portions are huge). The front veranda is a great spot for balmy nights and the service is excellent.

ICE COLD BEER Map pp74–5   Bar
☎ 6735 9929; 9 Emerald Hill Rd; 🕑 6pm-2am Sun-Thu, 6pm-3am Fri & Sat; Ⓜ Somerset
A raucous, boozy establishment at the top of the Emerald Hill bar strip, offering a huge range of chilled beers from around the world to a rock soundtrack. Like most bars in Emerald Hill, it's housed in a 1900s Peranakan shophouse, though the frontage is pretty much all that remains.

MUDDY MURPHY'S
Map pp74–5   Bar/Irish Pub
☎ 6735 0400; Orchard Hotel Shopping Arcade, 442 Orchard Rd; 🕑 11.30am-1am Mon-Thu, 11.30am-2am Fri & Sat, 11.30am-midnight Sun; Ⓜ Orchard
Located below street level in a courtyard, Muddy's is more appealing than the standard fake-Irish pub. The quieter Ballymoon top bar is narrow and smoky, and only opens in the evening.

QUE PASA Map pp74–5   Bar
☎ 6235 6626; 7 Emerald Hill Rd; 🕑 6pm-2am Sun-Thu, 6pm-3am Fri & Sat; Ⓜ Somerset
An extremely pleasant wine and tapas bar with a convincingly run-down interior reminiscent of a real Spanish bar – except for the icy air-con. The wine list is impressive and, in keeping with the rest of Emerald Hill, extravagantly expensive. Tapas are uniformly excellent – try the mushrooms and the ubiquitous spicy sausage.

THUMPER BAR Map pp74–5   Bar/Live Music
☎ 6737 3845; reservations@thumper.com.sg; 22 Scotts Rd; Ⓜ Orchard
Taking up a fair chunk of the 1st floor of the beautiful and *très* elegant Goodwood hotel, Thumper is as high-class a joint as you'd expect – collared shirts, no shorts, and for god's sake, if you're wearing Crocs, don't even think about it. Thumper offers live bands five nights a week (Wednesday is quiet night, and Sundays it's closed), and has a lovely dance-floor attracting a hip twenty-something crowd.

ZOUK Map pp74–5   Club
☎ 6738 2988; www.zoukclub.com; 17 Jiak Kim St; Ⓜ Somerset
Considered by many to be one of Singapore's best clubs (it was actually voted best club in Asia not long ago), the name Zouk stands for Ziggurats of Unbelievable Kolours. While it doesn't make much sense, we have to admit that it has a cool ring. The club, built inside a restored waterfront warehouse, pulses nightly, its dance-floors filled with Singapore's beautiful people gyrating to house and techno beats. Zouk plays host to some of Asia's hottest and trendiest DJs and musicians; even its website is cinematic (and noisy). If it's party people you're looking for, look no further.

HOLLAND ROAD & BUKIT TIMAH

Chic, serene and mostly undiscovered by the tourist crowd, Holland Village is an eating and entertainment zone tucked away inside a quiet residential neighbourhood a couple of miles west of the crowded concrete valleys of Orchard Rd. Lorong Mambong (the main chill-out street) is closed to traffic evenings and weekends, making it a good place to stroll while tipsy. There are a number of restaurants and bars in the area, as well as a hawker centre that stays open late for the party crowd.

DEMPSEY'S HUT Map pp92–3   Bar
☎ 6473 9609; 130E Minden Rd; 🚌 7 from Orchard Blvd
This jovial open-air bar is deep in the thickly forested former British army barracks around Dempsey Rd. Like its nearby wine-bar rivals, it's worth a visit as one of the few places near the city where you can enjoy a spot of unbridled nature – at a reasonable price too. The tables are laid out under the trees (bring repellent) and the beer costs a meagre $5 per mug, or $20 a jug. There's also a decent menu.

WINE NETWORK Map pp92–3 Bar

☎ 6479 2280; Block 13, Dempsey Rd;
🕑 11am-midnight Sun-Thu, 11am-1am Fri & Sat;
🚍 7 from Orchard Blvd

Tucked away in the Dempsey Rd furniture and antiques ghetto, this is a real find. A small, intimate bar with rough wooden floors and crumbling brick walls lined with wine bottles, where the wine is as cheap or expensive as you like (bottles start at $18, or it's $7 a glass). Sit inside, or enjoy the sight of the semiderelict colonial barracks and the sound of twittering birds on the deck. Pizzas, German sausages and cheese platters fight off hunger. Get off the bus at stop B03 on Holland Rd; from here it's a 10-minute walk.

WALA WALA CAFE BAR

Map pp92–3 Bar/Live Music

☎ 6462 4288; www.imaginings.com.sg;
31 Lorong Mambong; taxi

This two-storey restaurant and bar is increasingly popular with the smart set in Holland Village, not least because it features an excellent bar on the 1st floor (complete with highway billboard–sized flat screens broadcasting live sporting events from around the world) and a smoking-hot rock band on the second.

2AM: DESSERT BAR

Map pp92–3 Wine/Dessert Bar

☎ 9173 4340; 21a Lorong Mambong; taxi

Hip, sweet and chic are the three words that best describe this concept bar and restaurant that pairs the finest wines with some of the best desserts you'll find in Singapore. The menu itself is fantastic, offering suggestions for what combinations work best, be it tiramisu and Shiraz or caramel mousse and Pinot Noir. Comfort-

able couches ensure you'll want to hang around for seconds.

EASTERN SINGAPORE

The designation 'Eastern Singapore' covers a huge swath of real estate, from Geylang and Joo Chiat, to East Coast Park, to Changi Village, which has a few interesting watering holes, on the far eastern end of the island. (Geylang, though chock-full of bars, has few we can readily recommend in a family guidebook. See our Geylang section, p77, for more on this.)

CALIFORNIA JAM Map pp46–7 Bar

☎ 6542 2139; Block 1 Changi Village Rd; 🚍 2

A cool little rock 'n' roll bar in Changi Village. Jimi Hendrix posters, beer on tap and the occasional transvestite hooker gives this place a 'Walk on the Wild Side' vibe. California Jam is part of the strip of bars on Changi Village Rd that's somewhat popular with locals looking to escape the trendy crush of central Singapore.

ARTOHOLIC Map p80 Bar/Club

☎ 6348 7793; www.artoholic.sg;
422 Joo Chiat Rd; taxi

It would have been all too easy for the proprietors of Artoholic to have opened up in an already-happening neighbourhood, but they chose instead the more challenging route of the pioneer. As well as being a showcase for local artists, this cool happening space on Joo Chiat Rd also hosts small-music performances, open-mic nights, and even the occasional comedy performance starring our friend, Singapore-based comic Jonathan Atherton (p154). Beer, wine and cocktails flow freely (but not for free) all night.

ST JAMES POWER STATION

The new poster child of Singapore's night scene, St James Power Station (☎ 6270 7676; www.stjamespowerstation .com; 3 Sentosa Gateway; Ⓜ HarbourFront) is a 1920s coal-fired power station ingeniously converted into an entertainment complex. All the bars and clubs are interconnected, so one cover charge (men/women $12/10) gets access to all of them. Some bars – the Bellini Room, Gallery Bar, Lobby Bar and Peppermint Park – have no cover charge at all. Minimum age is 18 for women and 23 for men at all except Powerhouse, where the age is 18 for both.

The bars include Bellini Room (🕑 8pm-3am Mon-Thu, 8pm-4am Fri & Sat), a stylish jazz and swing club; Dragonfly (🕑 6pm-6am), a Mandopop and Cantopop club; Movida (🕑 6pm-3am), a latin live-band dance club; Powerhouse (🕑 8pm-4am Wed, Fri & Sat), a large dance club aimed at the younger crowd; and the Boiler Room (🕑 8.45pm-3am Mon-Thu, 8.45pm-3am Fri & Sat), a mainstream rock club featuring live bands.

SUNSET BAY GARDEN BEACH BAR
Map p80   Bar/Restaurant
☎ 6448 9060; sunbay@pacific.net.sg;
1300 East Coast Park (Car Park F2); taxi
What could be finer than relaxing with
cocktails in a car-free beachside park in the
early evening? Sunset Bay offers just that,
and with an excellent menu you can show
up for dinner and while the night away to
the far-off thrumming of hundreds of cargo
ships moored just off Singapore's southern
shore. A rare find, indeed!

SENTOSA ISLAND
Fans of Groove Armada ('If you're fond of
sand-dunes and salty air') might not find
exactly what they're looking for in Sentosa,
but the island's artificial beaches and tanker-
tinged ocean air is about as close as Singapore gets to the beach vibe. Thanks to the
recently built monorail system, Sentosa's
laidback ambience isn't much further from

the downtown hubbub than Holland Rd or
Joo Chiat.

SUNSET BAY Map p100   Bar/Club
☎ 6275 0668; www.sunsetbay.com.sg; 60 Siloso
Beach Walk; shuttle bus from Ⓜ HarbourFront
A bona fide beach bar where it's perfectly
OK to wear very little – most of the young
customers seem to. For groups of at least
20, they'll throw a mini beach-games tour-
nament, and for $750 you can have your
own DJ Dance Party on weekdays.

KM8 Map p100   Club
☎ 6274 2288; Tanjong Beach; ⏰ 11am-midnight
Sun-Thu, 11am-1am Fri & Sat; shuttle bus from
Ⓜ HarbourFront
If you're in the mood for sea, sand, thumping
music and oily tanned bodies punching the
air, this is the place. It's successfully staked a
claim as Sentosa's top party spot – with its
late closing time, free-for-all Jacuzzi, shame-
lessly Ibizan design and expensive alcohol.

ARTS & LEISURE

top picks

What's your recommendation? www.lonelyplanet.com/singapore

ARTS & LEISURE

What puts Singapore at the top of the 'cities beloved by tourists' list year after year? Astounding quantities of amazing cuisine? Hot and cold running shopping night and day? A plethora of possibilities for arts, entertainment and nightlife?

Well yes, these things probably are factors. But the Lion City's charms run deeper than that, deeper even than the words and images found in the myriad tourist brochures that await travellers in airport kiosks and hotel lobbies. Good things come in small packages, and Singapore's strength lies not in any one specific monument, neighbourhood or attraction, but in its endless wealth of activities offered in the space of one easily traversed (by metro, bus, foot, bicycle, rollerblade or any combination thereof) metropolitan area. Art fans will enjoy checking out numerous small and medium-sized galleries offering glimpses into Singapore's burgeoning art scene. Film-lovers won't have any problem finding excellent venues in which to watch, and theatre-goers may be a bit surprised at how far the boundaries of polite speech in this once-circumspect society have been pushed over the past decade.

Those looking for less-cerebral, more physical gratification will find no shortage of activities, from bicycling, jogging (or even skating) on well-maintained park roads to water parks, swimming pools, sailing and even skiing (on an enclosed indoor slope, probably more of an equatorial novelty than anything else). Golfers will be surprised at the number of driving ranges and golf courses boasted by the tiny city-state, and there are plenty of schools and studios offering short-term rates and drop-in packages for visiting yoga enthusiasts. Naturally, Singapore has great spas and massage parlours for relaxation seekers of all budgetary levels.

THE ARTS

Visiting culture vultures needn't worry about artistic starvation in Singapore; indeed, the main challenge will be figuring out how to cram so much into a limited timeframe. Though once thought of as a cultural desert ('New York City without artists' was one less-than-charitable description bandied about in the 1990s), the Lion City's cultural renaissance seems to be well underway; from galleries to museums, comedy to symphony, Singapore has something for almost everyone (as long as it's not politically, religiously or sexually controversial!).

GALLERIES

In addition to having excellent museums – many of which we've listed in the appropriate neighbourhood sections – Singapore is also home to myriad smaller galleries. Most galleries in Singapore keep casual hours of around 11am to 7pm, but some stay open later for various events. Published monthly and available for $3.90 at most bookstores, the *Singapore Art Gallery Guide* (www.sagg.com.sg) is an excellent resource for current happenings in the local arts scene. The following reviews are just a smattering of what you'll find in Singapore.

ART SEASONS Map pp62–3
☎ 6221 1800; www.artseasons.com.sg; 5 Gemmill Lane; Ⓜ Chinatown
You can't miss this gallery, located as it is inside the distinctive architecture award-winning steel-and-glass building known locally as 'The Box'. Art Seasons offers sculpture and painting, primarily that of artists from Singapore, China and Burma.

ART-2 GALLERY Map pp52–3
☎ 6338 8713; www.art2.com.sg; 140 Hill St; Ⓜ Clarke Quay or City Hall
A smaller gallery in the same building as Gajah, Art-2 offers a melange of mediums ranging from sculpture and ceramics to painting and paperwork from Southeast Asia.

ARTOHOLIC Map p80
☎ 6348 7793; www.artoholic.sg; 422 Joo Chiat Rd; Ⓜ Paya Lebar, walk to Joo Chiat Rd, head south 6 blocks
This new venue over in the Joo Chiat neighbourhood takes up the 1st floor of a beautifully renovated and retrofitted shophouse. In addition to doubling as a bar and a performance centre, Artoholic also showcases original works of some of Southeast Asia's ultratalented painters, sculptors and print artists.

GAJAH GALLERY Map pp52–3

☎ 6737 4202; www.gajahgallery.com; 140 Hill St;
Ⓜ Clarke Quay or City Hall

One of Singapore's most respected galleries, Gajah has been around since the mid-1990s, and specialises in contemporary art from South and Southeast Asia. The gallery hosts regular exhibits and forums; in 2008 Gajah played host to the International Buddhist Film Festival.

ISAN GALLERY Map p80

☎ 6442 4278; www.isangallery.com.sg;
42 Jalan Kambangan; Ⓜ Kambangan

The home gallery of Percy Vatsaloo showcases intricately crafted and exquisitely beautiful clothing and other textiles made by tribal craftspeople of Isan in northeast Thailand. Visitors are welcome by appointment, and most of the items on display are also for sale. Percy works closely with the craftspeople themselves, and half of the sale price goes directly to them.

KETNA PATEL STUDIO GALLERY
Map pp92–3

☎ 6479 3736; www.ketnapatel.com; 35 Jalan Puteh Jerneh, Chip Bee Gardens, Holland Village; taxi

Ketna Patel and her husband Jonathan run a home gallery best described as a 'residential laboratory for like-minded people'. The studio's specific goal is to promote dialogue between developed and developing nations, using art as the means of communication. While the gallery is open by appointment only, like-minded artists visiting Singapore should consider contacting Ketna (ketna@ketnapatel.com) to find out about ongoing projects and happenings.

LUKISAN ART GALLERY Map pp62–3

☎ 6410 9663; www.lukisan-art.com; 26 Smith St;
Ⓜ Chinatown

Lukisan provides a venue for contemporary Asian artists both known and emerging. At the time of writing, Lukisan was featuring the works of renowned Filipino abstract artist Carlo Magno; check the website for upcoming events.

XUANHUA ART GALLERY Map pp52–3

☎ 6339 3836; www.xuanhuaart.com; 231 Bain St 02-71; Ⓜ City Hall

Dedicated to showcasing the finest works of contemporary Chinese ink painters from Singapore and China, Xuanhua also hosts exhibitions and other events. Lovers of sweeping charcoal-and-ink landscapes featuring the karst mountains of Guilin and other picturesque scenes of middle-kingdom splendour, this is the place for you.

MUSIC

Although not a musical city on the level of London or New York City, the Lion City does have a fair number of venues for concerts and other musical happenings.

ESPLANADE – THEATRES ON THE BAY
Map pp52–3

☎ 6828 8222; www.esplanade.com; 1 Esplanade Dr;
Ⓜ City Hall

The 1800-seater state-of-the-art concert hall at the Esplanade – Theatres on the Bay is the home of the highly respected Singapore Symphony Orchestra (SSO), but it also plays host to scores of music, theatre and dance performances. Check out their regularly updated website, especially for information on upcoming free shows and other programs.

SINGAPORE CHINESE ORCHESTRA

☎ 6557 4034; www.sco.com.sg;
Singapore Conference Hall, 7 Shenton Way;
Ⓜ Tanjong Pagar

A performance by SCO, Singapore's only classical Chinese orchestra, is definitely worth catching for anyone interested in Asian music. Befitting their position as an orchestra in multi-ethnic Singapore, the orchestra also plays Indian and Malay music.

SINGAPORE INDIAN ORCHESTRA & CHOIR

☎ 6340 549; 9 Stadium Link; Ⓜ Kallang

Under the baton of Mrs Lalitha Vaidyanathan, the SIOC performs classics from all over the Indian subcontinent on traditional Indian instruments such as the sitar and tabla.

FILM

Take an affluent society with a highly educated citizenry somewhat lacking in creative outlets and chuck it in the sweltering sun for 12 months a year and blammo, you've got the perfect recipe for country full of movie buffs. Singaporeans love to watch movies, and at around $8.50 per ticket, it's great value. Multiplex cinemas abound, and you can find city centre ones at Parco Bugis Junction (Map pp52–3), Shaw Towers (Map pp52–3) on Beach Rd, Suntec City (Map pp52–3), Marina Square Complex (Map pp52–3), Cathay Cineleisure Orchard (Map pp74–5), Plaza Singapura (Map pp74–5) and Shaw House (Map pp74–5), all on or near Orchard Rd, among other places. For screening times, check the *Straits Times*. Singapore's cinemas are notoriously chilly places, so bring something warm to wear.

See also p33 for more on Singapore's homegrown film scene.

ALLIANCE FRANÇAISE Map pp74–5
☎ 6737 8422; www.alliancefrancaise.org.sg;
1 Sarkies Rd; Ⓜ Newton
Screens classic and contemporary French films Tuesday at 8pm. Tickets are $8 for nonmembers. Check the website for screening times. The British Council (Map pp92–3; ☎ 6473 1111; 30 Napier Rd; Ⓜ Orchard) has occasional screenings of British movies.

GOLDEN VILLAGE Map pp74–5
☎ 6735 8484; www.gv.com.sg;
1 Kim Seng Promenade; Ⓜ Somerset
For the ultimate pampered cinematic experience, $25 gets you a ticket to this 'gold class' cinema on the 3rd floor of the Great World City mall. There are seats that can be reclined and adjusted with little levers, little tables for your food and drinks, and waiters who take your order. It also has regular theatres (some with huge screens) with normal-priced tickets.

PICTUREHOUSE Map pp74–5
☎ 6235 1155; www.thepicturehouse.com.sg;
levels 5 & 6, 2 Handy Rd; Ⓜ Dhoby Ghaut
The first 'art-house' cinema in Singapore, the Picturehouse is the place to go for screenings of independent films from A to Z. Check the website for screening times.

LECTURES & READINGS
All-night partying aside, Singaporeans are studious folk with great appreciation of didacticism; thus, it's no surprise that even on a Saturday afternoon, scheduled lectures and talks on myriad subjects may wind up standing room only. Museums are the best places to catch a talk.

BOOKS ACTUALLY Map pp62–3
☎ 6221 1170; www.booksactually.com;
5 Ann Siang Rd; Ⓜ Tanjong Pagar
Opened by three friends with a shared passion for books and located on the 2nd floor of a renovated shophouse south of Chinatown, this neat little bookstore holds poetry readings and open-mic sessions. Call or check the website for scheduling.

OPERA
CHINESE THEATRE CIRCLE Map pp62–3
☎ 6323 4862; www.ctcopera.com.sg; 5 Smith St;
Ⓜ Chinatown
A low-key introduction to Chinese opera can be had at one of the teahouse evenings organised by the nonprofit opera company, the Chinese Theatre Circle. Every Friday and Saturday evening at 8pm there is a brief talk (in English) on Chinese opera, followed by a short excerpt from a Cantonese opera classic, performed by professional actors in full costume. Delicious lychee tea and little tea cakes are included in the price ($20). The whole thing lasts about 45 minutes and you are able to take photos. Some Cantonese operas are even sung in English, though how much is lost in translation we can't say. Bookings are recommended. For $35, turn up at 7pm and you can enjoy a full Chinese meal beforehand.

THEATRE
The Singapore Arts Festival (www.singaporeartsfest.com), which features many drama performances, is held in June. Music, art and dance are also represented at the festival, which includes the Fringe Festival, featuring plenty of street performances. Esplanade – Theatres on the Bay (p51) is one of the brightest spots in Singapore's vibrant theatre and dance scene.

ACTION THEATRE Map pp52–3
☎ 6837 0842; www.action.org.sg; 42 Waterloo St;
Ⓜ Dhoby Ghaut
Set in a two-storey heritage house, this established theatre group shows local and international plays with contemporary themes in its small, 100-seat upstairs theatre and in the two open-air venues.

NECESSARY STAGE Map p80
☎ 6440 8115; www.necessary.org; B1-02 Marine Parade Community Bldg, 278 Marine Parade Rd;
🚌 12, 14 or 32

Since the theatre's inception in 1987, current artistic director Alvin Tan (see also p35) has collaborated with resident playwright Haresh Sharma to produce over 60 original works such as 'Good People', 'Frozen Angels', and 'Top or Bottom'. Innovative, indigenous, and often controversial, the Necessary Stage is one of Singapore's best known theatre groups.

SINGAPORE DANCE THEATRE
Map pp52–3

☎ 6338 0611; www.singaporedancetheatre.com; 2nd fl, Fort Canning Centre, Cox Tce; Ⓜ Dhoby Ghaut
This top dance company performs traditional ballets and contemporary works. The group's Ballet under the Stars season at Fort Canning Park is very popular. There are regular classes in ballet, jazz ballet and Pilates.

SINGAPORE REPERTORY THEATRE
Map pp52–3

☎ 6221 5585; www.srt.com.sg; DBS Arts Centre, 20 Merbau Rd; 🚌 54 from Ⓜ Clarke Quay
Based at the DBS Arts Centre, but also performing at other venues, this theatre group offers up repertory standards such as works by Shakespeare, Tennessee Williams and Arthur Miller, as well as some modern Singaporean plays.

THEATREWORKS Map pp52–3

☎ 6338 4007; www.theatreworks.org.sg; Black Box, Fort Canning Centre, Cox Tce; Ⓜ Dhoby Ghaut
This is one of the more experimental and interesting theatre companies in Singapore. Theatreworks often performs at the Black Box theatre, as well as other venues around Singapore.

TOY FACTORY THEATRE ENSEMBLE
Map pp62–3

☎ 6222 1526; www.toyfactory.com.sg; 15A Smith St; Ⓜ Chinatown
A cutting-edge bilingual theatre company (in English and Mandarin, naturally), Toy Factory is known for staging controversial overseas plays, as well as producing Singaporean works. Where else could you see a performance like Shopping and F***ing?

WILD RICE Map p68

☎ 6223 2695; www.wildrice.com.sg; 3A Kerbau Rd; Ⓜ Little India

Possibly Singapore's most accomplished theatre group, due in no small part to the talents of artistic director Ivan Heng. Wild Rice's productions range from farce to serious politics and fearlessly wade into issues not commonly on the agenda in Singapore.

COMEDY
Despite the absence of a dedicated comedy club (the city's only comedy club, 1Night-Stand in Clarke Quay, shut its doors as this book was going to press), comedy is alive and well in Singapore. A number of venues host travelling comics, and Singapore is a major stop-over for touring stand-ups heading from England to Australia and New Zealand. Check local papers for listings of upcoming shows.

LEISURE ACTIVITIES
Lest the reader assume a trip to Singapore is an excuse to give the body short shrift, the Lion City also boasts a thousand different paths to exhaustion, and nearly as many spas and massage parlours to work out the kinks after a hard day's workout.

CYCLING & SKATING
Sweltering heat and humidity doesn't drive everyone into the cool embraces of the nearest mall or movie theatre, and Singapore has plenty of high-speed outdoor activities for those undaunted by climate. Somewhere in the region of a quarter of the island is taken up by parks, many of which are joined by a series of underground park connectors and overhead bridges. This means that you can bicycle or skate through much of the city without having to fight traffic. Most hostels rent bikes, and there are a few places in the city to rent in-line skates as well.

BIKE BOUTIQUE Map pp62–3

☎ 6298 9528; www.thebikeboutique.com; 98 Amoy St; Ⓜ Raffles Place
Though few casual visitors to Singapore will spend their time shopping for bicycles, those who lust after bicycles might want to drop into this shop just to salivate over its beautiful high-end machines. The shop is also noteworthy for offering bike storage and showers to office workers commuting in from the outskirts.

WHAT MAKES SINGAPORE LAUGH? *Jonathan Atherton*

I've often heard it said that Singaporeans lack a sense of humour; I say bollocks to that. While it may be true that Singapore's political system is a tad authoritarian and somewhat lacking – devoid, really – when it comes to having a sense of humour, really, aren't all governments wet blankets when it comes to fun? But stick-in-the-mud governance or not, your average Singaporean is always up for a good laugh.

Laughter, after all, is the best stress reliever, and in a society as focused on work, materialism and endlessly getting ahead in life, stress relief ranks high on the must-have list. In Singapore, a lot of humour can be gotten out of poking fun at the system. Now of course, actually complaining about the system is discouraged. For this reason, Singaporeans have elevated *whingeing* about the system to the status of a national sport.

Singapore is an ethnic stew, and while laws forbidding racism are very much enforced, friends of different ethnic groups have no problem poking fun at each other's customs or languages. It's all done in fun, with any jokes made out of shared experience rather than ignorance. Singaporeans genuinely respect the tenets of multiculturalism – you have to in a place so crowded with cultures. Singaporeans appreciate the distinction between an archetype and a stereotype, and this is just one of the things that I really like about the country.

But herein lies a comedic dilemma: the very multiculturalism that distinguishes Singapore from many other states also makes it difficult to pinpoint the essential character of its wit. Singapore is made up of dozens of cultures. 'Chinese', 'Malay' and 'Indian' are often cited as the main ethnic groups, but even within these groups lie marked differences.

Not to overgeneralise – it's politically incorrect, I know – but after 14 years as a touring stand-up comic in Southeast Asia, I feel it's safe to say that there are some observable patterns in what the various Singaporean subcultures find funny. The Hokkien Chinese enjoy ribald, bawdy humour, while their Cantonese cousins tend to favour slapstick more. Punjabis have a highly developed sense of irony, whereas Tamils love puns and word play. Gujuratis are fond of anecdotal material but Sindhis prefer a more philosophical slant. And Malays – they're a crowd any comic would appreciate. A fun-loving bunch, Malays will laugh at anything (as long as it's funny, that is!).

So the idea that Singaporeans lack senses of humour is nonsense; most folks you'll meet here will likely have a great sense of humour, so have some fun with locals over a cold beer or a hot cup of tea. But if you're hoping to get a laugh as a put-down comic, better think twice. Singaporeans have a strong sense of respect, both for themselves and for others. Nothing will fall flatter than fishing for laughs at the expense of others.

Australian-born comic Jonathan Atherton was Resident Master of Ceremonies at the now-closed 1NightStand. If anyone knows what makes Singapore laugh, it's him.

SKATELINE Map pp52–3

☎ 6339 7707; www.skateline.com.sg; Peninsula Shopping Centre, 3 Coleman St 04-37A; Ⓜ City Hall
Inline skating is very popular in Singapore and with five shops throughout the city Skateline is a great place to buy your blades. Skateline also run the rental kiosk at East Coast Park (near Burger King and car park C3).

BODY MODIFICATION

Art is no mere spectator sport, at least not to those who consider their body to be art's mobile canvas. To these, Singapore offers many fine places in which to be inked, pierced, studded, or otherwise corporeally modified. Probably the best place to shop for artists is at Far East Plaza (p113), which has about half a dozen shops to chose from.

Visitors looking for a tattoo shop with a definite pedigree should know about Exotic Tattoo (Map pp74–5; ☎ 6834 0558; 04-11 Far East Plaza 14 Scotts Rd; Ⓜ Orchard), for it's here that you'll be able to get exquisite work from Sumithra Debi. One of the few female tattoo artists in Singapore, Sumithra is also the granddaughter of Johnny Two-Thumbs, probably Singapore's most legendary tattoo artist. Though there's another shop in the plaza bearing the Two-Thumbs name, Exotic Tattoo is the actual heir to the Two-Thumbs lineage. In addition to ink work, the shop also does piercing.

BOWLING

Tenpin bowling is popular in Singapore, though it seems that several bowling alleys have closed down over the past few years – not surprising in a city where indoor space is at such a premium. The cost per game is between $4 and $4.50 per person per game, depending on the time of day you play (it's also more on weekends and less on weekdays). Shoe hire is around $1 and operators will even sell you a pair of fetching white ankle socks for $0.50.

Orchid Bowl @ E!hub (Map pp46–7; ☎ 6583 1622; basement, Downtown East Mall; ☽ closes 2am)

Victor Superbowl (Map pp48–9; ☎ 6223 7998; 7 Marina Grove, Marina South; ⊗ 9am-3am Sun-Thu, 24hr Fri & Sat; Ⓜ Marina Bay)

GOLF

Opening a golf course in a tiny city-state with extremely limited resources and open space seems an act of hubris against nature. Really, wouldn't miniature golf be more appropriate? If you're really intent on golfing, you're better off heading across the Causeway to the wide-open spaces at Sebana Golf and Marina Resort (p184). If you must golf in Singapore, most clubs are members-only so they charge visitors a premium and usually don't allow you to play on weekends. Expect to pay around $100 per game on weekdays and up to twice that on weekends.

Jurong Country Club (Map pp46–7; ☎ 6560 5655; www.jcc.org.sg; 9 Science Centre Rd; Ⓜ Jurong East)

Marina Bay Golf Course (Map pp48–9; ☎ 6345 7788; www.mbgc.com.sg; 80 Rhu Cross)

Laguna National Golf & Country Club (Map pp46–7; ☎ 6541 0289; www.lagunagolf.com.sg; 11 Laguna Golf Green; Ⓜ Tanah Merah)

Raffles Country Club (Map pp46–7; ☎ 6861 7655; www.rcc.org.sg; 450 Jalan Ahmad Ibrahim; 🚌 SBS 182 from Ⓜ Boon Lay)

Sentosa Golf Club (Map p100; ☎ 6275 0022; www.beaufort.com.sg/resort_golf.html; 27 Bukit Manis Rd, Sentosa Island; 🚌 shuttle bus from HarbourFront MRT)

HORSE RACING

SINGAPORE TURF CLUB Map pp46–7

☎ 6879 1000; www.turfclub.com.sg; 1 Turf Club Ave; Ⓜ Kranji

This is a hugely popular day out – not nearly as manic as Hong Kong, but a rousing experience nonetheless. There is a four-level grandstand with a seating capacity of up to 35,000. Admission to the non-air-conditioned seating is $3, or $7 for the upper air-conditioned level (and foreigners must bring their passports to get in). For $15 tourists can access the air-conditioned Gold Card Room, or for $20 the exclusive@ Hibiscus lounge. Like Raffles, dress code is enforced: smart casual in one section and suits and ties in another.

Races take place on Friday, Saturday or Sunday during racing months (check the *New Paper* for details and coverage), starting at 6.30pm, 2pm and 2.30pm respectively.

ROCK CLIMBING

DAIRY FARM QUARRY Map pp46–7

🚌 65, 170, 75, 171

Near Bukit Timah, Dairy Farm Quarry, which boasts 20 routes, is the only legal place to rock climb in Singapore. Most routes are bolted and can be done with a 50m rope; you'll need to bring your own gear. To find out about joining up with climbers who come here regularly on weekends, or to learn about indoor venues to climb in Singapore, check out www.indoorclimbing.com/singapore.html for a complete list of climbing walls in Singapore.

SKIING, SNOWBOARDING & TUBING

SNOW CITY Map pp46–7

☎ 6560 1511; www.snowcity.com.sg; 21 Jurong Town Hall Rd; adult/child per hr $15/13; ⊗ 9.45am -5.15pm Tue-Sun; Ⓜ Jurong East

A hangar-sized deep freeze chilled to a numbing -5°C, Snow City features a slope three-storeys high and 70m long, accessed via a silvery *Star Trek*–style airlock. Each session gives you an hour to throw yourself at high speed down the slope on a black inner tube and throw snowballs. Two-hour ski and snowboarding lessons are available in the evenings for $55 from Snow Line (☎ 6425 0801), located in the same building as Snow City. Snow Line also rents jackets and other equipment.

SWIMMING

Care for a dip in the world's most crowded waterways? Many do, despite the fact that none of Singapore's beaches are particularly great for swimming. Should you feel like joining them, the most popular beaches in Singapore are on Sentosa Island and East Coast Park.

A better option, if you're not staying at a hotel with its own pool, is the excellent public swimming complexes at Farrer Park (Map p68; ☎ 6299 1002; 2 Rutland Ave; ⊗ 8am-9.30pm; Ⓜ Little India) or River Valley Swimming Complex (Map pp52–3; ☎ 6337 6275; 1 River Valley Rd; ⊗ 8am-9.30pm; Ⓜ Clarke Quay) at the foot of Fort Canning Park. Admission to both is $1/0.50 per adult/child ($1.30/0.60 on weekends).

SPAS & MASSAGE

Spas, massage and paid-for relaxation are big business in Singapore. Telok Ayer St, right around the vicinity of the Thian Hok Keng Temple, seems to have become spa central, with at least half a dozen mid-priced spas and massage places on one short stretch of road.

Another place worth a visit is Chinatown's People's Park Complex (p109), which boasts several floors of stalls offering reflexology, shiatsu and even places where you can soak your feet in a pool of dead skin–eating fish for $12. There are hundreds of others scattered around Singapore, with rates varying from around $25 for a foot massage to more than $200 for a full-day package.

AMRITA SPA Map pp52–3

☎ 6336 4477; www.amritaspas.com; Level 6, Raffles, The Plaza, 2 Stamford Rd; Ⓜ City Hall
Amrita boasts of being Asia's most extensive spa with 35 treatment rooms, a fitness centre, a variety of plunge and bubble pools and a long menu of spa treatments; the day-spa escape package with back massage and express facial is $150. There are branches at Swissôtel (p162), Merchant Court Singapore and Raffles Hotel (p56).

ARAMSA, BISHAN PARK Map pp46–7

☎ 6456 6556; www.aramsaspas.com; Bishan Park, 1382 Ang Mo Kio Ave 1, Ⓜ Bishan, 🚌 410
Aramsa has five different outlets in Bishan park, including an amazing spa, a vegetarian cafe, a huge dining room, and a Pilates studio. The serene park location makes Aramsa a scene unto itself, a place where locals and travellers alike can escape the busy mainstream and spend the day getting back to the garden of the soul.

KENKO WELLNESS SPA Map pp62–3

☎ 6223 0303; www.kenkofootreflexology.com; 211 South Bridge Rd; Ⓜ Chinatown

GETTING HIGH IN SINGAPORE

Who doesn't love to get high, especially on vacation? Despite a reputation for level-headedness, Singaporeans love being high, and the city offers a plethora of opportunity to visitors looking to get high. Floating 40 storeys above terra firma, the DHL Balloon (Map p68; ☎ 6338 6877; Tan Quee Lan St; adult/child $23/13; 🕙 11am-10pm; Ⓜ Bugis) will leave you singing the Jimmy Webb tune 'Up, up and away in my beautiful balloon'. Filled with 6000 cu metres of helium, the bright yellow balloon with the DHL logo on both sides is a regular feature in the sky over Bugis – you can't miss it. There's a rumour that the balloon will be moving to a new location in 2009, so keep your eyes on the skies.

If you like your highs quick, intense and somewhat brutal, the G-max Bungy (Map pp52–3; ☎ 6338 1146; www.gmax.com.sg; 3E River Valley Rd; per ride $30; 🕙 3pm-late Mon-Fri, noon-late Sat & Sun; Ⓜ Clarke Quay) might be for you. You and two other thrill-seekers will be strapped into padded chairs enclosed inside a metal cage, which is propelled skyward to a height of 60m at speeds exceeding 200km/h before being pulled back down by gravity. Though the ride offers spectacular views to those who can keep their eyes open, it's best avoided by people prone to velocity-induced vomiting.

A relatively gentle high ('relatively' is the key here) is offered right next door on the GX5 (Map pp52–3; ☎ 6338 1146; www.gmax.com.sg; 3E River Valley Rd; per ride $40; 🕙 3pm-late Mon-Fri, noon-late Sat & Sun; Ⓜ Clarke Quay). Whereas the G-max offers a straight-up face-peeling vertical trip, the GX5 swings riders up and over the Singapore River with somewhat less nauseating velocity. The trip also lasts longer, though which one provides more bang for your buck is a matter of personal choice.

But the most celebrated – certainly the most family-friendly way to get high in the Lion City comes via the newly opened Singapore Flyer (Map pp52–3; ☎ 6333 3311; www.singaporeflyer.com.sg; 30 Raffles Ave; adult/child/senior $29.50/20.65/23.60; 🕙 8.30am-10.30pm; Ⓜ City Hall). Billed as 'The World's Largest Giant Observation Wheel', this monumental Ferris wheel carries riders up 165m before bringing them gently down into a rainforest covered park (part of a shopping complex, naturally – wouldn't want to get high and not be able to shop afterwards). Various packages are offered for those looking to get high in style, such as the signature cocktail flight for $69, in which drinks are served for that extra lift.

Getting high in Singapore is anything but cheap, but those in the know can do it for close to nothing if they're willing to resort to humbler methods. One way, known mostly to locals, is to take a trip on bus 33; a London-style double-decker doing the east–west route, it skirts the southern edge of downtown on the seven-storey East Coast Parkway, offering impressive views of the skyscrapers to the north and the harbour to the south. Not quite the same rush as the reverse bungee, but for under a buck who's complaining? Grab a seat up top for some extra elevation!

Kenko is the McDonald's of reflexology, with outlets all over the city centre, including two on Tanglin Rd (Map pp74–5). This 'wellness boutique', located in Chinatown, is the most upmarket of its operations.

NGEE ANN FOOT REFLEXOLOGY
Map pp74–5

☎ 6235 5538; 4th fl, Midpoint Orchard, 220 Orchard Rd; Ⓜ Somerset
Offers foot and body massage by visually impaired masseuses in friendly and refreshingly unpretentious surroundings.

ST GREGORY JAVANA SPA Map p68

☎ 6290 8028; www.stgregoryspa.com; Level 3, The Plaza, 7500A Beach Rd; Ⓜ Bugis
With spas all over Asia, St Gregory's is a major player in relaxation. Its three facilities in Singapore are all inside upper-end hotels, we've listed the one at the Park Royal on Beach Rd; the other two are at the Marina Mandarin and the Conrad Centennial.

SANCTUM Map p68

☎ 6225 4381; www.sanctumsg.com; 11 Haji Lane; Ⓜ Bugis
'Nourishment for mind, body and soul' is how this place bills itself, and with tarot readings, meditation events, past-life regression, shiatsu and reiki, we see no reason to argue. Sanctum has three beautiful and uniquely set-up rooms for sessions and chilling out, and offers online booking.

SPA BOTANICA Map p100

☎ 6371 1318; www.spabotanica.com; Sentosa Resort & Spa; ⏱ 10am-10pm; 🚌 shuttle bus from Orchard Rd Paragon Shopping Centre
Singapore's original indoor and outdoor spa. The signature treatment here is the galaxy steam bath, a 45-minute wallow in medicinal chakra mud in a specially designed steam room. It also has a mud pool outside as well as landscaped grounds and pools.

WATER PARKS

ESCAPE THEME PARK Map pp46–7

☎ 6581 9112; www.escapethemepark.com.sg; adult/child/family $17.70/8.90/42.80; ⏱ 10am-10pm Sat, Sun & school holidays; 🚌 354 from Ⓜ Pasir Ris
Who doesn't love a tropical waterslide, roller coasters, go-karts, bumper-boats and

wave pools? The wet and wild flume ride is said to be Asia's highest.

JURONG EAST SWIMMING COMPLEX
Map pp46–7

☎ 6563 5052; 21 Jurong East St 31; adult/child $2/1; ⏱ 9am-7pm; Ⓜ Chinese Gardens
The cheapest place in Singapore for swimming; has a lap pool, wading pool, wave pool, and three water slides.

WILD WILD WET Map pp46–7

☎ 6581 9135; www.wildwildwet.com; adult/child $13.80/9.40; ⏱ 1-7pm Mon & Wed-Fri, 10am-8pm Sat, Sun & school holidays; 🚌 354 from Ⓜ Pasir Ris
Part of the same Downtown East complex occupied by Escape Theme Park, this water fun-park offers rides in a similar vein.

WATER SPORTS

CHANGI SAILING CENTRE Map pp46–7

☎ 6545 2876; www.csc.org.sg; 32 Netheravon Rd; 🚌 2 from Ⓜ Tanah Merah
This centre rents out j-24s (24ft keel boats) on one-day charters for $180 a day, including petrol. You will need to show a sailing proficiency certificate.

MACRITCHIE RESERVOIR'S PADDLE LODGE Map pp46–7;

☎ 6258 0057; kayak rental per 1/2hr $10/15; ⏱ 9am-6pm Tue-Sun; 🚌 162
Offers paddle-boating and other water sports. For details, on which other parks offer water sports, see the website of the National Parks Board (www.nparks.gov.sg).

SCUBA CORNER Map p68

☎ 6338 6563; www.scubacorner.com.sg; 04-162 Kitchener Complex, Block 809 French Rd; Ⓜ Lavender
Diving trips and courses can be arranged through the outfit Scuba Corner; it's office is located conveniently close to Lavender MRT station.

SKI360° Map p80

☎ 6442 7318; www.ski360degree.com; 1206A East Coast Parkway; per hr weekdays/weekends $32/42; ⏱ 10am-10pm Mon-Fri, 9am-midnight Sat & Sun; Ⓜ Bedok then bus 401 (weekends only) 🚌 196, 197
What better way to cool off than strap on some water skis, a kneeboard or a wakeboard and get dragged around a lagoon

on the end of a cable? OK, you could just go swimming, but where's the fun in that? Best visited on weekday mornings, when there's usually hardly anyone there. The pose quotient goes through the roof at weekends, when it's just as entertaining sitting around hoping someone will come a cropper on the ramps.

YOGA

Yoga has caught on in a big way in Singapore – perhaps this accounts for the newfound mental flexibility of the denizens of this city-state once known for dogmatic stiffness. Most schools offer drop-in courses, but these aren't cheap; expect to pay between $20 and $30 for a 60- or 90-minute class. If you're in town for a few weeks and plan to practice regularly, you're better off purchasing a one-month or 10-class package. If you're just in town for a few days, you can take advantage of the 'first-timer' rates offered by some studios to attract new students, hopping from school to school for the duration.

Alternately, Sri Muneeswaran Hindu Temple (Map pp92–3; 3 Commonwealth Drive, Commonwealth MRT) offers free yoga classes on Sunday from 4pm to 5pm and 6pm to 7pm, and again on Monday from 7pm to 8pm.

The following schools offer short-term classes and drop-ins.

ABSOLUTE YOGA
☎ 6732 6007; www.absoluteyogasingapore.com
This large studio offers 'Hot Yoga', and has drop-in classes for $34 and 10-class cards for $270.

ANANDA MARGA Map p80
☎ 6344 6519;1 www.anandamarga.org.sg; Marine Parade Central, 07-01 Parkway Centre
In a world of corporate-run yoga studios, Ananda Marga is a breath of fresh air. Its Singapore studio offers small daily classes, dedicated instructors, and short-term class packages. Well worth coming east for.

TRUE YOGA Map pp62–3
☎ 6336 3390; www.trueyoga.com.sg; 20 Raffles Place, 27-00 Ocean Towers; Ⓜ Raffles Place
Probably the largest of Singapore's corporate yoga centres, True Yoga offers classes in a variety of styles and levels. It also has a branch on Orchard Rd, and often list one-time promotions on its website.

SLEEPING

top picks

- Raffles Hotel (p161)
- Fullerton (p162)
- Goodwood Park Hotel (p169)
- New Majestic Hotel (p165)
- Gallery Hotel (p163)
- Robertson Quay Hotel (p164)
- Siloso Beach Resort (p174)
- Betel Box (p173)
- Sleepy Sam's (p166)
- Lloyd's Inn (p171)

When it comes to accommodation in Singapore, there's good news and bad news. First, the good: despite the fact that you may run into one fully-booked hotel after another during major events, there have never been more hotels in Singapore than there are now. Now the bad: though not exactly across the board, prices have gone up in the last couple of years. Many former budget hotels have crept into the midrange category – sometimes, but not always, accompanied by corresponding improvements. Prices for many midrange and top-end hotels have also gone up, though not in all cases. (Indeed, there are some fine bargains to be found around town, especially through the internet.) While some new budget hotels have opened up (particularly those offering 'transit', or hourly rates), others have been driven out of business by rising property values.

Thanks to the peerless public transport system, it doesn't really matter where you stay in central Singapore. Everywhere is less than half an hour from everywhere else. If you're looking for atmosphere and character, we recommend Chinatown or Little India, both of which harbour most of the budget accommodation and boutique hotels in shophouse conversions. If you don't mind being a bit further out, there is a cluster of new hostels in the Joo Chiat area.

Orchard Rd and its environs are crammed with identikit upmarket hotels (with a few distinctive exceptions), as is the area around Marina Bay, where you'll find the Esplanade complex and Suntec City mall. There are also good options dotted close by the redeveloped quays of the Singapore River.

If you want to experience the grittier side of Singapore outside your hotel room, then Geylang is worth considering; we've found two hotels in that area that are high in cultural interest and low in sleaze. If you want the sea and a beach close at hand, Sentosa's the go, but avoid weekends, when rates and occupancy are higher.

LONGER-TERM RENTALS

For medium- to long-term stays, Singapore has a number of serviced apartments. It is also possible to rent rooms in private flats (check the classified pages of the *Straits Times* for listings). Rents are high, regardless of how near or far from the city centre you are. Note that the prices quoted include all taxes.

Probably the best place to start looking for long-term rental in Singapore is Singapore Expats (www.singaporeexpats.com), which has detailed information on the different districts, outlines the whole rental procedure and carries an apartment search engine. The Singapore section of www.craigslist.org is also a good place to look for long-term stays.

SOMERSET BENCOOLEN

Map pp52–3   Serviced Apartments $$$
☎ 6730 1811; www.somerset.com;
51 Bencoolen St; 1-bedroom apt per week from $2590;
Ⓜ Dhoby Ghaut; 🖥 🛝

If you're going to live large in Singapore, the Somerset Bencoolen might be the place to do it. Fully furnished service apartments are big and beautiful with floor-

---

ACTUAL PRICES MAY VARY

In Singapore's midrange and top-end hotels, room rates are about supply and demand, fluctuating daily.

Travellers planning a trip to Singapore need to keep this in mind, especially if youy're planning to come here during a major event. Be aware that reservation desk staff in top hotels usually add a casual (and often barely audible) 'plus plus plus' after the rate they quote you. Ignore this at your peril. The three plusses are service charge, government tax and GST, which together amounts to a breezy 16% on top of your bill.

To further complicate matters, Singapore's high-end hotels offer a stunning array of pricing packages, from rooms for a few hundred a night to Bill Gates–class suites costing thousands (with many incremental, ever-fluctuating price levels in between).

All prices quoted in our listings are from the day of our visit; your own price may vary. Don't thank us: that's the invisible hand of capitalism at work.

to-ceiling windows offering spectacular views. The rooftop pool is an especially nice touch, as are the guided floor-lights in the lobby, presumably to guide your footsteps when you come home drunk.

PARKLANE SUITES
Map pp74–5   Serviced Apartments $$$
☎ 6730 1811; www.goodwoodparkhotel.com/
parklanesuits.htm; 22 Scotts Rd; ste per month
$4500-6000; Ⓜ Orchard; 🖳 🖳
A real dose of style, these 64 split-level luxury suites are in a separate building next to the Goodwood Park Hotel. Immaculately done out with timber louvres, timber floors, black-slate wall panels, curved ceilings, plus your own balcony. Facilities include two swimming pools, a gym and a launderette.

METRO-Y APARTMENTS
Map pp74–5   Serviced Apartments $$
☎ 6839 8100; apt@mymca.org.sg; 58 Stevens Rd;
studios per month $3200; Ⓜ Orchard; 🖳 🖳
Next to the Metropolitan Y, Metro-Y has its own swimming pool, gym and washing machines, a bonus at this price and this close to Orchard Rd. The rooms are recently renovated, and all come with compact kitchenettes and cable TV. Larger family-sized suites are also available for varying prices dependent on size.

RESERVATIONS
'Build it and they will come', or so goes the Kevin Costner quote in *Field of Dreams*. In Singapore, the 'it' is lots of hotels, and the 'they', well, that's you. The more hotels that go up, the more travellers (and less hotel rooms) there seem to be. Though most travellers won't have too much of a problem finding a place to stay, Singapore is definitely not the place to just rock up without reservations if

you can help it – especially if you arrive during holidays (like Chinese New Year) or during major sporting events.

So book ahead and online when possible, if not for peace of mind then for the often available (and sometimes substantial) internet discounts. Hotel websites and discount websites like www.asiabesthotels.com, www.hotels.online.com.sg, or www.agoda.com are all good resources.

COLONIAL DISTRICT & THE QUAYS
This sprawling nerve centre of tourist activity contains the widest variety of accommodations, from the cheapest of the cheap no-frills hostels to the priciest luxury hotels. Though precise definition of where this area begins and ends is a bit difficult to pin down, for the purposes of our listings we're including anything close to the Clarke Quay, Dhoby Ghaut, City Hall or Bugis MRT stations, which includes the vast nexus of hotels on and around Bencoolen St.

RAFFLES HOTEL Map pp52–3   Hotel $$$
☎ 6337 1886; www.raffleshotel.com; 1 Beach Rd;
ste from $650; Ⓜ City Hall; 🖳 🖳
Hotels that double as tourist attractions are sometimes a let-down. This one isn't. With its wooden floors, high ceilings, unshakeable colonial decor and even its famous Sikh doorman, it stands alongside the Peninsula

PRICE GUIDE
$$$	over $200 a night
$$	$100-200 a night
$	under $100 a night

Hong Kong and the Oriental Bangkok as one of Asia's truly special hotels. Whether you're coming to stay or simply to soak up some air-conditioned elegance, be advised: dress code is in effect, and Raffles' turbaned doorman will not allow those in sleeveless shirts, sandals, or grubby backpacker attire to enter.

FULLERTON HOTEL Map pp52–3   Hotel $$$
☎ 6733 8388; www.fullertonhotel.com; 1 Fullerton Sq; r from $400; Ⓜ Raffles Place; 🖥 🖳

The Fullerton has the distinction of being both one of Singapore's most magnificent pieces of colonial architecture and the only hotel we've ever heard of that's also a restored post office. The heritage principles involved in the restoration mean some of the Armani-beige rooms overlook the inner atrium. Spend a bit extra to gain access to the hotel's private Straits Club and upgrade to river- or marina-view rooms, all of which are stunning. Though easily as elegant as the famed Raffles, the Fullerton is a bit less restrictive when it comes to welcoming casually dressed tourists.

RITZ-CARLTON
Map pp52–3   International Hotel $$$
☎ 6337 8888; www.ritzcarlton.com/hotels /singapore; 7 Raffles Ave; s/d from $465/515; Ⓜ City Hall; 🖥 🖳

This place was clearly designed with sex in mind, right from the striking entrance dominated by a Frank Stella sculpture. The rooms are an aphrodisiac all on their own, with stunning harbour views from the raised beds and even from the bathrooms, which are located, unusually, on the exterior wall. A must for romantic occasions.

SWISSÔTEL, THE STAMFORD
Map pp52–3   International Hotel $$$
☎ 6338 8585; www.singapore-stamford.swissotel .com; 2 Stamford Rd; r from $420, executive club from $550; Ⓜ City Hall; 🖥 🖳

More like an indoor town than a hotel, this massive hotel offers all the five-star comfort and amenities that you'd expect for the price, not to mention amazing views, numerous restaurants and bars, and plenty of shopping. Prices include breakfast, and if you get a room on the 57th floor executive club, breakfast (or any meal) will come with endless high-grade coffee, compliments of your room's personal Lavazza espresso machine.

HOTEL INTERCONTINENTAL
Map pp52–3   International Hotel $$$
☎ 6338 7600; www.ichotelsgroup.com; 80 Middle Rd; standard r from $360, shophouse r $410; Ⓜ Bugis; 🖥 🖳

A top-class hotel with impeccable Singaporean style, the most interesting rooms at this hotel are the shophouse rooms, which are done up in a mixture of Peranakan and colonial style down to the wooden floors, oriental rugs and hand-painted lampshades. Less expensive rooms are also lovely, though decorated more along standard five-star lines. Facilities include a fitness centre, a pleasant rooftop pool and several good restaurants.

ORIENTAL SINGAPORE
Map pp52–3   International Hotel $$$
☎ 6338 0066; www.mandarinoriental.com; 5 Raffles Ave, Marina Sq; r from $410; Ⓜ City Hall; 🖥 🖳

The sumptuous rooms here have stunning views, either over Marina Bay and the 'durians' of the Esplanade theatre, or the city skyline. A bonus is the large baths and your own DVD player.

FURAMA RIVERFRONT
Map pp52–3   International Hotel $$$
☎ 6333 8898; www.furama.com; 405 Havelock Rd; s/d/ste from $400/450/650; Ⓜ Outram Park; 🖥 🖳

Occupying the old Novotel building, the Furama is swank in every way, from its stunning indoor waterfall to the hip, modern-art decor in the lobby. Rooms are lovely, offering views of both city and river, and staff are extremely helpful in making your stay a memorable one. Internet discounts are available.

PAN PACIFIC HOTEL
Map pp52–3   International Hotel $$$
☎ 6336 8111; http://singapore.panpac.com; 7 Raffles Blvd, Marina Sq; r from $355; Ⓜ City Hall; 🖥 🖳

Taking the prize in the flash lobby stakes, the Pan Pacific soars up 35 storeys. The rooms are decorated in neutral tones and a contemporary style (the business rooms even have ergonomic Aeron desk chairs); those with a balcony and a view are a bit pricier, though worth every penny.

RAFFLES, THE PLAZA
Map pp52–3   International Hotel $$$
☎ 6339 7777; www.raffles-theplazahotel.com;
80 Bras Basah Rd; r from $330; Ⓜ City Hall; ⛊
It shares the same facilities as its twin
Swissôtel, but the rooms here are markedly
different in design from the usual flowers-
and-magnolia look of many hotels. Stylish
and understated, this place is top-notch.

GRAND PLAZA PARKROYAL HOTEL
Map pp52–3   International Hotel $$$
☎ 6336 3456; www.parkroyalhotels.com;
10 Coleman St; r from $320; Ⓜ City Hall; ⛊
It's won an award for its architecture apparently, and though the rooms are virtually
indistinguishable from many other top
hotels, there is an in-house spa that will
appeal to frazzled shoppers. Look out for
dramatic online discounts.

HOTEL RENDEZVOUS
Map pp52–3   International Hotel $$$
☎ 6336 0220; www.rendezvoushotels.com;
9 Bras Basah Rd; s/d from $300/330;
Ⓜ Dhoby Ghaut; ▯
Overlooking Bras Basah Park, the rooms
here are a little heavy on the pastel, but
well worth it if you can get a discount rate.
The interior lobby is quite elegant, and
there's an attractive bar next to a cool,
imposing courtyard.

NOVOTEL CLARKE QUAY
Map pp52–3   International Hotel $$$
☎ 6338 3333; www.novotelclarkequay.com.sg;
177A River Valley Rd; s/d from $300/320;
Ⓜ Clarke Quay; ▯ ⛊
The no-nonsense approach you expect
from the Novotel chain. No bells or whis-
tles, no surprises or extravagant extras;
plain, clean, comfortable and professional.

GRAND COPTHORNE WATERFRONT HOTEL
Map pp52–3   International Hotel $$$
☎ 6733 0880; http://millenniumhotels.com;
392 Havelock Rd; s/d from $295/325;
▯ 123 from Ⓜ Tiong Bahru; ▯ ⛊
Of the several hotels clustered at the Rob-
ertson Quay end of the river (the closest
MRT is Tiong Bahru, but it's not walking
within distance), the fanciest is this im-
posing place. This is the best of the Cop-
thorne group of hotels, with light-filled,
comfortable rooms.

GALLERY HOTEL
Map pp52–3   Hotel $$$
☎ 6849 8686; www.galleryhotel.com.sg;
76 Robertson Quay; r incl breakfast from $320;
Ⓜ Clarke Quay; ⛊
With its primary-colour fixtures and
fittings, hi-tech room facility control
panels and its gorgeous lap pool, the
Gallery Hotel is the crème de la crème of
Singapore's boutique hotels. The subdued minimalist lobby is so hip it hurts,
and room decorations are sexy without
being lewd. Broadband and wireless are
free, as is the indoor recreation area. The
one drawback to this otherwise excellent hotel is that the construction being
carried out next door might not be done
until sometime in 2009.

HOLIDAY INN ATRIUM
Map pp52–3   International Hotel $$$
☎ 6733 0188; www.holiday-inn.com; 317 Outram Rd;
s/d from $300/350; Ⓜ Outram Park; ▯ ⛊
This 27-storey dazzler has a charm be-
lying both its age and its chain-hotel
pedigree. The interior glass elevators give
the atrium a particularly futuristic feel.
Rooms are fairly standard, though quite
comfortable, making this hotel near the
Robertson Quay entertainment district
and Great World City shopping centre a
good choice.

ALLSON HOTEL
Map pp52–3   Hotel $$$
☎ 6336 0811; allson.sales@pacific.net.sg;
101 Victoria St; r from $320; Ⓜ City Hall; ⛊
Fitting its location in the museum district,
the Allson has an old-fashioned feel, despite its modern exterior. Rooms are tastefully done out with dark wood and leather
furniture. There are nonsmoking floors,
and facilities include a pool and several
restaurants.

RIVER VIEW HOTEL
Map pp52–3   Hotel $$$
☎ 6732 9922; www.riverview.com.sg;
382 Havelock Rd; s/d from $220/240;
Ⓜ Clarke Quay; ▯ ⛊
Excellent value if one of its generous
discounts is on offer, this uninspiring off-
white tower opposite Robertson Quay has
an excellent riverside location and large
comfortable rooms. A free shuttle service
runs to Orchard Rd, Suntec City and
Chinatown.

HOTEL ROYAL@QUEENS

Map pp52–3   Hotel $$$

☎ 6725 9988; www.royalqueens.com.sg; 12 Queen St; r from $230; Ⓜ Bugis; ⊉

Soft lighting, dark mahogany furnishings, and a smattering of hip wall paintings give this boutique hotel a cool hipster vibe. The best rooms are the ones with the view of St Joseph's cathedral, but all are clean and comfortable. Hotel Royal also has a swimming pool and health centre. Book online for deep discounts.

ROBERTSON QUAY HOTEL

Map pp52–3   Hotel $$$

☎ 6735 3333; www.robertsonquayhotel.com.sg; 15 Merbau Rd; s/d $150/180; Ⓜ Clarke Quay; ⌨ ⊉

Definitely one of the best value hotels in the area, the Robertson is a circular building that vaguely resembles a medieval castle tower. Rooms, though not large, are well furnished with all the mod-cons you'd hope for at the price; those on the higher floors offer excellent views. Perhaps the loveliest feature of this hotel is the unusual rooftop swimming pool landscaped with large boulders. The Robertson is close to both the Quays and the CBD, making it ideal for business and leisure travellers. Generous internet booking discounts are often available, too.

PARK VIEW HOTEL

Map pp52–3   Hotel $$$

☎ 6338 8558; www.parkview.com.sg; 81 Beach Rd; s/d $140/160, deluxe r $180; Ⓜ Bugis; ⌨

Not a bad little midrange hotel, Park View is centrally located to the Bugis shopping area (though where the park is we can't say). Though all rooms have bathtubs, some of the cheaper rooms are windowless. And while breakfast is included, wireless internet costs an additional $6 per hour, fairly expensive for a hotel of this middle calibre.

BEACH HOTEL Map pp52–3   Hotel $$

☎ 6336 7712; www.beachhotel.com.sg; 95 Beach Rd, s/d $135/150, deluxe r $170; Ⓜ Bugis

Just down the block from the Park View (which views no park) is the Beach Hotel (which has no beach). Rooms, prices and amenities are much the same here as there, though rack-rate at the beach is a few dollars less.

YWCA FORT CANNING LODGE

Map pp52–3   Hotel $

☎ 6338 4222; reservations@ywcafclodge.org.sg; 6 Fort Canning Rd; s/tw from $99/115, family ste $180; Ⓜ Dhoby Ghaut;

This is probably the best of the three Ys, boasting large, comfortable rooms complete with wooden floors and a decent range of facilities including a cafe, swimming pool and tennis court. It's sandwiched between busy roads, but it's a short walk from both Orchard Rd and the serenity of Fort Canning Park.

HOTEL BENCOOLEN Map pp52–3   Hotel $$

☎ 6336 0822; www.hotelbencoolen.com; 47 Bencoolen St; s/d $110/120; Ⓜ Dhoby Ghaut; ⊉

With a rooftop spa, good location and reasonable rates, Hotel Bencoolen is among the better-value places in this area, now brimming over with hotels. Rooms themselves are clean and comfortable, though about as exciting as Al Gore's wardrobe. Rates include breakfast.

YMCA INTERNATIONAL HOUSE

Map pp52–3   Hostel/Hotel $$

☎ 6336 6000; www.ymcaih.com.sg; 1 Orchard Rd; dm $30, s from $180, family ste $215; Ⓜ Dhoby Ghaut; ⊉

Like the YWCA, this place has large, clean rooms, a handy location and good facilities, including a fitness centre, rooftop swimming pool, squash and badminton courts, and a billiard room. There's also a restaurant, which offers a cheap set meal daily. All rooms have a telephone.

OXFORD HOTEL Map pp52–3   Hotel $$

☎ 6332 2222; www.oxfordhotel.com.sg; 218 Queen St; s/d $180/200; Ⓜ Bugis; ⌨

Another new medium-sized hotel in the Bencoolen hub. The main selling point of the Oxford is its uniform rooms (all are clean and perfectly serviceable, if somewhat dull) and its central location, pretty much equidistant from the Quays, Little India and the Bugis shopping district.

VICTORIA HOTEL Map pp52–3   Hotel $$

☎ 6622 0909; www.santa.com.sg; 87 Victoria St; s/d $128/168, deluxe r $208; Ⓜ Bugis; ⌨

Popular with businesspeople and casual travellers alike, this hotel offers comfortable rooms furnished with bed, TV, desk and chair. Single rooms are a bit on the cramped side, but the deluxe rooms feature queen-sized beds and bathtub-equipped bathrooms. There's also a nice little coffeeshop downstairs with free wireless.

WATERLOO HOSTEL Map pp52–3 Hotel $$
☎ 6336 6555; fax 6336 2160; 4th fl, Catholic Centre Bldg, 55 Waterloo St; s with shared/private bathroom $80/100, d $80/120; Ⓜ Dhoby Ghaut, City Hall or Bugis
Another victim of the area's change from hostel to upscale, the Waterloo Hostel is a hostel no longer (though the name, oddly enough, remains unchanged) but a hotel instead, having deleted dorm beds in favour of private rooms. The hotel is still clean and well run, with rooms equipped with TVs, fridges and phones. It's within reasonable walking distance of Orchard Rd, the Colonial District and Bugis. Breakfast is included.

SUMMER TAVERN Map pp52–3 Hostel $
☎ 6535 6601; www.summertavern.com; 31 Carpenter St; dm/s/d $35/90/180; Ⓜ Clarke Quay; 🖥
Still among the most popular hostels in Singapore despite the high price of its dorm beds, Summer Tavern Hostel offers fine dorm beds, medium-sized rooms good for one or two guests, and a fine rooftop beer lounge. Summer Tavern has recently expanded to include a second building across the street, in which you'll find deluxe rooms with queen-sized beds and attached bathrooms. Rooms can be booked online, and rates include breakfast.

AH CHEW HOTEL Map pp52–3 Hostel $
☎ 6837 0356; 496 North Bridge Rd; rooftop/fan/air-con dm $8/10/12, r with fan/air-con $26/30; Ⓜ Bugis
Above the Tong Seng Coffee shop, with its frontage facing the restaurant-bar strip on Liang Seah St, this dusty old flophouse has a certain dingy charm and the cheapest, noisiest beds in Singapore. Certain to make your stay a memorable one.

BACKPACKER COZY CORNER GUESTHOUSE Map pp52–3 Guesthouse $
☎ 6339 6128; www.cozycornerguest.com; 490 North Bridge Rd; dm with fan/air-con $11/16, d fan/air-con $33/48; Ⓜ Bugis; 🖥

It feels a little like a kindergarten, with its 'museum' and its flags, kitsch reading corner and government-issue paint, but at these rates who's complaining? It's clean, friendly and well located, with free breakfast, free internet and a rooftop lounging area as well.

CHINATOWN & THE CBD

Riding the shophouse restoration wave, Chinatown has some particularly fine midrange tourist hotels; here you'll find everything from elegant old-world charm to funky designer guesthouses, all in proximity to some of Singapore's best eating and nightlife. The area also has a few cheap hostels.

M HOTEL Map pp62–3 Hotel $$$
☎ 6224 1133; www.mhotel.com.sg; 81 Anson Rd; r from $380; Ⓜ Tanjong Pagar; 🖥
On the southern edge of the CBD, this is a place for Chanel-handbag and Armani-suit business types. It oozes chic, from the flat-screen TVs in the rooms to the neon blues of the bar. The only downside is the location, next to the expressway and a fair way from Singapore's main attractions. Good discounts are available on the website!

NEW MAJESTIC HOTEL
Map pp62–3 Boutique Hotel $$$
☎ 6511 4700; www.newmajestichotel.com; 31-37 Bukit Pasoh Rd; r from $350-700; Ⓜ Outram Park; 🖥 ⓡ
The New Majestic offers occupants 30 unique rooms – so unique each room features the artwork of a different artist – done up in a mix of vintage and designer furniture. Among the highlights are the private garden suite, attic rooms with loft beds and 6m-high ceilings, and the fabulous aquarium room, in which the central feature is a glass-encased bathtub. A technophile's paradise, all rooms are fitted with sophisticated high-end gadgetry like LCD TVs, Bose stereos with iPod docks and in-room coffee-makers provided by Nespresso. Undoubtedly the hippest hotel in Singapore, the newly opened New Majestic Hotel is destined to become an icon of cool.

BERJAYA HOTEL SINGAPORE

Map pp62–3   Boutique Hotel $$$
☎ 6227 7678; www.berjayaresorts.com;
83 Duxton Rd; r from $250, ste $450;
Ⓜ Tanjong Pagar

If you're looking for a boutique hotel with luxury to spare, this elegant shophouse conversion is one of your best bets – all wooden fixtures and old-world charm. All rooms are beautifully furnished and the suites have an unusual mezzanine bedroom reached by a spiral staircase.

ROYAL PEACOCK HOTEL

Map pp62–3   Boutique Hotel $$$
☎ 6223 3522; www.royalpeacockhotel.com;
55 Keong Saik Rd; s/d $145/165, executive r $205,
attic s/d $115/135; Ⓜ Outram Park

Though the wooden floors are uneven in spots and some of the antique furniture seems frayed around the edges, the Royal Peacock – one of the area's original shophouse-boutique hotels – has stood the test of time fairly well. Attic rooms are the best bargain, if you can live without a window. The lobby and attached restaurant are charming, to say the least.

HOTEL 1929

Map pp62–3   Boutique Hotel $$$
☎ 6347 1929; www.hotel1929.com; 50 Keong Saik
Rd; s/d $210/250; Ⓜ Outram Park; ▣

Once the most eclectic of Chinatown's boutique hotels, 1929 now takes second place to the nearby New Majestic – though since they're both owned by the same companies, there probably aren't any hard feelings. Still, the 1929 manages to please both style-wise and comfort-wise, with small but wonderfully and uniquely furnished rooms, an outdoor 4th-floor Jacuzzi, complimentary wireless, and all the class you'd expect from one of Singapore's pre-eminent boutique hotels. Discounts available through the website.

CHINATOWN HOTEL

Map pp62–3   Boutique Hotel $$$
☎ 6225 5166; www.chinatownhotel.com; 12-16
Teck Lim Rd; s/d/r $155/175/205; Ⓜ Outram Park

Though prices have risen dramatically at this one-time budget hotel, overall quality doesn't seem to have kept pace, resulting in budget hotel ambience at a boutique hotel price. Though not a bad place, rooms aren't as nice as the nearby 1929

or the cheaper Tropical next door. Worth a stay if everything else in the neighbourhood is full.

TROPICAL HOTEL Map pp62–3   Hotel $$
☎ 6225 6696; fax 6225 6626; 22 Teck Lim Rd;
s/d from $90/120; Ⓜ Outram Park

Rooms in this converted shophouse are a bit frayed around the edges, but not wholly lacking in charm. Some singles are without windows and the larger rooms at the front with balconies go for $100, but they're open to bargaining for longer stays.

SERVICE WORLD BACKPACKERS HOSTEL

Map pp62–3   Hostel $
☎ 6226 3886; 5 Banda St 02-82; dm $20;
Ⓜ Chinatown

Located behind the Buddha Tooth Relic Temple, this is a small family-owned hostel offering little in the way of frills but much in the way of friendliness and a central location. The hostel is in a traditional Singaporean housing development, giving budget travellers a valuable chance to experience life the way that 85% of Singaporeans do. Andrew Yip, who runs Service World with his wife, is an author and photographer who is exceptionally passionate about Singapore's traditional culture and art.

LITTLE INDIA & KAMPONG GLAM

From upmarket swank to low-key boutique hotels and even a few cheap and decent hostels, this area is a traveller's hot spot for tourists of all budget levels. Hotels in this area include those accessible from Boon Kong, Farrer Park and Little India, as well as some closer to Bugis and Lavender MRT stations.

GOLDEN LANDMARK HOTEL

Map p68   Hotel $$$
☎ 6297 2828; www.goldenlandmark.com.sg;
290 Victoria St; r from $240; Ⓜ Bugis; ▣ ▣

One of the few upmarket hotels in the Arab St area, rooms at the Golden Landmark are spacious and well-furnished, featuring full bathtubs and in-room espresso machines. The onion-domed glass elevators in the lobby are a particularly nice touch. Try to get a room facing the nearby mosque for the most spectacular views.

ALBERT COURT HOTEL

Map p68   Boutique Hotel $$$

☎ 6339 3939; www.albertcourt.com.sg; 180 Albert St; standard/deluxe r $200/220; Ⓜ Little India; 💻 At the southern edge of Little India, this is a splendid, colonial-era boutique hotel in a shophouse redevelopment that now shoots up eight storeys. All rooms have the usual mod cons, and include a choice of fan or air-con. The promotional rates go as low as $120.

PERAK HOTEL Map p68   Hotel $$$

☎ 6299 7733; www.peraklodge.net; 12 Perak Rd; s/d $174/233; Ⓜ Little India; 💻 A long-time favourite, the newly reno-vated Perak Hotel (formerly called Perak Lodge) mixes a colonial exterior with an oriental interior complete with Buddha statues and quaint sitting and meditation spaces. Rooms are lovely and well fur-nished, and rates include free wireless and breakfast.

SUMMER VIEW HOTEL Map p68   Hotel $$

☎ 6338 1122; www.summerviewhotel.com.sg; 173 Bencoolen St; d $200; Ⓜ Bugis Clean and comfortable, the rooms here are quite large for a midrange hotel and it's handily located. The MRT is a bit of a hike, so the shuttle service to Orchard Rd and Suntec City might come in useful.

FORTUNA HOTEL Map p68   Hotel $$

☎ 6295 3577; fax 6294 7738; 2 Owen Rd; r from $125; Ⓜ Farrer Park Looks more like an office building than a hotel, but the rooms are actually quite ap-pealing – and very large – and staff mem-bers are very welcoming. If you can get one of the $80 promo rates, snap it up.

DICKSON COURT HOTEL

Map p68   Hotel $$$

☎ 6297 7811; dicksonl@magix.com.sg; 3 Dickson Rd; d from $120; Ⓜ Little India Cobbled together from a row of old shop-houses, the lobby and courtyard areas of the Dickson Court Hotel have a touch of refinement about them. The rooms are clean, although some of them are small and dark. The hotel has a restaurant and a cafe as well as a broad range of services.

You will almost always find a promotional rate on offer, which can see prices drop to $89.

SOUTH-EAST ASIA HOTEL

Map p68   Hotel $

☎ 6338 2394; www.seahotel.com.sg; 190 Waterloo St; standard/superior d $80/98; Ⓜ Bugis Next to a couple of the area's most colour-ful temples on one of Singapore's most bustling, lively pedestrian precincts, this hotel is clean, friendly and good value, though you can barely swing a mouse in the bathrooms. Highly recommended, particularly for its location.

MADRAS HOTEL Map p68   Hotel $

☎ 6392 7889; www.madrassingapore.com; 28-32 Madras St; s/d/tr $95/105/175; Ⓜ Little India; 💻 Simple, clean and reliably hospitable are the main bullet points of the Madras Hotel, which, while offering little in the way of frills, still maintains its reputation as a trust-worthy place for travellers on a budget. Madras also offers a discounted price of $79 for any room checked into after mid-night (same check-out time applies). Prices include breakfast.

ASPHODEL INN Map p68   Hotel $

☎ 6296 92989; www.asphoinn.com; 80 Race Course Rd; s/d $85/95; Ⓜ Ferrer Park; 💻 A four-storey converted shophouse on a quiet street in between Little India and Bugis, the Asphodel Inn offers a reason-ably priced place to stay for those whose budgets fall between backpacker and boutique. What this establishment lacks in frills it makes up for in cleanliness and quaintness. The location isn't bad either: set across from a row of charming mul-ticoloured residential homes and a small Chinese temple.

ASPINALS HOTEL Map p68   Hotel $

☎ 6392 3944; www.aspinals.com.sg; 83 Syed Alwi Rd; s/d/tr $85/95/105; Ⓜ Little India; 💻 An inexpensive hotel in that it bridges nicely the budget gap between hostel and boutique hotel, Aspinals is clean, reason-ably well furnished, and definitely conven-ient to all the scent and splendour that little India has to offer.

BROADWAY HOTEL Map p68   Hotel $$
☎ 6292 4661; www.geocities.com/broadwayhotel; 195 Serangoon Rd; r $128; Ⓜ Little India
In the heart of Little India, this fairly plain looking but well-maintained hotel seems to attract a mixed crowd of business people and tourists. The Broadway offers free wireless internet, and is close to all the action of the area.

HAISING HOTEL Map p68   Hostel $
☎ 6298 1223; www.haising.com.sg; 37 Jalan Besar; s/d/f $50/55/100; Ⓜ Bugis; ▯
Across from Sim Lim Tower, rooms at this budget hotel are stuffy, charmless and cheap. But the place is reasonably clean, and did we mention it was cheap?

HANGOUT@MT.EMILY Map p68   Hostel $$
☎ 6438 5588; www.hangouthotels.com; 10A Upper Wilkie Rd; dm/s/d $40/94/117; Ⓜ Little India or Dhoby Ghaut; ▯
A sleek and trendy boutique hostel set among the leafy glades of Mt Emily, though the walk up the hill is a bit of a drag for those with bags. Hangout is a hybrid hostel–boutique hotel that's not too far from Orchard Rd and Little India. Done out in vibrant colours, with murals by local art students, the unisex and mixed dorms and private rooms are immaculate, as are the bathrooms. It also has a magnificent rooftop terrace, complete with Balinese sculptures, as well as a library, a cafe, free internet and cosy lounging areas. Knock $10 off the rates for internet bookings. Private room rates include breakfast.

SLEEPY SAM'S Map p68   Hostel $
☎ 9277 4988; www.sleepysams.com; 55 Bussorah St; dm/s/d $25/49/79; Ⓜ Bugis; ▯
With its boutique-hotel ambience, pier-and-beam ceilings, beautiful book-filled common area-cafe and well-furnished dorm rooms, Sleepy Sam's once again comes in as one of the finest hostels in Singapore. It's located just down from the imposing Sultan Mosque on the historical, burgeoning Bussorah St bohemian district, making it a great place to people watch. Sam's also features mixed or female-only dorms, private rooms and free internet.

BUGIS BACKPACKERS Map p68   Hostel $
☎ 6338 5581; 162B Rochor Rd; mixed/female dm $26/36, d $88; Ⓜ Bugis

In the bustling centre of Bugis Village, this clean, functional, appealing hostel (with the usual facilities) is particularly well located to sample the lively night markets and other nocturnal activity in the area – and it's a short walk from Arab St.

INNCROWD Map p68   Hostel $
☎ 6296 9169; www.the-inncrowd.com; 35 Campbell Lane; dm/d/tr $20/48/68; Ⓜ Little India; ▯
If Sleepy Sam's is avant-garde jazz, then Inn Crowd is more drum-and-bass, attracting a younger, party-hearty crowd. Located in the heart of Little India, the funkily painted hostel has become so popular that it's opened a second location (73 Dunlop St) around the corner. The air-con dorms, common bathrooms and kitchens are spotless and there's even a washing machine. Add to that a sun deck, a pub, a minimart, a foosball table, free internet, free breakfast, extremely friendly staff and a branch of the Singapore Visitors Centre, and you may well have the ultimate hostel.

NEW 7TH STOREY HOTEL Map p68   Hostel $
☎ 6337 0251; www.nsshotel.com; 229 Rochor Rd; dm/s $19/62 superior/deluxe r $92/95; Ⓜ Bugis; ▯
Sitting in splendid isolation on a patch of cleared land, this well-run, very friendly place has clean dorms with rather spindly bunks and very good-value private rooms. Other good points include delightful garden patios, close proximity to the DHL hot-air balloon ride (p156), a games room and bike rental.

HIVE Map p68   Hostel $
☎ 6341 5041; www.thehivebackpackers.com; 269A Lavender St; dm/s/d $20/32/42; Ⓜ Boon Keng; ▯
The Hive's friendliness and cleanliness more than makes up for a slightly inconvenient location. Dorms are fairly standard, lacking in natural light but otherwise fine. There's free breakfast, free internet and a comfortable lounge room.

PRINCE OF WALES BACKPACKER HOSTEL Map p68   Hostel $
☎ 6299 0130; www.pow.com.sg; 101 Dunlop St; dm $18, d with fan/air-con $42/50; Ⓜ Little India
Australian-style pub and hostel, featuring a spit-and-sawdust live-music pub down-

stairs (see p144) with excellent Australian beers and clean dorms upstairs painted in bright oranges and blues. The noise won't suit everyone, but it's a fun place to stay and is deservedly popular. POW is currently running a four-night $60 special, for those inclined to stay a bit longer.

HAWAII HOSTEL Map p68 Hostel $
☎ 6338 4187; www.hawaiihostel.com.sg; 2nd fl, 171B Bencoolen St; 4-bed dm $12, s/d $28/35; Ⓜ Bugis
One of the few places in the Bencoolen area that hasn't changed in the last few years; dorm beds, singles and doubles are still cheap and basic in this hostel located on the 2nd floor of an unassuming look-ing concrete building and as close to the epitome of cheap sleeps as you're likely to find in Singapore.

TREEHOUSE BACKPACKER'S HOSTEL
Map p68 Hostel $
☎ 6392 5331; www.treehouse.sg; 197 Jalan Besar; dm $20; Ⓜ Bugis
A smallish backpackers hostel with two dorm rooms; your host at Treehouse is the heavily tattooed Adrian Neo, who's always happy to advise visitors on what activities the area has to offer. The price includes free internet, breakfast, DIY laundry services, hot and cold showers, bath towels and bedding, and free tattoo advice.

DRAGON INN HOSTEL
Map p68 Hostel $
☎ 6296 0776; 1 Kelantan Rd; dm $16; Ⓜ Bugis; 🖥
Looking like a converted warehouse space, this fairly new hostel has 30 beds, free wire-less, a barely furnished common area with a TV and chairs, and a communal kitchen. Price includes breakfast.

ORCHARD ROAD

When many think Singapore, they think Or-chard Rd; undoubtedly the veritable heart of chic-ness in the Lion City, this area also has some of its poshest hotels. Though there aren't any budget options coming anywhere close to those found in Little India, the area does offer a few midrange hotels worth checking out. This section encompasses hotels served by the Somerset, Orchard and Newton MRT stations.

FOUR SEASONS HOTEL
Map pp74–5 International Hotel $$$
☎ 6734 1110; www.fourseasons.com/singapore; 190 Orchard Blvd; s/d from $435/475; Ⓜ Orchard; 🖥 🛋
In a quiet, tree-lined street just off Orchard Rd, the Four Seasons has a beautiful lobby matched by elegant antique-style rooms. Among its many facilities are air-conditioned tennis courts. Check out its weekend special, which starts at $248.

SHERATON TOWERS
Map pp74–5 International Hotel $$$
☎ 6737 6888; www.sheraton.com/towerssingapore; 39 Scotts Rd; deluxe/executive r $430/500; Ⓜ Newton; 🖥 🛋
Oozes opulence and has all manner of facilities. The rooms are decorated in mossy greens with beautiful pictures of flowers, and the service is efficient and pleasant. The grand lobby is a lovely place for tea.

GOODWOOD PARK HOTEL
Map pp74–5 Hotel $$$
☎ 6730 1811; www.goodwoodparkhotel.com; 22 Scotts Rd; r from $385; Ⓜ Orchard; 🛋
This historic hotel has an old-fashioned feel but bags of class, from its two swim-ming pools to the hotel's pet cat roam-ing the lobby. Nice touches in the rooms include arty black-and-white photos of Singapore, Persian rugs and neatly hid-den TVs and minibars. If you have $3000 to spare, treat yourself to a night in the opulent Brunei suite.

MERITUS MANDARIN SINGAPORE
Map pp74–5 International Hotel $$$
☎ 6737 2200; www.mandarin-singapore.com; 333 Orchard Rd; south-/main-tower r from $360/400; Ⓜ Somerset; 🖥 🛋
An elegant yet informal place. The cheapest rooms are in the south tower, while those in the main tower (the one with the obser-vation lounge and the revolving restaurant Top of the M) are decorated in warm tones with Oriental-themed furniture and fresh orchids in the bathrooms.

REGENT HOTEL
Map pp74–5 International Hotel $$$
☎ 6733 8888; www.regenthotels.com; 1 Cuscaden Rd; r from $350; Ⓜ Orchard; 🖥 🛋
Walking from the far west end of Orchard Rd, this is the first hotel you'll come across

and one of the best. It's a classy operation with all the colourful, spacious rooms arranged around its airy central atrium. There are acres of marble and gorgeous furnishings in the lobby, which is a top place for afternoon tea.

LE MERIDIEN SINGAPORE

Map pp74–5   Hotel $$$

☎ 6733 8855; www.lemeridien-singapore.com; 100 Orchard Rd; s/d from $290/320; M Somerset; 🖳 🐾

The atrium lobby, with its glass-panel elevators and line drawings, is beginning to look dated, but this is still a decent hotel. The rooms are quite pleasant and the Chinese screens on the walls add a distinctive touch.

GRAND HYATT SINGAPORE

Map pp74–5   International Hotel $$$

☎ 6738 1234; http://singapore.grand.hyatt.com; 10-12 Scotts Rd; r from $380; M Orchard; 🖳 🐾

Redesigned in 1998 to feng shui principles, this is a very grand place. The lovely rooms, decorated in a soothing lemon colour, have louvred wooden shutters and small patios. An excellent range of facilities is complemented by two tennis courts. Grand Hyatt offers complimentary breakfast and a very liberal check-out policy. For a truly indulgent experience, try the Grand Club rooms, which offer personalised service and use of an exclusive lounge.

SHANGRI-LA HOTEL

Map pp74–5   International Hotel $$$

☎ 6737 3644; www.shangri-la.com/singapore; 22 Orange Grove Rd; Tower wing deluxe r from $355; M Orchard; 🖳 🐾

This vast, opulent hotel, set in the leafy lanes surrounding the west end of Orchard, boasts a luxurious interior featuring a 15-acre tropical garden and large rooms done out in rich, butterscotch tones with the odd Asian touch. For long-term stayers with plenty of spare cash, there are 127 serviced apartments (at $7500 a month or $315 a day) and 55 private apartments.

TRADERS HOTEL

Map pp74–5   International Hotel $$$

☎ 6738 2222; 1A Cuscaden Rd; s/d from $355/380; M Orchard; 🖳 🐾

Attached to Tanglin Mall, this hotel has stylish, plush rooms, a lovely cloud-shaped outdoor pool and an attractive water wall running the length of its spacious lobby (flowing at peak times only). Traders also has a decent gym and spa on the 4th floor.

HILTON INTERNATIONAL

Map pp74–5   International Hotel $$$

☎ 6737 2233; www.singapore.hilton.com; 581 Orchard Rd; standard r $290, executive-floor r $350; M Orchard; 🖳 🐾

At the heart of Orchard Rd is the Hilton. Although nothing spectacular (apart from the distinctive sculpted exterior wall panels), this is a good choice for business

HISTORIC HOTELS

It's not just Raffles that has an illustrious past (see p56). Goodwood Park Hotel (p169), dating from 1900 and designed to resemble a Rhine castle, served as the base for the Teutonia Club, a social club for Singapore's German community, until 1914 when it was seized by the government as part of 'enemy property'. In 1918 the building was auctioned off and renamed Club Goodwood Hall, before it morphed again into the Goodwood Park Hotel in 1929, fast becoming one of the finest hotels in Asia.

During WWII it accommodated the Japanese high command, some of whom returned here at the war's end to be tried for war crimes in a tent erected in the hotel grounds. By 1947 the hotel was back in business with a $2.5-million renovation program bringing it back to its former glory by the early 1960s. Further improvements in the 1970s have left the hotel as it is today.

The Fullerton Hotel (p162) occupies the magnificent colonnaded Fullerton Building, named after Robert Fullerton, the first Governor of the Straits Settlements. When it opened in 1928, it was the largest building in Singapore and cost over $4 million. The General Post Office, which occupied the three floors of the building, was said to have the longest counter (100m) in the world at the time. Above the GPO was the exclusive Singapore Club, in which Governor Sir Shenton Thomas and General Percival discussed surrendering Singapore to the Japanese.

In 1958 a revolving lighthouse beacon was added to the roof; its beams could be seen up to 29km away. By 1996 the GPO had moved out and the entire building underwent a multimillion-dollar renovation and reopened in 2001 to general acclaim, receiving the prestigious Urban Redevelopment Authority Architectural Award the same year.

travellers – executive-floor guests have a buffet breakfast, use of the gym and other benefits included in the room cost. Rates can go much higher.

SINGAPORE MARRIOTT
Map pp74–5   International Hotel $$$
☎ 6735 5800; www.marriott.com/sindt; 320 Orchard Rd; deluxe/executive r $280/340; Ⓜ Orchard; 🖥 🔁
With its pagoda-like tower, this is one of the most distinctive buildings along Orchard Rd; it's located on one of Orchard Rd's busiest corners, next to the famous Tang's department store. The rooms are excellent and well decorated and the whole place has a bustling, big-city atmosphere.

ORCHARD PARADE HOTEL
Map pp74–5   Hotel $$$
☎ 6737 1133; www.orchardparade.com.sg; 1 Tanglin Rd; r from $310; Ⓜ Orchard; 🖥 🔁
Close to the bustle of Orchard Rd yet facing the greenery of Tanglin, the Orchard Parade offers good-sized rooms with huge beds and sofas – the cheapest ones are on the 6th floor (below the outdoor pool and pavilion) and below. There are a couple of good restaurants in the downstairs mall, and even a Starbucks.

ELIZABETH Map pp74–5   Hotel $$$
☎ 6738 1188; www.theelizabeth.com.sg; 24 Mount Elizabeth Rd; r from $290; Ⓜ Orchard; 🖥 🔁
In a quiet spot a short walk north of Orchard Rd, the Elizabeth has an exclusive feel, complemented by a wonderful waterfall-side dining room where staff serve excellent wood-fired pizzas at night. The rooms, accessed by external lifts, are warm and welcoming, with William Morris–style print bedspreads. There's a nifty shortcut to Scotts Rd through the lobby of the York Hotel opposite. Recommended.

METROPOLITAN Y
Map pp74–5   Hotel/Hostel $$
☎ 6737 7755; www.mymca.org.sg; 60 Stevens Rd; dm $45, s/d from $200/250; Ⓜ Orchard; 🔁
The cheapest rooms have no windows, but they're spacious and well-appointed and the excellent facilities include a gym and pool. It's a good 15-minute walk north of Orchard Rd, but a shuttle bus runs there Monday to Friday. For long-term visitors (see p161), apartments are also available. Booking online knocks $20 off the price.

HOTEL GRAND CENTRAL
Map pp74–5   Hotel $$
☎ 6737 9944; www.ghihotels.com; 22 Cavenagh Rd; r from $140; Ⓜ Dhoby Ghaut; 🖥 🔁
One of the few budget options in the Orchard Rd area, Grand Central lives up to its name, being suitably huge (390 rooms) and milling with endless tourist and business traffic. Rooms are tastefully appointed in the earth-tones so popular in Singapore, and all come with LCD TVs and four-star hotel amenities. As for location, if its Orchard Rd living you want at Bugis prices, you've come to the right place.

HOTEL SUPREME Map pp74–5   Hotel $$
☎ 6737 8333; supremeh@starhub.net.sg; 15 Kramat Rd; r from $150; Ⓜ Dhoby Ghaut; 🖥 🔁
Another Orchard Rd–area budget option, the inaptly named Supreme is smaller and, well, less grand than the Grand Central next door, offering smaller rooms for more money. On the plus side, it's quieter, not a bad place in its own right, and still cheaper than most other area hotels.

LLOYD'S INN Map pp74–5   Hotel $$
☎ 6737 7309; www.lloydinn.com; 2 Lloyd Rd; standard/deluxe r $100/120; Ⓜ Somerset
A quick walk south of the Orchard Rd hubbub is where you'll find this spread-out cool California 'motel-style' hotel on a quiet street surrounded by old villas. Rooms are clean, tidy, and fairly spacious, and some have lovely views of Lloyd's interior courtyard bamboo garden. Wireless internet and local calls are free. Bookings are advisable, as the low rates mean the place can fill up fast. Lloyd's is located a stone's throw from the ancestral home of former Prime Minister Lee.

EASTERN SINGAPORE

Far (for Singaporeans) from the maddening crowds, Eastern Singapore is a great place to stay for those seeking a different perspective on the Lion City. One of the main attractions of this exceptionally pleasant part of town is the chance to bookend every day amid the cooling breezes of East Coast Park.

The Eastern Singapore neighbourhood covers a large part of the island of Singapore, everything east of the Kallang MRT station.

GRAND MERCURE ROXY

Map p80   Hotel $$$

☎ 6344 8000; www.centuryhotels.com;
50 East Coast Rd; s/d from $230/250; Ⓜ Eunos
This hotel has a great location close to both Katong and the East Coast Park and 9km from the airport (the entrance is on Marine Parade Rd). The contemporary Asian design of the rooms is appealing and it has plenty of facilities. Rates include breakfast.

LION CITY HOTEL Map p80   Hotel $$

☎ 6744 8111; www.lioncityhotel.com.sg;
15 Tanjong Katong Rd; r from $165; Ⓜ Paya Leber
One of the best nontransit midrange hotels in the Joo Chiat area, the Lion City is a sight for sore eyes in an area in which many other hotels have gone for the quick 'rooms by the hour' buck. Rooms, though not fancy, are clean and well furnished, and all bathrooms have tubs. Two blocks south of the MRT and 20 minutes from the airport, Lion City is surrounded by excellent eating options, and is a good base from which to explore both eastern and central Singapore.

CHANGI VILLAGE HOTEL

Map pp46–7   International Hotel $$

☎ 6379 7111; www.changivillage.com.sg;
1 Netheravon Rd; r $180-200; 🚌 2 from
Ⓜ Tanah Merah; 🖥 🏊
Formerly known as Le Meridian Changi, this plush and stylish gem is located about as far away from the city centre as you can get without crossing the water. The hotel is nestled among some gorgeous gardens, offering superb views (especially at night) across to Malaysia and Pulau Ubin from its rooftop wooden deck (just steps away from its rooftop pool). Close to the Changi Golf Course, the sailing club, beach park, airport and the gentle pace of Changi Village, it's an excellent choice.

COSTA SANDS RESORT (EAST COAST)

Map p80   Chalets $$

☎ 6442 7955; www.costasands.com.sg; 1110
East Coast Parkway; 1-/2-storey chalets $140/170;
🚌 12, 14 or 32; 🏊
Smack on the beach at East Coast Park, this is a popular spot for Singaporeans to 'escape' for the weekend, offering an attractive, peaceful (except at weekends!) alternative to the usual city-centre accommodation, especially for travellers with kids. The chalets are comfortable and clean and there are plenty of facilities, from swimming to bike riding and fishing, plus the popular East Coast restaurants and pubs. Transport hassles into the city are the only downside.

HOTEL MALACCA Map p80   Hotel $

☎ 6345 7411; www.malacca.com.sg; 97 Still Rd;
s/d/f $89/99/119; Ⓜ Eunos; 🖥
Located on a somewhat busy street in the eastern end of the Joo Chiat district, your best bet at the Malacca is a room in the back if its peace and quiet that you're after. Rooms at this three-storey hotel are a decent size, and room service (on-call Chinese and Western dishes) is a nice touch.

FRAGRANCE HOTEL Map p80   Hotel $

☎ 6344 9888; www.fragrancehotel.com; 219 Joo
Chiat Rd, Katong; s/d Sun-Thu $58/59, Fri & Sat
$68/69; Ⓜ Payar Lebar
In fierce competition with the Hotel 81 chain for the 'quickie dollar', Fragrance has eight branches, most of them in Geylang, with gaudy names like Pearl and Crystal. The hotels, including this original branch, are attractive and clean enough, but when you consider that they can turn one room around five times a day at $20 per two hours, you might think twice.

HOTEL 81 JOO CHIAT Map p80   Hotel $

☎ 6348 8181; www.hotel81.com.sg/hotels_joochiat
.shtml; 305 Joo Chiat Rd, Katong; r Sun-Fri $49,
Sat $69; Ⓜ Paya Lebar
One of the burgeoning chain of no-nonsense business (and funny business) hotels sprouting up in central Singapore, this one, strung out behind a row of Peranakan shophouses, is among the best-looking, though all branches are identikit inside. It offers specially fitted rooms for the disabled. Check the website for other locations.

GATEWAY HOTEL Map p80   Boutique Hotel $

☎ 6342 0988; gwhotel@singnet.com.sg;
60 Joo Chiat Rd, Katong; r $48-148; Ⓜ Paya Lebar
The Gateway is one of the few boutique hotels in the area. Housed in a vaguely fortlike building with sloping tiled roofs, it offers modern rooms with louvred shutters, though the TV bolted to the ceiling

detracts from the general effect. Ask for a room with a window, even though Joo Chiat Rd can get a little noisy.

JING DONG HOTEL Map p80 Hotel $
☎ 6842 5828; 33-35 Lorong 12, Geylang Rd; r $50; Ⓜ Kallang

It'd be difficult to find a hotel better representing the strange dichotomy that is the Geylang district, Singapore's nexus of sleazy and spiritual. Just off to the side of the red-light district's heart, this two-storey hotel sits in the twin pious shadows of a stately mosque on the right and the Pu Ji Si Buddhist Research Centre (p77). Though Jing Dong rents rooms by the hour (as do all hotels in this part of town), the 2nd storey is reserved for more respectable (ie overnight) customers. Rooms are clean and as well furnished as could be expected for $50.

RUCKSACK Map p80 Hostel $
☎ 6443 3848; www.rucksackinn.com; 697E East Coast Rd; dm $30; Ⓐ 12 from Ⓜ Tanah Merah exit 2; 🖳

Offering the most expensive dorm beds in town, Rucksack has a cool vibe, a punk mural depicting a party of cubist mutants on the wall, and as much free information pamphlets, maps and what have you as you'll ever need. Located in the quieter eastern end of Joo Chiat, Rucksack has two eight-bed dorms, segregated by sex whenever possible. It's above Genesis Bistro Bar.

BETEL BOX Map p80 Hostel $
☎ 6247 7340; www.betelbox.com; 200 Joo Chiat Rd; mixed/female dm $20/22, d $50; Ⓜ Paya Lebar; 🖳

If it's a genuine Singapore experience you're looking for, you've come to the right place. This charming and traditionally furnished hostel is encased by a riot of some of the best local eateries in Joo Chiat and is reasonably near to East Coast Park as well. Betel Box boasts a cosy air-conditioned communal area with TV, DVDs, video games, computers and even a pool table (all of which are notorious for keeping guests in the hostel for too long). It's also equipped with tons of travel guides and a book-exchange corner. Friendly staff offer free tours for guests. If you want to taste a slice of Singapore life, look no further.

FERN LOFT Map p80 Hostel $
☎ 6444 9066; www.fernloft.com; 693 East Coast Rd; dm $18; Ⓐ 12 from Ⓜ Tanah Merah exit 2; 🖳

Cheaper than Rucksack Hostel next door, but not quite as tidy, Fern Loft has two dorm rooms, one mixed 10-bed dorm and one six-bed female dorm. Connected to the downstairs bar and cafe, patrons are offered a free welcome drink, 50% off meals and 20% off drinks at the bar. It also has a cool rooftop bar, free wireless, airport transport and breakfast. It's above George's Mad Bar & Cafe.

SENTOSA ISLAND

Sentosa, Singapore's island playground, where Singaporeans come to bicycle, roller-blade, and spend the weekend on the beach. You won't find any 'off the beaten track' accommodation here, but you will find a few lovely – nearly rustic – surprises. Sentosa can be reached by monorail, shuttle bus, and even cable-car, all of which leave from the HarbourFront MRT station.

SENTOSA SINGAPORE
Map p100 International Hotel $$$
☎ 6275 0331; www.beaufort.com.sg; 2 Bukit Manis Rd; r from $290; 🖳 🏊

A low-rise, elegantly designed five-star resort with a beautiful cliff-top setting. Contemporary furnishings in the rooms, the pleasant Terrace cafe, the very classy Cliff (p137) seafood restaurant and a garden spa with mud pools, Turkish baths and a curious meditation area make this a splendid choice for its target market. The promotional rate takes the price much ower midweek.

SHANGRI-LA'S RASA SENTOSA
RESORT Map p100 International Hotel $$$
☎ 6275 0100; www.shangri-la.com/singapore/rasasentosa/en/index.aspx; 101 Siloso Rd; hill-/sea-facing r from $290/320; 🖳 🏊

Singapore's only beachfront resort is shaped like a bent cruise ship and is ideal for a short family break. The rooms are very well designed to take maximum advantage of the sweeping views and there's a huge swimming pool for guests who don't quite fancy the Singapore Strait waters. Prices include breakfast.

SILOSO BEACH RESORT (SENTOSA)

Map p100   Hotel $$$

☎ 6722 3333; www.silosobeachresort.com; 51 Imbiah Walk; s/d $190/270; 🖵 🏊

The Siloso Beach Resort is the closest thing to a bona-fide jungle resort as you'll find on Sentosa. The concept behind this new resort is simple – rather than removing any of the trees, builders simply designed around them, with some pretty impressive results (several of the rooms are built around glass-encased jungle trees). There's a lovely tropical pool, a waterfall, and beautiful views. Definitely the antidote for antiseptic Singapore!

SIJORI RESORT SENTOSA

Map p100   Hotel $$

☎ 6271 2002; www.sijoriresort.com.sg/sentosa .htm; 23 Beach View; r from $180; 🏊

Despite the appealing setting in a colonial-era mansion at the centre of the island, this is the least fancy of Sentosa's upmarket hotels. The rooms and facilities, including a pool room and video arcade, are not terribly inspiring, but are reasonable value, and rates include breakfast.

COSTA SANDS RESORT (SENTOSA)

Map p100   Hotel $$

☎ 6275 1034; www.costasands.com.sg; 30 Imbiah Walk; kampong huts from $60, r from $140; 🖵 🏊

Reasonable budget choice, with 15 small air-conditioned wooden huts sleeping up to three people and using shared bathrooms. Use of the barbecue pit is $5 extra. Scoring a room over the weekend can be near impossible unless you book months ahead; during the week it shouldn't be a problem. Its hotel rooms are quite smart and good value. There's a small pool guests can use. Discounts are available online

EXCURSIONS

Nobody has ever accused Singapore of being the middle of nowhere. If anything, the island state is about as centrally located as it gets, and there are plenty of places a few hours (and in most cases a quick trip through immigration) from the cacophonous hubbub of central Singapore that are worth a visit.

For a quick plunge into bucolic splendour that leaves behind all of Singapore's overstimulating modernity, you don't even need to bring your passport; Pulau Ubin is one of the last inhabited (though barely) parts of the country that has yet to feel the cold scrape of construction crews armed with heavy machinery. Often billed as a glimpse into Singapore's past, life on this Singapore-controlled island nestled between Singapore and Malaysia hasn't changed much over the last hundred years. Most visitors come over for a day's walking or cycling along Singapore's best mountain-bike paths, but it's possible to spend a night under the stars (they're still there, even though you can only see half a dozen this close to the city lights), or at the island's lone but none-too-shabby resort.

Just across the causeway is where you'll find Johor, the state encompassing the southernmost tip of Peninsular Malaysia. It's home to amazing ecoparks, pretty seaside villages, beautiful cycling roads and plenty of lovely scenery; a few days exploring the area is time well spent. Even if you confine your excursion to the districts closest to Singapore, you'll run across some interesting surprises (ostrich farm, anyone?). And though it won't win any prizes in the 'excellence in urban planning' category, the city of Johor Bahru (a Frisbee toss across the Causeway) is a pretty interesting place to explore for an afternoon, not to mention a favourite shopping getaway for Singaporeans on the prowl for bargains.

Travel in Malaysia is covered in Lonely Planet's *Malaysia, Singapore & Brunei*. Lonely Planet's *Malay Phrasebook* may also come in handy.

PULAU UBIN

Ah, Pulau Ubin, Singapore in name alone! This small and heavily forested island is a mere 15-minute bumboat ride from Singapore, but once you get there you'll think you've stepped into a different century. With its double-digit population (most of whom still live in traditional kampong houses), mangrove swamps, dense forests and gorgeous hiking and cycling trails, Ubin offers an amazing natural escape from the overcrowded consumer frenzy of Singapore. Not surprisingly, Ubin is particularly popular with nature lovers, students and mountain bikers.

The bumboat from Changi Village's incongruously modern ferry terminal arrives at Ubin's village, a ramshackle time capsule of Singapore's past, where fish traps and the skeletal remains of abandoned jetties poke out of the muddy water, stray cats prowl for birds, and docile dogs flop unmolested on the sleepy streets. Still unconnected to the Singaporean electric grid, the businesses in this the only business centre on the island are still driven by gas-powered generators, which accounts for the din and – thankfully localised to the village – pollution.

TRANSPORT: PULAU UBIN

Distance from mainland Singapore 500m

Direction Northeast

Travel time 15 minutes

Boat Getting to Pulau Ubin is easy. A taxi from the city centre to the Changi Village ferry terminal will cost about $20 and take about 20 minutes. Public transport is cheaper, naturally, so if you can spare an hour or so, get the MRT to Tanah Merah, then bus 2 or 29 to the Changi Village interchange; from there it's a two-minute walk to the ferry terminal. Ferries leave whenever there are 12 people to fill a boat and ostensibly run 24 hours a day, though there are unlikely to be regular departures much beyond 8.30pm. The trip each way costs $2.50 per person, and bicycles are an extra $2.

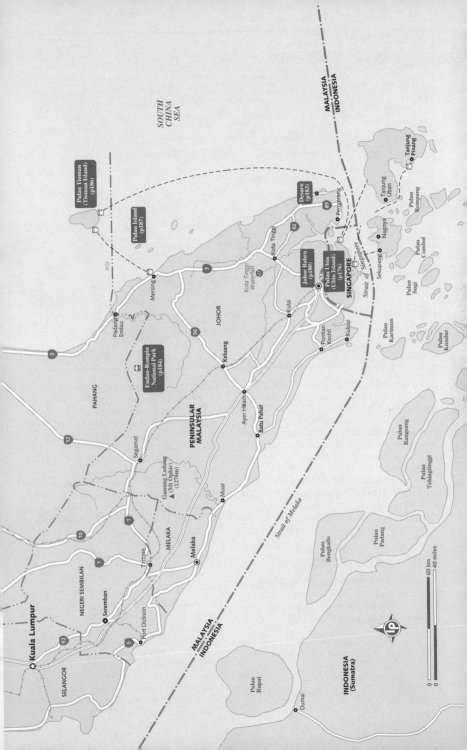

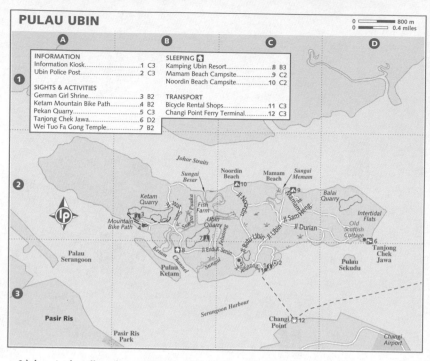

PULAU UBIN

0 — 800 m
0 — 0.4 miles

INFORMATION	
Information Kiosk	1 C3
Ubin Police Post	2 C3

SIGHTS & ACTIVITIES	
German Girl Shrine	3 B2
Ketam Mountain Bike Path	4 B2
Pekan Quarry	5 C3
Tanjong Chek Jawa	6 D2
Wei Tuo Fa Gong Temple	7 B2

SLEEPING	
Kamping Ubin Resort	8 B3
Mamam Beach Campsite	9 C2
Noordin Beach Campsite	10 C2

TRANSPORT	
Bicycle Rental Shops	11 C3
Changi Point Ferry Terminal	12 C3

It's here in the village that you'll find a half-dozen bicycle rental shops offering everything from cheap Chinese-made clunkers ($4 per day) to good-quality mountain bikes (Specialized, Trek and Giant, mostly) complete with shock absorbers, for anywhere between $10 and $20. If you're just here to cruise around the island, the cheap ones are fine, but if you're planning to tackle the newly constructed trails on Ubin's western end, the better bikes are well worth the investment. Whatever you choose, make sure you test gears and brakes before sealing the deal; Zen though Ubin may

be, the art of bicycle maintenance doesn't seem to be a local strong point.

The village is also where the island's restaurants, souvenir stands and grocery stores are. There are a few spots scattered around the island where you can buy snacks and drinks, but if you're planning to wander too far its best to stock up on provisions here.

Biking, hiking, bird-watching, culture and nature are what bring people to Ubin, so unless you enjoy the hum of diesel generators, you'll want to pass through the village before too long. From the village, head out to the eastern edge of the island to check out the Tanjong Chek Jawa, a beautiful wetlands area teeming with mangroves and boasting a 21m-high tower for viewing wildlife and a 1km coastal boardwalk for strolling. Until recently, the area was off limits to casual tourists and accessible only through guided tours. Nowadays individual travellers are permitted without a guide, though you'll still be asked to register and obey strict regulations against disturbing local flora and fauna. While guides are no longer mandatory, you may want to consider hiring the services of two sisters who collectively run a unique business known as the Ubin Experience (see left).

THE UBIN EXPERIENCE

Kamariah and Samsiah Abdullah, co-operators of the Ubin Experience (☎ 9100 6958), lead botanical tours introducing visitors to the natural and cultural aspects of the island that their family has called home for generations.

Costing $120 per group (the minimum suggested number being six, though the sisters often lead groups of up to 20), tours include a jungle walk, herb gathering, and a Malay cooking class followed by a feast inside the sister's 200-year-old kampong home, the oldest structure on the island.

THE GERMAN GIRL SHRINE

The curiously named German Girl Shrine is a bright yellow shack housing a large white urn next to an assam tree. The shrine is filled with all manner of charms, offerings, folded lottery tickets, a medium's red table and chair, burning candles and joss paper. Legend has it that the young German daughter of a coffee plantation manager, running away from British troops who had come to arrest her parents during WWI, fell to her death into the quarry behind her house. Discovered a day later, she was initially covered with sand, though Chinese labourers eventually gave her a proper burial. Her ghost supposedly haunts the area to this day.

However, somewhere along the way, this daughter of a Roman Catholic family became a Taoist deity, whose help some Chinese believers seek for good health and, particularly, good fortune. A small, devoted collection of Singaporeans regularly make the trek to the shrine, dodging mountain bikers who've taken over the area to seek the spectral maiden's favours. Some reportedly even bring German-speaking mediums along.

Pekan Quarry sits on the right side of the road heading out towards the eastern end of the island. The quarry is a beautiful deep pool ringed with granite cliffs, the sort of place that looks like it's custom-made for lazy days spent swimming; it's a pity that swimming is strictly forbidden in all of Ubin's quarries. This one is fenced off, though the fence is drooping and somewhat half-hearted in sections. In any event, no-one's going to arrest you for taking a look.

After the first bridge, a dirt track on the right leads you to Wei Tuo Fa Gong temple. This 80-year-old Buddhist temple sits on a hill overlooking a pond filled with carp and turtle, and contains a number of impressive shrines and statues of the Buddha meditating atop lotus blossoms. A truly living place of worship, the temple is surrounded by gardens meticulously maintained by worshippers, and is home to a dozen or so stray dogs that are fed and cared for by resident monks.

Back on the main road, another 500m of some mildly strenuous uphill cycling takes you past the chocolate-brown chalets and the impressive climbing wall tower of the Kampung Ubin Resort (p180). The climbing wall and surrounding action-toys (zip-lines and rappelling cables) are mostly used for corporate 'team-building' events, though resort guests are permitted to use them as well by advance arrangement. The resort also has a private beach, complete with beach chairs and sea-kayaks.

Just after the resort the road climbs to the northwest and into the part of Ubin least-visited by pedestrians and most beloved by cyclists; it's here, surrounding the Ketam Quarry, that you'll find the Ketam Mountain Bike Park. Though not as fraught with opportunities for orthopaedic injury as, say, the parks around Moab, Utah, by Singapore standards the park is pretty cool, and definitely built for mountain bikers of at least intermediate level.

With over a dozen trails of varying skill levels, the newly built park is a mountain-bikers wet dream, and – hopefully – proof that the Singapore government intends to keep Ubin wild and free for the next decade at least.

Incongruously enough, the mountain bike park is also home to one of Singapore's quirkier religious offerings, the German Girl Shrine (above).

Past the bike park the road becomes an unpaved pathway. Here you'll find yourself truly wandering (or riding) through the most rustic area that Singapore has to offer. It's in this last chunk of Ubin that free-range chickens and wild pigs (there are said to be scores of the latter) roam free, making it the only part of Singapore where being mauled by a wild animal is an actual possibility.

How long Ubin will remain unspoilt depends on both government plans, and the considerable strength of public pressure to preserve the island in its current state. It's hoped by many that in the near term the government's resources will be tied up in the Herculean task of building casinos in the newly reclaimed downtown waterfront area (not to mention its continuing efforts to transform Sentosa Island into Singapore's Disneyland), keeping Ubin wild for at least the foreseeable future. There's little doubt that eventually the government would like to bring Ubin's transport and facilities into line with Singapore's policy of relentless modernisation. For now, its jungle charms remain unsullied.

Information

Focus Ubin (www.focusubin.org) A good website with current listings.

Information Kiosk (☎ 6542 4108; ☽ 8am-5pm)

Ubin Explorer (www.ubinexplorer.com) Organises trips to and around the island.

Ubin Police Post (☎ 6542 8664)

Eating

There are four Chinese restaurants and one Halal Muslim restaurant located in Ubin Village, and another eatery inside the Kampung Ubin Resort. A few private homes have set up small drink and snack stalls along the roads as well. If you want a serious Malay feast, arrange it through Kamariah and Samsiah Abdullah of the Ubin Experience (p178).

Sleeping

Kampung Ubin Resort (☎ 6388 8388; www.marinacountry club.com.sg; 1-/2-bedroom chalets $90/175) This recently renovated chalet resort is a good alternative for outdoor types and activity junkies looking for a definitively different Singapore experience. The resort has its own ferry to Singapore, making it quite doable as a general base of exploration for those who want to see Singapore from the green fringes. Rates go down slightly on weekdays.

Noordin Beach & Mamam Camping (☎ Information kiosk 6542 4108; ⏰ 8am-5pm) Pleasant free camping spots with imported white-sand beaches. Watch out for otters, bats and the odd python! If planning group camping, consult the national park officers at the Information Kiosk for more details. Campers are advised to drop by the Ubin Police Post to register, so they know where to look for your remains should you be eaten by wild pigs.

HURRY UP AND WAIT (OR PAY)

Changi Point ferry terminal is the jumping-off point for trips to Pulau Ubin and Pengarang, on the southeastern tip of the Malay peninsula. But don't let the terminal's sparklingly modern exterior fool you into expecting regular schedules; in actuality, the terminal is more a central hangout for a dozen or so privately owned 12-seater bumboats, which do the runs across the straits. In order to make each journey profitable, the captains wait until there are 12 paying customers before leaving. Going to Pulau Ubin, this is rarely an issue – at least not during daytime hours.

But unless you're travelling with 11 of your friends, you may have to wait before heading across to Malaysia (then again, you may be that magical passenger who offers the green-light for 11 others). The boat captains don't actually care how many passengers under they are, just as long as they're paid for 12. For this reason, it's not uncommon for a group of eight or so to just agree to pony up the cash for the extra tickets to get the journey underway.

JOHOR BAHRU

☎ 07

Connected to Singapore by the 1038m-long Causeway, Johor Bahru (or JB as it's commonly known) is to Singapore what Shenzhen is to Hong Kong: a vastly cheaper, grittier sister city across the border with an ever-so-slight edge of lawlessness that visitors from the 'safe' side of the border blow way out of proportion. Though dingier than over-polished Singapore, JB is actually more like a mash-up of a few Singapore neighbourhoods. The Peranakan-style shophouses in the area just above the Straits of Johor are much like the newly renovated ones found in Joo Chiat (minus the 'newly renovated' part). The area surrounding the Sri Mariamman Temple looks and smells like Little India, right down to the small shops selling silks and saris.

JB is almost considered a suburb of Singapore. Thousands of people – Singaporeans included – live there and commute through the crowded Woodlands checkpoint, which handles about 50,000 people a day. Singapore residents flock over here at weekends and on public holidays to take advantage of cheaper grocery and petrol prices, and stock up on pirated CDs and DVDs. For those staying in Singapore past the usual visa period, a trip to JB is the easiest way to get around a trip to the immigration office. JB also has a few places worth visiting in their own right, not to mention some excellent (and inexpensive) eating options and, of course, pirated DVDs galore.

AROUND JOHOR BAHRU

One day is enough time to take in most of JB's sights. As you leave the immigration checkpoint, walking west will take you through the neighbourhood of Peranakan-style shophouses just south of the blue-domed **Indian Mosque**, the Muslim counterpoint to the nearby Sri Mariamman Temple. Wandering through this area gives a good idea of what Singapore might have looked like 20 years ago.

Continuing westward along the esplanade of Jalan Ibrahim, you'll find one of JB's main attractions, the **Royal Abu Bakar Museum** (☎ 223 0555; Jalan Ibrahim; adult/child US$7/3; ⏰ 9am-5pm Sat-Thu). The former Istana Besar (main palace) of the Johor royal family, it was built in Victorian style on a small hill overlooking the Johor Strait by the Anglophile sultan Abu Bakar in 1866. The palace is now a museum chock-full of the sultan's posses-

JOHOR BAHRU

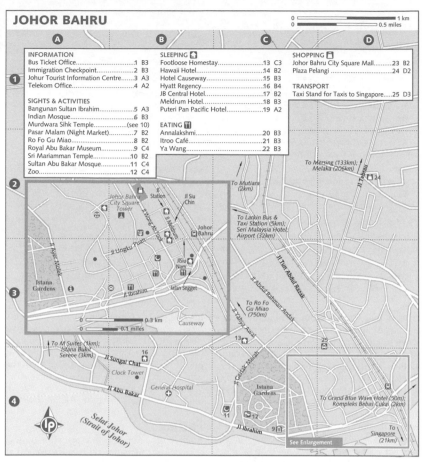

0 — 1 km
0 — 0.5 miles

INFORMATION
Bus Ticket Office................................1 B3
Immigration Checkpoint.....................2 B3
Johur Tourist Information Centre.......3 A3
Telekom Office..................................4 A2

SIGHTS & ACTIVITIES
Bangunan Sultan Ibrahim..................5 A3
Indian Mosque...................................6 B3
Murdwara Sihk Temple...............(see 10)
Pasar Malam (Night Market)............7 B2
Ro Fo Gu Miao..................................8 B2
Royal Abu Bakar Museum................9 C4
Sri Mariamman Temple...................10 B2
Sultan Abu Bakar Mosque..............11 C4
Zoo...12 C4

SLEEPING
Footloose Homestay.........................13 C3
Hawaii Hotel....................................14 B2
Hotel Causeway...............................15 B3
Hyatt Regency..................................16 B4
JB Central Hotel..............................17 B2
Meldrum Hotel.................................18 B3
Puteri Pan Pacific Hotel...................19 A2

EATING
Annalakshmi.....................................20 B3
Itroo Café..21 B3
Ya Wang...22 B3

SHOPPING
Johor Bahru City Square Mall.........23 B2
Plaza Pelangi...................................24 D2

TRANSPORT
Taxi Stand for Taxis to Singapore.....25 D3

sions, furniture and hunting trophies. There are some superb pieces, making it worth a visit for those interested in perusing royal bric-a-brac. Even if you aren't going into the museum, the magnificent surrounding grounds (admission free) are a lovely place for a stroll.

West of this is a small zoo (adult/child Rm2/1; 8am-6pm), but with one of Asia's best zoos just across the water it's hardly worth the effort.

A little further west, off Jalan Gertak Merah, is the impressive Sultan Abu Bakar Mosque (Jalan Gertak Merah); like some of the mosques in Singapore, it features a mish-mash of architectural influences – including Victorian. Also like the mosques in Singapore, it took some time to build (eight years from 1892 to 1900), but you can see why. Hailed in Singapore as one of the most magnificent mosques, it occupies

large grounds and, according to its caretaker, can hold up to 2000 people.

If you continue west (you'll have to take a taxi), you can see the real residence of the Sultan of Johor, the Istana Bukit Serene (Jalan Straits View), but of course you're not allowed to wander in and say hello.

For those who want to keep to a walking-only JB tour, head back east along the waterfront until you get to the most impressive Bangunan Sultan Ibrahim (State Secretariat Bldg; Bukit Timbalan), which overlooks the city centre. An imposing fortress-style building that looks like it was transported from Mogul India, the fortress was built in the 1940s, and is, sadly, not open to tourists. Follow Jalan Ungku Puan, which runs away from this building and you'll pass on your left the Sri Mariamman Temple, a beautiful Hindu temple with ornate carvings and devotional

TRANSPORT: JOHOR BAHRU

Distance from Singapore 1km

Direction North

Travel time 30 minutes to one hour

Bus Many bus companies run bus services from Singapore to Malaysia. Visit http://plusliner.com for online and off-line ticketing services for Plusliner and NiCE Executive coaches plying between Malaysia and Singapore. The Singapore–Johor express coach leaves every 15 minutes from the Queen St bus terminal (Map p68) between 6.30am and 11pm and costs $2.40. Alternatively take the public bus 170, which also runs from the Queen St terminal every 15 minutes, between 5.20am and 12.10am and costs $1.70. Yet another, quicker, option is to go to Kranji MRT station by train and catch bus 160, or Maisiling MRT and catch bus 950, either of which cuts down on your bus time dramatically.

In all cases, when you get to the Singapore checkpoint, take all your belongings and get off. After clearing immigration, you have to wait for the next bus (but don't have to pay again, as long you have your ticket). Repeat the process at the Malaysian side, or simply take a two-minute walk into Johor Bahru city centre. The public bus stops at the Komtar Shopping Centre and then the Larkin bus terminal 5km north of the Causeway, while the coach stops only at the bus terminal.

Coming back, the public bus costs Rm1.20 and the coach Rm2.40.

If at all possible, avoid crossing at weekends, when it gets infernally busy and the whole process can become a frustrating waste of time. Coming back into Singapore on a Sunday evening is little short of a nightmare.

Taxi A taxi from the city into Johor Bahru will cost around $28, more if there is a long wait at immigration. Alternatively, you can try to pick up a share taxi from the Queen St bus terminal (Map p68); the price will depend on how many people are going and how long a line you have at both immigration checkpoints.

artwork that is the heart of JB's Hindu community. Almost under the temple sits the Pasar Malam (night market), a favourite eating spot where you can also find some souvenirs and clothes. Starting at 5.30pm, it is divided into three sections (Chinese, Malay and Indian) and has a great selection of dishes. Also next to the Hindu Temple is the Murdvara Sihk Temple, and across the street (overlooked by the Puteri Pan Pacific hotel) is the Ro Fo Gu Miao, a beautiful, elaborately painted Chinese temple with a large wooden door. It is reputedly the only temple in Johor that survived WWII and is hence a highly sacred place for Chinese Malays.

From here, you can stroll back towards the border crossing, or spend more time in JB shopping or eating.

Information

Johor Tourist Information Centre (☎ 222 3590; www.tourismmalaysia.gov.my; 2 Jalan Ayer Molek; ☒ 8am-5pm Mon-Fri)

Shopping

For shopping most people head to the big malls like the fancy Johor Bahru City Square (☎ 226 3668; 108 Jalan Wong Ah Fook), along the chaotic, somewhat dirty Jalan Wong Ah Fook thoroughfare just across from the immigration post. Plaza Pelangi, an even fancier mall featuring handicrafts, fashion and food, seems to

have surpassed City Square in the modernity stakes, while Kompleks Bebas Cukai duty-free shopping complex (☎ 922 2611; Bukit Kayu Hitam), about 2km east of the Causeway, proudly proclaims itself one of the largest duty-free complexes in the world, with more than 160 shops. In general, you won't get much in JB that you can't get in Singapore, though prices tend to be lower.

Eating

Johor Bahru can be a fine place for dining; many of our Singaporean friends swear that Malay dishes here are simply 'more authentic' than they are at home. (Keep in mind that Singaporeans are hands-down the most 'obsessed with culinary minutia' people on the planet!) The streets and alleys just across the border are filled with excellent street-food options.

Annalakshmi (☎ 227 7400; www.annalakshmi.com.sg; 39 Jalan Ibrahim) This lovely vegetarian restaurant is sister to the one of the same name over in Singapore. Their 'pay what you like' policy ensures that spirituality and good food is placed over profit.

ITRoo Cafe (☎ 222 7780; jjchong@pc.jaring.my); 17 Jalan Dhoby A popular cafe with very friendly service in JB's colonial district. The best iced cappuccino in Malaysia.

Ya Wang Restaurant (☎ 224 8624; 28 Jalan Segget) *Ya wang* is Mandarin for 'duck king', which gives you a fair idea of what this little restaurant a few blocks from the Causeway border crossing specialises in. Savoury, juicy, delicious and half the price of what you'll pay in Singapore.

Sleeping

From cheap flophouses to decent mid-priced hotels, sleeping options are mostly clustered in the Jalan Meldrum neighbourhood, just east of the railway station. Upper-end travellers have a few other options away from the hub.

Meldrum Hotel (☎ 227 8988; hotel_meldrum@po.jaring .my; 1 Jalan Meldrum; r Rm66) Smart, clean rooms with air-con, TV and shared toilets. Superior room has its own toilet and shower for Rm99.

Hotel Causeway (☎ 224 8811; causewayhotel@yahoo.com; 6a-6f Jalan Meldrum; r Rm100) Slightly nicer than the Meldrum for about the same price, this is one of the more reliable choices in the area. However, for a few ringgit more you're better off staying at the brand new Hotel JB Central.

JB Central Hotel (☎ 222 2833; www.jbcentralhotel -johorbahru.com; Merlin Tower, Jalan Meldrum; r from Rm120) Though testing the upper end of the budget category (for JB at least), this brand new hotel on the northern end of Jalan Meldrum is by far the cleanest and most comfortable of the downtown sleeping options. Upper-floor rooms offer excellent views of northern Singapore and JB.

Puteri Pan Pacific Hotel (☎ 219 9999; www.puteripacific .com; Kotaraya Plaza; r from Rm270) This top-end hotel is close to town and overlooks some of JB's most impressive temples and mosques. It's often packed on weekends, so book in advance. Best top-end bet close to town. Big discounts.

Hyatt Regency (☎ 222 1234; hyatt@hrjb.po.my; Jalan Sungai Chat; s/d from Rm430/450) A stylish, top-end joint, the Hyatt is a bit far out of town for most casual JB tourists, but might be what you're looking for if you plan on an extended stay during which expense isn't an object.

GREATER DESARU

☎ 07

Desaru is in the Kota Tinggi district, the most southeasterly area of Peninsular Malaysia. Unlike nearby Johor Bahru across the Johor Delta, this region is sparsely populated, far less developed, and virtually undiscovered by tourists save for the few Singaporeans who head to Sungai Rengit (the southernmost town of note) for extravagant seafood meals on the cheap.

Close enough to Singapore for an afternoon trip, the area is pretty, filled with Malaysian charm, and home to a number of surprising attractions. The beaches aren't exceptional this far south (thanks to oil exploration and heavy shipping), but the road wrapping around the coast offers exceptional scenery, making it a favourite for cyclists from Singapore.

Pengerang port served as a British Operations Centre during WWII, giving it a certain historical cache. But aside from a Malaysian navy base, there isn't much to see right off the bumboat from Singapore; there are usually a few taxis waiting to take passengers up to the town of Sungai Rengit, 8km up the peninsula.

Sungai Rengit is a good town in which to base yourself for exploration around the area, though Sebana Golf & Marina Resort (p184) is a nice treat, if you can afford it. There are a couple of cheap hotels, cheap and midrange restaurants, and the main street is worth a stroll. Check out the large steel lobster statue by the waterfront, apparently the town mascot. There are a few sandy beaches just north of town, but water quality is really dependent on tidal activity. Locals do swim there, but you're probably better off further away from Singapore.

The real attraction of the area is sightseeing, soaking in the flavour of the Malay peninsula without really leaving Singapore's orbit. Northeast of Sungai Rengit the road is lined with palm trees punctuated occasionally by kampong houses and small clearings from which locals sell traditional Malay snacks and drinks. There are also some attractive temples and mosques along the road. Keep your eyes open at about the 3km mark out of town for a lovely single-storey shrine to Kuan Yin, goddess of

TRANSPORT: GREATER DESARU

Distance from Singapore 12km (to Pengerang port)

Direction Northeast

Travel time One hour (from Singapore)

Bus/boat The cheapest way to get to this chunk of Johor is by catching a ferry from the Changi Point ferry terminal (the same one the boats to Pulau Ubin leave from) to Pengerang. The bumboats hold 12 and leave when they're full, so be prepared to either wait or pay extra to convince the captains to leave. Generally speaking, 10 to 12 boats leave each way per day. Once there, you can hire a taxi at the dock. Alternatively, there are four boats per day from Tanah Merah Terminal in Singapore that go directly to Sebana Golf & Marina Resort.

mercy. Built in a traditional southern-Chinese style, the shrine features a small pagoda with a golden statue of the goddess out front.

Five kilometres out of town on the left you'll come across the Ostrich Showfarm (☎ 826 5846; adult/child Rm10/6), a 2-hectare ostrich farm and petting zoo that travellers with kids won't want to miss. Activities range from ostrich feeding and riding to, on some days, watching baby ostriches emerge from their huge shells. Ostrich Showfarm–owner Joyce Teh does a good job teaching groups about the huge birds, making the place a popular stop for school field trips. Burgers and satay are sold out front – made from ostrich meat, naturally.

From the Ostrich Farm, you can continue heading along the coastal road, which eventually curves northward. As the coast shifts from south-facing (Singapore) to east-facing, the beaches actually become quite nice. Teluk Punggai Beach is one of the more popular ones in the area, and probably the day-trip limit of all but the strongest cyclists.

Eating

Sungai Rengit has a dozen or so restaurants to chose from. If you're just looking for snacks, head to the waterfront – just east of the giant lobster statue there are a few stalls selling Malaysian snacks for a few ringgits. On the north side of town on Jalan Kerisi are three semi-enclosed seafood restaurants frequented mostly by Singaporeans. We found the food at Jade Garden Seafood Centre to be good, but we were overcharged despite previous negotiation.

Sleeping

Sungai Rengit has a couple of cheap and decent hotels to chose from. If you're looking for something at the top end, check out Sebana Golf & Marina Resort (right).

Tai Hoe Hotel (☎ 826 3855; www.taihoe.com.my; 36 Jalan Haji Abu Bakar; r Rm100) Oddly expensive for the area, the Tai Hoe is nonetheless clean and comfortable. Deluxe rooms (Rm 130) have antique rosewood furniture and flat-screen TVs.

Hotel Hiap Hwa (☎ 826 3111; 52 Jalan Siakap; s/d Rm68/88) Another comfortable hotel, deluxe rooms have ocean views (and views of Sungai Rengit's iconic metal lobster) from the balcony. Add Rm20 to the price on weekends.

RESORTS

After a few weeks in Singapore, you may find yourself looking for luxury that won't leave your bank account bleeding. If so, this end of the Malay peninsula has much to offer. Gener-

ally filled to capacity on the weekends (with Singaporeans, naturally), these places are uncrowded and usually cheaper on weekdays.

Sebana Golf & Marina Resort (☎ 826 6688, Singapore 6333 3363; www.sebanacove.com; r from Rm200, 🖳 🕎) Probably the largest of the resorts, this may be just the ticket. A full-fledged resort located on the beautiful Sebana River Delta, it offers swimming pools, spas, two beautiful restaurants and, of course, amazing golfing. Management can help arrange visits to all the sights around Desaru, and the resort has its own boat going to and from Singapore several times daily. Discounted rates available through the website.

Desaru Golden Beach Hotel (☎ 822 1101, Singapore office 6235 5476; r from Rm150; 🖳 🕎) Offers beautiful rooms and villas in a lush tropical setting up the coast from Sebana. The hotel also has a good golf course, and offers ferry transit to and from Changi ferry terminal in Singapore.

The Pulai Desaru Beach (☎ 622 2222; www.thepulai.com.my; r from Rm200; 🖳 🕎) Another favourite with Singaporeans looking for a break from urban hustle, this resort offers beautiful accommodation and plenty of land- and ocean-geared activities. Check out the website for regular promotional packages.

ENDAU-ROMPIN NATIONAL PARK
☎ 07

The standard quick getaways from Singapore are often beachy (Bintan, Desaru, Rawa, Tioman…) but in fact it's possible to hop on a train in the morning and by lunchtime

---

TRANSPORT: ENDAU-ROMPIN NATIONAL PARK

Distance from Singapore 180km

Direction North

Travel time Four to five hours

Bus/train/car The vast majority of people visit the reserve on an organised tour, which will pick you up from Mersing or Kluang. To get to Mersing, take the Transnasional bus from Lavender St bus station (Map p68; $16.50, 9am and 10am, four to five hours). To reach Kluang, hop on the 7.40am train from Tanjong Pagar railway station (adult/child $16/12, two to three hours). If coming by road, take Rte 50, travelling east, and turn off around 4km after Kahang at the 'Batu 26' marker. From there it's a bumpy 58km ride to the visitor centre.

THE BIGFOOT

Yes, another one. In recent years there have been several highly publicised sightings of an apelike creature (called *hantu jarang* in Malay) dwelling in the remote and largely unexplored forests of Endau-Rompin. Descriptions follow the standard format repeated in Nepal, North America and other 'bigfoot' locations: a large, shy, hairy hominid, about 2.5m to 3m tall, walking on two legs.

In 2005, a group of labourers reported seeing a group of primates near a river, and there have been a handful of unsubstantiated claims of sightings and shootings over the years. A zoologist claimed that a bigfoot was shot dead in 2001, but that loggers (conveniently) destroyed its remains.

Predictably, the rash of recent sightings has spawned the usual laughable hoaxers, attention seekers and melo-dramatic TV 'investigations'. Serious attempts to find evidence of such a creature have yielded a few inconclusive footprints and little else.

The *Orang Asli* guide we asked about the bigfoot laughed dismissively and said: 'If people come here and are told it is real, we are cheating them.'

Enough said? Perhaps, but like all such mysteries, a few rational voices are unlikely to stop the speculation. And perhaps, just *perhaps*, it really exists...

---

be in the thick of a 280-million-year-old rainforest.

Endau-Rompin National Park, overshadowed by the more famous Taman Negara to the north, encompasses around 870 sq km of forest atop the site of a tremendous ancient volcanic eruption. Fed by three rivers that slide down from two plateaus, the park is home to Malaysia's last Sumatran rhino (only an estimated two or three remain), as well as tigers, tapir, gibbons, deer, boar, countless birds, fish and rare plant species.

Despite its rich endowment of wildlife, Endau-Rompin's animals are not easy to spot, because much of the park is wisely closed off to visitors. However, it is an excellent place for bird-watching and trekking, and it's often possible to spot wild elephants, deer, boar and the occasional gibbon and tapir.

The park is closed during the wet season between November and February.

It's possible to get to the park in your own vehicle (see opposite), but once at the park it's wise to hire a guide (at Rm50 to Rm60 per day) to explore the park, as it's easy to get lost. The majority of visitors come on organised trips booked through Malaysian agents (see p186).

Come prepared for the jungle, with light clothing that dries easily (you'll be crossing rivers on foot), lots of insect repellent, a sleeping bag (if camping), sunscreen and a torch. There are also lots of leeches in the forest – Wellington boots and long pants tucked into long socks (speciality leech-proof socks can be bought at outdoor-activities shops) are the best defence against these blood-sucking pests, which easily penetrate even the stoutest walking boots.

Treks

There are several walks, ranging from easy to strenuous. The most popular begins from the Nature Education & Research Camp (NERC) or Kuala Jasin camp and follows the Jasin River along a fairly flat stretch to the Kuala Marong camp, which sits at the confluence of the Jasin and Marong Rivers. From there you have two options. For a shorter one-day walk, you cross the Jasin River on foot and continue for about 1km to the Upeh Guling falls. An imposing 100m cascade when the river is up, during the driest months it's no less impressive, as the drop in water level reveals a surreal landscape of cauldron-like depressions gouged out of the rock, formed over millennia by trapped stones.

Descending the falls again, another 30 minutes brings you to Tasik Air Biru, a beautiful turquoise natural swimming hole with what is claimed to be the clearest waters in Malaysia –

THE RIDER'S LODGE

Tucked away up a dirt road amid rolling hills and plantations, this grand white manor house (☎ 652 5330; www.riderslodge.com.my; r incl breakfast from Rm298), with its ample stables, looks like it was built in the 1920s, but in fact was only finished in 2000. Most people come to ride the magnificent horses (or play golf at the neighbouring club), but even if you're not interested in riding, it's a beautiful, peaceful weekend retreat, with extremely friendly staff. There are special packages for horse riders, beginner or expert.

The best way to get there is with your own (or a hired) vehicle – it's 45 minutes from the Tuas checkpoint. Alternatively, take a train from Singapore to Kulai and the manor will pick you up.

the perfect spot to cool off. From there turn and retrace your steps to your camp.

A longer walk takes a short rope bridge from Kuala Marong and follows a faint, tiring trail to the Buaya Sangkut falls. If you're camping, you can sleep at the Batu Hampar site around 2km from Kuala Marong. Then, the next morning, set out for the 4km hike to Buaya Sangkut. It's a long uphill walk, but the rewards when you hit the top of the falls are worth it.

It's possible to camp at the top of the falls, rather than at Batu Hampar – waking up in such a magical location is unforgettable.

Tours

Visiting Endau-Rompin independently is a little tricky, unless you have your own vehicle, which you can leave at the visitor centre or at the NERC, once you've secured your entry permit from the visitor centre.

Tour packages typically involve a two- or three-night stay and will pick you up in Mersing, or at the railway station in Kluang, or in Kahang. Accommodation is either in dorms or A-frame chalets at Kampung Peta, NERC or Kuala Jasin. If you have a group of four or more people, you can usually customise your trip and specify where you want to go and where you want to sleep. Some trips include tubing down the river and village visits. Online travel operators include the following:

Journey Malaysia (☎ 03-2692 8049; www.journey malaysia.com; 3-day 2-night packages per person or in a group of 4 or more from Rm500)

Cuti (☎ 03-3343 2884; www.cuti.com.my; 3-day 2-night package from Rm505)

Alternatively, contact Omar's Backpacker's Hostel (☎ 799 5096) in Mersing, which arranges trips to the reserve.

PULAU TIOMAN

☎ 09

The largest and most spectacular of Malaysia's east coast islands (though cynics say it's

PULAU TIOMAN

SLEEPING
ABC Beach Resort.................................1 A2
Bamboo Hill Chalets............................2 A2
Berjaya Tioman Beach Resort.............3 A2
Ella's Place..4 A1
Japamala Resort..................................5 A3

been overdeveloped), Tioman has beautiful beaches, clear water, good snorkelling and some excellent dive sites.

Tioman is the most popular destination on the east coast and it can get very crowded, especially at weekends and during public holidays. The main budget accommodation areas are in the villages of Air Batang (usually called ABC), Salang, Juara and Tekek, all of which have good beaches and swimming. Of all these, Salang is the most popular, with the highest number of beach chalet operations, the best nightlife on the island, and proximity to the Monkey Bay and Pulau Tulai snorkelling and diving sites. Tekek is the administrative centre of Tioman. It contains the airport, hospital, shops, moneychangers and post office, but it's not very attractive.

SANDFLIES

Pulau Tioman, Pulau Rawa, and all of the Seribuat Archipelago islands are blighted by sandflies. These minuscule bloodsucking pests are capable of ruining your beach holiday more effectively than any mosquito – and they are a lot harder to spot. Their bites are acutely itchy and have the tendency to develop into hard lumps topped with a blister, which can last for weeks. Highly potent repellent is effective to an extent, but if you find yourself being targeted, the only way to avoid them is either to stay off the beach, or spend all day in the sea.

TRANSPORT: PULAU TIOMAN

Distance from Singapore 178km

Direction Northeast

Travel Time Air/overland 35 minutes/five hours

Air If you have plenty of cash and not much time, Berjaya Air (Map pp62–3; ☎ 6227 3688; berjaya-air.com; 67 Tanjong Pagar Rd) operates daily flights ($305) direct to Tioman's airport from Singapore's Seletar Airport, departing at either noon, 1.35pm or 3.05pm. The flight takes 35 minutes.

Bus/boat Early birds can catch the Kaiho Coaches (☎ 07-241 8208) bus to Mersing ($35 return), except during the monsoon between October and February. The bus departs from Newton MRT station at 6.30am and takes three to four hours. Alternatively, hop on the Transnasional (☎ 6294 7034; $16.50) bus, which leaves the Lavender St bus terminal (Map p68) at 9am and 10am. When you arrive at Mersing, you have two options. The speedboats (Rm45 one way) are quickest, taking a bit more than an hour, but many find them unpleasantly fast. The normal ferries (Rm35 one way) leave around five times a day and take up to three hours, stopping off at the various beaches in a south-to-north direction. Departures are dependent on tide, conditions and number of passengers.

Sleeping & Eating

There's a huge range of accommodation on Tioman, the majority of it identical basic wooden beach chalets, typically with a bed, fan and bathroom. Most of them offer food, with varying degrees of skill.

ABC (☎ 419 1154; Air Batang; chalets Rm120) Long-standing favourite, located slightly away from the bulk of the ABC operations. Reasonable chalets in a garden setting.

Bamboo Hill Chalets (☎ 419 1339; Air Batang; r Rm70, chalets Rm100-120) Perched on a hillside, this small collection of simple chalets boast verandahs and spectacular views.

Ella's Place (☎ 419 5005; Salang; chalets Rm25-60) The best of the Salang cheapies, with friendly owners, decent food and a great stretch of beach.

Japamala Resort (☎ 603 4256 6100; www.japamala resorts.com; chalets Rm390-1450) The best upmarket resort on Tioman, located on the quiet southwest corner of the island, it claims to be open during the monsoon.

Berjaya Tioman Beach Resort (☎ 419 1000; chalets Rm275-385) This is the largest and fanciest resort on Tioman, although it's slightly rough around the edges. It offers a huge range of activities.

PULAU RAWA

☎ 07

For those who find Tioman a bit too over-developed and overcrowded, Pulau Rawa is a better option. More peaceful, with beautiful crystal-clear water and fine white sands, it's extremely popular with Malaysian and Singaporean weekenders, so book weeks in advance (especially for public holidays) or go on a weekday.

There's only one place to stay, the Rawa Safaris Island Resort (☎ 799 1204; www.rawasfr.com; chalets Rm280-430), and since the running of it passed out of the hands of some Johor royalty, the service has improved considerably. There are full-board packages available, which considering you don't have a choice of where to eat anyway, are probably a good idea.

Ask for one of the five waterfront chalets, which sit on stilts over the sea and have fantastic views.

Unlike much Tioman accommodation, Rawa is open year-round. The island is tiny and there's not much exploring to do, but most people come to lie around, do a bit of snorkelling and perhaps indulge in a spot of volleyball or kayaking. It's the perfect place to do nothing at all.

If you're planning a boozy trip, smuggle your own, as resort prices are high. Officially you're not allowed to bring your own, but as long as you're discreet, nobody will notice.

TRANSPORT: PULAU RAWA

Distance from Singapore: 170km

Direction: Northeast

Travel time: Five hours

Bus/boat: Get the bus to Mersing from Singapore (see above). The Rawa ferry (30 minutes, Rm35 one-way) leaves around noon every day, though they'll wait if they know you're coming.

TRANSPORT

Having invested vast sums in its public transport infrastructure, Singapore is undoubtedly the easiest city in Asia to get around. With a typical mixture of far-sighted social planning and authoritarianism, the government has built, and continues to extend, its Mass Rapid Transit (MRT) rail system and its road network.

If you're going to be using public transport heavily, buy the TransitLink Guide ($2.50 from MRT ticket offices), which lists all bus and MRT routes. Maps show the surrounding areas for all MRT stations, including bus stops.

For online bus information, including a searchable bus guide and the useful IRIS service (which tells you in real time when your next bus will arrive), see www.sbstransit.com.sg. For train information, see www.smrt.com.sg. Book flights, tours and rail tickets online at www.lonelyplanet.com/travel_services.

AIR

Singapore's location and excellent facilities have made it a natural choice as a major Southeast Asian aviation hub, with direct services all over the world. It is also serviced by four budget airlines, which often offer extremely cheap deals if you book well in advance.

Websites worth checking out for flights to and from Singapore include the following:

www.bezurk.com Similar to Zuji, but helpfully lists fares *including* the taxes and charges.

www.cheapestflights.co.uk This site really does post cheap flights (out of the UK only), but you have to get in early to get the bargains.

www.lastminute.com This site deals mainly in European flights but does have worldwide flights, mostly package returns. There's also an Australian version (www.lastminute.com.au).

www.statravel.com This is STA Travel's US website. There are also sites for the UK (www.statravel.co.uk) and Australia (www.statravel.com.au).

www.travel.com.au This is worth checking out for cheap flights from Australia.

www.travelonline.co.nz This is a good site for New Zealanders to find worldwide fares from their part of the world.

www.zuji.com.au This site offers decent deals on a range of top-notch carriers.

Airlines

Below are some of the major airline offices in Singapore. Check the Business Yellow Pages for any that are not listed here.

British Airways/Qantas (Map pp74–5; ☎ British Airways 6622 1747; www.britishairways.co.uk; 06-05 Cairnhill Pl, 15 Cairnhill Rd)

Cathay Pacific Airways (Map pp62–3; ☎ 6533 1333; www.cathaypacific.com/sg; 25-07 Ocean Towers, 20 Raffles Place)

Garuda Indonesia (Map pp74–5; ☎ 6250 5666; www.garuda-indonesia.com; 12-03 United Sq, 101 Thomson Rd)

KLM-Royal Dutch Airlines (Map pp62–3; ☎ 6832 2220; www.klm.com.sg; 06-01, 79 Anson Rd)

Lufthansa Airlines (Map pp74–5; ☎ 6245 5600; www.lufthansa.com; 05-01 Palais Renaissance, 390 Orchard Rd)

Malaysia Airlines (Map pp52–3; ☎ 6336 6777; www.malaysiaairlines.com; 02-09 Singapore Shopping Centre, 190 Clemenceau Ave)

Qantas (Map pp74–5; ☎ 6415 7373, www.qantas.com.sg; 06-05 Cairnhill Place, 15 Cairnhill Rd)

Singapore Airlines (Map pp74–5; ☎ 6223 8888; www.singaporeair.com; Level 2, Paragon Bldg, Orchard Rd)

Thai Airways International (Map pp62–3; ☎ 6210 5000; www.thaiairways.com.sg; the Globe, 100 Cecil St)

The following budget airlines operate out of Singapore. They are changing their networks all the time, so check websites for details. Bookings are made almost entirely online, though Air Asia tickets can also be bought at post offices.

Air Asia (☎ 6733 9933; www.airasia.com)

Cebu Pacific (☎ agents 6735 7155, 6737 9231, 6220 5966; www.cebupacificair.com)

Jetstar Asia (☎ 6822 2288; www.jetstarasia.com)

Tiger Airways (☎ 6538 4437; www.tigerairways.com)

GETTING INTO TOWN
Bus

Public bus 36 runs from terminals 1, 2 and 3 to Orchard Rd and the Colonial District ($1.70, one hour). They leave roughly every 15 minutes, the first departing at 6.09am and the last just after midnight.

Faster and more convenient are the airport shuttle buses (adult/child $9/6, 20 to 40 minutes) that leave from all main terminal arrival halls and drop passengers at any hotel, except for those on Sentosa and in Changi Village. They leave from Terminals 1 and 2 and the Budget Terminal (6.15pm to midnight, every 15 minutes; all other times every 30 minutes) and Terminal 3 (6am to 10am and 6pm to 2am, every 15 min; all other times every 30 minutes). Booking desks are in the arrival halls.

Train

The MRT is the best low-cost way to get into town. The station is located below Terminals 2 and 3, the fare to Raffles Place is adult/child $2.70/$1.50 (including a $1 refundable deposit) and the journey takes around 35 minutes. You have to change trains at Tanah Merah (just cross the platform). The first train leaves at 5.30am and the last goes at 12.06am.

Taxi

Taxi lines at Changi are usually fast-moving and efficient. Even at the Budget Terminal you rarely have to wait long. The fare structure is complicated, but count on spending anywhere between $18 and $35 into the city centre, depending on the time of travel. The most expensive times are between 5pm and 6am, when a whole raft of surcharges kick in. A limousine transfer service operates 24 hours a day and costs a flat $45 to anywhere on the island.

Airports
CHANGI AIRPORT

Unless you are travelling from Tioman or Redang Islands in Malaysia, your plane will land at one of the three main terminals or the Budget Terminal at Changi Airport (☎ 6542 1122, flight information 1800 542 4422; www.changiairport.com.sg).

Regularly voted the world's best airport, Changi Airport is vast, efficient and amazingly well organised. Among its many facilities you'll find free internet, courtesy phones for local calls, foreign-exchange booths, as well as the following:

Left luggage (24hr; cabin bag 1st/subsequent 24hr $3.15/4.20, suitcase $4.20/5.25) Terminal 1 (☎ 6214 0628; Basement West); Terminal 2 (☎ 6214 1683; Level 1, Arrival Hall North); Terminal 3 (Basement 2 South)

Medical centres Terminal 1 (☎ 6543 1113; Level 2, Transit Mall West; 8am-2am); Terminal 2 (☎ 6543 1118; Basement South; 24hr) Terminal 3 (☎ 6241 8818; Basement 2 South, 24hr)

Napping rooms Terminal 1 (☎ 6541 8518; www.rainforestbysats.com; Rainforest Lounge, Level 3, Transit Mall West; per person per hr single-occupancy only $10); Terminal 2 (☎ 6541 9107; www.airport-hotel.com.sg; Level 3; Transit Mall South; per 6hr $40.45)

Post offices (6am-midnight) Terminal 2, Level 2, Departure Hall South; Level 2, Transit Mall North.

Shower/spa/massage/gym Terminal 1 (☎ 6541 8518; www.rainforestbysats.com; Level 3, Transit Mall West);

Terminal 2 (☎ 6545 0388; www.plaza-ppl.com/sg_en/index.ppl; Level 3, Transit Mall South)

Swimming Pool (☎ 6546 5357; www.airport-hotel.com.sg; Level 3, Transit Mall East, Terminal 1; per visit $13.90; 7am-11pm)

SELETAR AIRPORT

This small, modern facility is more used to corporate flyers and visiting luminaries. You may come here to catch the daily Berjaya Airways flights to Tioman Island in Malaysia.

Seletar is in the north of the island, and the easiest way to get there is to take a taxi; otherwise bus 103 will take you from Serangoon MRT or outside the National Library (Map pp52–3) to the gates of the Seletar Air Force base, from where you take a local base bus to the airport terminal.

BICYCLE

Singapore's roads are not for the faint-hearted. The roads are not only furiously hot, but also populated by fast, aggressive drivers who tend to be unsympathetic to the needs of cyclists. Fortunately there's a large network of parks and park connectors, and a few excellent dedicated mountain-biking areas at Bukit Timah Nature Reserve, Tampines and Pulau Ubin.

Other excellent places for cycling include East Coast Park, Sentosa, Pasir Ris Park and the new route linking Mt Faber Park, Telok Blangah Hill Park and Kent Ridge Park.

CLIMATE CHANGE & TRAVEL

Climate change is a serious threat to the ecosystems that humans rely upon, and air travel is the fastest-growing contributor to the problem. Lonely Planet regards travel, overall, as a global benefit, but believes we all have a responsibility to limit our personal impact on global warming.

Flying & Climate Change

Pretty much every form of motor transport generates CO_2 (the main cause of human-induced climate change) but planes are far and away the worst offenders, not just because of the sheer distances they allow us to travel, but because they release greenhouse gases high into the atmosphere. The statistics are frightening: two people taking a return flight between Europe and the US will contribute as much to climate change as an average household's gas and electricity consumption over a whole year.

Carbon Offset Schemes

Climatecare.org and other websites use 'carbon calculators' that allow jetsetters to offset the greenhouse gases they are responsible for with contributions to energy-saving projects and other climate-friendly initiatives in the developing world – including projects in India, Honduras, Kazakhstan and Uganda.

Lonely Planet, together with Rough Guides and other concerned partners in the travel industry, supports the carbon offset scheme run by climatecare.org. Lonely Planet offsets all of its staff and author travel.

For more information check out our website: www.lonelyplanet.com.

Hire

In the city, the best place to rent top-quality bikes is Treknology Bikes 3 (Map pp92–3; ☎ 6466 2673; www.treknology3.com; 24 Holland Grove Rd; per day $35; ☼ 11am-7.30pm). It's probably the best bike shop in Singapore.

Bikes can also be rented at several places along East Coast Parkway, on Sentosa Island and Pulau Ubin, with prices starting from $5.

If you have your own bike, be aware that it's not allowed on public transport.

BOAT

You can take a bumboat (motorised sampan) tour up the Singapore River from several points along the bank, or to go to the islands around Singapore (see Excursions chapter, p176).

The big cruise centre at the World Trade Centre (Map p100; ☎ 6513 2200; www.singaporecruise.com.sg), next to HarbourFront MRT station, is the main departure point for cruises and ferries to Indonesia; a host of agents here handle bookings.

There are regular ferry services from Changi Point to Pulau Ubin ($2) and two destinations in Malaysia. To get there, take bus 2 from Tanah Merah MRT.

The Tanah Merah ferry terminal (Map pp46–7) south of Changi Airport handles ferries to the Indonesian island of Bintan and one destination on Batam. To get to the Tanah Merah ferry terminal, take the MRT to Bedok and then bus 35. A taxi from the city will cost from $18 to $30, depending on the time of day.

Malaysia
TANJUNG BELUNGKOR

The ferry from Changi Ferry Terminal (Map pp46–7; ☎ 6546 8518) to Tanjung Belungkor, east of Johor Bahru, is primarily a service for Singaporeans going to Desaru in Malaysia. The 11km journey takes 45 minutes and costs $16/22 one-way/return. Services leave at 10am, 5pm and 8.15pm Monday to Thursday, 7.15am, 10am, noon, 5pm and 8.15pm Friday and Saturday, 7.15am, 10am, 6pm and 8.15pm Sunday. From the Tanjung Belungkor jetty, buses operate to Desaru and Kota Tinggi.

PENGERANG

From Changi Point ferry terminal (Map pp46–7), boats go to Pengerang, a back-door route into Malaysia (see Excursions, p183). There's no fixed schedule; ferries leave throughout the day when a full quota of 12 people ($6 per person) is reached.

Indonesia

Direct ferries run between Singapore and the Riau Archipelago islands: Pulau Batam, Pulau Bintan, Tanjung Balai and Tanjung Batu. Services to Bintan and to Nongsapara on Batam run from the Tanah Merah ferry terminal. Services to Batam, Balai and Batu run from the cruise centre at HarbourFront.

From Batam, boats go to Sumatra, a popular way to enter Indonesia. The ferries are modern, fast and air-conditioned.

BUS

Singapore's extensive bus service is, needless to say, clean, efficient and regular, reaching every corner of the island.

Bus fares range from $0.90 to $1.80 (less with an Ez-link card). When you board the bus, drop the exact money into the fare box (no change is given), or tap your Ez-link card or Tourist Pass on the reader as you board, then again when you get off.

For information, contact SBS Transit (☎ 1800 287 2727; www.sbstransit.com.sg).

Train operator SMRT (www.smrtbuses.com.sg) runs three free shuttle buses (11am to 10pm Saturday and Sunday, every eight minutes) on three routes: Dhoby Ghaut MRT station to Little India, Dhoby Ghaut MRT station to Chinatown, and Outram Park MRT station to Chinatown.

SMRT also runs two late-night weekend bus services running between the city and the suburbs: Nite Owl ($3 flat fare, midnight to 4am Friday and Saturday) and NightRider ($3 flat fare, 11.30pm to 4.30am Friday and Saturday). See the website for route details.

Tourist Buses

Singapore Airlines runs the SIA Hop-On (☎ 9457 2896; www.siahopon.asiaone.com.sg) tourist bus, traversing the main tourist arteries every 30 minutes daily, starting at Raffles Blvd at 9am, with the last bus leaving at 5.30pm and arriving back at 7.35pm.

There's also a Sentosa Hop-On bus running between Raffles Boulevard, Orchard Rd, Lau Pa Sat hawker centre and Sentosa. The first bus leaves Sentosa at 10am and the last at 5.30pm. Tickets cost $12/6 per adult/child, or $3 with a Singapore Airlines or Silk Air boarding passes or ticket. Buy tickets from the driver.

Malaysia

For information on getting to Johor Bahru, see p180.

If you are travelling beyond Johor Bahru, the simplest option is to catch a bus straight from Singapore, though there are more options and lower fares travelling from Johor Bahru.

In Singapore, long-distance buses to Melaka and the east coast of Malaysia leave from and arrive at the Lavender Street bus terminal (Map p68; cnr Lavender St & Kallang Bahru), Queen Street bus terminal (Map p68; Queen St) or Golden Mile Complex (Map p68; Beach Rd). Public transport options to all three are poor, so it's best to take a taxi.

Konsortium Transnasional (☎ 6294 7034) is Malaysia's biggest coach company and has services throughout the country. Grassland Express (☎ 6293 1166; www.grassland.com.sg) has services to Kuala Lumpur, Penang, Melaka, Perak and other destinations.

Thailand

The main terminal for buses to and from Thailand is at the Golden Mile Complex (Map p68; Beach Rd). Among the travel agents specialising in buses and tours to Thailand are Grassland Express (☎ 6293 1166), with buses to Hat Yai ($42), and Phya Travel (☎ 6294 5415) and Kwang Chow Travel (☎ 6293 8977), both with bus services to Hat Yai ($35) and beyond. Most buses leave around 6pm and travel overnight.

CAR & MOTORCYCLE

Singaporeans drive on the left-hand side of the road and it is compulsory to wear seat belts in the front and back of the car. The *Mighty Minds Singapore Street Directory* ($12.90) is invaluable.

Driving

If you plan on driving in Singapore, bring your current home driver's licence and an international driving permit issued by a motoring association in your country.

Singapore once boasted fairly clear roads, but in recent years congestion has significantly worsened. The roads themselves are immaculate, but don't let that lull you into a false sense of security – nowhere is the infamous *kiasu* (Hokkien for 'afraid to lose') Singaporean character more evident than on the roads. Aggressive driving is common, speeding and tailgating endemic, use of signals rare, and wild lane-changing universal. Given Singapore's reputation for strict punishment, penalties for serious offences – even killing pedestrians while drunk – are breathtakingly lenient.

In short, we don't recommend driving in Singapore, but if you do, practise extreme defensive driving, and have your road rage under control!

As for motorcycles, they are held in very low esteem (we speak from experience here). At best, drivers display almost no regard for bike safety. At worst, they appear to violently object to the right of a lowly motorcycle to be in front of them and try to hunt you down.

Hire

If you want a car for local driving only, it's worth checking smaller operators, whose rates are often cheaper than the big global rental firms. If you're going into Malaysia, you're better off renting in Johor Bahru, where the rates are significantly lower (besides, Malaysian police are renowned for targeting Singapore licence plates).

Rates start from around $60 a day. Special deals may be available, especially for longer-term rental. There are hire booths at Singapore Changi Airport as well as in the city. These are some of the major companies:

Avis (Map pp52–3; ☎ 6737 1668; www.avis.com.sg; 392 Havelock Rd, 01-07)

Express Car (Map p80; ☎ 6842 4992; www.expresscar .com.sg; 1 Sims Lane)

Hawk (Map pp46–7; 6469 4468; www.hawkrentacar .com.sg; 32A Hillview Terrace;)

Hertz Rent-a-Car (Map pp74–5; ☎ 6734 4646; 15 Scotts Rd, 01-01 Thong Teck Bldg)

Premier (Map pp74–5; www-singapore.com/premier /index.html; 03-05 Balmoral Plaza, 271 Bukit Timah Rd)

Restricted Zone & Car Parking

From 7.30am to 7pm weekdays, as well as from 10.15am through to 2pm Saturday, the area comprising the CBD, Chinatown and Orchard Rd is considered a restricted zone. Cars are free to enter but they must pay a toll. Vehicles are automatically tracked by sensors on overhead gantries, so cars must be fitted with an in-vehicle unit, into which drivers must insert a cashcard (available at petrol stations and 7-Elevens). The toll is extracted from the card. The same system is also in operation on certain expressways. Rental cars are subject to the same rules.

Anyone whose vehicle is not fitted with a unit, or whose card does not have sufficient credit, is automatically photographed and fined.

Parking in the city centre is expensive, but relatively easy to find – almost every major mall has a car park. Outdoor car parks and street parking spaces are usually operated by the government – you can buy booklets of parking coupons, which must be displayed in the window, from post offices and 7-Elevens.

MASS RAPID TRANSIT

The superb MRT subway system is the easiest, quickest and most comfortable way to get around Singapore. The system operates from 5.30am to midnight, with trains at peak times running every three minutes, and off-peak every six minutes. For a map of the system, see the maps section at the back of this book.

In the inner city, the MRT runs underground, emerging overground out towards the suburban housing estates. It consists of three lines: North-South, North-East and East-West, with a fourth – the Circle Line – on the verge of opening at the time of writing.

Fares & Fare Cards

Single-trip tickets cost from $1.10 to $1.90 (plus a $1 refundable deposit), but if you're using the MRT a lot it can become a hassle buying and refunding tickets for every journey. A lot more convenient is the Ez-link card ($15, including a $5 nonrefundable deposit), which you can top up as necessary and use on all buses and trains. Alternatively, a Singapore Tourist Pass (www.thesingaporetouristpass.com) offers unlimited train and bus travel ($8) for one day.

TAXI

Poor old Singapore has endless problems with its taxi system. Despite an interminable cycle of debate, reform, complaint and adjustment, finding a taxi in the city at certain times (during peak hours, at night, or when it's raining) remains a major headache. The fare system is also hugely complicated, but thankfully it's all metered, so there's no tedious haggling over fares. The basic flagfall is $2.80, then $0.20 for every 385m.

The one exception is at Tanjong Pagar Railway Station, where there's no Changi Airport–style system. It's not unknown for taxi drivers to swoop on new arrivals and demand outlandish fares for short distances. Demand that they use the meter; it's against the law if they don't. Credit card payments incur a 10% surcharge.

These are the taxi companies:

Comfort and CityCab CabLink (☎ 6552 1111)

Premier Taxis (☎ 6363 6888)

SMRT Cabs (☎ 6555 8888)

Ordering a taxi by phone from any of these companies during nonpeak hours is usually quick, but during peak hours you'll often be waiting a long time. Just tell them your location, then wait for an automated message to give you the taxi registration number and estimated time of arrival.

You can flag down a taxi any time, but in the city centre taxis are not allowed to stop anywhere except at designated taxi stands.

TRAIN
Malaysia & Thailand

Singapore is the southern termination point for the Malaysian railway system, Keretapi Tanah Malayu (KTM; www.ktmb.com.my). Malaysia has two main rail lines: the primary line going from Singapore to Kuala Lumpur, Butterworth, Alor Setar and then into Thailand; and a second line branching off at Gemas and going right up through the centre of the country to Tumpat, near Kota Bharu on the east coast.

The booking office at Singapore railway station (Map pp62–3; ☎ 6222 5165; Keppel Rd) is open 8.30am to 2pm and 3pm to 7pm.

Three express trains depart every day to Kuala Lumpur (1st/2nd/3rd class $68/34/19) roughly around 7.40am, 3.30pm and 9pm, and takes between seven and nine hours; check the website or call the booking office for the exact times. One-way fares range from $19 for Economy to $111 for 'Premier Night Deluxe'. There are also three daily services to the northeast.

The luxurious Eastern & Oriental Express (☎ 6392 3500; www.orient-express.com) runs between Singapore and Bangkok, then onward to Chiang Mai and Nong Khai (for Laos). The sumptuous antique train takes 42 hours to do the 1943km journey from Singapore to Bangkok. Don your linen suit, sip a gin and tonic, and dig deep for the fare: from $3430 per person in a double compartment to $6650 in the presidential suite.

BUSINESS HOURS

In Singapore, government offices are usually open from Monday to Friday and Saturday morning. Hours tend to vary, starting between 7.30am and 9.30am and closing between 4pm and 6pm. On Saturday, closing time is between 11.30am and 1pm.

Shop hours vary. Small shops generally open from 10am to 6pm weekdays, while department stores and large shopping centres open from 10am to 9pm or 9.30pm, seven days a week. Most small shops in Chinatown and Arab St close on Sunday, though in Little India, Sunday is the busiest shopping day.

Banks are open from 9.30am to 3pm weekdays (to 11.30am Saturday), while top restaurants open at lunchtime and in the evenings.

CHILDREN

Singapore is a safe, healthy and fun country for children, provided you make provisions for the heat. Singaporean society is very family-oriented and kids are welcome pretty much everywhere. Eating out as a family is considered normal and hotels are usually able to provide family rooms, extra beds or cots, and babysitting. Lonely Planet's *Travel with Children* by Cathy Lanigan is packed with useful information for family travel.

In this book, sleeping and eating venues that are child-friendly show the 🐘 icon. For things to see and do with children, see p87.

CLIMATE

Singapore is hot and humid all year round and though it gets regular rainfall, it's usually in the form of heavy tropical showers that last an hour or two and leave clear skies behind them. There's little distinction between seasons but

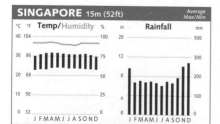

the hotter months are usually between May and September.

COURSES

Singaporeans are mad on courses, but town councils provide them at subsidised rates to citizens or permanent residents. For visitors, the most popular short-term courses are in cookery (see p122).

CUSTOMS REGULATIONS

Visitors to Singapore are allowed to bring in 1L of wine, beer or spirits duty-free. Electronic goods, cosmetics, watches, cameras, jewellery (but not fakes), footwear, toys, arts and crafts are not dutiable; the usual duty-free concession for personal effects, such as clothes, applies.

It is forbidden to bring any tobacco products into Singapore, though they'll turn a blind eye to the odd pack of smokes.

Duty-free concessions are not available if you are arriving in Singapore from Malaysia or if you leave Singapore for less than 48 hours.

Fire crackers, toy currency and coins, obscene or seditious material, gun-shaped cigarette lighters, endangered species or their by-products, and pirated recordings and publications are prohibited. The importation or exportation of illegal drugs carries the death penalty for more than 15g of heroin, 30g of morphine or cocaine, 1.2kg of opium, 500g of cannabis, 200g of cannabis resin, 1000g of cannabis mixture or 250g of methamphetamine. Trafficking in ecstasy (more than 150 tablets) carries a penalty of 30 years' jail and 15 strokes of the *rotan* (a rattan cane).

Penalties for trafficking in lesser amounts range from two years in jail and two strokes of the *rotan* to 30 years and 15 strokes. If you bring in prescription drugs, you should have a doctor's letter or a prescription.

There is no restriction on the importation of currency.

DISCOUNT CARDS

There are no discount cards as such, but anyone flying into Singapore on Singapore Airlines or Silk Air can get discounts at multiple shops, restaurants and attractions by pre-

senting their boarding pass. See singaporeair
.com/boardingpass for information.

ELECTRICITY

Electricity supplies are dependable and run
at 220V to 240V and 50 cycles. Plugs are of
the three-pronged, square-pin type used in
the UK. Most malls have electronic or hardware
stores, all of which stock a full range of
adaptors. For more information on travellers'
electrical issues, see www.kropla.com.

EMBASSIES

For a list of Singaporean missions abroad,
check out www.visitsingapore.com, where
you'll also find a full list of foreign embassies
and consulates in Singapore. Contact details
for some foreign embassies and consulates
include the following:

Australia (Map pp92–3; ☎ 6836 4100; www.australia
.org.sg; 25 Napier Rd; Ⓜ Orchard, then 🚌 7 or 123)

Canada (Map pp62–3; ☎ 6854 5900; www.cic.gc.ca;
11-01, One George St; Ⓜ Tanjong Pagar)

China (Map pp74–5; ☎ 6418 0246; www.chinaembassy
.org.sg; 150 Tanglin Rd; Ⓜ Orchard, then 🚌 7 or 123)

France (Map pp74–5; ☎ 6880 7800; www.france.org.sg;
101-103 Cluny Park Rd; Ⓜ Newton, then 🚌 48, 66 or 170)

Germany (Map pp62–3; ☎ 6533 6002; www.singapur
.diplo.de; 12-00 Singapore Land Tower, 50 Raffles Place;
Ⓜ Raffles Place)

India (Map pp74–5; ☎ 6737 6777; www.embassyofindia
.com; 31 Grange Rd; Ⓜ Orchard, then 🚌 7 or 123)

Indonesia (Map pp74–5; ☎ 6737 7422; 7 Chatsworth Rd;
Ⓜ Orchard, then bus 7 or 123)

Ireland (Map pp74–5; ☎ 6238 7616; www.ireland.org
.sg; 08-00 Liat Towers, 541 Orchard Rd; Ⓜ Orchard)

Israel (Map pp74–5; ☎ 6235 0966; 58 Dalvey Rd;
Ⓜ Orchard)

Japan (Map pp74–5; ☎ 6235 8855; www.sg.emb-japan
.go.jp; 16 Nassim Rd; Ⓜ Orchard)

Malaysia (Map pp74–5; ☎ 6235 0111; 301 Jervois Rd;
Ⓜ City Hall)

New Zealand (Map pp74–5; ☎ 6235 9966; www.nz
embassy.com; 15-06/10 Ngee Ann City, 391A Orchard Rd;
Ⓜ Orchard or Somerset)

Thailand (Map pp74–5; ☎ 6737 2644; 370 Orchard Rd;
Ⓜ Orchard)

UK (Map pp92–3; ☎ 6424 4200; www.britain.org.sg; 100
Tanglin Rd; Ⓜ Orchard, then 🚌 7 or 123)

USA (Map pp92–3; ☎ 6476 9100; http://singapore.us
embassy.gov; 27 Napier Rd; Ⓜ Orchard, then 🚌 7 or 123)

EMERGENCY

Useful emergency numbers:

Ambulance (☎ 995)

Fire (☎ 995)

Police (☎ 999)

SOS Helpline (☎ 1800 774 5935)

GAY & LESBIAN TRAVELLERS

Sex between males is illegal in Singapore,
carrying a minimum sentence of 10 years.
In reality, nobody is ever likely to be prosecuted,
but the ban remains as a symbol of
the government's belief that the country is not
ready for the open acceptance of 'alternative
lifestyles'.

Despite that, there are lots of gay bars and
you'll see lots of openly gay people around
the city.

A good place to start looking for information
is on the websites of Utopia (www.utopia-asia
.com) or Fridae (www.fridae.com), both of which provide
excellent coverage of venues and events
across Asia.

Singaporeans are fairly conservative about
public affection, though it's becoming much
more common to see displays of familiarity
among straight and lesbian couples these days
(the latter don't seem to attract any attention).
A gay male couple doing the same would definitely
draw negative attention.

HEALTH

As well as being a healthy place, Singapore has
excellent facilities that draw lots of 'medical
tourists'. For a complete rundown on what's
available, see www.singaporemedicine.com.

Hygiene is strictly observed and the tap
water is safe to drink. However, hepatitis A
does occur. You only need vaccinations if you
come from a yellow-fever area. Singapore is
not a malarial zone but dengue fever is an
increasing concern.

Lonely Planet's *Asia & India: Healthy
Travel Guide* is a handy pocket-sized and
packed with useful information including
pretrip planning, emergency first-aid, immunisation
and disease information, and what to
do if you get sick on the road. Lonely Planet's
Travel with Children also includes advice on
travel health for younger children.

Medical Problems & Treatment

Self-diagnosis and treatment can be risky, so you should always seek medical help. An embassy, consulate or hotel can usually recommend a local doctor or clinic. Singapore has many pharmacies (check www.yellowpages.com.sg).

DENGUE FEVER

Singapore has suffered a sharp rise in cases of this nasty viral disease in recent years. Spread by day-biting *Aedes aegypti* mosquitoes – recognisable by their black-and-white striped bodies – it is characterised by sudden high fever, extremely painful joint pains (hence its old name 'breakbone fever'), headache, nausea and vomiting, which peaks and settles after a few days, after which a rash often spreads across the body. The illness usually disappears after 10 days, but the resulting weakness can take months to recover from. The biggest danger is dengue haemorrhagic fever and dengue shock syndrome, which causes internal bleeding and can be fatal. If you suspect dengue, seek medical treatment immediately.

HEAT EXHAUSTION

It's important to avoid dehydration in Singapore's constant heat – it can lead to heat exhaustion. Take time to acclimatise to high temperatures; drink sufficient liquids and do not do anything too physically demanding. Salt deficiency, another cause of dehydration, is characterised by fatigue, lethargy, headaches, giddiness and muscle cramps; salt tablets may help, but adding extra salt to your food is better.

HEPATITIS A

Hepatitis A can be found in Singapore and is transmitted through contaminated food and drinking water. Symptoms include fever, chills, headache, fatigue, feelings of weakness, and aches and pains, followed by loss of appetite, nausea, vomiting, abdominal pain, dark urine, light-coloured faeces, jaundiced (yellow) skin and yellowing of the whites of the eyes. People who have had hepatitis should avoid alcohol for some time after the illness, as the liver needs time to recover.

You should seek medical advice, but there is not much you can do apart from resting, drinking lots of fluids, eating lightly and avoiding fatty foods.

The hepatitis A vaccine provides long-term immunity (possibly more than 10 years) after an initial injection and a booster after six to 12 months.

PRICKLY HEAT

This is an itchy rash caused by excessive perspiration trapped under the skin. It usually strikes people who have just arrived in a hot climate. Keep cool, bathe often, dry the skin and use a mild talcum or prickly heat powder, or resort to air-conditioning.

SUNBURN

In the tropics you can get sunburnt surprisingly quickly, even through cloud. Use a sunscreen, a hat (or umbrella), and a barrier cream for your nose and lips. Calamine lotion or a commercial after-sun preparation is good for mild sunburn. Protect your eyes with good-quality sunglasses.

HOLIDAYS

Public Holidays

Listed are public holidays in Singapore. For those days not based on the Western calendar, the months they are likely to fall in are provided. The only holiday that has a major effect on the city is Chinese New Year, when virtually all shops shut down for two days.

New Year's Day 1 January

Chinese New Year Three days in January/February

Good Friday April

Labour Day 1 May

Vesak Day May

National Day 9 August

Hari Raya Puasa October/November

Deepavali October

Christmas Day 25 December

Hari Raya Haji December/January

School Holidays

There are two long breaks; the first is a four-week break in June and the second is usually the entire month of December.

INTERNET ACCESS

Every top hotel has internet access and will help get you set up if you bring your own laptop or palmtop computer. The newer backpacker hostels all offer free internet access.

Singapore's island-wide broadband network and thousands of wireless hotspots

---

WI-FI ACCESS

Singapore has an ever-expanding network of around 1000 wireless hotspots – and most cafes and pubs operate them. A list of hotspots can be found by following the Wireless@SG link at www.infocomm123 .sg. Logging on is free until 31 December 2009 – you can get a user ID and password by dialling ☎ 186 on the SingTel Mobile network.

---

means you don't have to worry about telephone cables, but if you need dial-up internet access, ensure that you have at least a US RJ-11 telephone adaptor that works with your modem. You can almost always find an adaptor that will convert from RJ-11 to the local variety.

Major Internet service providers such as CompuServe (www.compuserve.com), AOL (www.aol.com) and AT&T (www.attbusiness.net) have dial-up nodes in Singapore. SingTel (www.singtel.com.sg) and StarHub (www.starhub.com) are the two biggest local providers.

If you intend to rely on internet cafes, you'll need your incoming (POP or IMAP) mail server name, your account name and your password from your internet service provider.

LEGAL MATTERS

Singapore's reputation for harsh laws is not undeserved – don't expect any special treatment for being a foreigner. Despite the surprisingly low-key police presence on the street, they appear pretty fast when something happens. Police have broad powers and you would be unwise to refuse any requests they make of you. If you are involved in an incident, it's worth noting that the first person who calls the police tends to be the one who gets believed. If you are arrested, you will be entitled to legal counsel (who will usually advise you to plead guilty if it's a minor offence, even if you're not) and contact with your embassy.

MAPS

Good-quality free tourist maps are available at tourist offices, the airport on arrival, and at some hotels, hostels and shopping centres. The *Official Map of Singapore*, available free from the Singapore Tourism Board (STB) and hotels, is very good and very easy to follow. Of the commercial maps, Nelles and Periplus

are good. The *Mighty Minds Singapore Street Directory* ($12.90) is superb and essential if you plan to drive.

MEDICAL SERVICES

Singapore's medical institutions are first-rate and generally cheaper than private healthcare in the West. Needless to say, insurance cover is advisable. Check with insurance providers what treatments and procedures are covered before you leave home.

Clinics

Raffles SurgiCentre (Map p68; ☎ 6334 3337; www.raffles hospital.com; 585 North Bridge Rd; ⊙ 24hr; Ⓜ Bugis) A walk-in clinic.

Singapore General Hospital Accident & Emergency Department (Map pp62–3; ☎ 6321 4311; Outram Rd; ⊙ 24hr; Ⓜ Outram Park) Located in Block 1 of this big compound.

Emergency Rooms

The following operate 24-hour emergency rooms:

Gleneagles Hospital (Map pp74–5; ☎ 6470 5688; 6A Napier Rd)

Mount Elizabeth Hospital (Map pp74–5; ☎ 6731 2218; 3 Mt Elizabeth Rd)

Raffles Hospital (Map p68; ☎ 6311 1111; 585 North Bridge Rd)

Singapore General Hospital (Map pp62–3; ☎ 6321 4113; Level 2, Block 1, Outram Rd)

MONEY

The country's unit of currency is the Singapore dollar, locally referred to as the 'singdollar', which is made up of 100 cents. Singapore uses 5¢, 10¢, 20¢, 50¢ and $1 coins, while notes come in denominations of $2, $5, $10, $50, $100, $500 and $1000. The Singapore dollar is a highly stable and freely convertible currency.

Changing Money

Banks change money, but virtually nobody uses them because the rates are better at the moneychangers dotted all over the city. Usually Indian-run, these tiny stalls can be found in just about every shopping centre (though not in the more modern malls).

NEWSPAPERS & MAGAZINES

English dailies in Singapore include the broadsheet *Straits Times* (which includes the *Sunday Times*), the *Business Times,* the afternoon tabloid *New Paper,* and *Today,* a free paper.

The *Straits Times* is a drab affair that acts as the mouthpiece of the government, though its coverage of Asia is OK. Stablemate the *New Paper* is Singapore's attempt at lurid tabloid journalism, and also offers obsessively detailed coverage of English football.

Today looks like a dog's breakfast, but most agree it's a better read than either of its rivals.

Foreign current affairs and business magazines are widely available, though you won't find the *Far Eastern Economic Review,* which was banned after displeasing the government. Pornographic publications are strictly prohibited, but *Cosmopolitan* and racy lads' magazines like *FHM* and *Maxim* are allowed.

ORGANISED TOURS

Singapore is easy for self-navigation, but there are a number of worthwhile tours that can open up the city and its history, or simply offer a unique experience. Recommended:

Culinary Heritage Tour (☎ 6238 8488; www.eastwest planners.com) Taking on Singapore's vast food culture can be daunting for the newcomer, so these tailor-made tours are a good way not just of sampling the most famous dishes, but having someone show you the best places to eat them. Aimed at the more affluent visitor. Prices and itineraries are available on request.

Imperial Cheng Ho Dinner Cruise (☎ 6533 9811; www .watertours.com.sg; adult/child daytime cruises $27/14, dinner cruises $55/29) Singapore's port and harbour has long been its lifeblood, and though it may be very touristy, there's no better way to see it than from this replica Chinese junk that picks its way through the giant container ships. The food is nothing spectacular, but the views are.

Original Singapore Walks (☎ 6325 1631; www.singapore walks.com; adult/child from $25/15) If you just do one tour in Singapore, make it one of these. Led by informed, enthusiastic guides, these walks through various parts of the city – including Chinatown, Little India and the Quays – provide a fascinating insight into Singapore's past, including the down-and-dirty stuff you won't hear about anywhere else. The WWII tour is excellent, too. No booking necessary, just check the website for meeting times and places, then turn up.

Singapore DUCK Tours (☎ 6333 3825; www.ducktours .com.sg; adult/child $33/17) We're including this because the vindictive streak in us likes the idea of subjecting people to the cringing embarrassment of being driven around the city in a brightly coloured amphibious vehicle playing a tinny soundtrack, before plunging into the harbour. So excruciating you'll never forget it.

Singapore Nature Walks (☎ 6787 7048; serin@swiftech .com.sg) Singapore's natural assets are often overlooked and hard to find, but freelance guide Subaraj has a passion for nature and an intimate knowledge of the island's pockets of wilderness.

Singapore Zoo Management Tour (☎ 6269 3411; www .zoo.com.sg; adult/child $20/10; ⏰ 11am, 2pm & 4pm) Excellent behind-the-scenes tours of various exhibits with zoo staff, sure to be a hit with the kids. Fragile Forest at 11am, Reptile Garden at 2pm and baboons at 4pm.

River Cruises

They're a little short and vaguely unsatisfying, but the bumboat cruises that ply the stretch between Clarke Quay and Marina Bay are a pleasant way of soaking up some history. Festooned with Chinese lanterns, they are best taken at night, when they make a romantic pre-dinner excursion. Cruises depart from several places along the Singapore River including Clarke Quay, Raffles Landing and Boat Quay. They generally run between 8.30am and 10.30pm.

One company **Singapore River Cruises** (☎ 6336 6111; www.rivercruise.com.sg) operates glass-top boats and bumboats up and down the river (adult/child 30-minute tours $13/8, 45-minute $18/10); for atmosphere, the chugging bumboats are by far the most preferable. There are two tour lengths: one goes as far as Clarke Quay, while the longer tour takes in Robertson Quay as well, which is not really worth the extra 15 minutes.

POST

Postal delivery in Singapore is very efficient. Most post offices are open 8am to 6pm Monday to Friday, and 8am to 2pm Saturday. Call ☎ 1605 to find the nearest branch or check www.singpost.com.sg.

Letters addressed to 'Poste Restante' are held at the **Singapore Post Centre** (Map p80; ☎ 6741 8857; 10 Eunos Rd; Ⓜ Paya Lebar), which is next to the Paya Lebar MRT station. It's open on Sunday, as is the post office on **Killiney Rd** (Map pp74–5; ☎ 6734 7899; 1 Killiney Rd; Ⓜ Somerset). There's another branch on **Orchard Rd** (Map pp74–5; ☎ 6738 6899; 04-15 Takashimaya, Ngee Ann City, 391 Orchard Rd; Ⓜ Orchard). Terminal 2 at Changi Airport (Map pp46–7) has two branches, one open from 6am to midnight, the other from 8am to 9.30pm.

Airmail postcards and aerograms cost $0.50 to anywhere in the world. Letters weighing 20g or less cost from $0.65 to $1.10, depending on the destination.

RADIO

The Media Corporation of Singapore (Media-Corp for short) runs the largest radio network, with 12 local and four international radio stations. It has five English-language stations: Gold 90.5FM, Symphony 92.4FM, NewsRadio 93.8FM, Class 95FM and Perfect 10 98.7FM. International Channel 96.3FM, also run by MediaCorp, specialises in French, German, Japanese and Korean programmes. Private stations include Safra Radio's English-language Power 98FM, a 24-hour station aimed at the 18- to 35-year-old market. The BBC broadcasts on 88.9FM.

Most of the island's radio stations have web streaming if you want to get a taste of mid-Atlantic accents with a Singaporean twang before you come.

RELOCATING

Singapore is one of the easiest places in the world to settle, with thousands upon thousands of expatriates streaming in and out constantly. But while the immigration and bureaucratic procedures are smooth and streamlined, the process of becoming socially established can be difficult. Probably the most popular online meeting point is www.singaporeexpats.com, which has a wealth of information on relocating, a real estate service, online forums on every possible topic, a popular dating and friendship service, and online classifieds where you can find lots of goods being discarded by people on their way out.

The spouses and partners of people coming to Singapore on work contracts can apply to the Ministry of Manpower (www.mom.gov .sg) for permission to work. The procedure is a formality, but many find the process of finding jobs a dispiriting slog – Singaporean employers are generally very reluctant to hire foreigners inside the country. Another option is to register a sole proprietorship company and work freelance; the paperwork can be completed at post offices and is usually a formality. Once approved, registering the company and getting the work permit are simple.

TAXES & REFUNDS

As a visitor you are entitled to claim a refund of the 7% Goods & Services Tax on your purchases, provided you meet certain conditions (see p105).

TELEPHONE

You can make local and international calls from public phone booths. Most phone booths take phonecards.

Singapore also has credit-card phones that can be used by running your card through the slot. At SingTel centres, there are also Home Country Direct phones – press a country button to contact the operator and reverse the charges, or have the call charged to an international telephone card acceptable in your country.

Useful numbers include the following:

Directory information (☎ 100)

Flight information (☎ 1800 542 4422) Voice activated.

STB 24-hour Touristline (☎ 1800 736 2000)

There are no area codes within Singapore; telephone numbers are eight digits unless you are calling toll-free (☎ 1800).

To call Singapore from overseas, dial your country's international access number and then ☎ 65, Singapore's country code, before entering the eight-digit telephone number.

Calls to Malaysia (from Singapore) are considered to be STD (trunk or long-distance) calls. Dial the access code ☎ 020, followed by the area code of the town in Malaysia that you wish to call (minus the leading zero) and then your party's number. Thus, for a call to ☎ 346 7890 in Kuala Lumpur (area code ☎ 03) you would dial ☎ 02-3-346 7890. Call ☎ 109 for assistance with Malaysian area codes.

Mobile Phones

In Singapore, mobile phone numbers start with ☎ 9. As long as you have arranged to have 'global roaming' facilities with your home provider, your GSM digital phone will automatically connect with one of Singapore's networks. Singapore uses GSM900 and GSM1800 and there is complete coverage over the whole island. Check roaming rates with your operator, as they can be very high.

Alternatively, you can buy a local SIM card for around $28 (including credit) from post offices and 7-Eleven stores – by law you must show your passport to get one.

Phonecards

Phonecards are particularly popular among Singapore's migrant workers – the domestic maids and construction workers that keep the city ticking over – so there are plenty on sale. There's a small thriving phonecard stall outside the Centrepoint shopping centre (p113) on Orchard Rd, and plenty of retailers around Little India, but check which countries they service before you buy.

TIME

Singapore is eight hours ahead of GMT/UTC (London), two hours behind Australian Eastern Standard Time (Sydney and Melbourne), 13 hours ahead of American Eastern Standard Time (New York) and 16 hours ahead of American Pacific Standard Time (San Francisco and Los Angeles). So, when it is noon in Singapore, it is 8pm in Los Angeles and 11pm in New York the previous day, 4am in London and 2pm in Sydney.

TOILETS

It will come as no surprise that Singapore's public toilets are widely distributed and immaculate, even those in public parks and train stations. Many places, the zoo for example, have the latest fancy 'outdoor' designs. Occasionally you'll need to pay $0.10 or $0.20 to use them – particularly at hawker centres – but ironically these are often the least well-kept.

TOURIST INFORMATION

Before your trip, a good place to check for information is the website of the Singapore Tourism Board (www.visitsingapore.com).

In Singapore, there are several tourism centres offering a wide range of services, including tour bookings and event ticketing, plus a couple of electronic information kiosks.

Liang Court Tourist Service Centre (Map pp52–3; ☎ 6336 7184; Level 1, Liang Court Shopping Centre, 177 River Valley Rd; ☉ 10am-10pm; M Clarke Quay)

Singapore Visitors Centre@Little India (Map p68; ☎ 6296 4280; 73 Dunlop St, InnCrowd Backpackers Hostel; ☉ 10am-10pm; M Little India)

Singapore Visitors@Orchard Information Centre (Map pp74–5; ☎ 1800 736 2000; cnr Orchard & Cairnhill Rds; ☉ 8am-10.30pm; M Somerset)

Suntec City Visitors Centre (Map pp52–3; ☎ 1800 332 5066; 01-35/37/39/41 Suntec City Mall, 3 Temasek Blvd; ☉ 10am-6pm; M City Hall)

TRAVELLERS WITH DISABILITIES

Facilities for wheelchairs used to be nonexistent in Singapore, but in recent years a large government campaign has seen ramps, lifts and other facilities progressively installed around the island. The pavements in the city are nearly all immaculate, MRT stations all have lifts and there are even some buses equipped with wheelchair-friendly equipment. Check out *Access Singapore,* which is a useful guidebook by the Disabled Persons Association of Singapore; it has a complete rundown on services and other information, and can be found online at www.dpa.org.sg. The booklet is also available from STB offices (see left) or from the National Council of Social Services (☎ 6210 2500; www.ncss.org.sg).

VISAS

Citizens of most countries are granted 30-day visas on arrival by air or overland (though the latter may get 14-day visas). The exceptions are the Commonwealth of Independent States, India, Myanmar, China and most Middle Eastern countries. Extensions can be applied for at the Immigration Department (Map p68; ☎ 6391 6100; 10 Kallang Rd; M Lavender).

WOMEN TRAVELLERS

Singapore is probably the safest Asian country in which to travel and sexual harassment is very rare – though women might be a little uncomfortable in Little India during the weekends, when tens of thousands of male migrant workers throng the area. Women are not cloistered in Singaporean society and enjoy considerable freedom and equality.

WORK

Work opportunities for foreigners inside the country are limited – the vast majority of foreigners get hired from overseas. One of the main reasons for this is the high cost of accommodation and car ownership, which overseas companies often cover for top executives.

However, foreigners do find work inside the country and there is a huge skills gap in many industries, including digital media, finance and hospitality. Business experience, marketable job skills and impressive qualifications are your best bet – like the rest of Asia, Singapore often places a higher value on your paperwork than your experience. Contact Singapore (www.contactsingapore.sg) should be your first stop for job-hunting, though there are also dozens of headhunting firms on the lookout for skilled foreigners.

Doing Business

Singapore prides itself on being a dynamic and efficient place to do business. Leaving Barings Bank and a couple of other scandals aside, Singapore has stable financial markets, a stable government and negligible corruption.

Singapore has aggressively attracted foreign capital, and big money from overseas has played a large part in the dramatic rise in Singapore's wealth. As a free-trading promoter of foreign investment with minimal restrictions, Singapore is an easy place to set up a business. Though it primarily directs its energies and substantial concessions to large investors in export-oriented industries, the current focus on boosting tourism, arts and entertainment has opened up a new world of opportunity. The domestic economy is very much directed by the government through the auspices of the Economic Development Board (www.sedb.com).

Singapore pursues a free-trade policy and, other than the GST for the importation of goods, very few goods are dutiable or restricted for import or export. International Enterprise Singapore (Map p68; ☎ 6337 6628, Singapore only 1800 437 7673; www.iesingapore.gov.sg; Level 10, Bugis Junction Tower, 230 Victoria St) has simplified import and export procedures, and trade documents can be processed through TradeNet, an electronic data system. Check its website for a list of its offices worldwide, usually located at the Singaporean diplomatic missions.

You may also find the *Business Times* newspaper useful.

Bring plenty of business cards with you – business meetings typically begin with the exchange of cards, which are offered with two hands in a humble gesture signifying that you are presenting yourself to your contact. Expect to be liberally dined and entertained. Establishing personal rapport is important and your business contacts are unlikely to let you languish in your hotel at the end of a working day.

Volunteering

Singapore prides itself on its volunteer culture. If you're living in the city, volunteers are usually welcome at any of the customary places: rest homes, disability associations, Society for the Prevention of Cruelty to Animals (SPCA), the Singapore zoo, environmental groups etc. Don't be surprised if you're asked to go through extensive procedures and/or training sessions before being accepted, however.

The four official languages of Singapore are Malay, Tamil, Mandarin and English. Malay is the national language, adopted when Singapore was part of Malaysia, but its use is mostly restricted to the Malay community.

Tamil is the main Indian language; others include Malayalam and Hindi.

Chinese dialects are still widely spoken, especially among older Chinese, with the most common being Hokkien, Teochew, Cantonese, Hainanese and Hakka. The government's long-standing campaign to promote Mandarin, the main nondialectal Chinese language, has been very successful and increasing numbers of Singaporean Chinese now speak it at home.

English is becoming even more widespread. After independence, the government introduced a bilingual education policy aimed at developing the vernacular languages and lessening the use of English. However, Chinese graduates found that this lessened their opportunities for higher education and presented them with greater difficulties in finding a job. English was the language of business and united the various ethnic groups, and the government eventually had to give it more priority. It officially became the first language of instruction in schools in 1987. In 2000 the government launched a 'speak good English' campaign to improve the standard of English.

All children are also taught their mother tongue at school. This policy is largely designed to unite the various Chinese groups and to make sure Chinese Singaporeans don't lose contact with their traditions.

SINGLISH

You're unlikely to spend much time in Singapore without finding yourself at some point staring dumbly at someone, trying to work out what on earth they are on about. Unnecessary prepositions and pronouns are dropped, word order is flipped, phrases are clipped short and stress and cadence are unconventional, to say the least. Nominally English, the Singaporeans' unique patois contains borrowed words from Hokkien, Tamil and Malay.

There isn't a Singlish grammar as such, but there are definite characteristics, such as the long stress on the last syllable of phrases, so that the standard English 'government' becomes 'guvva-men'. Words ending in consonants are often syncopated and vowels are often distorted. A Chinese-speaking taxi driver might not immediately understand that you want to go to Perak Road, since they know it as 'Pera Roh'.

Verb tenses tend to be nonexistent. Past, present and future are indicated instead by time indicators, so in Singlish it's 'I go tomorrow' or 'I go yesterday'.

The particle 'lah' is often tagged on to the end of sentences for emphasis, as in 'No good lah'. Requests or questions may be marked with a tag ending, since direct questioning can be rude. As a result, questions that are formed to be more polite often come across to Westerners as rude. 'Would you like a beer?' becomes 'You wan beer or not?'

SPEAK MANDARIN, PLEASE!

Singapore is a country with many languages and people, but Chinese ultimately predominate.

When their forebears came from China they brought with them a number of Chinese languages and dialects, including Hokkien, Teochew, Hakka, Cantonese and Mandarin. So dissimilar are these dialects that they might as well be separate languages. The British temporarily solved the problem by making English the lingua franca (common language) of its tropical colony, and to a large degree that still remains the case today.

Since 1979 the Singapore government, in an effort to unite its disparate Chinese peoples, has been encouraging minority-language speakers to adopt the language of administration used by Beijing, namely Mandarin. It is hoped that in this way disunity and differences can be eliminated and the concept of a Singaporean nation can be better realised.

The campaign was initially targeted at monolingual Chinese-speakers, but over the years it has spread to English-educated Chinese who have begun to show an increasing willingness to use Mandarin as their main vehicle for communication in business and pleasure. The government is so intent on its 'Speak Mandarin Campaign' that it even has a website where would-be converts can get themselves motivated – it's at www .mandarin.org.sg.

You'll also hear Singaporeans addressing older people as 'uncle' and 'auntie'. They are not relatives and neither is this rude, but more a sign of respect.

Following are a few frequently heard Singlishisms. For a more complete exploration, get hold of the hilarious Coxford Singlish Dictionary on the satirical website **Talking Cock** (www.talkingcock.com).

a bit the – very; as in *Wah! Your car a bit the slow one*

ah beng – every country has them: boys with spiky gelled hair, loud clothes, the latest mobile phones and a choice line in gutter phrases; his fondest wish, if not already fulfilled, is to own a souped-up car with an enormous speaker in the boot, so that he may pick up the cutest *ah lian*

ah lian – the female version of the *ah beng*: large, moussed hair, garish outfits, armed with a vicious tongue; also known as *ah huay*

aiyah! – 'oh, dear!'

alamak! – exclamation of disbelief or frustration, like 'oh my God!'

ang mor – common term for Westerner (Caucasian), with derogatory undertone; literally 'red-haired monkey' in Hokkien

ayam – Malay word for chicken; adjective for something inferior or weak

blur – slow or uninformed

buaya – womaniser, from the Malay for crocodile

can? – 'is that OK?'

can! – 'yes! That's fine.'

char bor – babe, woman

cheena – derogatory term for old-fashioned Chinese in dress or thinking

confirm – used to convey emphasis when describing something/someone, as in *He confirm blur one* (He's not very smart)

go stun – to reverse, as in *Go stun the car* (from the naval expression 'go astern')

heng – luck, good fortune (Hokkien)

hiao – vain

inggrish – English

kambing – foolish person, literally 'goat' (Malay)

kaypoh – busybody

kena – Malay word close to meaning of English word 'got', describing something that happened, as in *He kena arrested for drunk driving*

kenna ketok – ripped off

kiasee – scared, literally 'afraid to die'; a coward

kiasu – literally 'afraid to lose'; selfish, pushy, always on the lookout for a bargain

kopitiam – coffee shop

lah – generally an ending for any phrase or sentence; can translate as 'OK', but has no real meaning, added for emphasis to just about everything

lai dat – 'like that'; used for emphasis, as in *I so boring lai dat* (I'm very bored).

looksee – take a look

makan – a meal; to eat

malu – embarrassed

minah – girlfriend

or not? – general suffix for questions, as in *Can or not?* (Can you or can't you?)

see first – wait and see what happens

shack – tired

shiok – good, great, delicious

sotong – Malay for 'squid', used as an adjective meaning clumsy, or generally not very switched on.

steady lah – well done, excellent; an expression of praise

Wah! – general exclamation of surprise or distress

ya ya – boastful, as in *He always ya ya*

FOOD

Before sampling the delights of a hawker centre, it's a good idea to arm yourself with the names of a few dishes and ingredients, to avoid bewilderment.

Food Glossary
CHINESE

ah balling – glutinous rice balls filled with a sweet paste of peanut, black sesame or red bean and usually served in a peanut- or ginger-flavoured soup

bak chang – local rice dumpling filled with savoury or sweet meat and wrapped in leaves

bak chor mee – noodles with pork, meat balls and fried scallops

bak choy – variety of Chinese cabbage that grows like celery, with long white stalks and dark-green leaves

bak kutteh – local pork rib soup with hints of garlic and Chinese five spices

char kway teow – Hokkien dish of broad noodles, clams and eggs fried in chilli and black-bean sauce

char siew – sweet roast-pork fillet

cheng ting – dessert consisting of a bowl of sugar syrup with pieces of herbal jelly, barley and dates

choi sum – popular Chinese green vegetable, served steamed with oyster sauce

congee – Chinese porridge

Hainanese chicken rice – a local speciality; chicken dish served with spring onions and ginger dressing accompanied by soup and rice

hoisin sauce – thick seasoning sauce made from soya beans, red beans, sugar, vinegar, salt, garlic, sesame, chillies and spices; sweet-spicy and tangy in flavour

ka shou – fish-head noodles

kang kong – water convolvulus, a thick-stemmed type of spinach

kway chap – pig intestines cooked in soy sauce; served with flat rice noodles kway teow – broad rice noodles

lor mee – local dish of noodles served with slices of meat, eggs and a dash of vinegar in a dark-brown sauce

mee pok – flat noodles made with egg and wheat

popiah – similar to a spring roll, but not fried

spring roll – vegetables, peanuts, egg and bean sprouts rolled up inside a thin pancake and fried

won ton – dumpling filled with spiced minced pork

won ton mee – soup dish with shredded chicken or braised beef

yu char kueh – deep-fried dough; eaten with congee

yusheng – salad of raw fish, grated vegetables, candied melon and lime, pickled ginger, sesame seeds, jellyfish and peanuts tossed in sweet dressing; eaten at Chinese New Year

yu tiao – deep-fried pastry eaten for breakfast or as a dessert

INDIAN

achar – vegetable pickle

fish-head curry – red snapper head in curry sauce; a famous Singapore-Indian dish

gulab jamun – fried milk balls in sugar syrup

idli – steamed rice cake served with thin chutneys

keema – spicy minced meat

kofta – minced meat or vegetable ball

korma – mild curry with yoghurt sauce

lassi – yoghurt-based drink, either sweet or salted

mulligatawny – spicy beef soup

pakora – vegetable fritter

paratha – bread made with ghee and cooked on a hotplate; also called *roti prata*

pilau – rice fried in ghee and mixed with nuts, then cooked in stock

raita – side dish of cucumber, yoghurt and mint, used to cool the palate

rasam – spicy soup

roti john – fried roti with chilli

saag – spicy chopped-spinach side dish

sambar – fiery mixture of vegetables, lentils and split peas

samosa – fried pastry triangle stuffed with spiced vegetables or meat

tikka – small pieces of meat and fish served off the bone and marinated in yoghurt before baking

vadai – fried, spicy lentil patty, served with a savoury lentil sauce or yoghurt

MALAY & INDONESIAN

ais kacang – similar to *cendol* but made with evaporated milk instead of coconut milk; it is also spelt 'ice kacang'

belacan – fermented prawn paste used as a condiment

belacan kankong – green vegetables stir-fried in prawn paste

cendol – local dessert made from a cone of ice shavings filled with red beans, *attap* (sweet gelatinous fruit of the attap palm) and jelly, then topped with coloured syrups, brown-sugar syrup and coconut milk

gado gado – cold dish of bean sprouts, potatoes, long beans, *tempeh,* bean curd, rice cakes and prawn crackers, topped with a spicy peanut sauce

itek manis – duck simmered in ginger and black-bean sauce

itek tim – a classic soup of simmered duck, tomatoes, green peppers, salted vegetables and preserved sour plums

kari ayam – curried chicken

kaya – a toast topping made from coconut and egg

kecap – soy sauce, pronounced 'ketchup' (we got the word from them, not the other way around)

kepala ikan – fish head, usually in a curry or grilled

kueh mueh – Malay cakes

lontong – rice cakes in a spicy coconut-milk gravy topped with grated coconut and sometimes bean curd and egg

mee siam – white thin noodles in a sourish and sweet gravy made with tamarind

mee soto – noodle soup with shredded chicken

nasi biryani – saffron rice flavoured with spices and garnished with cashew nuts, almonds and raisins

nasi minyak – spicy rice

pulut kuning – sticky saffron rice

o-chien – oyster omelette

rojak – salad made from cucumber, pineapple, yam bean, star fruit, green mango and guava, with a dressing of shrimp paste, chillies, palm sugar and fresh lime juice

sambal – sauce of fried chilli, onions and prawn paste

soto ayam – spicy chicken soup with vegetables, including potatoes

tempeh – preserved soya beans, deep-fried

PERANAKAN

ayam buah keluak – chicken in a rich, spicy sauce served with buah keluak (a unusually flavoured black, paste-like nut)

carrot cake – omelette-like dish made from radishes, egg, garlic and chilli; also known as *chye tow kway*

kueh pie ti – deep-fried flour cup filled with prawn, chilli sauce and steamed turnip

otak – spicy fish paste cooked in banana leaves; a classic Peranakan snack, also called *otak-otak*

papaya titek – type of curry stew

satay bee hoon – peanut sauce–flavoured noodles

shui kueh – steamed radish cakes with fried preserved–radish topping

soup tulang – meaty bones in a rich, spicy, blood-red tomato gravy

GLOSSARY

Also see the glossaries for Chinese (p203), Indian (p204), Malay and Indonesian (p204) and Peranakan (p204) cuisine.

adat – Malay customary law
akad nikah – Malay wedding ceremony
ang pow – red packet of money used as offering, payment or gift

Baba – male Peranakan
bandar – port
batik – technique for printing cloth with wax and dye
batu – stone, rock, milepost
bendahara – Sultan's highest official
bercukur – Malay haircut
bertunang – to become engaged
bukit – hill
bumboat – motorised *sampan*
bumiputra – indigenous Malays (literally 'sons of the soil')

chettiar – Indian moneylender
chinthes – half-lion, half-griffin figure
chou – clown character in Chinese opera

godown – river warehouse
gopuram – colourful, ornate tower over the entrance gate to Hindu temple
gurdwara – Sikh temple

hajj – Muslim pilgrimage to Mecca; man who has made the pilgrimage to Mecca
hajjah – woman who has made the pilgrimage to Mecca
hantar tanda – family's permission to marry
haveli – traditional, ornately decorated Indian residence
hawker centre – undercover eating area with food stalls; known as hawker market, food court and food centre
HDB – Housing & Development Board; state body responsible for the provision of public housing

imam – Islamic leader
istana – palace

jalan – road

kallang – shipyard
kampong – traditional Malay village
kasot manek – slippers
kavadi – spiked metal frames decorated with peacock feathers, fruit and flowers used in the Thaipusam parade
kebaya – blouse worn over a sarong
kelong – fish trap on stilts
kenduri – important Malay feast
keramat – Malay shrine
kerasong – brooches, usually of fine filigree gold or silver
kiasu – Hokkien word expressing the Singaporean philosophy of looking out for oneself
kongsi – Chinese clan organisations for mutual assistance known variously as ritual brotherhoods, heaven-man-earth societies, triads and secret societies

kopitiam – traditional coffeeshop
kota – fort, city
kramat – Malay shrine
KTM – Keretapi Tanah Malayu (Malaysian Railways System)
kuala – river mouth, place where a tributary joins a larger river

lorong – narrow street, alley

masjid – mosque
merlion – half-lion, half-fish animal and symbol of Singapore
moksha – the Hindu notion of spiritual salvation
MRT – Singapore's Mass Rapid Transit underground railway system
muezzin – the official of a mosque who calls the faithful to prayer

namakarana – Indian name-giving ceremony
Nonya – female Peranakan

padang – open grassy area; usually the city square
pantai – beach
PAP – People's Action Party; main political party of Singapore
pasar – market
pasar malam – night market
penjing – Chinese bonsai
Peranakan – literally 'half-caste'; refers to the Straits Chinese, the original Chinese settlers in Singapore, who intermarried with Malays and adopted many of the Malay customs
pintu pagar – swing doors seen in Chinese shophouses
po chai pills – traditional remedy for travellers' diarrhoea and minor stomach problems
pulau – island

raja – prince, ruler
Ramadan – Islamic month of fasting
rotan – cane made of rattan used to punish criminals

sampan – small boat
shen – local deities
Singlish – variation of English spoken in Singapore
STB – Singapore Tourism Board
STDB – Singapore Trade Development Board
sungei – river

tai tai – wealthy lady of leisure
tanjung – headland
temenggong – Malay administrator
thali – necklace worn by bride during Indian wedding ceremony; buffet of rice, curried vegetables, soup, curries and bread (Indian)
thola – Indian unit of weight
towkang – Chinese junk
towkays – Chinese business chiefs

wayang – Chinese street opera
wayang kulit – shadow puppet play
wet market – produce market
WTC – World Trade Centre

BEHIND THE SCENES

THIS BOOK

This 8th edition of *Singapore* was researched and written by Mat Oakley and Joshua Samuel Brown. The 7th edition was written by Mat Oakley. Simon Richmond updated the 6th edition. This book was commissioned in Lonely Planet's Melbourne office, and produced by the following:

Commissioning Editors Holly Alexander, Shawn Low

Coordinating Editors Victoria Harrison, Simon Williamson

Coordinating Cartographers Jolyon Philcox, Peter Shields

Coordinating Layout Designer Indra Kilfoyle

Senior Editors Helen Christinis, Katie Lynch

Managing Cartographer David Connolly

Managing Layout Designer Celia Wood

Cover Designer Pepi Bluck

Project Manager Chris Love

Language Content Coordinator Quentin Frayne

Thanks to Chris Girdler, Nicole Hansen, Laura Jane, Yvonne Kirk, Lisa Knights, Wayne Murphy, Andy Rojas

Cover photographs Palm fronds in Botanic Gardens, Rodney Hyett/Lonely Planet Images (top); Chinese New Year's Parade, David Noton Photography (bottom)

Internal photographs Internal photographs by Lonely Planet Images: p2 Christian Aslund; p6 (#1), p8 (#2) Mervin Chua; p8 (#1), p9 (#2) Tom Cockrem; p4 (#1), p5 (#2), p7 (#3, #4), p10 (#1), p11 (#3), p12 (#1, #3) Felix Hug; p3, p4 (#3), p5 (#3), p9 (#1), p11 (#4), Richard I'Anson/; p10 (#2) Paul Kennedy; p5 (#1) Aun Koh; p4 (#2), p6 (#2), p12 (#2) Phil Weymouth

All images are copyright of the photographer unless otherwise indicated. Many of the images in this guide are available for licensing from Lonely Planet Images: www .lonelyplanetimages.com.

THANKS
MAT OAKLEY

Thanks to Ros Lim and Tracy Gan for eating suggestions, and all the other countless informed suggestions on where to eat the best this and find the best that. Thanks as always to Shiwani for putting up with bouts of grumpiness and to Mae, who road-tests everything for kid-friendliness. A special mention must also go to Kristy Weller, a paragon of integrity and honesty and an inspiration to us all. And finally a big thanks to Lily, Leo and Lulu – the three Ls who made the whole experience of writing this book a lot more colourful.

JOSHUA SAMUEL BROWN

Heartfelt gratitude to all the friends in Singapore who made doing this book less a job and more a lifestyle: Ginny, Dawn, Ruqxana, Jonathan, Asako and the kids, Wesley, Colin, Hanshih, Sakina Bridgit and, of course, the amazing Tony Tan, without whom this book would be only half as good (at best). Special thanks to Alex Au, Victor Yue and Alvin Tan for their interviews and expertise. This book is dedicated to the memory of Cliff Heller, without whom I might have faced my first visit to Singapore all those years back alone and sober.

THE LONELY PLANET STORY

Fresh from an epic journey across Europe, Asia and Australia in 1972, Tony and Maureen Wheeler sat at their kitchen table stapling together notes. The first Lonely Planet guidebook, *Across Asia on the Cheap*, was born.

Travellers snapped up the guides. Inspired by their success, the Wheelers began publishing books to Southeast Asia, India and beyond. Demand was prodigious, and the Wheelers expanded the business rapidly to keep up. Over the years, Lonely Planet extended its coverage to every country and into the virtual world via lonelyplanet.com and the Thorn Tree message board.

As Lonely Planet became a globally loved brand, Tony and Maureen received several offers for the company. But it wasn't until 2007 that they found a partner whom they trusted to remain true to the company's principles of travelling widely, treading lightly and giving sustainably. In October of that year, BBC Worldwide acquired a 75% share in the company, pledging to uphold Lonely Planet's commitment to independent travel, trustworthy advice and editorial independence.

Today, Lonely Planet has offices in Melbourne, London and Oakland, with over 500 staff members and 300 authors. Tony and Maureen are still actively involved with Lonely Planet. They're travelling more often than ever, and they're devoting their spare time to charitable projects. And the company is still driven by the philosophy of *Across Asia on the Cheap*: 'All you've got to do is decide to go and the hardest part is over. So go!'

OUR READERS

Many thanks to the travellers who used the last edition and wrote to us with helpful hints, useful advice and interesting anecdotes:

Mark Ackermoore, Bazga Ali, Marea Bass, Jeffree Benet, Itay Birger, Redvers Brandling, Jared Brubaker, Blake Brunner, Pensa Carlo, Julian Chin, Matt Collins, Roger Cornish, David Covill, Pamela Dawson, Rosanna D'Costa, Marja De Man, Mervyn Evans, Pat Eyre, Michael Fussthaler, Sally Gladstone, Fredrik Graffner, Donat Grgurovic, Spencer Han, Susanne Horras, Christoph Houben, Eveline How, Sharon How, Mike Howieson, Adrian Ineichen, Martha Iskyan, Rachel Janssen, Gillian Jeens, Martin Junginger, Eero Keränen, Yuncheul Kim, Darrel Kingham, Chan Kris, Rachel Lee, Louis Lehenaff, Dieter Von Lepel, Julian Lloyd, Woon Sien Loh, Borja Luque, Dominique Majecki, Mark Mallari, Oliver Munn, Wee Kee Nah, Karin Ohlin, Kerry Paterson, Haus Patterson, Jennifer Quong, Rishi Ramchand, Peter Randall, Rupert Reed, Shaun Rowley, Karl Ruloff, Helga Schinkel, Lukas Schmid, Anke Schwabbauer, Scott Secker, Serene Seow, Ann Shield, Terry Sikora, Rogowski Stephen, Klaus Suemmerer, Craig Tehan, Ching Ching Tew, Jeyaram

SEND US YOUR FEEDBACK

We love to hear from travellers – your comments keep us on our toes and help make our books better. Our well-travelled team reads every word on what you loved or loathed about this book. Although we cannot reply individually to postal submissions, we always guarantee that your feedback goes straight to the appropriate authors, in time for the next edition. Each person who sends us information is thanked in the next edition – and the most useful submissions are rewarded with a free book.

To send us your updates – and find out about Lonely Planet events, newsletters and travel news – visit our award-winning website: lonelyplanet.com/contact.

Note: We may edit, reproduce and incorporate your comments in Lonely Planet products such as guidebooks, websites and digital products, so let us know if you don't want your comments reproduced or your name acknowledged. For a copy of our privacy policy visit lonelyplanet.com/privacy.

(Jack) Thangagelu, Kimon Theodossis, Stephen Wilson, David Yalin, Rodney Zandbergs, Sophia Zhang

Notes

Notes

INDEX

A

accommodation 160-74, see also Sleeping subindex
costs 160, 161
rentals 160-1
reservations 161
activities 153-8, see also Arts & Leisure subindex, individual activities
Adam, James 36
air travel 188-9
ambulance 195
antiques 116, see also Shopping subindex
aquariums 101-2
Arab Street 67
architecture 34-7
art galleries, see Arts & Leisure, Shopping subindexes
arts 31-4, 150-3, see also Arts & Leisure, Shopping subindexes
International Film Festival 17
Mosaic Music Festival 17
Singapore Arts Festival 18
Singapore Buskers Festival 19
WOMAD 18
Atherton, Jonathan 154

000 map pages
000 photographs

B

bargaining 106
bars 140-8, see also Drinking & Nightlife subindex
bathrooms 200
beaches, see Sights subindex
bicycle travel, see cycling
bigfoot 185
bird-watching 185
Birthday of Matsu 94
Birthday of the Monkey God 18, 94
Birthday of the Third Prince 17
Boat Quay 57
boat travel 190-1, 198, see also Arts & Leisure subindex, kayaking, sailing
body modification 154
books, see also Shopping subindex
politics 39
restaurant guides 126
Yew, Lee Kuan 39
Botero, Fernando 32
bowling 154-5
Buaya Sangkut falls 186
Buddha Tooth Relic Temple 61, **10**
Buddhist centres, see Sights subindex
Bukit Timah 87, 91-4, **92-3**
Bukit Timah Nature Reserve 91
bumboats, see boat travel
bus travel 191
bushwalking, see hiking, walking tours
business hours 105-6, 122, 140, 194
business travellers 201
Bussorah Street 110

C

cable-car rides 95
car travel 191-2
cathedrals, see Sights subindex

CBD 60-6
drinking 143-4
nightlife 143-4
shopping 108-10
cell phones 199-200
central business district, see CBD
central Singapore 86-90
walking tour 88-90, **89**
Changi 79-83
Changi Airport 189
children, travel with 87, 98, 194
Chinatown 60-6, **62-3**
accommodation 165-6
drinking 143-4
food 126-8
nightlife 143-4
shopping 108-10
walking tours 64-6, **65**
Chinatown Heritage Centre 35, 60
Chinese medicine 60, 108
Chinese New Year 16
Chinese New Year's Eve 94
Chinese opera 32-3, 152
Chinese Revolutionary Alliance 88
Chingay 16-17
Christmas 19
churches & cathedrals, see Sights subindex
cinema 33-4, 151-2, see also Arts & Leisure subindex
International Film Festival 17
Clarke Quay 57, **3**
classical music 32, 151
climate 16, 194
climate change 190
clothes, see Shopping subindex
clothing sizes 113
clubs 140-8, see also Drinking & Nightlife subindex
colonial buildings, see Sights subindex
Colonial District 51-9, **52-3**
accommodation 161-5
drinking 140-3
food 123-6

nightlife 140-3
shopping 106-7
walking tour 58-9, **58**
colonisation 22-4
comedy 153, 154
consulates 195
cooking courses 122
costs 19, 20
accommodation 160, 161
drinking 140
food 122, 123
taxes 105, 199
courses 194
Coward, Noel 56
crab 120
crafts, see also paper making, Shopping subindex
pewter 106
cultural centres, see museums
culture 29-30, 105, 114, 154
customs regulations 194
cycling 153-4, 189-90
Ketam Mountain Bike Park 179
Pulau Ubin 176

D

Dali, Salvador 32
dance 32
Deepavali 19
development 3, 37
DHL Balloon 156
disabilities, travellers with 200
discount cards 194-5
diving 186
Dragon Boat Festival 17-18
drinks 140-8, see also Drinking & Nightlife subindex
driving, see car travel
driving licence 191-2

E

East Coast Park 79, 87
eastern Singapore 77-85, **80**
accommodation 171-3
drinking 147-8

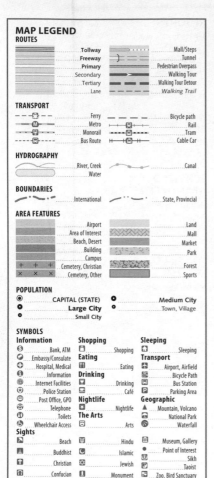

MAP LEGEND
ROUTES

- Tollway
- Freeway
- Primary
- Secondary
- Tertiary
- Lane
- Mall/Steps
- Tunnel
- Pedestrian Overpass
- Walking Tour
- Walking Tour Detour
- Walking Trail

TRANSPORT

- Ferry
- Metro
- Monorail
- Bus Route
- Bicycle path
- Rail
- Tram
- Cable Car

HYDROGRAPHY

- River, Creek
- Water
- Canal

BOUNDARIES

- International
- State, Provincial

AREA FEATURES

- Airport
- Area of Interest
- Beach, Desert
- Building
- Campus
- Cemetery, Christian
- Cemetery, Other
- Land
- Mall
- Market
- Park
- Forest
- Sports

POPULATION

- CAPITAL (STATE)
- **Large City**
- Small City
- **Medium City**
- Town, Village

SYMBOLS

Information
- Bank, ATM
- Embassy/Consulate
- Hospital, Medical
- Information
- Internet Facilities
- Police Station
- Post Office, GPO
- Telephone
- Toilets
- Wheelchair Access

Sights
- Beach
- Buddhist
- Christian
- Confucian

Shopping
- Shopping

Eating
- Eating

Drinking
- Drinking
- Café

Nightlife
- Nightlife

The Arts
- Arts

- Hindu
- Islamic
- Jewish
- Monument

Sleeping
- Sleeping

Transport
- Airport, Airfield
- Bicycle Path
- Bus Station
- Parking Area

Geographic
- Mountain, Volcano
- National Park
- Waterfall

- Museum, Gallery
- Point of Interest
- Sikh
- Taoist
- Zoo, Bird Sanctuary

Published by Lonely Planet Publications Pty Ltd
ABN 36 005 607 983

Australia Head Office, Locked Bag 1,
Footscray, Victoria 3011,
☎03 8379 8000, fax 03 8379 8111,
talk2us@lonelyplanet.com.au

USA 150 Linden St, Oakland, CA 94607,
☎510 250 6400, toll free 800 275 8555,
fax 510 893 8572, info@lonelyplanet.com

UK 2nd fl, 186 City Rd, London, EC1V 2NT,
☎020 7106 2100, fax 020 7106 2101,
go@lonelyplanet.co.uk